上海帕丁顿双语学校志

School Annals of Shanghai Paddington Bilingual School

《上海帕丁顿双语学校志》编纂委员会　编

方志出版社

图书在版编目（CIP）数据

上海帕丁顿双语学校志 /《上海帕丁顿双语学校志》编纂委员会编. —北京：方志出版社，2017.10
ISBN 978-7-5144-2667-0

Ⅰ.①上… Ⅱ.①上… Ⅲ.①上海帕丁顿双语学校—校史 Ⅳ.①G527.513

中国版本图书馆CIP数据核字（2017）第279884号

上海帕丁顿双语学校志

编　　者：《上海帕丁顿双语学校志》编纂委员会
责任编辑：王　俊
出 版 人：冀祥德
出 版 者：方志出版社
　　　　　地址　北京市朝阳区潘家园东里9号（国家方志馆4层）
　　　　　邮编　100021
　　　　　网址　http：//www.fzph.org
发　　行：方志出版社发行中心
　　　　　电话　（010）67110500
经　　销：各地新华书店
印　　刷：上海光扬印务有限公司
开　　本：787×1092　1/16
印　　张：22
字　　数：364千字
版　　次：2017年10月第1版　2017年10月第1次印刷
印　　数：0001-1500册
ISBN 978-7-5144-2667-0　定价：260.00元

1997年1月，奉贤县委副书记、县长金建忠（右二），县委副书记刘正贤（右三），县委常委、常务副县长朱德龙（右一）听取奉浦工业区教育园区学校规划建设的工作汇报

1998年10月，中共奉贤县委副书记刘正贤（中）考察学校时与校领导合影

1998 年 10 月，奉贤县教育局局长庄锦荣（中）考察学校食堂

1998 年 11 月，上海市教育委员会主任张伟江（左一）到学校考察，听取学校汇报

1998 年 12 月，奉贤县人大常委会副主任朱顺江（左六）等到学校考察教育

1999 年 10 月，奉贤县政协主席姜金余（左一）考察学校，与学生亲切交谈

2006年9月，上海市人大常委会教科文卫副主任委员夏秀蓉（左二）、奉贤县教育局原局长蒋辉蘽(右一）考察学校学生宿舍

2008年11月21日，奉贤区教育局党委书记王森龙（右），副书记张杰（左）到学校指导工作

2012年10月22日，奉贤区政协主席陈洪凡（左二）、区政协秘书长金国强（左三）到学校考察，听取汇报

2013年12月，奉贤区副区长钱雨晴（中）到学校考察工作

2014 年 4 月 16 日，上海市慈善基金会副理事长袁采（右二）到学校考察工作

2015 年 4 月 23 日，上海交通大学教育集团总裁吴竹平（左一）参加上海交通大学教育集团现代教育示范园区暨上海帕丁顿双语学校揭牌仪式

2015 年 6 月 1 日，奉贤区人民政府区长庄木弟（前右二）考察学校

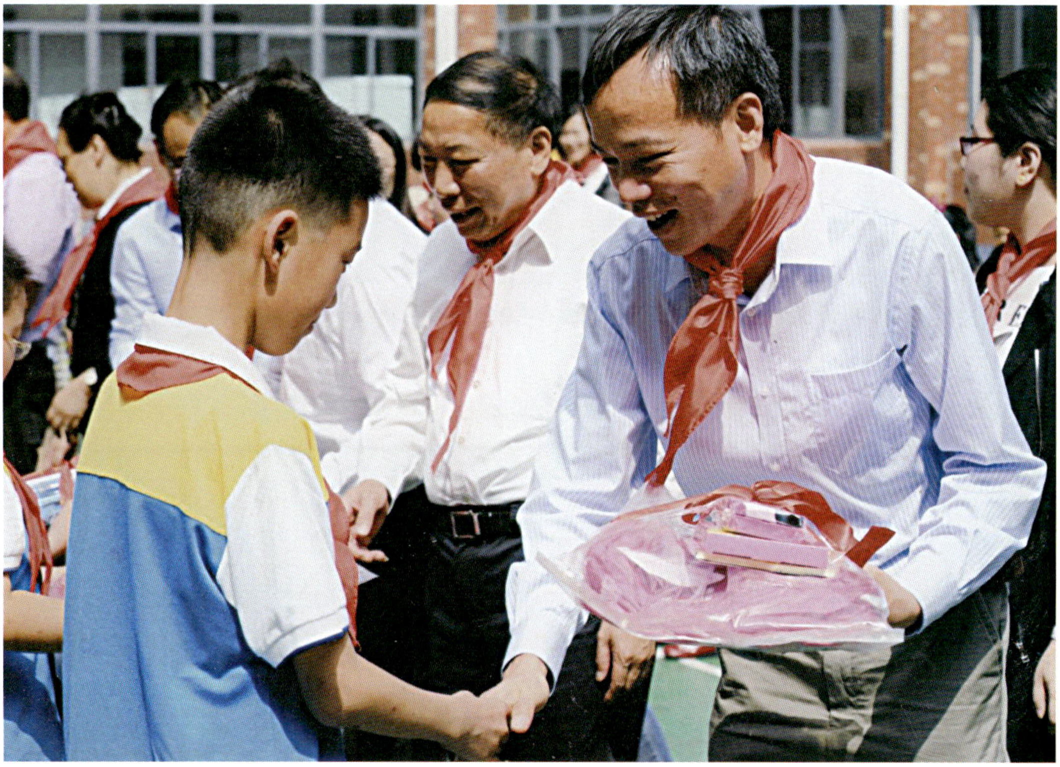

2015 年 6 月 1 日，奉贤区教育局局长施文龙（右一）到学校参加儿童节庆祝活动，向少先队员赠送节日礼品

2015 年 12 月，上海申生投资有限公司董事长王新其（右一）、上海奉浦社区党工委书记王少峰（右二）、奉贤区总工会党组书记王森龙（右三）、上海工业综合开发区总经理陈建庆（右四）、党委书记朱国平（右五）参加学校校区的奉浦体育俱乐部开张仪式

2015 年 12 月，学校校区奉贤区奉浦体育俱乐部成立，奉贤区政协副主席吴梅（左）、学校董事长王丹花（右）为俱乐部揭牌

2015 年 12 月，奉贤区副区长倪闽景（中）、区教育局党委书记陆琴（左一）到学校考察工作，听取汇报

2016 年 1 月，奉贤区人大常委会副主任陆建国（右一）到学校为优秀教师颁奖

2015 年，学校校区上海交通大学教育集团国际教育交流中心（左）、学校教学大楼（右）

学校校门

2016 年，安装 2 部观光电梯的国际教育交流中心大楼

学校教学大楼外景

学校庭园式教学大楼

上海帕丁顿外国语幼儿园

学校校区的国际现代教育中心大楼全景

学校餐饮楼外景

学校游泳球类馆外景

学校校园长廊（露天）

学校校园长廊（平顶）

学校校园长廊（帐篷式）

学校三号宿舍楼

学校操场全景

学校休闲餐厅

学校教师公寓

学校一号宿舍楼

学校二号宿舍楼

1999年10月，奉贤县教育局局长蒋辉蘷在学校第一届教师节上作“让课堂充满生命活力”的讲话

2007年，学校顾问张思中与民办奉浦学校教师探讨英语教学工作

外籍教师在学校讲授英语课

奉贤区教育局教研室主任李逢五在学校授课

学校教师曾均婷为学生上古筝课

学校中外教师研讨教学工作

2006年6月，上海市特级教师、名校长于漪（左二）到学校指导工作

2008年10月，上海市语文学科专家徐鹄到学校授课

2008年11月，上海社会学家陆震到学校授课

学校坚持每周举行升国旗仪式

学校每年开展学生军训活动

2001年，学校组织学生赴奉贤区爱国主义教育基地中共奉贤县委旧址参观学习

学校组织学生到爱国主义教育基地李主一烈士陵园开展学习活动

2008年10月，学校组织全校师生参加迎上海世博“城市让生活更美好，我签字我承诺”活动

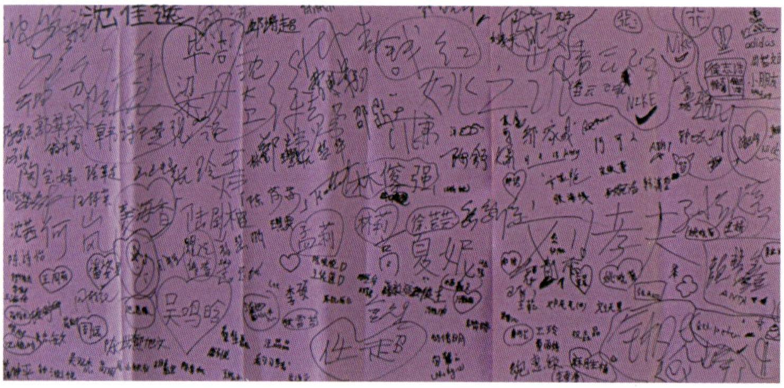

2009年，学校举办“迎世博，我签字、我承诺”签名活动

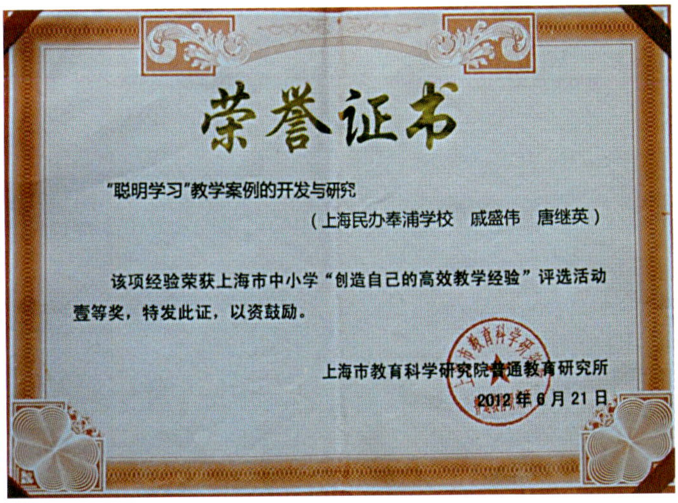

2012年6月21日，学校"聪明学习"教学案例的开发与研究，获上海市中小学"创造自己的高效教学经验"评选一等奖

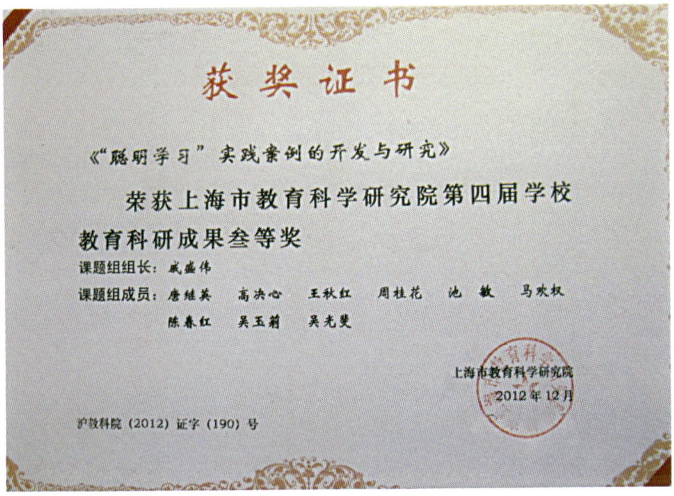

2012年12月，学校《"聪明学习"实践案例的开发与研究》获上海市教育科学研究院第四届教育科研三等奖

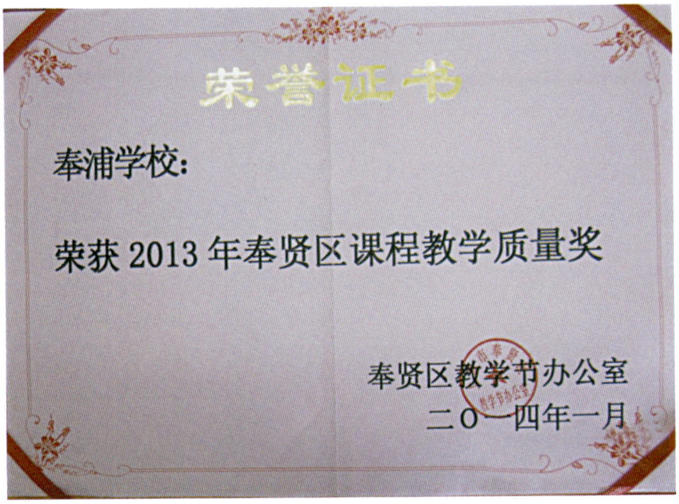

2014年1月，学校被奉贤区教学节办公室评为2013年度奉贤区课程教学质量奖

学校举办文化艺术节活动

学校管弦乐队

学校举办学习雷锋好榜样歌唱活动

2002年10月，学校学生与菲律宾学生举行文艺联欢

2012年6月27日，学校举办中德学生文化交流活动

2014年12月，学校举办迎新年文艺会演

证书
ZHENG SHU
2001上海市第三届学生艺术节
中小学优秀节目调演
二等奖
学校：
节目：
2001上海市第三届学生艺术节组委会

2001年，学校管乐队合奏曲在上海市第三届学生艺术节调演中获奖证书

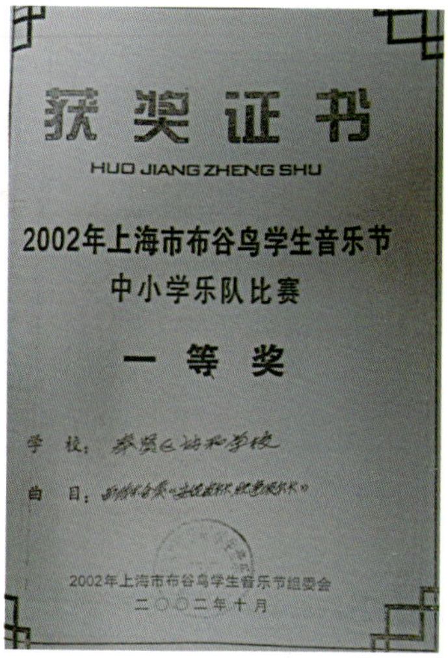
获奖证书
HUO JIANG ZHENG SHU
2002年上海市布谷鸟学生音乐节
中小学乐队比赛
一等奖
学校：
曲目：
2002年上海市布谷鸟学生音乐节组委会
二〇〇二年十月

2002年，学校西洋乐合奏获上海市布谷鸟学生音乐节中小学乐队比赛一等奖证书

Shanghai Fengpu Private School
果行园
校风：品行朴实 学业扎实 身体结实
校训：果行毓德
教风：关爱学生 严于治学 因材施教 探索创新
学风：志存高远 勤思好问 笃学不倦 求知求真
2012年4月25日 星期三 第1期
上海民办奉浦学校(主办) 网址:http://www.fp-edu.net 邮箱:fengpuxuexiao@163.com
创刊词
彰显民办特色 建设智慧校园

2012年4月，学校校报《果行园》印行

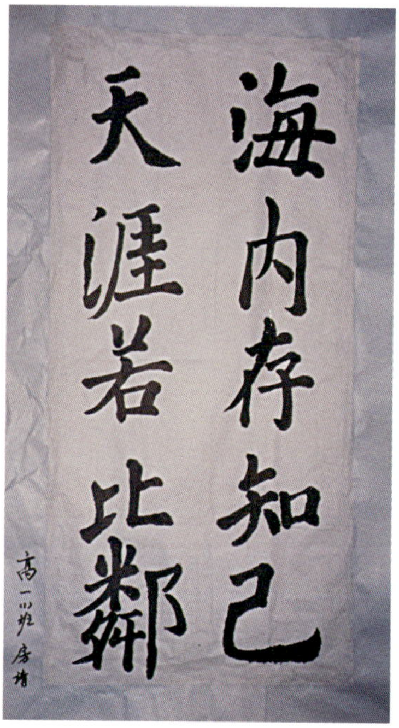

学校高一（1）班学生房靖书法：海内存知己，天涯若比邻

学校八（2）班学生凡婷婷（女）作品《古华公园》获2016年奉贤区中学生单元化课程美术课堂作品展一等奖

2008年10月，学校预初二班余露红（女）参加上海市中小学生绘画比赛作品——《海空凭鱼跃》

2016年学校学生社团旗帜

2006年学校校园石碑上的校训

2008年11月6日，学校举办第八届学生运动会主席台

学生运动会场

学生运动会团体操

学生武术操

学校学生体育代表队

2013年11月，学校在奉贤区第三届运动会上获体育道德风尚奖

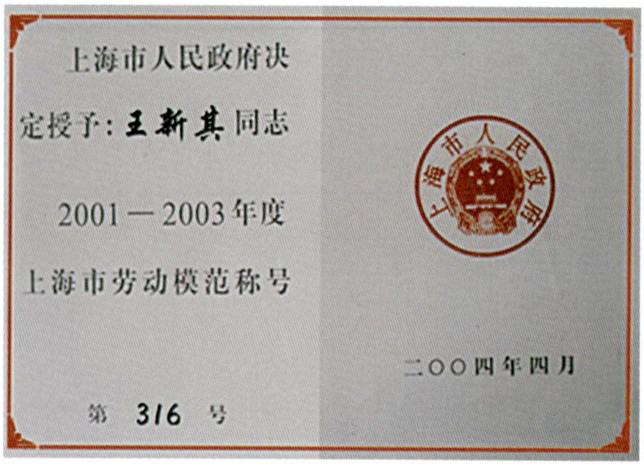

2004年4月，王新其获2001—2003年度上海市劳动模范称号证书和奖章

2015年4月，王益权获2010—2014年度上海市劳动模范称号证书和奖章

2008年4月，学校被奉贤区综治委、区教育局评为奉贤区2006—2007年度安全文明校园二等奖

2008年12月，学校在第二届上海市中小学生“小科学家”创新英语擂台赛上被评为优秀组织奖

2008年12月，学校被上海市科技艺术教育中心等部门列入2008年上海市优秀校园植物名录

2009年1月，学校被奉贤区教育局验收为行为规范示范校

2009年1月，学校被奉贤区教育局评为奉贤区师德先进集体

2009年3月，学校被上海市教育委员会、上海市知识产权局确认为知识产权试点学校

2009年，学校被上海市社会治安综合治理委员会评为平安单位

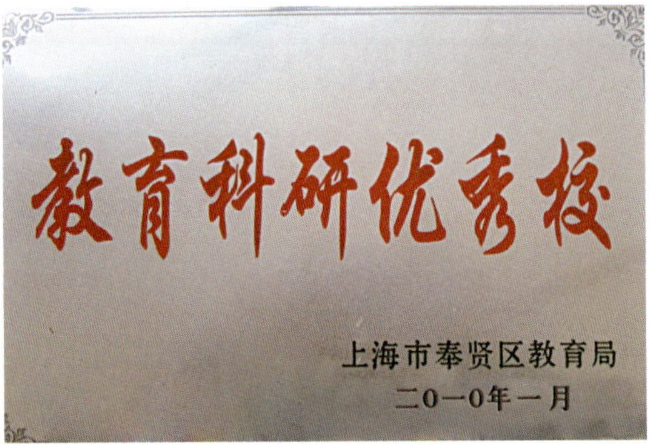

2010年1月，学校被奉贤区教育局评为教育科研优秀校

2010 年 10 月，学校被评为 2009 年度贯彻落实科学发展观加强改进学校德育工作活动优秀学校

2013 年 12 月，学校被奉贤区教育局评为奉贤区学校教育科研管理优秀校

2010 年 2 月，学校被评为 2008 — 2009 年度上海市安全文明校园

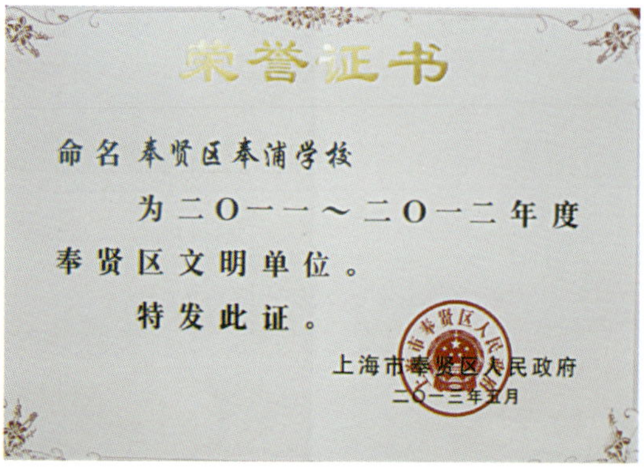

2013 年 5 月，学校被奉贤区人民政府再次命名为 2011 — 2012 年度奉贤区文明单位

2009 年 12 月，学校被评为上海市红十字工作达标学校

2013 年 2 月，学校被评为奉贤区 2012 年度消防安全先进集体

1999 年学校党政班子、部门负责人（前排右起：柏新鉴、夏明德、翁连云、沈靖华；后排右起：王益权、周时青、沈爱玉、陈建春、周林锋、朱锋、宋建伯）

2005 年学校领导班子及部门负责人（前排右起：周时青、程春影、戚盛伟、徐建、曹春华；后排右起：盛伟宾、李永卫、王益权、唐继英、沈靖华）

2012 年 10 月，学校行政、党支部及学校骨干（左起二顾行建、三戚盛伟、四刘平、五王益权、六李永卫、七沈靖华、八曹善明）

2015 年学校董事会、监事会成员（前排左起：朱德龙、董俊平、王丹花、顾行建、诸海萍；后排左起：王新其、靳寿德）

2016 年学校行政班子成员（左起：李志强、张臻、顾行建、董俊平、陆桂英、诸海萍）

上海交大教育集团设在学校校区的奉贤现代教育集团现代教育园区第一届理事会成员（左起：王永吉、朱德龙、王新其、常韶伟、王丹花、董俊平、诸海萍）

2017年8月15日，参加《上海帕丁顿双语学校志》评审会议的全体人员。前排左起：戚盛伟、陈建庆、庄锦荣、姚金祥、王新其、蒋辉蘽、施文龙、王少峰、陈炳章；第二排左起：周时青、曹春华、刘平、唐英、王丹花、胡婷婷、徐晓华、顾行健、王益权；第三排左起：李永卫、朱德龙、顾首育、王永平、周生明

《上海帕丁顿双语学校志》全体编务人员。左起：徐晓华、周生明、戚盛伟、王丹花、陈炳章、朱德龙、刘平

序　一

在改革劲风吹拂下，20世90年代初，奉贤成立奉浦工业区管理委员会和奉浦经济发展实业总公司，奉浦地区的开发、建设日新月异，一批一批中外企业落户奉浦，同时也吸引来自全国各地的各类建设人才。为解决奉浦工业区及就业于奉浦地区的外来建设者的子女就近入学的燃眉之急，1995年，奉浦工业区管委会决定创建十二年学制的上海民办协和实验学校，即现在的上海帕丁顿双语学校。

教育事业的发展与整个社会发展一样，革故鼎新，与时俱进，是亘古不变之理，也是谁都阻挡不了的历史潮流。然而旧制更新，利益所属又能造成发展进程中的复杂性与艰巨性。上海帕丁顿双语学校自1998年开学至今，曾经四次易名。学校频繁更名，既反映初创时期办学的艰苦奋斗历程，又真实记录由民办公助学校逐步变更为民营企业投资的民办学校的发展轨迹。

上海帕丁顿双语学校的诞生和发展，在奉贤教育改革发展的征途上创造了令人注目的三个“第一”：第一所民办性质的学校。真正意义上打破了奉贤教育公办体制一统天下的局面，解放后实现奉贤民办学历教育零的突破，开创了基础教育多元化多形式办学体制改革的新格局。第一所奉贤教育史上十二年学制的寄宿制学校。一方面可继续有利于工业区人才引进，满足随迁子女随年级就读的需要；另一方面可依托国家民办教育的法规、政策，大胆实验、探索学校管理的科学运行机制，突破公办学校管理上的瓶颈，大胆进行高中招生制度改革的实践，以真正实现义务教育和高中教育一体制的现代学校管理体系，同时为推进基础教育学制年限设置的改革，寻求学制经营高效的教育新路创设实验基地。第一所由民营企业投资的规模较大学校。2009年3月，以王新其为董事长的上海申生投资有限公司，成为上海民办奉浦学校的投资举办企业。2010年12月，已属民营企业的上海申生投资有限公司依法竞拍收购学校。公司先后投资4.79亿元扩建和改造学校，使教育教学设施设备现代先进。

改革开放以来，奉贤境内民营企业众多，其中亿万富翁也不少，但像王新其这样投资办学校、热心公益事业的，目前也是第一人。兴学筑路造桥，为民谋福祉，这样的人历来为民众所敬重，王新其成为上海市劳动模范，当之无愧。“崇奉贤人，见贤思齐”是奉贤的人文品质，王新其的兴学义举，也必然成为奉贤贤城中贤人贤事的楷模。

上海帕丁顿双语学校，虽然在历史长河中仅仅是近二十年的短暂一瞬，其中，有行进中的困惑，也有成功后的喜悦，这都给后人带来深远的启迪，也给奉贤教育改革发展的思考与实践提供了颇丰的借鉴实例。书写好这段办学历史无疑十分重要。古人说“疑今者察之古，不知来者视之往”，“善言古者之于今，能术远者考之于近”。《上海帕丁顿双语学校志》的编修，也是奉贤教育史上的一件大事。志书综合近二十年办学的各种信息、资料，客观、全面、系统地展示了新时期一所民办学校的办学历程，乃至奉贤民办学历教育的开创与实践路径。这部志书一定会便于后人通古知今、展望未来，也是上海帕丁顿双语学校深感创业艰难，而勇往前行的“果行懿德”之所在，更为奉贤各类学校编修校史、提供了一种新的存世典籍式的范例。

“雄关漫道真如铁，而今迈步从头越”。正如《上海帕丁顿双语学校志·总述》中所说：望未来，任重道远，相信在学校董事会的正确领导下，在探索十二年一体化新型教育体制、科学运行机制，推进课程改革，改善教与学的方式，造就一代名师等领域，进一步加强学校精神文化、制度文化、行为文化和物质空间文化的学校文化建设，持续增强办学的综合实力，为实现“奉贤美、奉贤强”的战略目标，培育和输送德、智、体全面发展的后备人才，做出应有的贡献。

以上数语，权代为序。

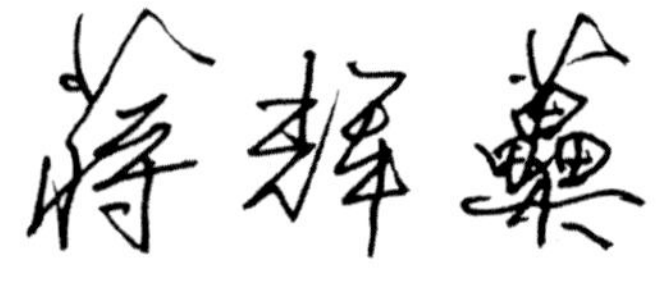

2017年3月26日

（作者系奉贤区教育学会会长、原奉贤教育局局长）

序　二

《上海帕丁顿双语学校志》在全国人民喜迎党的十九大召开，全区人民同心同德打造“奉贤美、奉贤强”的新时期付梓出版，这是我校“贤文化”建设的又一重大成果，更是一件慰藉前人，启迪后人的大好事，可喜可贺。

盛世修志，是中华民族的优良传统。编修《上海帕丁顿双语学校志》，是一项总结学校发展进程中的经验与教训的系统工程，是一项服务当代，开创未来，造福后代的重要工作。志稿记述了学校全体教职员工甘于奉献、莘莘学子奋发向上的精神风貌。是学校再度走向繁荣的体现，亦为学校增添了一笔“存史、资政、育人”的宝贵财富。在此，谨向为《上海帕丁顿双语学校志》不辞辛劳、勤奋笔耕的编纂人员和关心、帮助、指导的所有单位和个人，表示诚挚的感谢。

树有根，水有源。作为一名民营企业的法人代表，创业至今，深感企业的每一步发展和进步，都离不开党的改革开放的富民政策，离不开社会各界的支持和帮助，离不开企业全体员工的共同努力。致富思源，不忘感恩，回报社会成了我的一个宿愿。捐资兴教，为教育事业贡献力量，责无旁贷。正因如此，我毫不犹豫地投资收购学校，教育兴国。

取是一种能力，一种本事，舍是一种境界，一种悟性。一个人的真正价值正是为社会做贡献。出资办学是一种人才工程的舍。这项投资，功在当代，利在千秋。

教育兴则人才兴，教育强则国家强。重视教育就是重视未来，重视教育才能赢得未来。“育才造士，为国之本”。办好教育，为全面建设小康社会，为实现中华民族伟大复兴的中国梦提供强有力的智力支持和人才支撑。办好学校，培养德智体美劳全面发展的社会主义事业的建设者和接班人，这是我的毕生追求。锲而不舍，金石为镂，这就是我的信念。

以史为鉴可知兴衰。我对上海帕丁顿双语学校的未来充满信心，豪情满怀。

我坚信，学校的发展能赓续不断，再造辉煌。

是为序！

2017 年 8 月 15 日

（作者系上海申生投资有限公司董事长、上海帕丁顿双语学校监事长）

凡　例

一、本志记述上海帕丁顿双语学校的发展历史和现状，定名为《上海帕丁顿双语学校志》。

二、本志以马克思列宁主义、毛泽东思想、邓小平理论、“三个代表”重要思想和科学发展观为指导，贯彻落实习近平总书记系列重要讲话精神和治国理政新理念新思想新战略，坚持辩证唯物主义和历史唯物主义立场、观点和方法。详略记载学校的发展历程，力求达到思想性、科学性、发展性和资料性有机结合，成为具有民办学校特色与时代特征的志书。

三、本志记事时间上限为1994年学校创办投资方奉浦经济发展实业总公司成立，下限至2016年。为反映某些重要事物（事件）的发生和发展过程，其时间断限可以上溯下延。

四、本志坚持横排竖写、纵横结合的写法，除序言、总述、大事记外，采用章、节、目、子目四级排列的结构，设有创办发展、决策机构、管理机构、校务改革、党群组织、教职员工、课程教学、学生教育管理、综合管理、设施设备、校园文化科技体育、人物荣誉共12章38节151目216子目。以记、述、志、图、照、表、录为主要表达方式，卷首设彩照、地图、序言、总述、大事记等，其他照片、表、图、随文设置，力求做到图文并茂。各章设无题小序，展现本章特色和风貌。

五、由于学校几易其名，大事记和正文，表述时间与校名同步。凡涉及办校19年间的表格，表头学校名称均用上海帕丁顿双语学校。

六、本志资料主要来自学校档案室和部门，经核实的口述资料也予以记载。历年师生人数摘自《奉贤统计年鉴》。

七、本志使用计量单位一律采用法定计量单位。

八、本志目录、总述用中英文同时表述。

目 录

第一章 创办发展

第二章　决策机构

第三章　管理机构

第四章　校务改革

第五章 党群组织

第六章 教职员工

第七章 课程 教学

第八章 学生教育管理

第九章　综合管理

第十章　设施　设备

第十一章 校园文化 科技 体育

第十二章　人物　荣誉

Contents

Chapter Six Teaching and Administrative Staff

Chapter Seven Curriculum Teaching

III. Curriculum Concept

1. The Concept of Democratic Construction in 'Grass Roots' Form

2. The Concept of Situational Knowledge Construction

3. The Concept of School Institution Reorganization

IV. Training Objective and Curriculum Objective

1. Training Objective

2. Curriculum Objective

3. Specific Objective

V. Curriculum Structure and Curriculum Offered

1. Curriculum Offered in Senior Middle School

2. Curriculum Offered in Junior Middle School

3. Curriculum Offered in Primary School

VI. Characteristic School-based Curriculum

1. "Taking Root in National Spirit and Learning to Be Modern People" School-based Curriculum Concerning Moral Education

2. Characteristic Foreign Language School-based Curriculum

3. Characteristic Curriculum Concerning Art, Physical Education and Science and Technology

4. Mathematical Thinking Training Curriculum Offered in Primary School and Junior Middle School

5. Characteristic Chinese Curriculum Concerning Writing and Poetic Prose Chanting

VII. Curriculum Implementation

1. Transform of Teachers from Single-loop Learning to Double-loop Learning to Gradually Accomplish the Research, Development and Implementation of School-based Curriculum

2. Establishment of Cooperative Team Culture to Achieve the Integration of School Curriculum

3. Establishment of Common Vision to Construct a Learning Organization

VIII. Curriculum Evaluation

1. Evaluation System for Independent Growth of Students

2. Evaluation System for the Professional Development of Teachers

3. Evaluation System for the Sound Development of School Curriculum

IX. Curriculum Management

1. A Leading Group on Curriculum Reform Work

2. Special Funds for Curriculum Reform

X. Practice of School-based Curriculum

1. School-based Curriculum Concerning Moral Education

2. Zhang Sizhong English Curriculum

3. Characteristic Curriculum Concerning Art

4. Mathematical Thinking Training Curriculum

3. Experimental Class for Gifted Junior Middle School Students

III. Application of Modern Teaching Techniques

IV. Teaching Quality Monitoring

1. Form nature problem quantity monitoring

2. Monitoring the quality of results

Chapter Eight Students Education Management

Section One Moral Quality Education

I. Flag-raising Ceremony Education

II. Education on Concept of Honor and Disgrace and Core Values

III. National Defense Education

IV. Thousand Signatures Showing Love for Taiwan

V. Learning from Predecessors, Emulating the Advanced and Singing Patriotic Songs

Section Two Education on Code of Conduct

I. Education on Civilized Manners

II. Themed Class Meetings

III. Formative Education for Students

IV. Education for Students on Rules of Life

Section Three Characteristic Education

I. "Warm Classroom" Construction

II. "Resolute Action" School-based Moral Education

III. Education on Environmental Protection

IV. Education for Underachievers

V. Education on Psychological Health

Section Four Social Practice

I. Visit, Learning and Communication

II. Activities of Benevolence Dedication

Section Five Student Management

I. Management System

1. Daily Management System

2. Conventions for Resident Students

3. System of Asking for Leave and Shuttling

4. System of Excellent Junior Middle School Graduate Selection

5. Publicity System of Triple-A Student and Excellent Student Cadre Selection

6. System of Helping and Supporting the Poor

7. System of Psychological Consultation

8. System on Disciplinary Actions against Students Violating Discipline

II. Management Work

总　述

时光流金　岁月如歌　上海帕丁顿双语学校走过19个春秋。1995年11月5日，奉浦工业区管理委员会向奉贤县教育局提出创办九年制学校的立项报告。1997年1月，由奉浦经济发展实业总公司首期投资的学校基础设施在一片河道纵横、高低不平的土地上动工建设。1998年3月29日，奉贤县编制委员会批复同意建校。是年4月，学校基础设施竣工。是年4月20日，奉贤县教育局正式批准建立十二年制的上海协和实验学校。9月1日，举行上海民办协和实验学校开学典礼。之后学校先后易名为上海市教育科学研究院奉浦实验学校、上海市奉贤区教师进修学院附属奉浦实验学校、上海市民办奉浦学校、上海帕丁顿双语学校。1998年9月至2015年8月，学校为民办（公助）性质。2015年8月，上海帕丁顿双语学校公办教师、公办学生析出，成立公办性质的上海市奉贤区奉浦学校。自此，上海帕丁顿双语学校成为民企投资的民办学校。建校19年，先后经历乘势创办、困难曲折、改革进取、健康发展4个阶段。学校在投资举办方的正确决策、社会各界关心支持、师生员工共同努力下，交出了一份让社会满意的答卷。学校经上级有关部门验收评估，先后获得上海市安全文明学校、上海市知识产权试点学校、上海市AAAAA级社会组织、奉贤区文明单位、奉贤区二级甲等学校、奉贤区师德建设先进学校、奉贤区学生行为规范三星示范学校、奉贤区教学科研示范学校、奉贤区心理辅导优秀学校、奉贤区优秀家长学校、奉贤区绿色学校、奉贤区教育局师德档案管理试点学校、上海市红十字会达标学校。

学校创办　多方关爱　90年代初，奉贤县奉浦工业区创办、开发，陆续吸引一批批中外企业到这块热土上投资发展。解决来自全国各地各类人才、外来民工及工业区居民子女就近就学问题，摆上了工业区管理委员会的重要议事日程。百年大计教育为本。1995年春，奉浦经济发展实业总公司向奉贤县教育局提出在工业区规划的教育园区建立九年制学校的立项报告，先后得到奉贤县编制委员会、奉贤县教育局的批准。1997年1月，由奉浦经济发展实业总公司投资3500余万元的学校基础设施开工建设，1998年4月竣工。为保证当年9月正式开学，奉贤县教育局从全县各校抽调教职员工42人，在应届大学毕业生中选聘23人，组成学校教职员工队伍。学校组建由奉浦经济发展实业总公司、上海市教育科学研究院民办研究所、奉贤县教育局主要负责人参加的董事会。董事会任命由名校长、名教师组成的学校行政班子。学校于1998年9月1日正式开学。是年10月，中共西渡镇委员会批准建立中共上海民办协和学校支部委员会，11月又成立学校工会和共青团等群众组织。2000年3月，上海市教育委员会批准学校向全市招生。市内多所名校校长、名教师应聘担任学校顾问。1998—2015年，奉贤区（县）人民政府、区（县）政协、区（县）教育局、体育局等部门领导多次到学校检查指导教育教学工作。上海工业综合开发区、上海市民办教育研究所、上海申生投资有限公司先后投入资金，加大学校建设力度，增添学校设备，克服办校各种困难，不断改善学校条件。全校教师、学生分别从1998年的65人、765人发展到2016年的102人、1212人。2016年，上海帕丁顿双语学校占地面积5.99公顷，学校资产现值4.94亿元。教育教学设施、设备完善，教育教学质量稳定。分获上海市AAAAA社会组织、奉贤区二级甲等学校等10余项荣誉。

决策管理　组织健全　1998年9月开学前，建立学校董事会。至2016年，历任董事长为沈金龙、胡卫、李臻、王丹花(女)。在学校发展的几个关键阶段，学校董事会及时采取调整董事会主要成员和学校行政主要负责人等审慎果断措施，总揽学校发展建设大局，保证学校稳妥健康发展。学校董事会先后4次制订学校董事会章程，规范学校运作。1998—2016年，学校董事会不断加大投入力度，为学校发展奠定坚实基础。董事会关心与支持学校教育教学、安全保障等方面的改革与创新，推动学校制度化、科学化、规范化管理。学校实行董事会领导下的校长负责制。1998—2016年，历任校长为夏明德、马伯相、丰忠汉、杨连明、徐建（代）、戚盛伟、顾行健、董俊平。在历任学校校长主持下，先后制订每学年（学期）教育工作计划，明确目标任务。学校先后召开400多次行政会议，讨论校务工作议题3800多项，制定8个大项157个小项的学校管理制度，并坚持贯彻执行。实行校务公开，加强民主管理，根据学校实际，设置学校教学管理部门，推行考核、评价、激励机制，促进行政管理正常运行。学校党组织发挥政治核心作用，历任党支部书记为夏明德、马伯相、张遴贤、杨连明、徐建、戚盛伟、顾行健。1998—2016年，学校党支部先后在中青年教师中发展党员21名，充分发挥党员教师的先锋模范作用。王新其、王益权两名党员评为上海市劳动模范，受到奉贤区（县）表彰的党员30余人次。党支部重视校园文明创建，学校连续七届被评为奉贤区文明单位。学校行政、党组织关心支持学校工会、教职工代表会议、共青团、学生会、少先队等群众团体组织，开展有序活动，发挥积极作用。

稳定队伍 提高素质 上海帕丁顿双语学校为新办学校，师资队伍来自全区（县）各校，力量相对薄弱，教育教学能力、业务能力存在不少差异。加上公办、民办教师、退休聘用教师并存，一度影响了教师队伍的稳定，教师流动频繁。1998年10月，学校首次聘请外籍老师任教。2000年起，学校邀请或聘请奉贤区（县）名校长、名教师到学校开展工作或指导。2001年，学校举行中青年骨干教师、首席教师学科带头人评选活动。加强教师队伍管理，提高教师政治素质和业务水平。2002—2008年，采用请进来走出去的办法，聘请名校长名教师担任学校顾问，请名校长、名教师黄静华(女)、于漪(女)、蒋辉蘽、金建中等到校分别作“无悔的选择”“教师的责任”“中国传统与教师的人文素养”“增强教师发展的内需与激情”等专题报告，并委派工作成绩突出的教师赴美国访问学习。学校制订《奉浦学校师德规范九条》，提出“五提倡”“五不准”“五表率”“五发扬”教师行为准则，学校与教师签订师德承诺书100余份。为激励教师提高教学水平，推行“师徒结对”、以老带新并实行名师制度和低职高聘制度；完善教学科研奖，实施《绩效工资和年终考评奖励方案》《上海民办奉浦学校教师业务学期综合考评的步骤和奖励办法》《上海民办奉浦学校结构工资方案》；开展“我心目中的好教师”征文活动，多方面调动教师积极性，激励创新精神。2005年，董事会为58名教师配备手提电脑计58台。2009年开展“教育教学能手、新秀评选”活动。2011年，学校组织教师到名校取经学习，教育教学水平进一步提高。学校小学、初中、高中部多次获课程教学奖。2012年初中、高中课程分获奉贤教育系统二、三等奖。“聪明学习、智慧教学”被市教委列为特色项目。2015—2016年，上海帕丁顿双语学校广招教育人才，教师队伍分别来自江苏、安徽、重庆、江西、山东、河南、吉林等10多个省市（其中学士11名、硕士5名）。学校坚持与教职员工签订劳动合同，维护教职员工合法权益，保障教职工队伍稳定。1999—2016年，全校受到区（县）教育局以上机关表彰的教职员工100余人次。

教育教学 体现特色 1998年，学校针对生源来自全国各地、接受教育程度差异大的特点，提倡“适时、适度、适人”的适合教育，明确各学部的教学定位。小学部实行特色教育，适量增加活动课程、双语课程、艺体课程；初中部实行减负增效，增强学生的知识迁移能力及可持续发展能力；高中部针对生源现状，注重挖掘学生内在潜质，激发学习热情和动力，改变学习方法，提高学习策略运用水平，在个体发展上因人而宜、扬长避短。2001年，学校首届高中毕业生参加高考173名，大专以上上线159名，占高考总人数91.91%，其中提前录取学生4名。2005年，学校开展“聪明学习、智慧教学”，提倡让“学生想学会学、教师想教会教”的教育课程改革，发展文艺、科技、体育等特色课程，根据学生的兴趣爱好，引导学生课余读书、文艺、科技、体育活动，坚持组织学生社团，成立学校社团联合会，充分发挥学生个人特长。学校还与奉贤中学等学校结成教学联盟，取长补短，开展特色教育，提高教学质量。2009年，全校有12项科技发明被上海市知识产权局、上海市教育委员会认定为发明专利，其中6项获奖。在教学实践中，学校教师先后编辑出版反映聪明学习、智慧教学的《为了智慧型校园的理想》，反映特色教育的《色彩静物技法突破》《小学武术校本课程》等作品，内部汇编《聪明学习、智慧教学案例集》1～5册，收入教学实践案例145篇。汇编2015年教学节活动成果展示教学论文集，收入45名教师的教学论文46篇，从不同角度体现学校教学特色。有30多个教学课题列为区级以上教学课题，其中“聪明学习、智慧教学”课题被列为上海市市级课题，并评为三等奖。

学生管理　科学规范　1998年，学校明确提出以学生为本，开发青少年的技能为中心的指导思想，制订学生自学自律的10项基本要求（公——以公为先，爱国保国；义——见利思义，不失人格；仁——团结协作，助人为乐；信——真诚无妄，守信知报；礼——尊师敬长，谦恭礼让；律——严于律己，守法遵纪；智——追求真知，勤奋学习；美——注重仪表，情趣高尚；毅——力行坚毅，自强自立；俭——热爱劳动，戒奢尚俭），规范学生教育管理模式与制度，坚持在学生中开展以爱国主义、行为规范教育为主要内容的品德素质教育。2003年，在学生中组织文化、科技、体育等社团组织，建立学校社团组织联合会。引导学生从小养成好学上进、热爱劳动、参加公益事业的好习惯。2005年，学校针对学生管理有所松懈的情况，重新制订和完善学生教育管理的规章制度，装订成册下发各班级贯彻执行。学校建立以班主任为主体的学生管理责任制，发挥共青团、学生会、少先队组织和专职宿管员的作用。2008年，编辑3册适合小学、初中、高中学生自学的《学生成长手册》，熏陶学生高尚情操。2009年，学校政教处会同各团队，组织学生参加文明学校、文明社区创建系列活动，提高学生自我管理能力。学校还运用黑板报、广播等方式宣扬学生先进事例，鼓励学生参加各类学习征文、知识竞赛、演讲活动。学校坚持开展评选优秀学生（干部），实行对优秀学生的奖励和对困难学生的帮扶，每年有百余名学生受到各种表彰。学校坚持举办家长学校，采用家校结合的教育管理方式，加强学生教育管理力度。2013年，学校收集古今中国廉洁小故事65篇并汇编成册。2016年，上海帕丁顿双语学校根据民办学校的特点，进一步完善学校教育管理制度，把学校安全工作列为学生管理的重点之一，完善具体化、规范化管理措施30多项。推动学生德、智、体全面发展。

设施设备　日趋完善　学校重视与加强教学设施、生活设施等的建设与各类教学设备的添置或更新。1997年，学校投资举办方上海奉浦经济发展实业总公司在自身经济实力还不强的情况下，投资3500余万元，在开发区核心地带选址建校。学校第一期基础设施建成教学楼，宿舍楼。1998年8月开学前夕，奉贤县教育局为学校提供教学配套设备，保证学校按时开学。2000年，学校投资建设学生3号宿舍楼，改善学生住宿条件。2006年，学校出资把煤屑操场跑道改为塑胶跑道，为学生宿舍楼安装太阳能热水装置。2011年，学校投资举办方上海申生投资有限公司投资建设7层的教师公寓楼，为引进国内外教师提供硬件条件。2012年起，上海申生投资有限公司先后投入资金3.46亿元，新建5层新的教学大楼、15层国际教育交流中心、3层的学校食堂、4层的游泳球类馆，同时配套建设长380米、宽4.5米～6米、高3米～4米的校园长廊，使校区教学大楼、学校食堂、学生宿舍等5幢主体建筑南北通连，方便师生学习生活。2016年，全校基础设施形成以国际教育交流中心为标志的3幢教学大楼、4幢师生宿舍楼、1幢餐饮楼、1幢游泳球类楼、1道校园长廊、1块标准化绿色操场的总体格局，建筑面积7.46万平方米。学校重视教育教学及各类生活设备的建设，改善教学设备经费在历年学校经费支出中占有相当的比例。2004年，学校用于专用设备、办公设备、专用材料及其他设备支出158万元，占当年公用支出（教职员工工资以外）的68%。2013—2015年，学校投入以教学设备为主的经费支出1920万元，占学校3年经费总支出的30%。2016年，国际教育交流中心大楼增装观光电梯2部。至2016年，全校有各类设备9000余台（件），保障学校教学、生活正常有序运转。

综合管理　同步推进　学校重视与加强以校区为重点的安全保卫、后勤保障工作。1998年9月，制订的校长职责，把安全保卫工作列为校长工作的主要职责之一。全校施行包括治安工作内容的班主任责任制。2005年，确定校长、班主任为全校、班级的安全工作第一责任人，由校长与区教育局、校长（分管副校长）与班主任、专任教师签订安全工作责任书。2012年，学校总结历年安全工作经验教训，补充和完善学校的17项安全保卫规章制度，细化规章制度的具体措施，并参照兄弟学校的经验，制订学校应对突发性事件的应急预案，每年安排时间进行应对突发性事件的演练。2015年8月，上海帕丁顿双语学校实行公办、民办分设，延续执行学校系列安全保卫工作措施。2016年，上海帕丁顿双语学校再次修订学校安全保卫制度，把安保制度汇编成包括14个突发事件安全应急预案和35项安保措施在内的《上海帕丁顿双语学校安全手册》，在全校贯彻落实。学校加强以食堂、学生宿舍为重点的后勤保障工作。坚持组织食堂管理、学生宿舍管理人员开展学习教育和年度体检工作。全面推进食堂规范化建设，不断提高后勤保障服务水平，被评为上海市示范食堂 。学校坚持贯彻执行“统筹安排、量力而行、保证重点、略有节余”的财务方针，建立与实行经费预算、决算、审计财务公开制度。保障学校收支平衡。1998—2016年，全校历年经费总收入2.3亿元，总支出2.33亿元。学校建立档案室，配备专人管理。学校档案室藏有人事等文书档案万余件。

校园文化　丰富多彩　2003年8月，学校设计制作白底蓝字的上海民办奉浦学校校旗和白底绿色圆形校徽，实行全校学生统一着校服，制订校训“明理力行”。2005年，校训改为“果行懿德”。提出“品行朴实、身体结实、学业扎实”校风，意为学生德智体美劳全面发展；“关爱学生、因材施教、严于治学、探索创新”教风；“志存高远、笃学不倦、勤思好问、求知求真”学风。在校园制作校训石碑，在原教学大楼教室制绘“民族魂”红墙、“文武德艺”浮雕、“丝绸之路”油彩画。各班级开展形式多样的教室文化。举办艺术节、科技节、读书节和校园运动会，活跃校园文化、科技、体育活动。在学生中建羲之社、合唱社等文化社团10余个。开辟学校电子网站，学校新闻广播电视，创办“果行园”校刊，开展教师著作（论文）及学生文化作品展示活动。全校先后有12项学生科技创造发明获专利，其中组合式钥匙扣等6项分别在市创新设计竞赛中获奖。至2016年，学校先后举办校园运动会15届，参加的学生运动员万余人次，创学校田径赛纪录66项。学校坚持每天1小时体育活动制度。学校建立家长学校，结合实际丰富家教文化。开展“家风小故事”征文活动，传承好家训、培养好家风，弘扬贤文化，丰富校园文化生活。

人物先进 集体荣誉 在上海帕丁顿双语学校创办和发展过程中，涌现出许多应该铭记的人物和荣誉。其中有关心热爱教育事业的国有、民营企业负责人和社会各界人士，有区（县）教育局的历任领导，有对学校进行决策、推动学校健康发展的学校董事会成员，有长年累月坚守在教育岗位或退而不休的校长、教师，聘用来自全国各地具有中高级职称的老教师和外籍教师、优秀教师。学校也荣获10余次区（县）教育系统以上先进集体，其中连续7次被奉贤区人民政府授予奉贤区文明单位称号。

上海帕丁顿双语学校从创办至今，时间不算很长，但经历了创办成功的喜悦，也经受了困难曲折的考验，作为民办性质的学校，学校投资举办方始终不忘初心，不仅更加坚定办好学校的决心，也积累了办校治学的丰富经验。办学19年来，学校环境逐渐优化，学生生源充足稳定，教学质量稳步提高，这充分显示民办学校的发展特色和生机勃勃的魅力。

展望未来，任重道远。相信有上海帕丁顿双语学校投资举办方的果断决策，有学校党政组织和群众团体及全校师生员工共同努力，有上级党和政府部门的关爱和社会力量的支持帮助，学校定能坚持深化教育教学改革，开拓创新，为全面建成中国特色的社会主义小康社会，实现“奉贤美、奉贤强”的战略目标，为持续培育和输送德、智、体全面发展的后备人才，做出更大的贡献。

General Description

Time flies like a song and Shanghai Paddington Bilingual School has gone through 19 years. On November 5, 1995, Fengpu Economic Development Industrial Corporation proposed a project report of the establishment of Nine-year School to the Fengxian Bureau of Education. In January 1997, the construction of infrastructure of the school initially invested by Fengpu Economic Development Industrial Corporation began on the uneven land interwoven by vertical and horizontal rivers. On March 29, 1998, Fengxian Organization Commission approved the establishment of the school. In April, the infrastructure of the school was completed. On April 20, the Fengxian Bureau of Education formally approved the establishment of Twelve-year Shanghai Xiehe Experimental School. On September 1, the opening ceremony of Shanghai Xiehe Experimental School was held. Later, the school has been renamed the Shanghai Academy of Educational Sciences Fengpu Experimental School, Shanghai Fengxian Teachers Training Institute Experimental School, Shanghai Private Fengpu School, Shanghai Paddington Bilingual School. From September 1998 to August 2015, the school was a private school (government funding). In August 2015, public teachers and students were released from Shanghai Paddington Bilingual School to establish the public Shanghai Fengxian Fengpu School. Since then, Shanghai Paddington Bilingual School has become a private enterprises to set up the school. The school has been founded for 19 years and experienced 4 stages including establishment, difficulties and twists and turns, reform and endeavor, and healthy development. The school has done a good job in satisfying the community in the correct decision made by the investment organizer, care and support by all walks of life and joint efforts made by teachers and students. Inspected and assessed by the superior departments, the school has rewarded with Shanghai Safe and Civilized School, Shanghai Intellectual Property Experimental School, Shanghai AAAAA Social Organization, Fengxian District Secondary-level School, Fengxian District Advanced School of Ethics Construction, Fengxian District Students' Behavior Three-star Demonstration School, Fengxian District Advanced School of Teaching and Research, Fengxian District Excellent School of Psychological Counseling, Fengxian District Excellent Parents School, Fengxian District Green School, Fengxian Bureau of Education Teacher's Ethics File Management Pilot School and Red Cross Standard School.

The establishment of school was gotten lots of care In the early 1990s, Fengxian County Fengpu Industrial Park was founded and developed, which has attracted a number of Chinese and foreign enterprises to invest in this land. Solving the schooling of children from all kinds of talent from all over the country, migrant workers and residents of the industrial area has been on the important agenda of the industrial area. Education is the foundation of a country. In the spring of 1995, Fengpu Economic Development Industrial Corporation proposed a project report of the establishment of Nine-year School to the Fengxian Bureau of Education in the educational park in the industrial area as planned, which was approved by Fengxian Organization Commission and Fengxian Bureau of Education. In January 1997, the construction of infrastructure of the school initially with the investment of more than RMB 35 million by Fengpu Economic Development Industrial Corporation began and was completed in April 1998. In order to ensure that the school official opening in September, Fengxian Bureau of Education transferred 42 teaching staff from all schools of the whole county and recruited and selected 23 college graduates to make up teaching and administrative staff of the school. The school formed the Board composed of head of Fengpu Economic Development Industrial Corporation, Shanghai Academy of Educational Sciences Private Research Institute and Fengxian Bureau of Education. The board appointed the school administrative body composed of prominent school principals and teachers. The school was officially opened on September 1, 1998. In October, the CPC Xidu Commission approved the establishment of the Branch Committee of CPC Shanghai Private Xiehe School, and in November, School Trade Unions and the Communist Youth League and other mass organizations were established. In March 2000, the Shanghai Municipal Education Commission approved the school to recruit students from the whole city. Many elite school principals and teachers from other schools in the city applied to act as school counselors. From 1998 to 2015, heads of Fengxian District (County) People's Government, District (County) CPPCC, District (County) Bureau of Education, Sports Bureau and other departments have come to the school to inspect and guide the work of education and teaching many times. Shanghai Industrial Comprehensive Development Zone, Shanghai Private Education Institute and Shanghai Shensheng Investment Co., Ltd. successively invested to increase school construction, added school equipment, overcome all kinds of difficulties and constantly improved school conditions. The number of teachers and students has increased from 65 and 765 in 1998 to 102 and 1242 in 2016 respectively. In 2016, Shanghai Paddington Bilingual School covered an area of 5.99 hectares with the total assets of RMB 553 million. Perfect educational and teaching facilities and equipment, and stable quality of education and teaching. Rewarded with more than 10 honors including Shanghai AAAAA Social Organization and Fengxian District Secondary-level School.

Sound decision-making management organization Before the school opening in September 1998, the school board was established. To 2016, Chairman of the board had included Shen Jinlong, Hu Wei, Li Zhen and Wang Danhua. During several key stages in the development of the school, the school board timely took prudential and decisive measures including adjusting the leading member of the board and head of the school administration, assumed the responsibility of school development and construction and ensured school development in a safe and healthy way. The school board has formulated the charter of the school board 4 times to regulate the operation of the school. From 1998 to 2016, the school board continued to increase investment to lay a solid foundation for the development of the school. The Board cares about and supports the reform and innovation of school education and teaching, security and so on, and promotes systematic, scientific and standardized management of the school. The principal responsibility system under the leadership of the board is carried out in school. From 1998 to 2016, the successive principals included Xia Mingde, Ma Boxiang, Feng Zhonghan, Yang Lianming, Xu Jian (agency), Qi Shengwei, Gu Xingjian and Dong Junping. Under the auspices of the successive school principals, the school-year (semester) education work plan was developed and objectives and tasks were clarified. The school has held more than 400 executive meetings, discussed more than 3,800 issues, formulated 8 school management systems including 157 small items, and adhered to the implementation. Implement public affairs, strengthen democratic management, according to the actual situation of the school, set up the school teaching management departments, implement the assessment, evaluation and incentive mechanism and promote the normal operation of the administration and management. School Party plays the political core role, and Party Branch Secretary includes Xia Mingde, Ma Boxiang, Zhang Linxian, Yang Lianming, Xu Jian, Qi Shengwei and Gu Xingjian. From 1998 to 2016, the School Party recruited 21 Party members from young and middle-aged teachers, and gave full play to the exemplary vanguard role of Party members and teachers. Two Party members, Wang Xinqi and Wang Yiquan, were assessed Shanghai model workers, and more than 30 Party members were commended by Fengxian District (County). Party Branch attaches great importance to the establishment of the school civilization, and the school has been named the Fengxian District Civilized Unit twice. School Administration and Party are concerned about and support School Trade Unions, Teaching and administrative staff Representatives Meeting, the Communist Youth League, Student Union, Young Pioneers and other mass organizations, carry out orderly activities and play an active role.

Stabilize the team and improve the quality Shanghai Paddington Bilingual School is a new school with teachers from other schools in the whole district (county), the strength is relatively weak, and there are many differences in education teaching ability and professional ability. Coupled with the employment of public, private teachers and retired teachers, the stability of the teachers has been affected, and teachers flow frequently. In October 1998, the school employed foreign teachers to teach for the first time. Since 2000, the school has invited or hired prominent school principals and teachers in the Fengxian District (County) to come to the school to work or guide. In 2001, the school held the selection activities for young and middle-aged backbone teachers, chief teachers and leading teachers in different subjects. Strengthen the management of teachers, improve the political quality and professional skills of teachers. From 2002 to 2008, in the way of introducing and leading out, the school hired prominent school principals and teachers as school counselors, invited prominent school principals and teachers Huang Jing, Yu Yi, Jiang Huilei, Jin Jianzhong to come to the school to make special reports on "Regretless choice", "Teacher's responsibility", "Chinese tradition and the humanistic quality of teachers" and "Domestic demand and passion for enhancing teachers' development", and delegated the teachers with outstanding achievements to visit the United States to study. The school formulated the Nine Norms of Teacher's Ethics in Fengpu School, put forward teacher codes of conduct including "Five Advocates", "Five

Prohibitions", "Five Examples" and "Five Developments", and the school signed more than 100 copies of commitment to teachers' code of morality with teachers. In order to encourage teachers to improve the teaching level, it implements "masters and apprentices" to pair the old with the new and implements the top teacher system and system of appointing someone of a lower professional title to a senior position; Improve the Teaching and Research Award and implement Incentive Scheme of Performance Salary and End-of-year Evaluation, The Steps and Incentive Methods of the Semester Comprehensive Evaluation of the Teachers' Professional Work in Shanghai Private Fengpu School and Structural Wage Scheme of Shanghai Private Fengpu School; Carry out the essay activities of "good teacher in my mind", and mobilize the enthusiasm of teachers in many ways to stimulate the spirit of innovation. In 2005, the board equipped 58 laptops for 58 teachers. In 2009, it carried out "selection of education and teaching experts and new talent" activity. In 2011, the school organized teachers to learn from the famous school and the quality of education and teaching level was further improved. The primary school, junior high school and high school have won curriculum teaching awards many times. In 2012, the curriculum of junior high school and high school won the second and third prize respectively in education system in Fengxian. "Intelligent learning, wise teaching" is listed by the Municipal Education Commission as a featured project. From 2015 to 2016, Shanghai Paddington Bilingual School widely recruited education talents, and teachers were from more than 10 provinces and cities including Jiangsu, Anhui, Chongqing, Jiangxi, Shandong, Henan and Jilin. Including 11 bachelors and 5 masters. The school insists on signing labor contracts with faculty and staff, safeguarding the legitimate rights and interests of faculty and staff, and ensuring the stability of faculty and staff. From 1999 to 2016, more than 100 staff of the whole school was recognized by the above District (County) Bureau of Education.

Characteristics of education and teaching In 1998, the school, based on students from all over the country and big differences in educational status, advocated "timely, appropriate and personal" education and clarified teaching orientation of various divisions. The primary school implemented characteristic education, properly increased activity courses, bilingual courses and art courses; Junior high school implemented the unnecessary burden for more efficient learning to enhance students' ability to transfer knowledge and the ability of sustainable development; Based on the current situation of students, high school paid attention to tapping the inherent potential of students, stimulated the enthusiasm and motivation to learn, changed the learning methods, improved the application level of learning strategy, made best use of the advantages and avoided weaknesses in the individual development. In 2001, the first 173 high school graduates of the school participated in the college entrance examination, 159 students passed the college line or above, accounting for 91.91% of the total number of participants, including 4 students admitted in advance. In 2005, the school carried out "intelligent learning, wise teaching", advocated education curriculum reform of "students want to learn and can learn, teachers want to teach and can teach", developed literature, science and technology, sports and other special courses, according to the interest and hobbies of students, guided students in extracurricular reading, art, science and technology and sports, adhered to organizing student associations, established school organization federation and gave full play to students' personal specialty. The school formed the teaching alliance with Fengxian High School and other schools, learned from others' strong points to offset its weakness, carried out special education and improved the quality of teaching. In 2009, 12 scientific and technological inventions from the school were identified as invention patents by Shanghai Intellectual Property Office and Shanghai Municipal Education Commission, of which 6 won awards. In the teaching practice, the school teachers have edited and published many works such as Ideal for Intelligent Campus reflecting the intelligent learning and wise teaching, Breakthrough in Techniques of Color Still Life and School-based Curriculum of Primary School Martial Arts reflecting the characteristics of education, internally compiled Casebook of Intelligent Learning, Wise Teaching 1 ~ 5 volumes, and collected 145 teaching practice cases. Compiled the teaching papers of teaching festival activities results show in 2015, collected 46 teaching papers from 45 teachers, reflecting the characteristics of the school teaching from different angles. There are more than 30 teaching topics listed as teaching topics above the district level, including "Intelligent learning, wise teaching", which was listed as the Shanghai municipal-level project and won the third prize.

Scientific and standardized student management In 1998, the school clearly put forward the guiding ideology with focusing on the students and developing youth skills at the core, formulated 10 basic requirements for students' self-study discipline (public-public first, be patriotic; Righteousness-remember what is right at the sight of profit without losing the personality; Benevolence be united and collaborative, find pleasure in helping others; Sincerity- be honest, trustworthy and grateful; Courtesy-honor teachers and respect the elders, be humble and courteous; Law-self-disciplined, abide by the law; Wisdom-pursue knowledge, work hard; Beauty-focus on appearance, with noble taste; Persistence- perseverance, self-reliance; Frugal-love of labor, quit extravagance and thrift), standardized the management model and system of student education, adhered to implementation of moral character quality education among the students about patriotism and behavior norm education. In 2003, it organized culture, science and technology, sports and other social associations, established the association of school societies. Guided students to develop good habits of willingness to learn, love of labor and participation in public welfare undertakings from the young. In 2005, considering lax student management, the school re-developed and improved the rules and regulations for students' education and management, bound in volumes to hand over to each class for implementation. The school established the student management responsibility system with the head teacher as the main body, and played the role of Communist Youth League, Student Union, Young Pioneers and full-time dorm staff. In 2006, the school collected ancient and modern Chinese little stories on integrity, edited Student Growth Manual in 3 volumes for students in primary school, junior high school and high school to teach themselves to edify noble sentiment of students. In 2009, the politics and law department of the school, in conjunction with other teams, organized students to participate in a series of activities of establishment of civilized schools and civilized communities to improve the ability of self-management. The school also used blackboard newspaper, radio and other means to promote advanced examples of students, and encouraged students to participate in all kinds of learning essay, knowledge contest and speech activities. The school adhered to selection of outstanding students (cadres), awarded the outstanding student and helped the students having difficulties, and more than 100 students won various awards every year. The school adhered to hold the parent school, used home-school combination education management, and strengthened the management of student education. In 2016, Shanghai Paddington Bilingual School, according to the characteristics of private schools, further improved the management of school education system, listed the school security as one of the key points of student management, and improved more than 30 specific and standardized management measures. Promote the students to improve their moral, intellectual and fitness level.

Facilities and equipment are becoming more and more perfect The school attaches importance to and strengthen construction of teaching facilities, living facilities and acquisition or update of various types of teaching equipment. In 1997, the school's investment organizer Shanghai Fengpu Economic Development Industrial Corporation invested more than RMB 35 million to select a site and build the school in the core areas of development zone when it was not economically strong. The teaching buildings and dormitory buildings were finished as part of the first phase of the school infrastructure. On the eve of school opening in August 1998, Fengxian Bureau of Education provided teaching facilities for the school to ensure that the school could be open on time. In 2000, the school invested in the construction of No. 3 student dormitory building to improve students' accommodation condition. In 2006, the school invested to change cinder playground runway into plastic runway, and installed solar water heater for the student dormitory building. In 2011, the school's investment organizer Shanghai Shensheng Investment Co., Ltd. invested in the construction of 7-layer of teachers apartment building to provide hardware conditions to introduce teachers from home and abroad. Since 2012, Shanghai Shensheng Investment Co., Ltd. has successively invested RMB 346 million to build a new 5-layer teaching building, 15-layer International Education Exchange Center, 3-layer student canteen, 4-layer swimming sports hall, while supporting the construction of campus gallery that is 380 meters long, 4.5-6 meters wide and 3-4 meters high, so that 5 main buildings including campus teaching building, school canteens and dormitories are connected in the north-south direction, convenient for the school life of teachers and students. In 2016, the overall pattern of school infrastructure is composed of 3 teaching buildings, 4 dormitory buildings for teachers and students, 1 catering building, 1 swimming sports building, 1 campus gallery and one standardized green playground with the International Education Exchange Center as the symbol, as well as the building area of 74.6 thousand square meters. The school attaches great importance to the education and teaching and the construction of all kinds of living facilities, improves the funds for teaching equipment, which account for a considerable proportion of the school expenditure in the past years. In 2004, the school spent RMB 1.58 million on special equipment, office equipment, special materials and other equipment, accounting for 68% of the public expenditure of that year (except faculty salaries). From 2013 to 2015, the school spent RMB 19.2 million on teaching equipment, accounting for 30% of the total expenditure of the school in three years. In 2016, the International Education Exchange Center was equipped with 2 elevators. To 2016, the school had more than 9000 units (pieces) of various kinds of equipment to protect the normal and orderly operation of teaching and life of the school.

Integrated management were promoted at same time The school attaches importance to and strengthen the campus security and logistics support. In September 1998, the formulated principal duties regarded security work as one of the principal duties of the principal. The responsibility system of the head teacher including public security work was carried out in the school. In 2005, the principal and head teacher were determined to be in charge of the safety of classes of the school, and the principal and the District Education Bureau, the principal (vice principal in charge) and head teacher and full-time teachers signed the safety responsibility agreement. In 2012, the school summarized the experience and lessons of school security in the past years, supplemented and perfected 17 security rules and regulations of school, specified measures for rules and regulations, and referred to the experience from brother schools to develop the emergency response plan for the school to deal with emergencies and arrange time for emergency drills every year. In August 2015, the Shanghai Paddington Bilingual School set up public and private schools, and continued the implementation of measures to protect the safety of school. In 2016, Shanghai Paddington Bilingual School revised the school security system again, compiled the Shanghai Paddington Bilingual School Safety Manual including 14 emergency contingency plans for security and 35 security measures, and implemented it in the school. The school strengthened logistics support with the cafeteria and student dormitories as the focus. The staff of canteen management and dormitory management was adhered to carry out work on study and education and annual physical examination. Comprehensively promoted the "Standardized" construction of canteen, and constantly improved the level of logistics support services, and has been awarded as Demonstration Canteen of Shanghai City The school adhered to the implementation of the financial policy of "overall arrangement and acting according to capabilities, guarantee of the focus and slight surplus", established and implemented disclosure system of appropriation budget, final accounts and audit finance. Ensured the balance of payments of school. From 1998 to 2016, the total revenue of the school in the past years was RMB 230 million and the total expenditure was RMB 233 million. The school set up an archive, managed by dedicated personnel. The archive of the school had more than ten thousand documents including personnel files and other documentary archives.

Rich and colorful campus culture In August 2003, the school designed and produced the blue-on-white school flag and green-on-white round school badge of Shanghai Private Fengpu School, required all the students to wear school uniforms and made the school motto "sensible and diligent". In 2005, the school motto was changed to "cultivation of noble morality with decisive action". Put forward the school spirit of "morally simple, physically robust and academically solid", meaning students' all-round development; The teaching style of "caring for students, teaching students in accordance with their aptitude, rigorous scholarship, exploration and innovation"; The learning style of "ambitious, never tired of study, diligent thinking and seeking truth". Made the motto stone on campus, and painted "red wall of national spirit" and "civil and artistic relief" and "oil painting of Silk Road" in the classroom of the original teaching building. Various classes carried out a variety of classroom culture activities. Held art festival, science and technology festival, reading festival and campus sports games and animated campus culture, science and technology and sports activities. Built more than 10 cultural organizations among students including Xizhi club and chorus club. Opened the school electronic website, school news broadcast television, established "fruit garden" magazine, and carried out the exhibitions of works (thesis) of teachers and cultural works of students. 12 science and technology inventions by students in the school won patents, of which 6 items including combined key won respectively awards in the innovation design competition of the city. To 2016, the school had held 15 sports games on campus, more than ten thousand student athletes participated in them, and made 66 records in the school track and field meet. The school adhered to the physical activity system of 1 hour a day. The school established parent school and combined with the reality to enrich family culture. Carried out the "family story" essay activities, inherited good family instructions, cultivated good family tradition, promoted virtuous culture and enriched the cultural life of the campus.

Advanced figures and collective honors In the process of establishment and development of Shanghai Paddington Bilingual School, many figures and honors have emerged that should be remembered. There are heads of state-owned and private enterprises and people from all walks of life who care about education, successive leaders of District (County) Bureau of Education, members of the school board who make the decision to promote the healthy development, principals and teachers who stick in the position of education for a long time or are re-hired to teach, senior teachers with the medium-grade and senior professional title and foreign teachers, excellent teachers were recruited from all over the country. The school has also won above district (county) education system advanced collectives for more than 10 times. From 2003 to 2004 and from 2013 to 2014, the school was awarded the title of Fengxian District Civilized Unit by the People's Government of Fengxian District for twice.

It has not been for a long time since Shanghai Paddington Bilingual School was established, but it has gone through the joy of success of establishment, withstood the test of twists and turns, as a school with government subsidy and running by private, the school's investment organizer has never forgotten its original intention, it has not only become more determined to run the school well, but also accumulated rich experience in running the school. In the past 19 years, the school environment has been gradually optimized, the students' source has been sufficient and stable and the teaching quality has been improved steadily, which fully displays the development characteristics and vibrant charm of the private school.

Looking ahead, we have a long way to go. I believe that with the decisiveness of Shanghai Paddington Bilingual School's investment organizer, joint efforts by school's Party and government organizations, mass organizations and school staff and students, love from the Party and higher-level government and support from social forces, the school will be able to adhere to deepening the educational reform and innovation and make greater contribution to completely building a socialist well-off society with Chinese characteristics, achieve the strategic goal of "beautiful Fengxian, strong Fengxian", continue to cultivate and transport the reserve talents of all-round development of morality, intelligence and physique and make more contributions.

大事记

1994年

5月21日 奉贤县第十届人民政府第25次常务会议决定，成立上海市奉贤县奉浦工业区管理委员会和上海奉浦经济发展实业总公司。

1995年

11月5日 奉浦工业区管理委员会向奉贤县教育局提出《关于奉浦工业区建造九年一贯制学校的立项请示》。

1996年

8月22日 中共中央政治局委员、上海市委书记黄菊到奉浦工业区考察教育园区。

是年 奉浦工业区管理委员会着手筹备学校基础设施建设的前期工作：学校位置选择、规划设计、资金筹措、施工企业招标投标。设计单位为上海奉贤建筑设计院，承建单位为上海奉浦经济发展实业总公司奉浦工程公司。

1997年

1月7日 奉贤县委副书记、县长金建忠，副书记刘正贤，县委常委、常务副县长朱德龙到奉浦工业区听取教育园区学校规划建设工作汇报。

1月 由上海奉浦经济发展实业总公司投资的学校基础设施动工建设，次年4月竣工。

年末 奉浦工业区有外资企业5家，内资企业9家。商业服务业迅速发展，有职工5000余人，解决工业区员工和当地居民子女入学成为奉浦工业区管理委员会工作的重要议事日程之一。

1998年

3月11日 上海奉浦经济发展实业总公司向奉贤县教育局申请《关于开办

民办协和实验学校的请示》报告。3月29日，奉贤县机构编制委员会批复同意。4月20日，奉贤县教育局批准设立学制为12年的上海市民办协和实验学校（以下简称协和学校）

6月 协和学校面向社会招收新生。

8月 成立协和学校董事会。是月30日，召开协和学校首届第一次董事会，会议正式通过协和学校董事会章程、董事会分工。奉浦工业区党工委副书记沈金龙为董事长。董事会决定聘任夏明德为校长，翁连云为副校长。

9月1日 协和学校开学，奉贤县副县长管其昌、奉浦工业区管理委员会主任朱家骏到校考察并检查开学工作。奉贤电视台到校采访并播出学校开学新闻。

9月2日 中共奉贤县委常委、常务副县长朱德龙、副县长汪黎明(女)、县教育局局长庄锦荣等一行到校考察开学工作。

9月10日 协和学校举办教师节活动。

9月29日 协和学校举行国庆文艺会演。

10月 协和学校组织全校师生参观上海植物园、上海万人体育馆，观摩第八届世界中学生运动会。通过社会考察了解社会，激发师生爱国爱家乡热情。

10月8日 中共奉贤县西渡镇委员会批复，建立中共上海市民办协和实验学校支部委员会，夏明德任书记。

10月9日 协和学校首次聘用1名英籍女教师来校任教。

11月4日 协和学校第一届工会成立，民主选举产生工会委员会，翁连云任主席。

11月20日 共青团协和学校第一次代表大会召开，选举产生第一届团委，周林峰任书记。

11月24日 上海市教育委员会主任张伟江，副主任张民生，督导室副主任张岚(女)，县委常委、常务副县长朱德龙，副县长汪黎明(女)，县教育局局长庄锦荣，县教育局党委书记黄兆康等到校考察检查工作。

12月29日 协和学校举行首届艺术节暨元旦联欢会，同时展出美术、书法、摄影、篆刻、泥塑、集邮作品100余件。

12月30日 上海市教育委员会主任张伟江及教育系统老教师一行40余人到协和学校考察工作。

1999年

2月22日 奉贤县教育局局长蒋辉蘷到协和学校考察检查工作。

3月24日 协和学校举办教学节活动，主题为“让课堂充满生命活力”，全县中、小学校校长到校观摩教学节活动。

4月2日 经县有关部门核准，学校新学年收费标准为小学每学期1700元、初中2100元、高中3000元。

同日 香港特别行政区中学校长代表团到协和学校访问交流。

4月8日 协和学校开展“小眼睛看大上海”的社会考察活动，组织全校学生参观东方明珠、上海大剧院、金桥出口加工区、孙桥现代农业园区，感受改革开放的成就。

4月22日 协和学校举办宗旨为“开发学生运动潜能、选拔优秀体育人才、丰富学生业余生活”的首届春季运动会，共设10个项目360名运动员参加，县教育局副局长陆建国、县体委副主任李郁仙(女)出席开幕式并讲话。

4月29日 协和学校副董事长胡卫筹资300万元，以上海教科院民办教育中心名义兴建学校3号宿舍楼。

5月11日 奉贤县政协教育组到协和学校考察教学工作。

8月18日 国家教委脑潜能开发课题组上海组组长陈根宝及袁霞(女)，市教委教学研究室英语学科组组长陈少敏分别为全校教师作“数学实验教材教学”“英语实验教材教学”辅导报告。

9月初 上海市协和民办教育中心有关领导到协和学校检查工作，肯定学校一年来成绩，提出改进教学的9点建议。

9月28日 协和学校举行迎国庆文艺演出暨第二届艺术节，新成立的学校管弦乐队参加演出。

10月22日 协和学校语文组被推荐为奉贤县教育系统文明组室。

12月29日 协和学校举行迎“新千年”庆祝活动。

2000年

2月14日 奉贤县教育局副局长项智庄到校检查指导工作。

2月18日 协和学校购大巴1辆，接送教师上下班。

2月 召开协和学校第一届第二次董事会会议，调整董事会成员，胡卫任协和学校董事会董事长。

3月6日 协和学校董事会董事、上海奉浦经济发展实业总公司工程部经理王新其陪同德国某大学校长访问协和学校。

3月10日 协和学校举行“祖国宝岛台湾在我心中”千人签名活动。

3月 上海市教育委员会批准协和学校在全市招收中小学生。

4月初 经有关方面审核，学校调整收费标准，每学期小学2000元、初中3000元、高中5000元。

4月13日 协和学校董事会聘马伯相任协和学校校长。

4月20日 协和学校启动招生宣传计划，《文汇报》《解放日报》《新民晚报》登载招生广告，上海电台、奉贤电视台均作宣传。

4月 协和学校教师沈靖华被奉贤县人民政府授予荣誉称号并晋升一级工资。

5月12日 协和学校管弦乐队粗具规模，鼓号队统一服装，同时建立学校合唱队。

6月15日 奉贤县教育局局长蒋辉蘧到校考察检查工作。

6月18日 协和学校与日本青森大学结对为姐妹学校。

11月2日 协和学校举行第一届秋季运动会开幕式，设田径运动项目10余项，400多名运动员参加。

11月22日 协和学校开展教学展示周活动。

12月8日 协和学校通过县教育局验收，成为奉贤县行为规范合格学校。

12月10日 协和学校举办第三届艺术节活动。

是年 协和学校高中男子足球队在全县中学足球联赛中获第一名。

2001年

6月 协和学校开展中青年骨干教师、首席教师学科带头人评选活动。

8月20日 协和学校董事会聘任丰忠汉任校长，奉浦工业区党工委任命张遴贤为学校党支部书记。

11月21日 协和学校举行第二届秋季运动会开幕式。

12月10日 上海市教育科学研究院民办教育中心领导到校督导。

12月29日 协和学校举行迎新年元旦文艺会演。

12月 协和学校代表队表演的管弦乐队演奏的节目《舞曲》在2001年上海市第三届学生艺术节中小学优秀节目调演中获二等奖。

2002年

3月19日 上海市特级教师、全国模范班主任黄静华(女)应协和学校之邀到校向全校100余名教师作题为“无悔的选择”的报告。

4月10日 协和学校和区教育督导室联合举办教学展示活动，全区各镇教委、各学校均指定专人参加。

7月2日 协和学校董事会聘任周佩华(女)任副校长（分管教学工作)。

9月5日 上海市教育科学研究院民办教育中心专家一行到校，帮助指导制定协和学校三年发展规划。

10月22日 协和学校举行第三届秋季运动会开幕式。

10月 协和学校代表队的西洋乐合奏“安娜波尔卡快速波尔卡”节目，在2002年上海市布谷鸟学生音乐节中小学乐队比赛组中获一等奖。

12月5日 协和学校推行“绩效工资与年终考评奖励方案”。

12月20日 协和学校举行欢送菲律宾学生来校学习期满离校回国前联欢活动。

12月30日 根据上级教育部门批准，上海市民办协和实验学校更名为上海市教育科学研究院奉浦实验学校（以下简称实验学校)，中共奉贤区委常委、宣传部部长姚海、副区长汪黎明(女)参加揭牌仪式。

2003年

1月5日 奉贤区教育局为实验学校发放首次教师年终奖，人均1500元。考核等级分A、B、C、D四档，总奖金10余万元。

2月 学校被上海市绿化委员会评为“上海市绿化合格单位”。

4月12日 实验学校成立红豆豆艺术团，定期组织活动，挖掘学生文体潜能。

5月10日 学校开始组织开展预防“非典”（非典型肺炎）工作。

5月25日 上海市教育科学研究院民办教育中心专家一行到校调研师资

工作。

5月 实验学校举行董事会第三次会议，调整部分董事会成员。

8月29日 上海奉浦经济发展实业总公司终结原学校经营管理承办协议，委托奉贤区教师进修学院代管学校，上海市教育科学研究院奉浦实验学校更名为上海市奉贤区教师进修学院附属奉浦学校（以下简称奉浦学校）。成立奉浦学校董事会，李臻为董事长，决定聘任杨连明为校长（兼党支部书记），姚志强为常务副校长。

9月2日 奉浦学校董事会重新组建，奉贤区教育局局长王森龙为名誉董事长，奉浦工业综合开发区管委会主任李臻为董事长。

是年 奉浦学校教师池敏的论文《寄宿制学校学生存在的心理问题及应对策略》在上海市中小学德育教育论文评比中获三等奖、奉贤区德育教育论文评比一等奖。

是年 奉浦学校董事会董事、上海营巢房产开发有限公司董事长王新其被上海市人民政府授予“2001—2003年度上海市劳动模范”称号。

2004年

5月15日 奉浦学校教工合唱队参加区教育局歌咏比赛。

5月20日 奉浦学校举办“我心目中的好教师”征文活动结束。收到征文100多篇。

6月1日 奉浦学校举行“六一”国际儿童节庆祝活动，上海工业综合开发区领导前来参加，并捐款44万元，设立学校教育奖励基金。

6月15日 奉浦学校颁布《高考、中考奖励条例》。

6月 奉浦学校派代表队参加奉贤区中学生民防运动会获团体二等奖，模拟逃生演练获第一名。

7月23日 奉浦学校教师丁永花(女)在上海市中小学教学比武中获一等奖，后学校选派她去美国学习深造。

7月 奉浦学校教师曹春华(女)的论文《郊区学校学生西洋管弦乐队的组建与训练的研究》，在全国中小学音乐课程教学改革论文评选中，被中央教育科学研究院学校教学研究部评为一等奖。

11月 奉浦学校被奉贤区人民政府评为2003—2004年度奉贤区文明单位。

是年 奉浦学校在“和我们一起改变世界”《儿童权利公约》宣传海报设计大赛中获优秀组织奖。

是年 学生桑雨晨(女)的1篇作文获《中学生报》上海市作文竞赛一等奖。

是年 学生柳霜(女)的1篇作文在《21世纪中学生英语报》创刊3周年征文大奖赛中获二等奖。

2005年

1月15日 召开奉浦学校董事会会议，听取和审议学校2004年工作报告等事项。

3月10日 奉贤区教育局党委任命徐建为奉浦学校党支部书记，学校董事会决定徐建为代理校长。

7月 奉浦学校初三毕业班蔡佳骏获全区中考第一名。

8月5日 上海市奉贤区教师进修学院附属奉浦学校更名为上海民办奉浦学校（以下简称奉浦学校）。成立新一届学校董事会，李臻任董事长。奉浦学校第一届董事会会议通过《上海民办奉浦学校董事会章程》。

8月28日 奉浦学校董事会聘任戚盛伟为奉浦学校校长。

8月30日 奉浦学校董事会聘任程春影(女)为奉浦学校副校长。

9月1日 奉浦学校实施行政干部管理制度改革，明确职责细化目标。

9月16日 奉浦学校高一年级参加奉贤区学生军训，2个连队获一等奖，1个连队获三等奖。

9月27日 奉浦学校董事会会议决定增补戚盛伟、徐建为董事。

11月15日 奉浦学校颁布《上海民办奉浦学校教师业务学期综合考评的步骤与奖励办法》《上海民办奉浦学校结构工资方案》。

12月5日 奉浦学校建立与奉贤区实验中学、实验小学成绩对照常模。

12月23日 奉浦学校董事会会议决定为每名教师配置1台价值6700元的手提电脑，全校计58台，投入资金近40万元。

12月28日 奉浦学校聘请上海市名校长、上海世界外国语小学校长王小平，上海师范大学第一附属学校校长章绍岩，上海北郊中学校长郎建中为奉浦学校顾问。

2006 年

2 月 8 日 奉浦学校提出“根扎民族魂，学做现代人”的教育工作思路。

3 月 奉浦学校开展课程改革大讨论，收到教师提交的课程改革建议100份，经评议按质量分别颁发一、二、三等奖。

4 月 7 日 奉浦学校聘请上海市名教师于漪(女)、张思中、季洪旭为奉浦学校顾问。

4 月 25 日 奉浦学校顾问王小平为全校1000余名师生作“让学生学会做人”的报告。

4 月 奉浦学校提出“适合教育”的办学理念，形成奉浦学校课程方案，即“提供适合学生发展的学习经历”。该方案获上海市课程方案二等奖。

5 月 12 日 奉浦学校启动250米塑胶跑道和校园网建设，完成教室多媒体、宿舍楼太阳能热水供应系统建设。

6 月 8 日 奉浦学校顾问于漪(女)作题为“教师的责任”专题报告，全面介绍她的从教经历，鼓励全校教师扎根奉浦学校。

6 月 奉浦学校的教学科研实践研究课程“民族魂 · 现代人”被列为奉贤区教育系统重点课程。

6 月 奉浦学校推行全员聘用合同制，公办、民办教师实行同工同酬。

7 月 奉浦学校初三毕业班徐丹(女)获奉贤区中考成绩第一名。全校57%的初中毕业生进入市、区重点高中，高中上线率100%。

10 月 29 日 奉浦学校举办“健身育人”为宗旨的第七届秋季体育运动会开幕式。运动会设13个比赛项目，432名运动员参加。

是年 奉浦学校教师柳肖云(女)的论文《痴心一片终不悔 心血浇开希望花》在全国中小学德育教育论文评比中获一等奖。

是年 奉浦学校在教学楼（今为幼儿园）一楼、二楼制作“民族魂”红墙、“文、武、德、艺”浮雕、“丝绸之路”油彩画，在校园小花园竖校训石碑。

2007 年

3 月 奉浦学校颁布《教育教学能手和教育教学新秀评比方案》。

4 月 21 日 奉浦学校邀请上海市教委基教处副处长江铭初到校作《关于中

小学拓展课程建设与实施的思考》的报告。

4月 奉浦学校制订《年级团结合作竞争发展目标奖励方案》。

5月 奉浦学校部分学科开展“学习包”活动初见成效。

8月25日 区教育局局长蒋辉藁到校作“中国传统与教师的人文素养”报告。

10月6日 奉浦学校师生与在校的参加世界夏季特奥会的各国运动员进行联欢，学校武术队为客人作百人武术表演。

10月10日 奉浦学校开展“九九重阳，浓浓孝心”民族精神教育系列活动。

10月27日 上海工业综合开发区第二届运动会在奉浦学校举办。奉浦学校受上海工业综合开发区委托，谱写运动会会歌的歌词。

11月8日 奉浦学校“倡导适合教育，促进学生在高水平上的均衡发展”在奉贤区第十二届教学节中展示。

11月29日 奉浦学校举行“扬我民族文化，秀我学生风采”迎新年文艺演出。

11月30日 奉浦学校举办宗旨为“健康快乐、放飞希望”的第八届秋季运动会开幕式。运动会设16个比赛项目，562名运动员参加比赛。

12月14日 上海市普教研究所所长胡兴宏到校作“关于课堂教学的研究”专题报告。

2008年

1月8日 韩国教育界人士到奉浦学校参观考察。

2月20日 奉浦学校举办“聪明学习”现场教学活动，校长戚盛伟作“为了智慧校园的理想”专题报告，展示11期学生学习专刊与部分学生聪明学习方案、教师智慧教学方案，市教委副主任夏秀蓉(女)、区教育局局长陆建国出席。

4月2日 《21世纪英语》报刊区级公开课在奉浦学校举办。

4月10日 奉浦学校聘请市特级教师、邵光标小学校长金建中，市小学语文编写组成员徐鹄为学校顾问。

4月 奉浦学校举办“奥运歌曲校园行”演唱观摩活动，初中、高中学生参加。

5月 奉浦学校举行向四川汶川地震灾区捐款活动，全校捐款43万元。

8月23日 奉浦学校举办报告会，学校顾问金建中作“唤醒教师发展和内需与激情”报告。

9月14日 奉浦学校举办“迎世博盛会，做礼仪少年”系列活动。

10月20日 举行奉浦学校艺术节“艺术——让生命精彩”开幕式。

10月29日 奉浦学校举办宗旨为“健康成长、实现超越”的第九届秋季运动会开幕式。运动会设比赛项目18项，434名运动员参加。

10月 奉浦学校“聪明学习实践案例的开发与研究”被立为市级课题。

11月22日 奉浦学校建立心理咨询室。

11月30日 奉浦学校编制《学生成长指导手册》(小学、初中、高中各1册)在升旗仪式后发至每个学生。

12月31日 奉浦学校举行艺术节会演暨迎新年联欢活动。

是年 奉浦学校学生刘雨桐(女)的1篇作文在全国第十二届青少年“作家杯”作品比赛中获金奖。

是年 奉浦学校教师翁丹香(女)的1篇论文获全国中小学德育教育成果评比一等奖。

2009年

2月10日 奉浦学校教师完成学期“课堂教育改进计划”。

2月23日 奉浦学校董事会成员调整，董事会由11名成员组成，王丹花(女)任董事长，另设监事2人。

3月9日 上海营巢房产开发有限公司与上海奉浦经济发展实业有限公司出资组建上海申生投资有限公司，亦是上海民办奉浦学校的投资举办企业。

3月19日 区教育局主办、奉浦学校承办的“聪明学习—探索有效教学的途径”现场教学观摩活动在校举行。校长戚盛伟作“为建设智慧型校园的再思考”的报告，全区各校180余人参加，区教育局局长陆建国到会并讲话。

4月12日 奉浦学校工会换届，选举王益权为工会主席。

5月14日 奉浦学校举行“五月红歌会”活动。

5月18日 奉浦学校举行小学、初中、高中3个套本《读懂中国》的授书仪式暨读书节开幕式。

6月 奉浦学校汇编《聪明学习、智慧教学案例》第一册，至2014年6月，先后汇编5册，收入145人次教师的145篇教学案例，共44万字。

9月10日 奉浦学校防治禽流感工作全面展开。

9月20日 奉浦学校开展新一轮“教育教学能手·新秀”评选活动，并提高能手、新秀津贴。

10月15日 奉浦学校小学、初中、高中部课程教学均获奉贤区教育局颁发的课程教学奖。

11月2日 奉浦学校举行“奉浦学校——快乐成长的家园”艺术节开幕式。

11月5日 奉浦学校通过上海市红十字会达标校验收。

11月10日 奉浦学校举办宗旨为“激扬生命之活力”的第十届秋季运动会开幕式。运动会设13个比赛项目，468名运动员参加。

11月12日 在“学习包”基础上，奉浦学校启动校本练习编写工作。

11月13日 奉浦学校通过区教育局的教学科研合格学校的验收。

12月4日 区教育局副局长施文龙到校作“课程与课改”专题报告。

12月8日 奉浦学校启动《智慧教学论文集》编写工作。

12月30日 奉浦学校举行学校艺术节闭幕式暨元旦庆祝活动。

是年 由学生彭谦创新设计的新型钥匙扣获学生发明专利证书，并在上海市第十四届创新设计竞赛中获一等奖。

是年 由学生韩萧鋆设计的旧牙刷板刷获学生发明专利证书，并在上海市第十四届创新设计竞赛中获二等奖。

是年 奉浦学校被上海市教委、市知识产权局认定为“上海市知识产权试点校”。

是年 奉浦学校动漫社代表学校参加上海市动画配音比赛并获三等奖。

是年 奉浦学校教师柳肖云(女)的论文《用心经营、共创温馨教室》在全国中小学思想道德建设优秀成果展评比中获二等奖。

是年 奉浦学校被上海市社会治安综合治理领导小组评为“上海市安全文明学校”。

2010年

2月 奉浦学校发动全校教师参与拟定《学校三年发展规划》。

3月 上海申生投资有限公司投资建设学校教师公寓、新食堂设施，建筑面积9075平方米，投入资金2722万元，次年7月竣工。

4月23日 奉浦学校通过奉贤区教育局“道德教育四星级行为规范示范学校”的验收。

5月10日 奉浦学校与奉贤中学联办高中英语特长班。

5月15日 奉浦学校师生开展迎世博“观、读、书、演”活动。

10月25日 奉浦学校开展“文明促我们进步，和谐与我们同行”活动。

10月30日 为改革教育教学，奉浦学校召开岗位设置研讨会。12月2日，高中教师岗位设置专题研讨会再次召开。

11月1日 举行奉浦学校艺术节开幕式。12月30日召开艺术节闭幕暨元旦庆祝大会。

11月24日 奉浦学校举办第十一届秋季运动会开幕式。运动会设田径等比赛项目10余个，400多名运动员参加。

是年 奉浦学校教师诸海萍(女)被上海市民办教育协会授予“优秀德育工作者”称号。

是年 奉浦学校食堂被评为“上海市6T实务（天天处理、天天整合、天天清扫、天天规范、天天检查、天天改进）示范食堂”。

是年 奉浦学校体育组编写《上海武术校本课程》，全书共8章，张俊杰等参编。

2011年

1月 上海申生投资有限公司依法竞拍收购奉浦学校4290余万元全部资产，成为学校的投资方、举办方。

3月9日 奉贤区教师进修学院领导到校调研高中教学工作。

3月9日 召开奉浦学校岗位设置聘任委员会会议，根据学校专家评议组意见，11名教师评为八级，14名评为九级，11名评为十级。

4月6日 奉浦学校组织学校领导去金苹果学校取经学习。

5月17—18日 区教育督导室领导到校进行办学水平测评，评定结果为二级甲等。

5月21日 奉贤区国际象棋赛在奉浦学校举行。

8月10日 奉浦学校和奉贤中学联办超常儿童实验班，9月1日开班。

10月10日 奉浦学校召开“学校每天1小时校园体育活动”专题体育工作会议。

10月15日 奉浦学校小学、初中、高中部课程教学均获区教育局课程教学奖。

10月20日 奉浦学校举行开启“艺术感知通道，打开情感闸门”艺术节开幕式，12月31日艺术节闭幕，历时70天。全校层层演出节目百余个，1000余人次参演各类文艺节目。

11月2日 奉浦学校举行宗旨为“绿色课程、阳光健身”的第十二届秋季运动会开幕式。运动会设比赛项目20项，636名运动员参加。

11月8日 奉浦学校董事会聘任曹善明为副校长，分管教学工作。

11月28日 奉浦学校举行消防演习，普及消防知识，增强消防意识。

11月 奉浦学校制订“2011—2015年发展规划”，提出新时期办学理念和发展战略、发展定位和目标。

12月31日 奉浦学校董事会聘任顾行健为校长，王益权、曹春华(女)为副校长，戚盛伟为党支部书记。

是年 奉浦学校教师曹春华(女)的论文《郊区学校学生西洋管弦乐队组建与训练的研究》获全国中小学音乐课程教学改革论文一等奖。

是年 学校校区北部7层的教师公寓建成，建筑面积5208平方米。

2012年

1月20日 奉浦学校试行扁平化行政管理方案。

2月3日 奉浦学校执行“快乐星期五”方案。

2月 上海申生投资有限公司投资建设学校国际教育交流中心，建筑面积2.64万平方米，投入资金7914.44万元。2014年7月竣工。

4月4日 奉浦学校组织师生赴奉城李主一烈士墓扫墓，并开展扫墓征文活动，98篇征文评为优秀。

4月9日 奉浦学校工会换届，选举李永卫为工会主席。

4月13日 全校为小学三（1）班白血病患者王桓栋捐款8万余元。

4月15日 奉浦学校校报《果行园》第一期刊出。

4月29日 奉浦学校副校长王益权参加中华骨髓捐献配对成功，成为奉贤第七位干细胞捐献者。

5月7日 奉浦学校试办高中国际班——中加国际教学班，加拿大多伦多五湖学院领导到校参加签约仪式。

5月31日 上海营巢房产开发有限公司十周年庆典在校举行。该公司向“我心中的好教师”颁奖，向困难学生捐款，向图书馆赠书。

7月 奉浦学校全面修订学校各项管理制度，共分9篇157项，并汇编成册，分发全校贯彻执行。

9月 奉浦学校举办六、八年级语文公开课，全区相关年级语文教师200余人参加，区初中语文教研员宋姬(女)主持该项活动。

9月29日 奉浦学校初中部、高中部课程教学分获区教育局课程教学二、三等奖。

10月22日 奉浦学校举行宗旨为“丰富学生校园生活，提高运动技术”的第十三届秋季运动会开幕式。运动会设12个比赛项目，794名运动员参加。

10月28日 奉浦学校举办“积极向上，清新高雅，健康文明”为宗旨的艺术节开幕。

11月初 奉浦学校董事会成员调整，增加名誉董事长1人，增加董事2人，董事会成员增至14人，王丹花(女)续任董事长。

11月20—21日 教育部组织的上海教育均衡发展专项督导的督导人员到校督导，校长顾行健作“倡导适合教育，建设智慧校园”专题汇报。

11月29日 奉浦学校召开董事会会议。会议决定巩固和开拓高中国际课程项目；提高民办班学生学费和住宿费收费标准；进一步深化学校管理制度改革。

12月7日 市教委肯定奉浦学校的“聪明学习”特色项目，每年下拨专项经费20万元。

12月13日 奉贤资源联盟教师到奉浦学校观摩特色课，对小学数学、初中英语教学课程予以肯定。

12月14日 奉浦学校结合区“贤文化”推进工作，开展道德讲座活动。

12月29日 奉浦学校举办艺术节闭幕式暨迎元旦文艺联欢活动。6个专场评出一等奖节目8个、二等奖节目17个、三等奖节目28个。

12月 学校高中部教学楼、食堂启动建设，建筑面积1.41万平方米，其中食堂面积3829平方米。

12月 上海市人事局外国专家管理处向民办奉浦学校颁发聘请外国专家资格证书。

是年 奉浦学校教师戚盛伟、唐继英(女)的论文《"聪明学习"教育案例的开发与研究》被上海市普教所评为一等奖。

是年 奉浦学校学生顾家(女)的1篇作文在全国中学生作文比赛中被评为二等奖。

是年 学生薛昕悦设计发明的带吸管饮料瓶获傲阳杯设计竞赛一等奖。

是年 学生吴禛设计的升降洗手盆获上海市第二届"赛复创智杯"二等奖。

是年 学生薛彧豪设计发明的带手柄护手黑板擦套获陈嘉庚青少年发明二等奖。

2013年

2月 奉贤育秀学校教育资源联盟成员到校观摩奉浦学校小学武术公开课。

3月20日 区教研中心初中组教研员到校进行常态教学指导，听课30余节。

4月2日 奉浦社区、奉贤区晚晴诗社与奉浦学校联办"奉浦社区'忘年交'江南第一牡丹行诗歌会"。

4月 奉浦学校代表队参加奉贤区第二届体育运动会，在青少年组比赛中奖牌排名第六，其中金牌3枚，铜牌2枚，并获体育道德风尚奖。

5月28日 召开奉浦学校董事会会议，审议校长顾行健"关于奉浦学校开设普通高中国际课程试点工作的设想"报告。

5月 奉浦学校汇编《智慧教育，由此起步——聪明学习、智慧教育之班主任论文集》，收入28篇教师论文。

5月 奉浦学校教师戚盛伟主持的《聪明学习的案例开发实践研究》课题获上海市第四届学校教科研成果三等奖。

6月15日 奉浦学校教师唐继英(女)、许娟娟(女)在2013年《上海教育情报》第3~4期上发表题为《教师教学行为优化》论文。

6月30日 奉浦学校高考本科上线率92.3%，小学毕业班成绩名列全区同类学校第三，初中录取分数平均501.5分，高中高考上线率61%。

8月31日 教育部中学校长培训中心副主任、华东师范大学教授刘莉莉(女)到奉浦学校讲课。

9月29日 区教育局领导到校进行教育科研示范校验收。

10月13日 国家级艺术大师、上海立达学院艺术设计与传媒学院院长李斌到奉浦学校为高一高二师生主讲《景德镇陶瓷文化》的艺术讲座。

10月 奉浦学校教师唐继英(女)的论文《基于“聪明学习”的教师智慧教学的实践研究》，获奉贤区第十届教科研成果一等奖。

10月 奉浦学校教师张春辉与徐韧刚编辑的《色彩静物技术突破》一书由上海人民美术出版社出版，该书为指导学生提高美术水平的基础教材。

10月20日 奉浦学校举行“创和谐校园，展艺术风采”为宗旨的艺术节开幕式。

12月25日 为迎接上海市社会团体管理局到校评估，奉浦学校理事会成立，褚继平任理事长。

12月27日 奉浦学校艺术节闭幕。

12月 奉浦学校自编印刷由党支部书记作序的《廉洁文化进校园》系列读本3册，小学读本内容为《革命先辈廉洁奉公的故事》，初中读本内容为《中国古代的廉吏》，高中读本内容为《知荣辱、践贤行》，全校学生人手1册。

2014年

3月21日 奉浦学校举办“传承好家训、培育好家风、弘扬贤文化”家庭教育研讨会，79个家庭的家长学生参加，评选出治家格言、小故事征文一等奖13篇、二等奖20篇、三等奖46篇。

3月28日 奉浦学校董事会召开董事会议并邀请奉浦社区、奉浦工业综合开发区的领导参加。董事会会议决定聘任董俊平为校长，原校长顾行健作“做细做实稳中求进”的工作报告。

4月4日 奉浦学校董事会在多功能厅举行校长董俊平就职仪式，董俊平作“春天来了”的发言。

4月4日 奉浦社区党工委批准顾行健任奉浦学校党支部书记。

4月 奉浦学校汇总编写《为了智慧型校园的理想》一书，全书设9章25节，论述“聪明学习、智慧教学”的研究和实践。中西书局出版，全书288千字，主编戚盛伟，副主编顾行健、唐继英(女)。

6月 奉浦学校小学毕业班考试成绩排名奉贤区小学系统第4名，高中本科上线率达92%。

7月 上海申生投资有限公司投资1447万元建设学校游泳球类馆，建筑面积4826平方米，2015年7月竣工。

9月2日 奉浦学校举办宗旨为“自信、阳光、健康成长”的校园运动会开幕式。运动会设16个比赛项目，885名运动员参加。

9月 奉浦学校小学、初中阶段参加上海弘文学校教育资源联盟，高中阶段加入奉贤中学教育集团。

10月10日 上海市教育委员会民办学校“聪明学习”特色项目结题。

11月 奉浦学校通过上海市社会团体管理局评估，获AAAAA级社会组织证书。

12月 奉浦学校被评为2013—2014年度奉贤区文明单位。

12月12日 奉浦学校2014年度教师考核优秀奖13人，其中公办教师6人，民办教师7人。

12月 奉浦学校校区成立上海交通大学教育集团现代教育示范园区。

是年 奉浦学校武术操在上海市中小学武术比赛中获第二名。

2015年

2月 奉浦学校顾行健撰写的论文《坚持依法治教，努力办人民满意的教育》在全区教育系统2014年度理论学习十八届四中全会征文活动中被评为一等奖。

3月30日 上海市奉贤区社会团体管理局向奉浦学校颁发民办非企业单位变更登记决定书。

4月23日 奉浦学校副校长王益权被上海市人民政府授予“2010—2014年度上海市劳动模范”称号。

4月24日 经奉浦学校董事会决定、上级教育部门批准，奉浦学校更名为上海帕丁顿双语学校（以下简称帕丁顿学校）。举行上海交通大学教育集团现代教育示范园区落成典礼暨上海帕丁顿双语学校揭牌仪式。

6月1日 奉贤区区长庄木弟等区委、区政府、区人大、区政协四套班子部分领导、区教育局局长施文龙等到校参加“六一”庆祝活动。

6月 帕丁顿学校小学学业考试全A，初中中考高中录取率60%，高考本科上线率达92%。

6月16日 董事会决定编写《上海帕丁顿双语学校志》，王新其为编纂委员会主任，王丹花(女)为主编，朱德龙等为顾问。

7月1日 帕丁顿学校的公办性质教师、学生从帕丁顿学校析出，建立公办上海市奉贤区奉浦学校，帕丁顿学校成为纯民办学校。

8月30日 帕丁顿学校建立第一届董事会，召开第一次会议，王丹花(女)续任董事长。会议讨论通过《上海帕丁顿双语学校章程》，聘任董俊平为上海帕丁顿双语学校校长，顾行健、陆桂英(女)为副校长等事项。

9月14日 中共上海民办奉浦学校支部委员会更名为中共上海帕丁顿双语学校支部委员会。

10月23日 帕丁顿学校工会委员会成立，校党支部书记顾行健兼任主席，施红妹(女)、程涛为委员，郎军红(女)为经济审查委员。

11月23日 帕丁顿学校举办第一届（学校连续计算为第十五届）运动会。运动会设田径19个项目及广播操比赛，429名运动员参加。

11月 帕丁顿学校教师发展中心编制《上海帕丁顿双语学校2015年教学节活动成果展示——教学论文案例集》收入教学论文46篇。

12月13日 帕丁顿学校召开第一届董事会第二次会议。会议审议“上海帕丁顿双语学校2014学年决算”“上海帕丁顿双语学校2015学年预算”“上海帕丁顿双语学校首轮薪酬改革方案”“2015学年学校工作计划”“学校收费标准调整方案”和上海帕丁顿双语学校后勤社会化管理事项等。

12月31日 帕丁顿学校举办“紧握羊毫留青史，奋挥猴棒辟征程”“亮教职工之情，展帕丁顿之彩”艺术节暨迎元旦联欢晚会，演出声乐、舞蹈、戏曲等6大类节目。

12月 奉浦体育俱乐部在上海帕丁顿双语学校校区成立，奉贤区人民政府副区长倪闽景等出席仪式。

是年 帕丁顿学校制订《上海帕丁顿双语学校外籍教师管理制度》。

2016年

1月10日 帕丁顿学校召开第一届第三次董事会会议，校长董俊平作“2015年学校工作述职报告”“关于学校副校长以上领导班子人员提名”“上海帕丁顿双语学校薪酬改革方案”的报告。会议还讨论了学校收费标准提高问题、学校后勤社会化服务问题。

2月2日 帕丁顿学校初一（1）班学生刘霖楠(女)在上海市第十四届古诗文阅读大赛初一组比赛中获一等奖。

2月22日 帕丁顿学校召开第一届第四次董事会会议。会议审议“上海帕丁顿双语学校2016年预算”“上海帕丁顿双语学校学费调整的报告”“关于实施薪酬改革方案的决议”“关于学校行政班子调整的方案”“2016年招生计划”“关于生均经费的报告”等文件。

4月7日 帕丁顿学校第一届第五次董事会会议聘任张臻为副校长，分管高中部。

4月 上海申生投资有限公司为改善学校条件，投资400万元，在国际教育交流中心大楼安装2部电梯，10月竣工使用。

4月 帕丁顿学校击剑队在“SECA之星”自由挑战赛重剑站比赛中获1金1银3铜好成绩。

5月5日 奉贤区教育局主办、帕丁顿学校协办、奉贤区青少年活动中心承办、“何球红”上海艺术教育名师工作室策划的“帕丁顿杯”奉贤区中小学生艺术单项（工艺）比赛在校举行。

5月 帕丁顿学校红十字会开展“爱心汇聚，花开贤城博爱月”活动，发展新会员112名，筹集善款6000余元，上缴区红十字会会费2000余元，并进行“三角包急救包扎技能”培训，组织防灾减灾逃生演练。

6月6日 帕丁顿学校召开全校教职工代表大会，校长董俊平、党支部书记顾行健分别作帕丁顿学校由公办民助学校改为民办学校一年来工作报告和总结，并表彰一批先进教师。

6月18日 召开帕丁顿学校领导班子会议，通过“上海交通大学现代教育示范区组织架构”“上海帕丁顿双语学校组织架构”等决议，对部门设置作了调整，竞选教学主任、德育主任、级部主任等人选。

7月4日 帕丁顿学校协同上海交通大学教育集团国际教育学院举办国际语言村入学教育体验营。

7月 帕丁顿学校22名教师被评为奉浦社区优秀教师，优秀班主任。

8月22日 帕丁顿双语学校举行“争当教育教学先锋”微故事演讲比赛，杜星(女)、黄艳红(女)、刘瑜会(女)等13名教师获奖。其中，一等奖2名，二等奖4

名，三等奖 7 名，学校为获奖者颁发奖金。

8 月 帕丁顿学校举办小学国际班，聘请外籍教师 3 人。

9 月 1 日 上海帕丁顿外国语幼儿园开学。

9 月 上海帕丁顿双语学校成立以上海市劳动模范王益权名字命名的“王益权公益体育劳模创新工作室”，工作室成员 10 人。主要从事公益体育人才成长、体育安全，高质量、高效率的公益体育事业的创新发展工作。

9 月 帕丁顿学校修订学校系列安全措施，把修改后的学校安全工作制度装订成《上海帕丁顿双语学校安全手册》，全书汇集应急（防治）预案 14 个，安全管理制度 35 项，推动学校安全工作常态化、规范化。

10 月 8 日 帕丁顿学校编写《走进学生心里》教育教学微故事集，收录校内 83 名教师 2015 学年教育教学微故事 84 篇。党支部书记顾行健作序——读教师微故事有感。

10 月 16 日 帕丁顿学校举办第二届（十六届）运动会。运动会设田径 19 个项目及广播操比赛，524 名运动员参加。高中组沈弘劼在 100 米跑比赛中成绩 11 秒 62，打破 2013 年刘易创造的 12 秒 15 的学校纪录。

11 月 21 日 奉贤区教育局到校进行区级行为规范示范学校评估，获得通过。

12 月 30 日 上海帕丁顿双语学校 2016 年教学成果—学生学习优秀项目展示等活动在奉浦体育馆举办。

是年 上海帕丁顿双语学校小二（1）班学生杨宇轩在全市 1000 余名新华小记者选拔中脱颖而出，确定与其他 3 名小记者一起于次年 3 月进京采访全国人民代表大会、政协全国代表大会会议代表。

第一章　创办发展

1995年10月，上海市奉贤县奉浦工业区正式挂牌。百年大计，教育为本。作为奉浦工业区开发主体的上海奉浦经济发展实业总公司，把教育工作纳入工业区总体规划。在交通便利、环境良好的工业区中心地段划出一片土地为教育园区的规划用地。是年11月，奉浦工业区管理委员会向奉贤县教育局递交《关于奉浦工业区建造九年制学校的立项请示》。1997年，奉浦工业区经过3年建设开发，逐渐形成规模，进入工业区的中外实业型企业、商贸服务型企业不断增加。其中，不乏携家带口千里迢迢到奉贤，在工业区周边租房创业者，外来民工、奉浦地区居民的子女就近上学成为工业区工作的当务之急。1998年4月，奉贤县教育局根据奉浦工业区发展远景和生源实际，批准建立民办公助十二年制学校。在奉浦经济发展实业总公司、奉贤县教育局等方方面面的关心支持下，经过半年时间的紧张筹备建设，是年9月，由奉浦工业区投资、面向社会招生、教育环境良好、师资配备较强的上海民办协和实验学校（以下简称协和学校）（注一）在奉浦工业区教育园区开学。全校占地4.66公顷，建筑面积1.89万平方米。2011—2012年上海申生投资有限公司又投入3亿余元建成教师公寓、食堂、新教学楼、校园走廊。2015年国际教育交流中心、游泳（球类）馆竣工。2016年，增建国际教育交流中心观光电梯。至2016年，全校占地5.99公顷，建筑面积7.45万平方米，教育教学设备齐全。学校拥有资产现值4.94亿元。纯民办教职员工、学生人数1300余人。学校开办后校名几经更改，先后分别为上海民办协和实验

新闻报 BUSINESSNEWS　INDUSTRY 工业

第4版　1998年11月10日　星期二

重点报道　□/禾子

一流投资环境要有一流人才储备

奉浦工业区建成教育基地

上海市奉浦工业区在经过国内外专家共同设计，以高标准的超前规划定位，以培养跨世纪人才为重点，规划建成了南上海的教育基地——奉浦教育基地。

奉浦教育基地位于该工业区的生活区内，占地300亩，其中占地70亩的投资3500万元的上海市民办协和实验学校，是全市唯一与上海市教育科学院联办的12年一贯制寄宿民办学校。学校每间教室均配备进口29英寸彩电和录像机、影碟机，采用多媒体的教学方法；两幢4层宿舍楼均配有电梯、电话，每两间寝室分享一个卫生间，学校拥有电脑房、语音室、各类物理、化学、生物实验室，以及占地17亩的标准体育馆和健身房，整个硬件配套全部达到市教委的一类标准。

协和学校在配套先进的教学设备同时，注重以人为本，狠抓师资力量。该校由上海市特级教师、数学专家夏明德担任校长，其余均是具有长期教学经验的市、县级优秀教师参与教学。为使学生从小接受标准的英语教育，该校还特聘两位外籍教师上课。在数学教育上引入奥林匹克竞赛训练机制。电脑教育以实践动手为主，60部电脑全部上网，学生在老师手把手指导下，不仅会电脑基本操作，还可上网遨游。学校对全部寄宿学生派出专门人员细心呵护，让他们享受家一般的温暖。“协和”从传统教育模式转向国际化标准教育之路，正成为培养跨世纪人才的摇篮。

紧靠协和的东侧，是奉浦教育基地的另一个主要教学中心——奉贤职业教育中心。作为市政府今年10个重大项目之一的职教中心，投资1.5亿元，占地220亩，建筑总面积5.5万平方米。建成后，设有机械制造、企业管理、文秘、计算机、化工等10个专业，可招生2400多人。学校分教学、文化体育活动和生活三个区。各类配套设施均达到市教委的一类标准。它的建成将源源不断地为奉浦工业区以及南上海的各类企业提供具有各种专业技能的青年人才。

现代企业必须拥有高层次的科研和管理人才。奉浦工业区不必为缺少高级人才而担心。一桥之隔就是具有百年历史的综合型大学——上海交通大学和以它为首的高标准教育基地，这是奉浦工业区高级科研、管理人才的摇篮。每年有4000多名的本科毕业生，再加上其他高校近万名毕业生，从校园的象牙塔迈入丰富多彩的社会大学。人才资源优势的凸现，将为奉浦工业区的可持续发展带来最强有力的支持，完全有理由相信奉浦工业区不久将来定能建成上海市郊一流的工业区。

1998年11月，《新闻报》登载奉浦工业区创办民办协和实验学校的报道

学校、上海教育科学研究院奉浦实验学校、上海市奉贤区教师进修学院附属奉浦学校、上海民办奉浦学校。2015年4月更为现名上海帕丁顿双语学校（注二）。

1998—2016年，上海帕丁顿双语学校经历顺势创办、艰难曲折、改革进取、健康发展4个阶段。尤其是2005年后，学校通过一系列改革，陆续摸索出民办学校开展的特色教育、管理模式和教学经验，教学质量稳步提高，社会信誉不断提升，学校各方面工作取得明显进步，多次受到区（市）教育部门的好评。至2016年，学校先后通过市、区有关部门的上海市安全文明学校、上海市AAAAA级社会组织、奉贤区二级甲等学校的验收评估。

注一：上海民办协和实验学校校名中“协和”两字，以团结协作、和衷共济之意，取“协、和”两字命名。

注二：帕丁顿为英国一小镇名。引用该镇名一则揭示人与自然、社会和谐美好的古老童话，展示学校在于爱、理解、关怀为办学理念而命名为上海帕丁顿双语学校（中文、英文）学校。

第一节　选址建校

一、学校位置

上海帕丁顿双语学校位于上海工业综合开发区中部，北依韩村路、南至八字桥路、东邻上海市奉贤工业中等专业学校、西以陈桥路为界。学校北门为韩村路

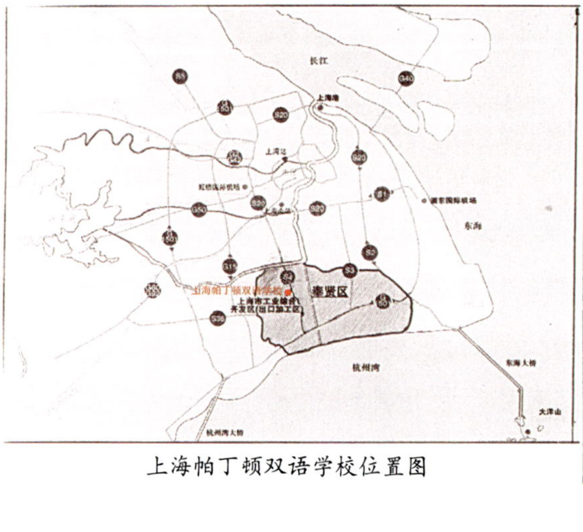

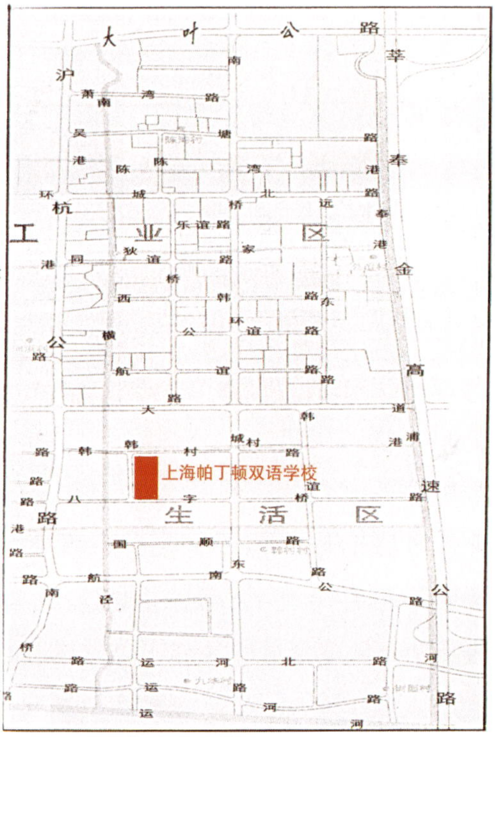

上海帕丁顿双语学校位置图

733号，南门为八字桥路686号。距上海市中心仅40余千米，与奉贤区人民政府所在地不足3千米。交通便捷，西有上海地铁5号线奉浦站、东有省道沪金高速公路（S4），南桥汽车站始发的公交南桥3线、南桥16线经过学校南门八字桥路陈桥路站。

二、学校面积

1．占地面积　1998年，学校占地4.66公顷。2010年，根据学校发展的需要面积扩大1.33公顷。2016年，全校总占地面积为5.99公顷。

2．建筑面积　1998年9月，学校创办初期，全校建筑面积1.89万平方米。随着学校的发展，教学设施不断完善，建筑面积不断扩大。2011—2015年，先后新建16层国际教育交流中心及教师公寓、高中部教学大楼等5.38万平方米。2016年，全

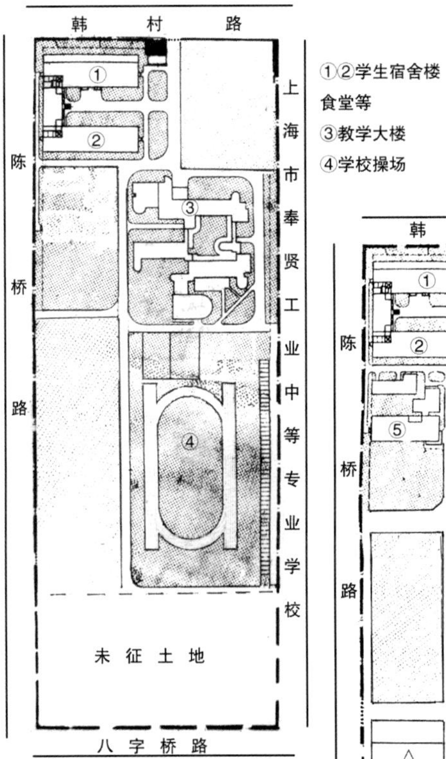

1998年上海民办协和实验学校平面图

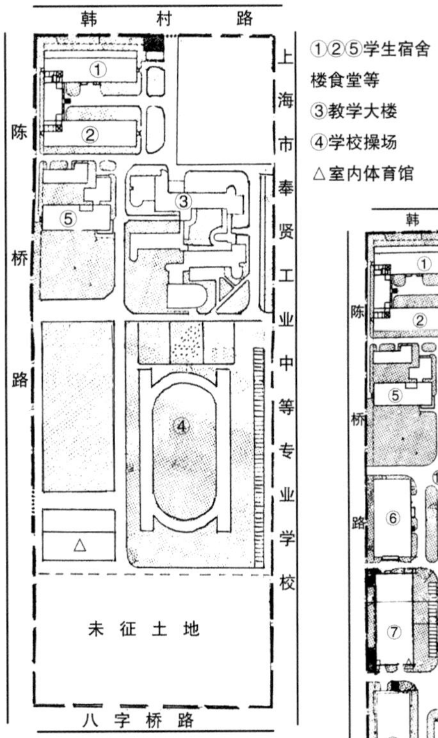

2004年上海民办奉浦学校平面图

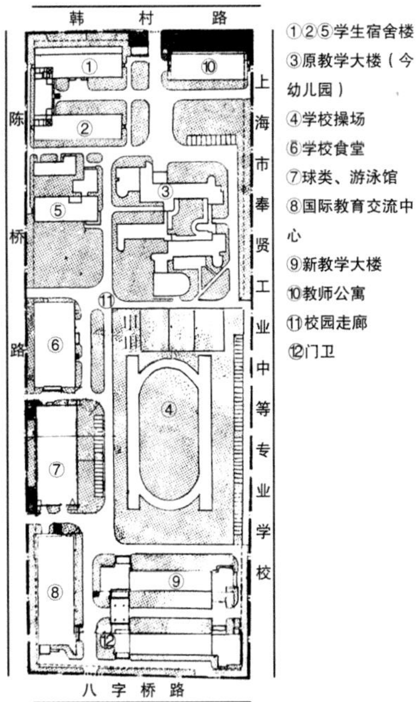

2016年上海帕丁顿双语学校平面图

校建筑总面积7.46万平方米。除自身使用外，还为其他公办、民办学校提供一流的从早教、幼儿园教育到特色专业教育的教学场所。

三、设计　建设

1．设计单位　上海奉贤建筑设计院。

2．承建单位　上海奉浦经济发展实业总公司奉浦工程公司。

1997年1月，由奉浦经济发展实业总公司首期投资的上海民办协和实验学校开工建设

2012年5月31日，上海营巢房产开发有限公司董事长王新其（左一）向民办奉浦学校捐赠50万元

3．投资主体单位　上海奉浦经济发展实业总公司、上海市奉贤区（县）教育局、上海教育科学研究院民办教育中心胡卫、上海申生投资有限公司。

4．资产转让　2011年1月，上海民办奉浦学校房（地）产等固定资产，经国家有关部门清理、核实、评估，并公开挂牌拍卖，上海民办奉浦学校全部资产转让给上海申生投资有限公司。转让总资产为4296.98万元。

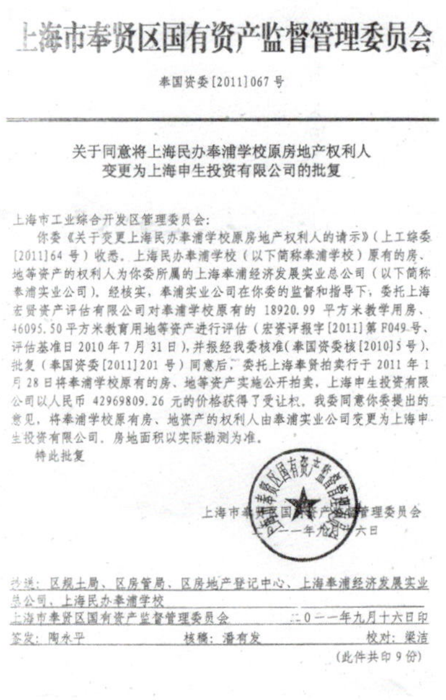

上海市奉贤区国有资产监督管理委员会

奉国资委[2011]067号

关于同意将上海民办奉浦学校原房地产权利人
变更为上海申生投资有限公司的批复

上海市工业综合开发区管理委员会：

你委《关于变更上海民办奉浦学校原房地产权利人的请示》（上工综委[2011]64号）收悉。上海民办奉浦学校（以下简称奉浦学校）原有的房、地等资产的权利人为你委所属的上海奉浦经济发展实业总公司（以下简称奉浦实业公司）。经核实，奉浦实业公司在你委的监督和指导下，委托上海宏贤资产评估有限公司对奉浦学校原有的18920.99平方米教学用房、46095.50平方米教育用地等资产进行评估（宏资评报字[2011]第F049号、评估基准日2010年7月31日），并报经我委核准（奉国资委核[2010]5号）、批复（奉国资委[2011]201号）同意后，委托上海奉贤拍卖行于2011年1月28日将奉浦学校原有的房、地等资产实施公开拍卖，上海申生投资有限公司以人民币42969809.26元的价格获得了受让权。我委同意你委提出的意见，将奉浦学校原有房、地资产的权利人由奉浦实业公司变更为上海申生投资有限公司。房地面积以实际勘测为准。

特此批复

上海市奉贤区国有资产监督管理委员会
二〇一一年九月十六日

抄送：区规土局、区房管局、区房地产登记中心、上海奉浦经济发展实业总公司、上海民办奉浦学校

上海市奉贤区国有资产监督管理委员会　　二〇一一年九月十六日印

签发：陶永平　　核稿：潘有发　　校对：梁洁

（此件共印9份）

2011年9月，上海市奉贤区国有资产监督管理委员会关于民办奉浦学校房地产权利人变更为上海申生投资有限公司的批复

四、投资主体单位简介

1．上海市工业综合开发区有限公司（原名上海奉浦经济发展实业总公司）

1994年5月21日，奉贤县第十一届人民政府第25次常务会议批准成立上海奉浦经济

发展实业总公司，为奉贤县人民政府的直属经济组织，奉浦工业区的开发主体，承载组织实施工业区开发建设的职能，主营实业投资、招商引资、科技开发、国内贸易、房地产开发、工业用房租赁、园林绿化、水利水电工程建设、物业管理、教育园区规划和投资，实行独立核算、自负盈亏的国有企业。注册资金1亿元。公司领导班子与工业区党（工）委、管委会交叉任职。1995年10月，上海奉浦经济发展实业总公司为发展奉浦工业园区教育，解决奉浦地区居民、外来民工子女上学问题，向奉贤县教育局提出创办奉浦学校立项申请，在得到奉贤县机构编制委员会、县教育局批复同意建校后，开始组织资金，进入学校筹备、建设工作。1998年4月，学校首期工程竣工后，又根据学校发展需要不断投入资金，加快学校建设。学校创办后，奉浦经济发展实业总公司主要负责人担任学校董事会重要职务，对学校建设与发展行使各项决策权，为学校持续发展奠定坚实基础。2000年2月，奉贤县人民政府与上海工业投资（集团）公司合资组建的上海市工业综合开发有限公司，为开发区的开发主体，注册资金2亿元，延续上海奉浦经济发展实业总公司的职能和经营范围。至2011年，上海市工业综合开发有限公司始终为学校的投资举办方与决策者。

从学校筹办建设至2016年，历任公司总经理为：朱德龙、朱嘉骏、管其昌、李臻、陈建庆。

2．奉贤区（县）教育局

1949年5月，成立江苏省奉贤县教育科。1955年8月，县教育科改称文教处。1958年10月，奉贤县行政区划从江苏省划入上海市，改称为上海市奉贤县教育局。“文化大革命”时期，曾数度改名。1980年恢复奉贤县教育局名称。2001年8月，奉贤撤县建区，改称上海市奉贤区教育局。奉贤区教育局为奉贤区（县）人民政府的组成部门，主管全区教育事业。2015年，全区有基础教育类学校160所，其中幼儿园80所，小学35所，初中14所，高中7所，九年一贯制学校22所，十二年一贯制1所，特殊教育学校1所。基础教学类学生9.49万人，其中小学生4.01万人，初中生2.17万人，高中生5936人。专任教师6897人。

1995年10月，奉贤县教育局受理上海奉浦经济发展实业总公司关于建立奉浦学校（初定名）立项报告。1998年3月，奉贤县教育局向奉贤县编制委员会提出创办奉浦学校的报告得到同意的批复。1998年9月，上海民办协和实验学校开办后，县教育局先后调配师资和领导骨干加强学校的领导和教育教学工作，局主要负责人担任学校董事会名誉董事长等重要职务，并经常到学校检查指导工作，对学校公办部分给予经费补助和设备投入，保证学校正常运行，与时俱进。

上海帕丁顿双语学校办学期间，历任区（县）教育局局长为庄锦荣、蒋辉藁、王森龙、陆建国、施文龙。

3．**上海教育科学研究院民办教育中心（研究所）**

为上海市教育委员会所属的教育科学研究部门，为民办教育研究专业机构。1998—2002年，民办教育中心主任胡卫先后担任上海民办协和学校副董事长、董事长职务，并以民办教育中心的名义投入资金300万元，建造学生宿舍等设施。帮助、关心、支持学校的创办和初期发展。2003年9月，胡卫以上海教育科学院民办教育中心名义投入的资金退出。

4．**上海申生投资有限公司**

2009年3月9日，由上海营巢房产开发有限公司与上海奉浦经济发展实业有限公司共同出资成立上海申生投资有限公司，为上海民办奉浦学校投资举办方，注册资金2000万元。其中上海营巢房产开发有限公司投资1803.04万元，占投资总额90.15%，上海奉浦经济发展实业有限公司投资196.96万元，占投资总额9.85%。经营范围：教育文化投资、文化用品、电脑软件销售、房屋租赁、维修、教育咨询。董事长王新其，董事李臻、徐定华、蔡德明、钟洪葵。总经理王丹花(女)，监事金忠卫、靳寿德。2011年8月23日，原投资人上海奉浦经济发展实业有限公司从上海申生投资有限公司撤资，上海营巢房产开发有限公司成为上海申生投资有限公司唯一出资方，总资产为1803.04万元。2012年11月2日，公司经营范围调整，在原经营项目基础上，增加建材批发、零售、房屋建筑工程施工、园林古建筑工程专业施工、自有房屋租赁。2014年10月27日，上海申生投资有限公司注册资金调整为1900万元，其中上海营巢房产开发有限公司投资1803.04万元，占94.9%；王新其投资96.96万元，占5.1%。从2011年8月起上海申生投资有限公司，新建上海民办奉浦学校教师公寓5208平方米、食堂3829平方米、高中部教学楼14137平方米、国际教育交流中心26037平方米、游泳球类馆4826平方米、新建校园长廊、改造原教学楼7614平方米、改造学校操场跑道等设施，总投入资金4.5亿多元。为学校后续发展奠定坚实基础。上海申生投资有限公司现任董事长王新其，总经理王丹花(女)。

五、性质 学制

1. 学校性质

1998年9月开办的上海协和实验学校（简称协和学校），以及后来先后易名的上海市教育科学研究院奉浦实验学校、上海市奉贤区教师进修学院附属奉浦学校（简称奉浦学校）、上海民办奉浦学校（仍简称奉浦学校）、2015年4月更名的上海帕丁顿双语学校（简称帕丁顿学校），均为民办公助性质的学校。2015年7月，上海帕丁顿双语学校析出公办教师、公办学生，成立九年一贯制义务教育的上海市奉贤区奉浦学校。由此，上海帕丁顿双语学校，成为民办性质学校，继续实行十二年制教学。

2. 学制设置

学制为十二年制（即小学五年、初中预备班一年、初中三年、高中三年）。学校根据社会生源需求，吸收各学段的学生入学，体现学制的规范性和招生的灵活性。

第二节 校名更迭

一、上海民办协和实验学校

1998年4月，经奉贤县教育局批准，奉贤县编制委员会审定，定名为上海民办协和实验学校。由投资方委托上海市教育科学院民办教育中心管理。2002年2月，更名为上海市教育科学研究院奉浦实验学校。

上海民办协和实验学校

上海市教育科学研究院奉浦实验学校

上海奉浦经济发展实业总公司

奉经总(98)字第003号

关于开办协和实验学校的请示

上海市奉贤县教育局：

上海市奉浦工业区是经上海市人民政府批准设立的市级工业开发区，规划面积18.8平方公里，首期启动4平方公里。为优化工业区功能配套，积蓄发展后劲，在工业区内辟建5平方公里的住宅小区，其中有投资1.5亿的职教中心，投资3千万的九年一贯制的中小学以及高中和幼儿园。目前来工业区投资客商不断增加，境内外人士来工业区居住、生活日益增多，大家对办有特色、高水准学校的呼声很高。经我公司与上海教科院协商后，拟在奉浦工业区创办一所高标准、现代化的十二年一贯制实验学校。

1. 学校名称：协和实验学校(十二年一贯制)
2. 学校地址：上海市奉浦工业区(八字桥)韩村路(南一路)2号
3. 办学性质：民办
4. 办学宗旨：为奉贤及上海21世纪发展培养高标准高水平的人才打好基础。
5. 办学目标：头脑灵活、身体健康、个性开朗，使每一个学生在德、智、体、生活能力和社会交往能力等诸方面得到发展、为升学和就业作好充分准备。
6. 办园特色：采用中外最新教材和先进的教学及管理方法，配套先进的教学设备，创造温馨的家庭式气氛，运用现代视听手段，努力提高教育质量，达到一流水平，与国际教育事业发展接轨。
7. 课程设置：执行上海市课程计划，并在数学、语文、外语、计算机、第二课堂中加强特色教学。
8. 教职工的聘用：教职工实行推荐和公开招聘、择优录用办法，对被录用的教职工实行聘任制。
9. 招生计划：98年校收一、二年级学生120名，初中一年级学生160名，高中一年级学生120名招生纳入县教育局的招生计划。
10. 收费说明：根据国家制定的收费标准，按市场经济规律、家长的承受能力和教育水平，制定收费标准；对奉浦开发区内的适龄学生(200名)按公办学校收费标准收费。

为此，请求奉贤县教育局同意将奉浦九年一贯制学校的房舍、场地和现有设备，作开办一所高水准的十二年一贯制实验学校使用，并给予办学者以办学自主权。

以上请示，望给予审查、批准

上海奉浦经济发展实业总公司
一九九八年三月十三日

主题词：学 校　　开 办　　请 示

主 送：上海市奉贤县教育局

上海奉浦经济发展实业总公司办公室　一九九八年三月十三日印发

签 发：沈金龙　　核 稿：王振宇　　校 对：王振宇

(此件共印8份)

1998年3月，上海奉浦经济发展实业总公司关于开办协和实验学校的请示

奉贤县编制委员会

奉编（1998）23号

关于建立上海协和实验学校的批复

县教育局：

奉教人（1998）字第5号《关于建立上海协和实验学校的请示》悉。经县机构编制委员会一九九八年三月二十五日会议讨论，同意在奉浦开发区新建一所九年一贯制及高中阶段学校，校名为上海协和实验学校，全民事业单位。独立建制，隶属于县教育局领导，编制内部调剂解决。

奉贤县机构编制委员会
一九九八年三月二十九日

抄送：政府办　财政局　西渡镇政府

主题词：建立　机构　批复

签发：金建忠　　核稿：王月英　　校对：汪英杰

1998年3月，奉贤县机构编制委员会关于建立协和学校的批复

上海市奉贤县教育局(　　)

奉教（1998）字第14号

关于同意设立上海市民办协和实验学校的批复

上海奉浦经济发展实业总公司：

你公司关于《上海市民办协和实验学校申办报告》收悉。经审核，同意设立上海市民办协和实验学校，学制为十二年（小学五年、初中预备班一年、初中三年、高中三年），以目前条件，同意县内招生，部分学生实行寄宿制。在奉浦开发区配套学校未建成前，对区内的小学、初中适龄儿童和青少年必须保证其入学，并按义务教育学校的收费标准收费。希望公司按《社会力量办学条例》以及《上海市民办学校管理办法》的规定，发挥企业办学优势，坚持非营利性社会公益事业的性质，不断改善办学条件，切实开展教育实验，努力提高办学质量。

特此批复。

奉贤县教育局
一九九八年四月二十日

主题词：学校　　机构　　建制　　批复

抄送：上海市民办协和实验学校、县教育督导室

奉贤县教育局办公室　　一九九八年四月二十日印发

签发：庄锦荣　　核稿：曹建国　　校对：袁军辉

1998年4月，奉贤县教育局同意设立上海市民办协和实验学校的批复

二、上海市奉贤区教师进修学院附属奉浦学校

2003年8月，奉浦经济发展实业总公司终结原学校经营管理承办者承办协议，学校投资举办方上海奉浦经济发展实业总公司委托奉贤区教育局所属的区教师进修学院代管，学校更名为上海市奉贤区教师进修学院附属奉浦学校。

上海奉贤区教师进修学院附属奉浦学校

三、上海民办奉浦学校

2005年8月，根据上级教育部门厘清办学主体的要求，经上海市教育委员会民办管理部门审核批准，学校更名为上海民办奉浦学校。

上海民办奉浦学校

四、上海帕丁顿双语学校

2011年1月，民办奉浦学校房（地）产等资产转让给上海申生投资有限公司，上海申生投资有限公司成为民办奉浦学校的投资方和学校经营管理方。2015年4月，上海民办奉浦学校更名为上海帕丁顿双语学校。是年8月，上海民办奉浦学校的公办成份从原校中析出，由公办教师和公办学生组成新校，校名为上海市奉贤区奉浦学校，校舍租赁上海帕丁顿双语学校。自此上海帕丁顿双语学校成为纯

上海帕丁顿双语学校

民办学校。

第三节 学校资产

上海帕丁顿双语学校经过19年的投资和积累，至2016年上海帕丁顿双语学校房产总值4.8亿元。设备原值1351.52万元，合计总资产现值4.94亿元。

一、学校房（地）产

1997年1月，上海奉浦经济发展实业总公司征用土地4.66公顷，为学校建设用地，并开始投资进行学校教学楼等基础设施的建设，一期工程投入资金3500余万元。1999年，胡卫以上海教育科学研究院民办教育中心名义投入300万元用于学校宿舍楼建设。2003年，胡卫以集体名义投入的资金由奉浦经济发展实业有限公司接管，胡卫投资资金予以偿还。2011年1月，上海民办奉浦学校校产经公开拍卖转让，受让方为上海申生投资有限公司。自此上海申生投资有限公司成为学校资产的所有者和学校投资方、举办方。2011年起，上海申生投资有限公司陆续投入资金4.5亿多元进行学校房屋建设，改善教育教学环境。2016年，全校房产建筑面积达7.46万平方米，房产现值约4.8亿元。

2016年上海帕丁顿双语学校房产现值情况表

表1-3-1

建筑名称	建筑面积（平方米）	建成时间	现值（万元）
合计	74642.08		47956.83
4层教学楼	7614.55	1998	3807.28
4层宿舍楼（一）	3026.86	1998	1531.43
4层宿舍楼（二）	7709.96	1998	3854.98
浴室	240.77	1998	120.39
门卫（老）	111.09	1998	55.55
7层教师公寓	5208.91	2011	3646.24
食堂	3829.34	2012	2680.54
6层教学楼（新）	14137.13	2012	9895.99
15层国际教育交流中心	26037.47	2015	18226.23
3层游泳（球类）馆	4826.00	2015	3378.20
校园长廊	1900.00	2015	360.00
国际教育交流中心增建观光电梯		2016	400.00

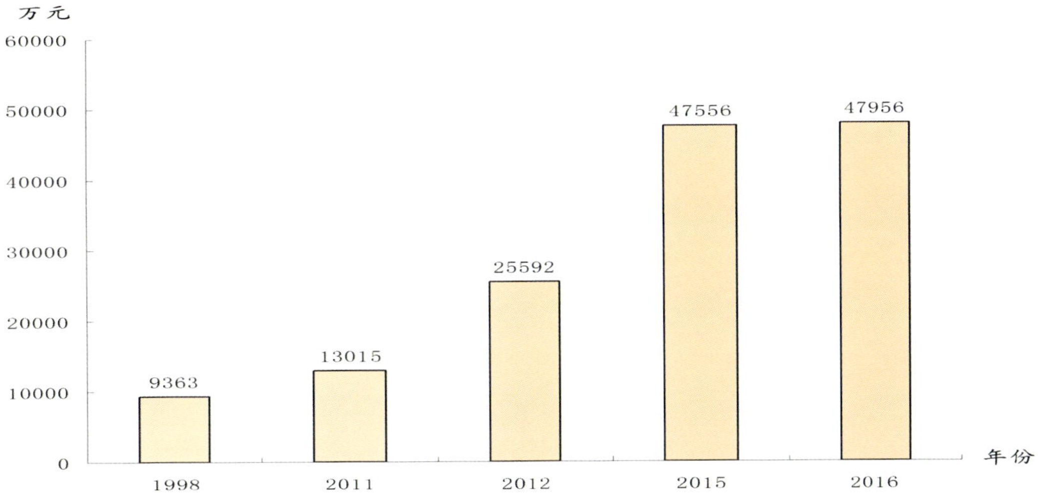

1998—2016年上海帕丁顿双语学校房产发展示意图

说明：以2016年价值计算

二、设备资产

为提高教育教学质量，上海帕丁顿双语学校在19年办学中，不断购进和更新各种教学设施、设备，逐步改善文化娱乐、会议活动、体育场所（地）和学校食堂、寄宿生住宿条件。2016年，全校拥有各种教学、办公、生活设施设备9400多件，历年累计投入资金4000余万元。现有设备原值1351.52万元。

2016年上海帕丁顿双语学校教学设备情况表

表1-3-2

设备类型	件（台）	原值（万元）	设备类型	件（台）	原值（万元）
合计	9427	1351.52	教室办公设备	5755	138.60
教学设备	1910	716.27	交通通信设备	47	85.21
文体卫生设备	621	187.42	宿舍食堂设备	1094	224.02

第四节　学校人口

1998年9月，上海民办协和实验学校开学，首批教职工由县教育局从全县各校抽调42人，从应届大学毕业生中招收23人，开始在学校驻地和外来人员子女中招收学生。2000年3月，市教育委员会批准协和实验学校可以在全市范围内招生。生源随上海工业综合开发区外来民工增加而增加。2007年以后学生人数稳定在1000人以上。2016年，帕丁顿学校已改为纯民办学校，全校师生1324人。其中学生1212人。

一、教职工

1998年9月，全校教职员工65人。2005年为62人，2016年2月为112人。分别比1998年增加23.08%、72.3%。

二、学　生

1998年9月，全校公办民办学生765人，2005年为863人，2010年突破1300人，2014年超过1500人，2015年8月改为纯民办学校，民办学生稳定增加。2016年民办学生1212人。

1998—2016年上海帕丁顿双语学校人口情况表

表1-4-1　　单位：人

年份	总人数	教职工	学生	年份	总人数	教职工	学生
1998	830	65	765	2008	1217	67	1150
1999	959	62	897	2009	1289	91	1198
2000	1133	85	1048	2010	1407	99	1308
2001	1050	54	996	2011	1481	116	1365
2002	987	71	916	2012	1587	146	1441
2003	1090	77	1013	2013	1667	162	1505
2004	855	72	783	2014	1723	167	1556
2005	925	62	863	2015	1123	109	1014
2006	931	63	868	2016	1354	112	1212
2007	1108	66	1042				

说明：教职员工、学生人数摘自《奉贤统计年鉴》。2015、2016年因公办、民办分设而人数减少

第五节　发展历程

一、顺势创办

1998年4月，学校基础设施即将竣工，奉贤县教育局批准上海民办协和实验学校于夏季正式面向社会招生。为解决新校师资力量，县教育局从全县部分学校调配教职工42人，招收应届大学毕业生23人。在“专家治校、名师执教”广告宣传效应和“学生进步、家长满意、社会信任”的教育目标、崭新优美的校舍

环境吸引下，许多家长携子拖女纷纷到学校报名。高中原计划招收2个班，因报名学生多，根据学生与家长的要求，又扩大招2个班。全校18个班级，学生765人。其中，小学部班级5个，学生175人；初中部班级9个，学生387人；高中部班级4个，学生203人。学校先后制订教育教学、师生队伍管理、安全卫生管理等一系列措施，并聘请1名市特级教师为校长。经过全校教职员工共同努力，民办寄宿制学校管理逐步完善，实现良好开局。2001年全校173名应届高中毕业生，高考录取大学本科28人，占毕业生人数16.18%，录取大学专科70人，占毕业生人数40.46%，两者相加录取98人，占毕业生人数的56.64%。学校教育教学引起社会关注。

二、艰难曲折

从学校创办到2000年虽开局顺利，但在现行教育体制下民办教育如何优化生源，发展、培育和激励师资队伍，开掘课程特色等方面尚缺乏经验；加上地域间的差异和体制机制上发生的矛盾未能及时妥善地加以化解，使学校丧失持续发展的良机，教育质量下滑，社会声誉下降。2000年4月至2005年7月，校董事会先后3次更换校长，但见效甚微。2003年上海工业综合开发区出资终结原委托管理协议，偿还社会投资学校的部分资金，委托奉贤区教育局所属的奉贤区教师进修学院管理，仍未挽回生源日减、教师辞聘的被动局面，学校教育教学正常运转受到严重影响。是年，学校高中毕业班学生参加高考139人，总录取率仅31.65%，为同类学校最低。初中毕业生中考录取率在全区28所初中学校中位列23位，学校社会声誉下滑。2005年，全校开设的班级由2000年29个班级下降至23个班级，学生人数由1048人下降至863人，分别下降20.69%、18.66%。

三、改革进取

2005年8月，面对学校困境，上海工业综合开发区管委会负责人兼任学校董事会的董事长。董事会作出断然决定，聘请奉贤名校校长2人，担任学校的正副校长。按照校长负责制原则授予学校改革职权。针对生源不足、教师信心不足的问题，学校领导班子提出“校荣我荣，校耻我辱”的共同价值观，采取多项行之有效措施，鼓励教师重拾兴校决心。并以“教师想教会教，学生想学会学”的校园愿望，在加强学校常规管理的基础上，把学校整体发展目标分解到年级组、教师；实行课程改革，形成体现民办学校特色课程；建立和优化考核考评机制，制订教职工学期综合考评指标和考评办法，以及学校各年级团队合作目标奖励条例；更新办学理念，倡导“聪明学习，智慧教学”的教学策略，同时先后聘请市内6名名校长、名教师为学校顾问，邀请名教师到学校进行教育教学指导等一系列改革措施，全校教育教学面貌逐渐改观。生源增加，教师稳定。《“聪明学习”的实践案例研究》课题为市级课题，获上海市教育科学研究所批准后付诸实施。2012年，小学毕业考试成绩在全区35所小学中名列第三名，初中中考成绩在全区31所学校中列第七名，从小学到初中、高中均获全区课程教学奖。2006—2007年连续2年，2名初中学生在全区中考中列总分第一。

四、健康发展

2012年，学校新一届董事会采取一系列措施，使学校教学工作逐渐走上稳定发展的轨道。是年，先后试行扁平化行政管理方案，试办高中国际班。年末“聪明学习”特色项目得到市教育委员会肯定。2014年9月，学校小学部、初中部阶段参加弘文学校教育资源联盟，巩固、完善、落实各项管理措施，高中阶段加入奉贤中学教育集团，取长补短不断提高教育教学水平。是年10月，学校被上海市社会团体管理局评为AAAAA级社会组织。2015年4月，学校改名为上海帕丁顿双语学校，8月由民办公助学校改为民办学校，成立新一届董事会，学校进一步实施薪酬改革方案，调整校领导班子，继续开展特色教学，教学质量逐步提高。2014年，学校小学毕业考试排名全区第四。是年小学学业考试全A，中考高中录取率60%。连续2年高考本科上线率92%。是年，学校被评为2013—2014年度奉贤区文明单位。2016年全校高考录取本科生92人，本科上线率98.2%，本科、大专总录取率100%。

第六节　验收　评估

一、二级甲等学校验收

2010年5月，上海民办奉浦学校经奉贤区教育督导室及基教科对学校的办学条件、师资队伍、课程教学、学校管理、招生管理、收费管理、财务管理、师生权益等10个方面进行检查评估，认定为二级甲等学校。

2010年上海民办奉浦学校达标升级评估情况表

表 1-5-1

评估主要内容	市规定指标	学校实际指标
校舍	独立使用	独立使用
占地人均面积平方米	>43.85 平方米	58.03 平方米
绿化人均面积平方米	>35.00 平方米	>35.00 平方米
建筑面积人均平方米	>6.94 平方米	23.84 平方米
活动场地人均平方米	>2.00 平方米	2.80 平方米
教学设施设备	齐全	齐全
专用教室设备	达到“94”标准	达到“94”标准
校长任职资格	一级一等校长资格	为奉贤首批名校长（原致远中学校长）
教师任职资格	专职教师达标	达标
课程教学	严格执行	严格执行
各项管理	依法执行	依法执行

二、上海市AAAAA级社会组织评估

2013年11月5日，上海民办奉浦学校向市社会组织规范化建设评估委员会提交对学校进行评估的申请。2014年4月，上海市社会组织规范化建设评估委员会组织专人对上海民办奉浦学校进行全面评估。评估委员会按照“上海市民办非企业单位规范化建设评估”的要求，通过听汇报、看现场、阅资料、内外调查征求意见等方法，对学校的基础设施（法人资格、章程、登记和备案、年度检查），内部治理（发展规划、组织机构、人力资源、领导班子建设、档案证章管理），业务活动和诚信建设（公益活动、提供服务、信息公开）社会评价（内部评价、外部评价）等4个方面14个大项239个小项进行全面检查评估，认为已基本符合AAAAA级社会组织要求。2014年向学校颁发AAAAA级社会组织称号证书。

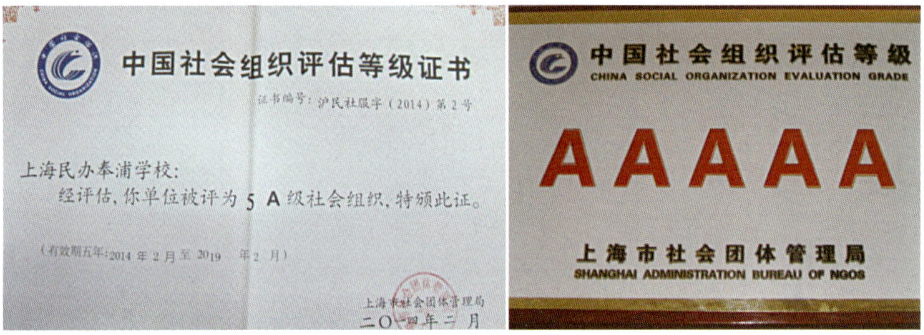

2014年2月，上海民办奉浦学校被评为AAAAA级社会组织的证书

三、其他荣誉

1998—2016年，上海帕丁顿双语学校，经过自身的努力与社会各界的关心帮助，学校各方面管理工作逐步规范、科学，学校面貌不断改观。经市、区的有关部门验收评估，还先后获得11项荣誉称号。2010年，学校食堂被中国饭店协会、上海餐饮行业协会评为餐饮业（六T实务）现场管理示范食堂。

2010年，学校食堂被中国饭店协会、上海餐饮行业协会评为餐饮业（六T实务）现场管理示范食堂

1998—2016年上海帕丁顿双语学校验收评估获得荣誉情况表

表1-5-1

荣誉名称	验收评估机关	授予时间
2008—2009年度上海市安全文明校园	上海市综治委周边治安治理领导小组	2010.2
上海市知识产权试点校	上海市教育委员会、上海市知识产权局	2009.3
上海市红十字会达标校	上海市红十字会	2009.11
奉贤区学生行为规范三星示范校	奉贤区教育局	2009.1
奉贤区心理辅导优秀校	奉贤区教育局	2009.10
奉贤区师德建设先进校	奉贤区教育局	2008、2011
奉贤区教育局师德档案管理试点校	奉贤区教育局、档案局	2012
奉贤区优秀家长学校	奉贤区教育局	2000
奉贤区教学科研先进校	奉贤区教育局	2010.1
奉贤区绿化合格单位	上海市绿化委员会	2003.2
奉贤区文明单位	奉贤区人民政府	2003年至今

第二章　决策机构

1998年8月，上海民办协和实验学校成立董事会，董事会成员由学校投资方上海奉浦经济发展实业总公司、上海教育科学研究院民办教育中心（协和集团）、奉贤县教育局及学校代表组成。1998—2015年8月，在民办（公助）学校期间，由于部分学校投资方的变动，董事会机构也作相应调整。2015年8月，学校由民办（公助）转为纯民办学校，学校董事会成员由投资举办方、学校代表组成。1998—2016年，先后产生5届董事会，产生董事长6人次，分别为沈金龙、胡卫、李臻、王丹花(女)，董事46人次。先后制订上海民办协和学校董事会章程、上海市奉贤区教师进修学院附属奉浦学校董事会章程、上海民办奉浦学校董事会章程、上海帕丁顿双语学校章程。召开董事会会议23次，决定学校重大事项72项。董事会成为学校不断全面规划建设、健康发展的决策机构。

第一节　民办（公助）学校董事会

1998年8月至2015年8月，学校为民办（公助）性质，期间董事会成员由出资举办单位、上级教育主管部门、学校推荐协商产生。董事会分别由名誉董事长、董事长、副董事长、董事若干人组成。董事会为学校的最高决策机构。

一、上海民办协和实验学校董事会

1. 第一届学校董事会

由名誉董事长1人、董事长1人、副董事长1人、董事4人共7人组成，任期1998年8月至2000年2月。

名誉董事长	朱嘉骏	上海奉浦经济发展实业总公司总经理
董　事　长	沈金龙	上海奉浦经济发展实业总公司常务副总经理
副董事长	胡　卫	上海市教育科学研究院民办教育研究所所长
董　　　事	王新其	上海奉浦经济发展实业总公司工程部经理
	夏明德	上海市教育委员会教研室原教研员、学校校长

	钱在森	上海教育科学研究所原所长
	庄锦荣	上海市奉贤县教育局局长

2．**第二届学校董事会**

由名誉董事长1人、董事长1人、副董事长2人、董事3人共7人组成，任期2000年2月至2002年5月。

名誉董事长	蒋辉蘗	上海市奉贤区（县）教育局局长
董事长	胡　卫	上海市教育科学研究院民办教育研究所所长
副董事长	庄锦荣	原上海市奉贤县教育局局长
	陆金莲(女)	上海市工业综合开发区党工委副书记
董事	王新其	上海奉浦经济发展实业总公司工程部经理
	夏明德	上海市教育委员会教研室原教研员、学校校长
	钱在森	上海教育科学研究所原所长

3．**第三届学校董事会**

由名誉董事长1人、董事长1人、副董事长2人、董事4人共8人组成。2002年7月，学校更名为上海市教育科学研究院奉浦实验学校，董事会成员延任。任期为2002年5月至2003年8月。

名誉董事长	王森龙	上海市奉贤区教育局局长
董事长	胡　卫	上海市教育科学研究院民办教育研究所所长
副董事长	陆建国	上海市奉贤区教育局副局长
	钟洪葵	上海市工业综合开发区党工委副书记
董事	王　强	上海市教育科学研究院民办教育研究所党委书记
	周远生	上海市教育科学研究院实验中学校长
	丰忠汉	上海市教育科学研究院奉浦实验学校校长
	钱在森	上海教育科学研究所原所长

二、上海市奉贤区教师进修学院附属奉浦学校董事会

2003年8月，学校由上海工业综合开发区接管，更名为上海市奉贤区教师进修学院附属奉浦学校。学校重新成立董事会，董事会由名誉董事长1人、董事长1人、副董事长3人、董事4人共9人组成，任期2003年8月至2005年8月。

名誉董事长	王森龙	上海市奉贤区教育局局长

董事长	李 臻	上海市工业综合开发区总经理
副董事长	钟洪葵	上海市工业综合开发区党工委副书记
	陆建国	上海市奉贤区教育局副局长
	杨连明	上海市奉贤区教师进修学院院长
董事	王明芳(女)	上海工业综合开发区教育管理办公室负责人
	王新其	上海营巢房产开发有限公司董事长
	王 斌	上海市奉贤区教育局计财科科长
	卫文若	上海工业综合开发区企业服务部主任

三、上海民办奉浦学校董事会

2005 年 8 月，为厘清办学主体，上海市奉贤区教师进修学院附属奉浦学校更名为上海民办奉浦学校。学校重新建立董事会。2009 年 2 月起，董事会另设监事 3 人。

1. 第一届学校董事会

由名誉董事长 1 人、董事长 1 人、副董事长 1 人、董事 7 人共 10 人组成。任期 2005 年 8 月至 2009 年 2 月。

名誉董事长	王森龙	上海市奉贤区教育局局长
董事长	李 臻	上海市工业综合开发区总经理
副董事长	钟洪葵	上海市工业综合开发区党工委副书记
董事	杨连明	上海市奉贤区教师进修学院院长
	王明芳(女)	上海工业综合开发区教育管理办公室负责人
	王新其	上海营巢房产开发有限公司董事长
	王 斌	上海市奉贤区教育局计财科科长
	卫文若	上海市工业综合开发区企业服务部主任
	戚盛伟	上海民办奉浦学校校长
	徐 建	上海民办奉浦学校党支部书记

2. 第二届学校董事会

2009 年初，由上海营巢房产开发有限公司、上海工业综合开发区联合组建上海申生投资有限公司，成为奉浦学校投资、举办企业。学校董事会重新建立，设名誉董事长 2 人，董事长 1 人，副董事长 2 人，董事 6 人，共 11 人组成。同时设监事3人，任期为2009年2月至2012年7月。

名誉董事长	陆建国	上海市奉贤区教育局局长
	李　臻	上海市工业综合开发区管委会主任
董　事　长	王丹花(女)	上海申生投资有限公司总经理
副董事长	钟洪葵	上海市工业综合开发区党工委副书记
	庄锦荣	原上海市奉贤县教育局局长
董　事	朱玉平	上海市奉贤区教育局副局长
	王　斌	上海市奉贤区教育局计财科科长
	戚盛伟	上海民办奉浦学校校长
	王益权	上海民办奉浦学校工会主席
	杨连明	上海奉贤区教师进修学院院长
	何建华(女)	上海市工业综合开发区教育管理办公室主任
监　　事	王新其	上海申生投资有限公司董事长
	靳寿德	上海市工业综合开发区财务部主任
	金忠卫	上海营巢房产开发有限公司财务总监

2012年7月，民办奉浦学校董事会人员调整，设名誉董事长3人，董事长1人，副董事长2人，董事8人，同时设监事1人。任期至2015年4月。

名誉董事长	陆建国	奉贤区教育局局长
	陈建庆	上海市工业综合开发区总经理
	王少峰	奉浦社区党工委书记、主任
董　事　长	王丹花(女)	上海申生投资有限公司总经理
副董事长	庄锦荣	原奉贤县教育局局长
	钱秀娟(女)	奉浦社区办事处副主任
董　　事	朱玉平	奉贤区教育局副局长
	杨连明	上海奉贤区教师进修学院院长
	袁军辉	奉贤区教育局计划财经科科长
	张培良	奉贤区教育局民办教育科科长
	靳寿德	上海市工业综合开发区财务部主任
	石士康	上海市工业综合开发区教育管理办公室负责人
	顾行健	上海民办奉浦学校校长

　　　　江仁章　　奉贤区奉浦社区教育干部
监　　事　金忠卫　　上海营巢房产开发有限公司财务总监

四、上海帕丁顿双语学校董事会

2015年4月，上海民办奉浦学校易名为上海帕丁顿双语学校，学校性质仍为民办（公助）。董事会成员由原上海民办奉浦学校董事会延任至2015年8月学校改为纯民办性质另组董事会止。

五、董事会会议

1998年8月至2015年8月，民办（公助）学校董事会先后召开董事会会议18次，重要的会议议程31项。5次调整董事会组成人员，聘任校长（代校长）8人次，并作出一系列重要决定。

1998—2015年8月上海帕丁顿双语学校部分董事会会议情况表

表2-1-1

会议时间	会议主要内容	主持人	出席人数
1998.8.30	1.决定董事会人员分工，设名誉董事长1名，董事长1人，副董事长1人，董事4人，沈金龙为董事长 2.讨论通过《上海民办协和实验学校董事会章程》 3.审议通过“上海民办协和实验学校1998—2000年办学规模三年规划” 4.决定上海民办协和实验学校行政班子组成人员，聘任夏明德为校长	沈金龙	7
2000.2.20	1.调整董事会部分人员，胡卫为董事长 2.调整协和实验学校行政班子，聘任马伯相为校长	胡　卫	7
2001.8.20	调整协和实验学校行政班子，聘任丰忠汉为校长	胡　卫	7
2002.7.2	决定聘任周佩华(女)为协和实验学校副校长	胡　卫	7

续表 2-1-1

会议时间	会议主要内容	主持人	出席人数
2003.8.29	1.决定终结委托上海教育科学研究院民办教育中心管理学校的协议，学校委托上海市奉贤区教师进修学院管理，更名为上海市奉贤区教师进修学院附属奉浦学校 2.决定学校董事会人员分工，设名誉董事长 1 人，董事长 1 人，副董事长 3 人，董事 4 人，李臻为董事长 3.讨论通过《上海市奉贤区教师进修学院附属奉浦学校董事会章程》 4.决定奉浦学校行政班子人员，聘任杨连明为校长 5.讨论通过《上海市奉贤区教师进修学院附属奉浦学校 2003 年 9 月至 2004 年 8 月经费支出预算》 6.听取《上海市奉贤区教师进修学院附属奉浦学校 2003 年 9 月至 2006 年 8 月生源情况调整报告》 7.听取与审议《上海市奉贤区教师进修学院附属奉浦学校 2003 年 9 月至 2006 年 8 月硬件设施规划及经费估算报告》	李　臻	9
2005.1.15	1.听取和审议《上海市奉贤区教师进修学院附属奉浦学校 2004 学年第一学期工作总结报告》 2.听取学校《关于 2005 年秋季招生调研及计划报告》 3.听取学校《2004 学年第一学期教学成绩分析报告》 4.讨论学校校舍总体规划布局 5.讨论通过《2004 年度学校财务报告》	李　臻	9
2005.3.1	学校董事会决定徐建为代校长	李　臻	8
2005.8.30	1.根据上级教育部门厘清办学主体要求，决定上海市奉贤区教师进修学院附属奉浦学校更名为上海民办奉浦学校 2.重新组建学校董事会，设名誉董事长 1 人，董事长 1 人，副董事长 1 人，董事 7 人，李臻为董事长 3.讨论通过《上海民办奉浦学校董事会章程》 4.决定调整学校行政班子，聘任戚盛伟为校长	李　臻	8
2005.9.27	学校董事会决定戚盛伟、徐建为学校董事会董事	李　臻	10
2005.12.23	学校董事会决定为全校每名教师配备每台 6700 元的手提电脑，共计 58 台	李　臻	10
2009.2.23	上海奉浦经济发展实业有限公司和上海营巢房产开发有限公司出资组建上海申生投资有限公司后，决定调整学校董事会人员，设名誉董事长 2 人，董事长 1 人，副董事长 2 人，董事 6 人，王丹花(女)为董事长，另设监事 2 人	王丹花(女)	11
2011.4.6	学校董事会组织学校行政班子人员去金苹果学校取经	王丹花(女)	

续表 2-1-1

会议时间	会议主要内容	主持人	出席人数
2011.12.31	学校董事会决定聘任顾行健为校长	王丹花(女)	11
2012.11.29	1.听取校长顾行健的工作汇报 2.讨论学校下一阶段工作，并作出巩固和开拓高中国际课程项目，关于提高民办学生收费标准，并向区有关部门报告，深化学校管理体制改革的3项决定	王丹花(女)	8
2013.5.28	听取与审议校长顾行健《关于奉浦学校开设普通高中国际课程试点工作的设想》工作报告	王丹花(女)	11
2014.3.28	1.决定聘任董俊平为校长 2.听取原校长顾行健《做细做实、稳中求进》的学校工作报告	王丹花(女)	11
2015.3.30	经上级教育部门批准，学校决定更名为上海帕丁顿双语学校	王丹花(女)	
2015.6.16	决定编写《上海帕丁顿双语学校志》，王新其为编委会主任，王丹花(女)为主编	王丹花(女)	11

第二节　民办学校董事会、监事会

一、上海帕丁顿双语学校董事会

2015年8月，上海帕丁顿双语学校的公办部分析出后，由民办（公助）性质改为纯民办性质，重建学校董（监）事会，其组成人员由学校举办方提名并协商确定。

1．董事会成员

2015年8月30日，学校召开董事会第一届第一次会议，决定董事会组成人员为5人。其中，董事长1人，董事4人。

董事长　王丹花(女)　上海申生投资有限公司总经理

董　事　董俊平　上海帕丁顿双语学校校长

顾行健　上海帕丁顿双语学校党支部书记、工会主席

诸海萍(女)　上海帕丁顿双语学校教师代表

朱德龙　原中共奉贤县委常委、奉贤县人民政府常务副县长

上海帕丁顿双语学校第一届届董事会成员名单

董事长	（学校法人代表、投资方）	王丹花
董　事	上海帕丁顿双语学校校长	董俊平
董　事	上海帕丁顿双语学校工会主席	（待　选）
董　事	上海帕丁顿双语学校教职工代表	诸海萍
董　事	社会知名人士	朱德龙

上海帕丁顿双语学校首届监事会名单

王新其	上海申生投资有限公司董事长
王永吉	上海申生投资有限公司法务部主任
靳寿德	上海市工业综合开发区有限公司财务总监

董事会全体成员一致举手，表示同意。

上海帕丁顿双语学校第一届董事会

二０一五年八月三十日

全体董事签字：

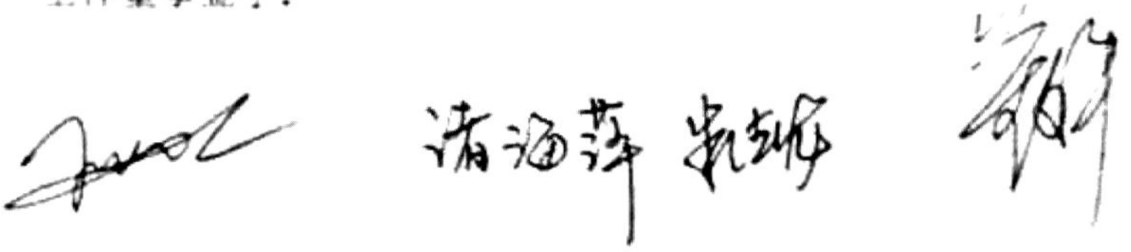

2015年8月30日，上海帕丁顿双语学校由5人组成董事会

2. **董事会会议**

2015年8月成立上海帕丁顿双语学校董事会后，至2016年2月先后召开5次董事会会议，作出重要决定35项。

2015年8月至2016年上海帕丁顿双语学校董事会会议情况表

表2-2-1

会议时间	届次	会议主要内容	主持人	出席人数	列席人数
2015.8.30	第一届第一次会议	1.讨论通过《上海帕丁顿双语学校章程》 2.通过“上海帕丁顿双语学校第一届董事会成员”王丹花(女)为董事长，通过上海帕丁顿双语学校首届监事会成员 3.决定聘任董俊平为上海帕丁顿双语学校校长，顾行健、陆桂英(女)为副校长 4.决定王丹花(女)为上海帕丁顿双语学校法人代表 5.讨论通过《上海帕丁顿双语学校“十三五”改革与发展规划纲要》《上海帕丁顿双语学校三年发展规划》 6.通过关于全面落实学校预算、决算管理的实施意见的决定	王丹花(女)	7	3
2015.12.13	第一届第二次会议	1.审议《上海帕丁顿双语学校2014学年决算》 2.审议《上海帕丁顿双语学校2015学年决算》执行情况 3.审议《上海帕丁顿双语学校首轮薪酬改革方案》 4.审议《上海帕丁顿双语学校2016学年学校工作计划》 5.审议《上海帕丁顿双语学校收费标准调整方案》 6.审议《上海帕丁顿双语学校后勤社会化管理事项》	王丹花(女)	9	1
2016.1.10	第一届第三次会议	1.听取审议《2015年上海帕丁顿双语学校校长工作述职报告》 2.听取《上海帕丁顿双语学校2016学年学校预算》报告 3.听取《关于帕丁顿双语学校副校长以上领导人员提名》报告 4.讨论学校提高收费标准，学校后勤社会化管理，小学一年级2016年春季扩班，成人高中班与普通高中班分离等事项	王丹花(女)	8	1

续表 2-2-1

会议时间	届次	会议主要内容	主持人	出席人数	列席人数
2016.2.22	第一届第四次会议	1.审议通过《上海帕丁顿双语学校学费调整报告》 2.通过《上海帕丁顿双语学校薪酬改革方案》的决议 3.通过《上海帕丁顿双语学校行政班子调整的决定》 4.讨论通过《2016 年上海帕丁顿双语学校招生计划》《关于生均经费的报告》 5.审议《上海帕丁顿双语学校购置空调的申请报告》 6.审议《上海帕丁顿双语学校每年董事会会议召开具体时间》 7.审议校长聘任事宜	董俊平	9	1
2016.4	第一届第五次会议	1.听取张臻自我介绍来帕丁顿双语学校工作的汇报。 2.决定聘任张臻为上海帕丁顿双语学校副校长，分管高中部	王丹花（女）	7	

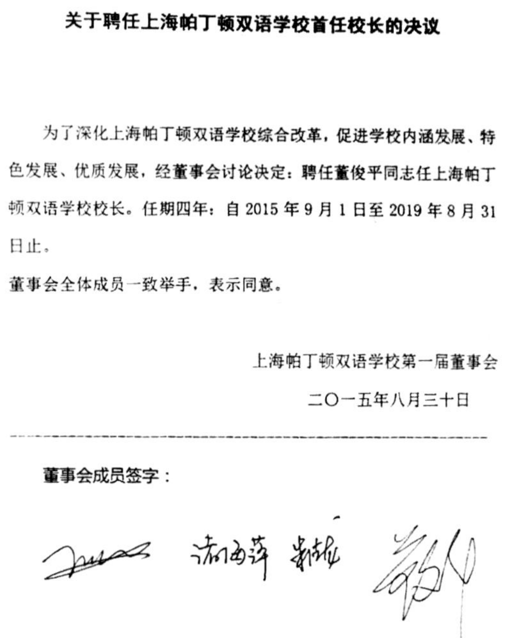
关于聘任上海帕丁顿双语学校首任校长的决议

为了深化上海帕丁顿双语学校综合改革，促进学校内涵发展、特色发展、优质发展，经董事会讨论决定：聘任董俊平同志任上海帕丁顿双语学校校长。任期四年：自 2015 年 9 月 1 日至 2019 年 8 月 31 日止。

董事会全体成员一致举手，表示同意。

上海帕丁顿双语学校第一届董事会

二〇一五年八月三十日

董事会成员签字：

2015 年 8 月 30 日，上海帕丁顿双语学校董事会聘任董俊平为校长的决议

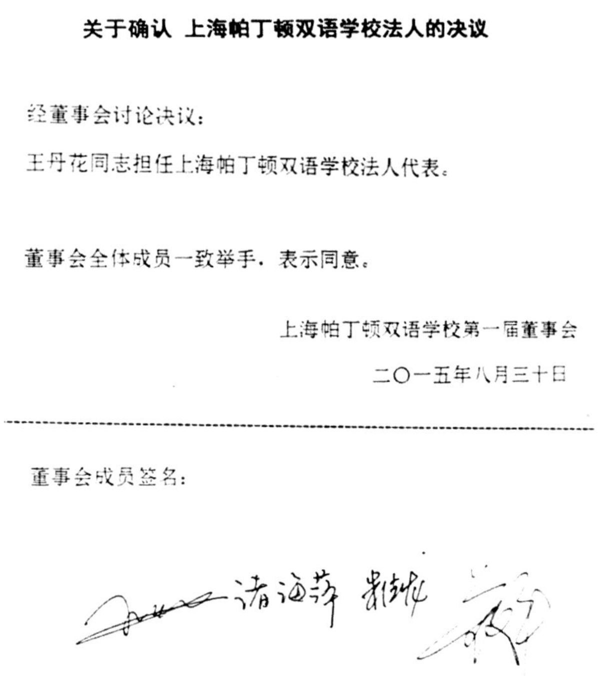
关于确认 上海帕丁顿双语学校法人的决议

经董事会讨论决议：

王丹花同志担任上海帕丁顿双语学校法人代表。

董事会全体成员一致举手，表示同意。

上海帕丁顿双语学校第一届董事会

二〇一五年八月三十日

董事会成员签名：

2015 年 8 月 30 日，上海帕丁顿双语学校董事会关于王丹花为学校法人代表的决议

二、上海帕丁顿双语学校监事会

上海帕丁顿双语学校监事会由举办者、学校从业人员或有关单位推荐的人选中产生或更换。由3人组成。

1．监事会人员

监事长	王新其	上海申生投资有限公司董事长
监　事	王永吉	上海申生投资有限公司法务部主任
监　事	靳寿德	上海市工业综合开发区有限公司财务总监

2．权利和义务

2015年8月，上海帕丁顿双语学校总结十几年来学校管理的经验教训，在成立学校董事会同时设立监事会，监事会监事长由学校投资举办方上海申生投资有限公司董事长担任，监事长采用定期或不定期方式，广泛听取学校师生、社会各界人士的意见，规范监事活动。监事会还认真检查本单位财务和会计资料；监督董事会、行政负责人遵守法律、法规、规章和章程的情况；发现问题时，有权对董事会、行政负责人提出质询和建议，并向登记管理机关和相关职能部门反映情况。

3．监事活动

监事会成员参加董事会会议；参与制订学校发展规划、学校教育教学工作计划，并监督学校行政等部门贯彻执行；参与制订学校经费预算，监督执行情况；对校长负责制，校务公开制等重要工作进行督促检查，反映学生家长与社会对学校工作的评价，提出监督意见和建议，改进董事会和学校行政工作，改善和提高教学水平。2015—2016年，高考总录取率93.29%。

第三章　管理机构

1998年9月，上海民办协和实验学校开学，后几易其名。历任学校校长由学校董事会聘任。历任校长先后为夏明德、马伯相、丰忠汉、杨连明、徐建（代校长）、戚盛伟、顾行健、董俊平。历任副校长8名。校长对内主持工作，对外代表学校，处理学校日常事务。学校实行董事会领导下的校长负责制。历任校长先后主持学校行政会议300余次，主持制订学年（学期）教育教学工作计划与学校发展规划、学校管理的规章制度等160项；学校实行校务公开制，对学校教师招聘、招生收费、评优推优、学校经费管理、学校重大事项实行公开，接受学校教职工与社会监督；学校先后聘任8名市区学校名校长担任顾问，帮助改善学校教育教学工作；提高教育质量，学校开展校际结对、交流，接受上级教育机关的工作指导，推动学校稳定发展。学校根据教育教学需要，设置若干工作部门，民办（公助）学校期间，设置校务办、政教处、教导处、总务处等部门及人事干部、财务人员；学校实行民办以后，设置教务中心、教师发展中心、学生发展中心、人力资源中心、后勤保障中心、财务科等部门，发挥职能部门的作用，同时培养选拔一批教育教学骨干。2012年，执行学校董事会“学校统筹、分级管理、条块结合、以块为主”的管理理念，发挥群体作用。2016年，在校长主持全面工作的框架下，实行由副校长牵头的学部管理负责制，减少管理层次，提高全校各方面的工作效率。

第一节　校长　副校长

1998年8月至2015年8月，学校在民办（公助）性质期间，校长由学校投资方、上级教育主管部门代表等组成的学校董事会聘任。2015年8月，上海帕丁顿双语学校改为纯民办性质后，校长由学校投资举办方、学校代表组成的董事会聘任。至2016年，学校董事会先后聘任学校正、副校长（代校长）16人次。

一、上海民办协和实验学校校长、副校长

1998年9月，上海民办协和实验学校开学，至2002年12月学校更名为上海教育科学研究院奉浦实验学校，学校先后聘任3任校长。

校长	夏明德	1998年9月—2000年4月
	马伯相	2000年4月—2001年8月
	丰忠汉	2001年8月—2003年8月
副校长	翁连云	1998年9月—2001年8月
	周佩华(女)	2002年8月—2003年8月

二、上海市奉贤区教师进修学院附属奉浦学校校长、副校长

2003年8月，学校由上海奉浦经济发展实业总公司接管，改名为上海市奉贤区教师进修学院附属奉浦学校，先后聘任两任校长（代校长），并配设副校长2人，校长助理4人。

校长	杨连明	2003年8月—2005年3月
代校长	徐建	2005年3月—2005年8月
常务副校长	姚志强	2003年8月—2005年8月
副校长	周时青	2004年8月—2005年8月

三、上海民办奉浦学校校长、副校长

2005年8月，为厘清学校投资主体，上海市奉贤区教师进修学院附属奉浦学校更名为上海民办奉浦学校，先后聘任2任校长。

校长	戚盛伟	2005年8月—2011年12月
	顾行健	2011年12月—2014年8月
副校长	程春影(女)	2005年9月—2010年2月
	周时青	2005年8月—2014年4月
	曹善明	2011年11月—2015年6月
	王益权	2011年12月—至今
	曹春华(女)	2011年12月—2014年8月

四、上海帕丁顿双语学校校长、副校长

2015年4月，上海民办（公助）奉浦学校更名为上海帕丁顿双语学校。2015年8月，学校中公办教师、公办学生析出，上海帕丁顿双语学校成为纯民办学校。

2014年3月，上海帕丁顿双语学校董事长王丹花向校长董俊平颁发校长聘书

校　　长 董俊平　2014年3月至今

副 校 长 顾行健　2014年8月至今

陆桂英(女)　2014年3月至今

张　臻　2016年4月至今

第二节　学校部门设置

1998年学校创办后，学校管理部门随着学校的发展需要设置。1998年8月至2015年8月，设校务办、人事、教导处、政教处、总务处等部门，2015年8月起设教务中心等若干中心及财务科等部门，履行各自管理职能。

一、民办（公助）学校部门设置（1998年7月—2015年8月）

1. 校务办公室（兼党务办公室）（1998年7月设置）

历任主任 柏新鉴　1998年7月—1999年8月

徐　英(女)　2000年9月—2002年8月

周时青　2002年10月—2015年8月

工作职责：负责会务、接待、档案管理、宣传、文秘、校园网、招生、人事、工资、职称评聘、教师招聘、校刊校报、党支部建设、学校工作督办、纪检、工会、妇联会、教工团支部工作。

2．**教导处**（1998 **年** 7 **月设置**）

主　　　任　沈爱玉(女)　1998 年 7 月—2001 年 5 月

　　　　　　陈小红(女)　2002 年 12 月—2003 年 6 月

　　　　　　余爱椿　　　2003 年 9 月—2004 年 8 月

　　　　　　程春影(女)　2005 年 9 月—2010 年 1 月，副校长兼

　　　　　　曹善明　　　2010 年 9 月—2015 年 8 月，副校长兼

副　主　任　周时青　　　1998 年 7 月—2003 年 6 月

　　　　　　陈小红(女)　2001 年 9 月—2002 年 12 月

　　　　　　何新莲(女)　2002 年 9 月—2003 年 6 月

　　　　　　唐国华　　　2003 年 9 月—2008 年 6 月

　　　　　　唐继英(女)　2004 年 9 月—2015 年 8 月

　　　　　　高决心　　　2006 年 9 月—2015 年 8 月

工作职责：负责教学常规管理、课程设置、教学任务安排、考务、学籍管理、教研、科研、教学评价、教师培训、学科竞赛、教学指导、专业发展、名师工作室、信息中心、语言文字、体卫艺科、图书馆、实验室管理等工作。

3．**政教处**（1998 **年** 7 **月设置**）

主　　　任　宋建伯　　　1998 年 8 月—2001 年 8 月

　　　　　　曹春华(女)　2001 年 10 月—2014 年 9 月

　　　　　　夏红波　　　2014 年 9 月—2015 年 6 月

副　主　任　曹春华(女)　1999 年 9 月—2001 年 10 月

　　　　　　沈晓红(女)　2000 年 9 月—2001 年 8 月

　　　　　　唐继英(女)　2003 年 9 月—2004 年 8 月

　　　　　　江仁章　　　2006 年 9 月—2010 年 8 月

工作职责：负责德育、班主任队伍建设、学生思想品德教育、共青团少先队工作、学生社会实践、学生社团、宿舍管理等工作。

4．**总务处**（1998 **年** 7 **月设置**）

主　　　任　沈靖华　　　1998 年 7 月—2011 年 8 月

　　　　　　王益权　　　2011 年 9 月—2015 年 8 月

副　主　任　王益权　　　1998 年 7 月—2011 年 9 月

　　　　　　詹　强　　　2014 年 7 月—2015 年 8 月

工作职责：负责财务科、采购、保管、维修、场馆管理、保安管理、水电、文印、食堂、小商店、绿化、清洁、安全措施、消防安全、食品安全等工作。

二、民办学校部门设置

2015年8月，上海帕丁顿双语学校改为民办性质，学校部门设置，有教务中心、教师发展中心、学生发展中心、人力资源中心、后勤保障中心、财务科。分别行使学校教育教学、教师队伍的发展管理、学生的招收管理服务、教职工的招聘管理、后勤保障安全保卫、财务管理等部门职能。2016年，学校部门设置进行调整。

学校发展中心	**主　任**	黄艳红(女)
教师发展中心	**主　任**	任其兵
	副主任	么凤娟(女)
学生发展中心	**主　任**	诸海萍(女)
	副主任	张建丽(女)
副主任兼科技总辅导员		李佳燕(女)
少先队大队辅导员		李　平(女)、李若男(女)

年级负责人：

小学1～2年级部	**主　任**	汤春燕(女)
小学3年级部	**主　任**	臧桂玲(女)
小学4～5年级部	**主　任**	施红妹(女)
初中年级部	**主　任**	刘　佳(女)
高一年级部	**主　任**	任其兵(兼)
高二年级部	**主　任**	刘晓敏(女)
高三年级部	**主　任**	黄艳红(女，兼)

教研组负责人：为了加强学校各教研组的管理，提高教研组业务水平，2015年9月，全校各教研组配备负责人11名。

2016 年上海帕丁顿双语学校教研组负责人情况表

表 3-3-1

教研组名称	负责人			
	小学部	初中部	高中部	初高中联合部
语文教研组	郑　妹(女)	么凤娟(女，兼)	蒋义素(女)	—
数学教研组	周华星(女)	尹　晶(女)	王树松	—
英语教研组	吴小燕(女)	陈晶晶(女)	任其兵(兼)	—
综合教研组	臧桂玲(女)	—	—	—
政史地教研组	—	—	—	孔维佳(女)
音体美教研组	—	—	—	程　涛

2016 年，根据学校发展实际，学校进一步推行扁平化管理，党政班子进行分工。校长主持学校全面工作。党支部书记兼副校长负责师德、学生德育、纪检、安全工作、工会教代会、共青团少先队、妇委会。副校长张臻担任高中学部执行校长。副校长陆桂英(女)担任小学学部、初中学部执行校长，小学、初中部下设小学部负责人分别为周华星(女)、刘佳(女)。

1999 年 12 月，学校语文组被评为奉贤县教育系统文明班组时合影

第四章　校务改革

1998年9月，上海民办协和实验学校开学，至2015年4月学校改名为上海帕丁顿双语学校，均实行学校董事会领导下的校长负责制。校长对外代表学校，对内全面主持学校行政工作。明确规定校长“坚持社会主义办学方向、按照教学规律办学、坚持民主集中制原则、全面主持学校行政工作、负责师生队伍的建设和管理、抓好学校安全、组织学校的经营和管理、廉洁从政以身作则”等8项职责。对分管教学、政教、后勤保障的副校长也相应规定职责。

学校实行校务公开制，坚持“学校发展规划、教职员工聘任、职称评定、推优评优、奖金福利津贴、招生收费、财务收支、重大活动经费”公开，推动学校工作实行民主管理。

学校实行顾问聘任制，先后聘请上海市8名名校长、名教师为学校顾问，帮助谋划学校发展，指导提高教学质量。

学校开展结对联盟、交流互访、到校指导活动，先后与国内外10所学校结对，与德国、日本、菲律宾及中国香港等学校开展交流互访，邀请上海市、奉贤区教育主管部门领导、专家到学校指导工作。促进学校教育教学创新发展。

第一节　校长负责制

1998年9月1日开学后，上海民办协和实验学校坚持实行董事会领导下的校长负责制。至2016年，学校董事会先后聘任学校正副校长（代校长）16人次，校长对外代表学校，对内主持学校全面工作，副校长协助校长工作。校长对学校董事会负责并报告工作。

一、校长职责

1．正校长职责

在董事会领导下，坚持社会主义办学方向，遵循《中华人民共和国宪法》《中华人民共和国义务教育法》确定的基本原则，全面贯彻国家的教育方针，组织开展学校的教育教学工作，依法保护师生的合法权益。按照教学规律办学，接受上级教育主管部门的领导和监督，全面完成教育教学工作任务。坚持民主集中制原则，充分发挥领导班子的集体智慧和力量，主动接受学校党支部的政治领导和监督，尊重教职员工的民主权利，接受教职员工代表大会监督。全面主持学校行政工作，组织制订和实施学校的发展规划和年度工作计划。负责师生队伍的建设和管理，不断提高教师队伍的政治思想，职业道德和文化业务水平，保证教育教学质量的稳步提高。抓好安全工作，防止事故的发生，保障师生的健康和人身安全。组织学校的经营和管理工作，合理使用经费，努力改善办学条件和教职工的福利待遇。廉洁从政，以身作则，不断提高自己的综合素质。

向学校董事会和教职工代表大会作述职报告，接受校内外的评议和批评意见，改进工作。

2．副校长职责

学校分管教导、政教、总务的副校长，在校长领导下，协助校长做好政治教育、教育教学、后勤保障等工作。

教学副校长工作职责　认真贯彻党和国家的教育方针、政策、法规，执行上级教育部门的指示，全面完成教育教学任务；负责组织领导学校教育教学工作，结合实际制定教导处工作计划，抓好实施、检查、总结等工作；审查批准任课教师学期教学计划并进行督导、检查，及时提出调控措施；协同校长研究选聘部门的负责人以及教师人事安排；主持有关教育教学工作会议；领导教育教学改革实践研究工作以及教学研究活动；领导教师教育教学质量的检查与评估；经常检查指导教师备课、课堂教学、课外辅导和作业批改，及时提出改进教学工作的意见；负责组织教学质量抽测的考试命题、评卷、检查学生试卷和做好质量分析等工作，及时掌握教学质量情况，采取措施改进和提高；安排学生的文体、卫生保健和劳动教育工作，组织领导学生的课外活动；负责教务行政工作，编制课程表、活动表、作息时间表；建立和管理教师业务档案；协助招办做好招生、毕业生、学籍管理工作；以教学为中心，组织制定学校教学常规，教学年历，教学月（周）历等，规范与完善教学过程各个环节，建立科学的、正常的教学秩序；领导教导处、科研室等教育教学部门的工作；深入教育教学第一线，了解、检查教师教学和学生学习的情况，帮助教师解决教学中困难与问题，抓好教育教学质量的管理；协助后勤副校长做好学校教育技术装备工作的管理工作，发挥教育教学设备、设施、仪器、资料等的功能与作用；建立健全教育教学管理的各项规章制度，认真实施与检查，使教育教学管理科学化、规范化。

政教副校长工作职责 主持政教处工作，主管学校德育工作；根据学校总体目标，提出政教处工作目标。贯彻执行《德育大钢》《中小学生守则》《中小学生日常行为规范》及校规校纪，负责制订政教处工作计划并组织实施，做好反馈总结。制定和完善教育管理制度；抓好政教处人员，班主任定岗定责以及评估、考核、奖惩等工作；负责班主任队伍、家长委员会和学生会建设，维持学校正常秩序和后进生的转化工作；组织开展先进班级评比，三好学生、先进个人及奖学金学生的确定，学生奖惩，毕业生思想品德鉴定的审核；负责学校值周、值日与学生各项纪律、卫生、出勤等检查评比工作；负责学生、家长对学校教师的测评和信息反馈工作；管理学校广播、黑板报、墙报、宣传栏等宣传工作；组织领导学生的军训及安全、保卫、护校工作；会同团委组织有益学生身心发展的各种社会活动；主持每周升旗仪式和各种节日纪念活动，指导年级学生大会、班会活动；指导班主任制定班级工作计划，定期召开班主任会议，组织班主任工作的检查总结和经验交流；协助校长、年级组长和班主任召开家长会，指导班主任写好学生评语。

后勤副校长工作职责 认真贯彻执行党和国家及上级教育部门关于学校总务后勤工作的政策、法规；协同校长制定学校建设发展规划，组织制订学校总务后勤管理工作规划、计划、制度、措施等，抓好实施、检查、总结等工作；做好总务后勤行政人员的管理工作，抓好总务后勤人员的学习进修和提高工作，做好管理与服务工作，做好教育教学设备、物品等保障工作；协调总务处、教导处、政教处等部门，为总务后勤人员创造良好的工作环境；主持总务后勤行政工作会议，听取、收集后勤管理工作的意见和建议，研究改进总务后勤工作；协同校长做好学校财务和物品管理工作；领导与组织好校园校舍建设、维修及绿化、美化等工作；领导与管理好校产，做到开源节流，增收节支；组织好学校的安全工作。

二、校长工作

1．主持学校行政会议

根据校长职责，主持学校行政会议。参加学校行政会议的人员有学校行政正副职领导干部、学校党支部书记、学校工会负责人、学校校务办、政教处、教导处、总务处等职能部门负责人，或邀请参加的教职工代表。行政会议主要交流讨论阶段性学校各方面工作，作出职权范围内的工作决定或提请董事会审批的事项，以及教职工代表会议讨论通过的事宜。行政会议一般1周至2周召开1次，校长因事不能主持会议时，可以委托1名副校长主持。2002年9月至2016年，学校召开行政会议389次，有3678人次参加，讨论学校日常事务议题1905项。

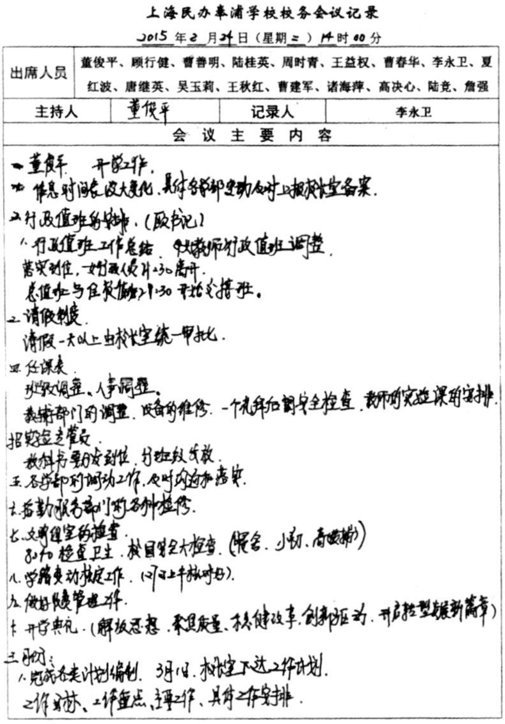

2015年2月24日，民办奉浦学校校务会议内容

2002—2016年上海帕丁顿双语学校行政会议情况表

表4-1-1

学年	会议次数（次）	参加人数（人）	讨论工作议题数（项）	学年	会议次数（次）	参加人数（人）	讨论工作议题数（项）
2002	32	357	102	2010	23	229	94
2003	17	174	95	2011	20	201	105
2004	32	302	128	2012	38	430	240
2005	25	272	116	2013	38	438	159
2006	14	137	57	2014	32	334	116
2007	24	152	69	2015	23	236	257
2008	7	43	60	2016	24	162	202
2009	30	211	105				

说明：2003、2006、2008学年只收集到1个学期数据

2．组织制订学校发展计划

1998年9月，组织制订《上海民办协和实验学校1998—2000年办学规模三年规划》。

2003年10月，总结学校教育教学实践，制订以招生工作和提高教育教学质量改善教学环境为重点的《上海市奉贤区教师进修学院附属奉浦学校2003—2005年8月学校总体规划》。2005年1月，根据2003—2005年学校规划执行情况和学校发展要求，制订学校校舍总体规划布局，同时开展2005年秋季招生调研，规划招生计划。

2006年8月，针对招生工作压力和师资队伍不稳的实际，提出“外借助力、内练硬功、韬光养晦、打造精品”的指导思想，聘请市区3名名教师担任学校顾问，提高小学、初中教学质量，高中形成特色教育；启动人事制度改革，推行全员聘用合同制；开展教学新秀、能手评选，树立“校荣我荣，校耻我辱”价值观。

2007年，围绕《奉贤区推进基础教育均衡发展行动纲要》营造良好的学校文化，坚持二期课改，落实《奉浦学校课程改革方案》。

2008年，以完善考核，激励机制为重点，缓解工作矛盾，建设稳定的教师队伍，提高教育教学质量，实现社会认可，家长放心，学生称心的目标。

2009年，学校提出各年级段学生的发展目标和实现目标的“三个加强”（加强学校安全，加强文化建设，加强师资队伍），重点落实德育、教学、课程、后勤保障措施。

2011年，学校经过认真分析，充分认识自身硬件设施标准较高，师资队伍相对稳定，基本素质提高的有利条件及与创精品小学、初中、特色高中存在的差距，制订2011—2015年学校发展规划。继续倡导适合教育，实行智慧型校园的办学理念。确立生源是财富，特色是生命，重视高素质教师队伍建设及“三本”（追求人本、寻求校本、讲究成本），提出发展定位和发展目标。

2013—2014年，学校提出坚持以法治校、以德立校、文化强校，努力把学校建成“师生员工高素质、教育教学高质量、管理运作高效率、校园高品位、办学条件高标准”的平安健康、文明的和谐校园的发展思路和具体措施。

2015—2016年，按照年初制订的工作计划，以利构建学部管理架构，制订《学校扁平化管理制度》，完善《薪酬改革制度》等5项制度。实施小学一年级双语课程，把单一的课程转化为4大课程与特色课程，开展“传承长征精神争当贤德少年”主题班会和适应双语教学环境的教师英语培训，适合科学教育的心理学培训，适合学生4项（文本解读、教案设计、上课、命题）关键技能培训等。全校发生4大变化，学生对学校认同度满意度提高，教师教学科研意识增强，爱学习风气蔚然成风，社会信誉提高。

3．组织制订学校规章制度

1998—2016年，学校为贯彻《中华人民共和国教育法》及市区（县）教育领导部门作出的有关规定，加强学校各项管理，促进学校各项工作有序展开，学校先后制订领导干部岗位职责，学校安全管理、教师管理制度、学生管理制度、教学管理制度、后勤保障管理制度等8个大项159个小项，成为全校师生执行的行动规范。

2016年上海帕丁顿双语学校主要规章制度情况表

表4-1-2

类别	制度项数	主要规章制度
岗位职责考核办法	14	校长（副校长）岗位职责；教导（政教）处主任岗位职责；科研主任岗位职责；总务主任岗位职责；工会主席、团支部书记岗位职责；中层干部聘用和考核办法（制度）；学校领导班子目标责任考核奖励办法（细则）；校务公开制度等
民主管理会议制度	10	民主决策制度；行政工作会议制度；董事会会议制度；教职工代表大会制度；党员民主评议制度；社会评价制度等
教师管理制度	24	教师办公室管理制度；教师文明办公室评比细则；师资招聘制度；“师徒结对”制度；“名师”制度；师德管理制度；教职工政治和业务学习制度；外籍教师管理制度；教师职务低职高聘制度；教学科研奖励办法；班主任奖励考核办法；教师评价激励制度；学科教师工作考核办法等
学生管理制度	34	小学、中学生日常行为规范；学生文明礼仪要求；初中毕业生推优方案；学生政治品德考核条例；三好学生、优秀学生干部、先进班级（集体）评选标准及办法；中考高考奖励制度；学生违纪处分实施条例；贫困生资助制度
安全管理制度	24	安全保卫工作制度；门卫制度；学校领导值班制度（细则）；学校值周班制度；学生在校安全管理制度；住宿学生安全纪律规定；班主任班级安全管理责任书；校园安全稳定事故应急预案；学校停电（突发事件）紧急疏散演练方案；食品安全卫生应急预案等
教学管理制度	15	教师教学工作考核考评办法；教学常规管理制度；高中美术特色班管理考核条例；校本课程制度；实验室管理制度；电子教室管理制度等
后勤保障制度	28	财务预决算制度；审计制度；财务管理制度；收费管理制度；物资采购制度；学校财产保管制度；现金、存款、收据管理制度；节约用水、用电、用纸规定等
其他制度	20	档案管理制度；关于学校印章使用管理规定；升降国旗制度；课外体育活动制度；工作监督制度；社会协调制度

4．实施教育教学改革

1998—2016年，学校坚持贯彻《中华人民共和国教育法》规定，在民办公助阶段，完成公办学生的九年制义务教育。在德育方面，开发“民族魂·现代人”教育课程，运用各种形式开展爱国主义教育，行为规范教育，组织参加社会实践活动；从学校生源实际出发，开展适人、适时、适度的适合教育和艺体特色教育，挖掘学生潜力，开展教学科研活动推动学生想学会学，教师想教会教的聪明学习和智慧教学逐步展开。

5．加强师生队伍管理

学校建立教师与学生的激励机制。在教师队伍中实行“名师”“师徒结对”“低职高聘”制度和优秀教师（班主任）评选制度，鼓励教师创新教育教学的奖励制度；根据校内寄宿生与走读生特点，加强各项管理教育，推动学生“三实”（品行朴实、学业扎实、身体结实），德、智、体全面发展。

6．组织开展学校重大活动

1998—2016年，学校组织举办了15届校园运动会，18届学校艺术节、科技节、读书节，涌现一批体育、科技、文艺人才和优秀作品，发明专利等。

7．落实学校安全保障工作

学校重视环境安全和食堂用餐安全，健全安全保障组织体系，制订安全保卫制度，实行安全工作责任制，实现安全保障工作落实到位。

8．坚持校长述职报告制

1998—2016年，校长每年向董事会、教职工代表会议作述职报告或学校工作总结，广泛听取教职工的意见与建议，接受学校董事会的领导和监督、社会评价，扬长避短改进学校工作。

第二节　校务公开制

一、校务公开内容

1．学校发展规划公开

学年工作计划公开由校长室提出，学校行政会议通过初步方案，并经过教职工代表会议审议，采纳教职工合理意见和建议，修改后报区教育部门审批。

2．教职员工聘任公开

教职工的聘任工作实行定编制、定岗位、定职能双向选择的原则，分管校长和校长提出初步聘任分工方案，在广泛征求教职工意见基础上，由学校行政会议作出决定。学校成立聘任工作领导小组，根据聘任工作指导思想、原则，体现公平、公正。聘任的教职工与学校签订聘任合同。合同明确双方权利与义务等项内容。年终由学校对聘任期间的工作进行考核，成为奖励和下年度能否续聘的依据之一。1998年9月学校开办以来，先后聘任教职工千余人次，签订聘任合同千余份。

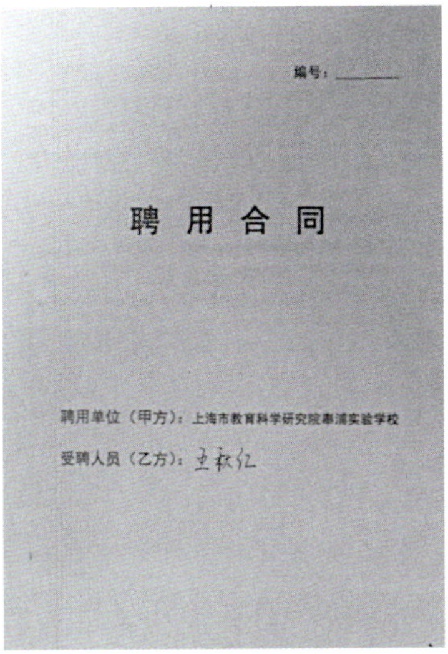
编号：________

聘 用 合 同

聘用单位（甲方）：上海市教育科学研究院奉浦实验学校

受聘人员（乙方）：王秋红

2000年奉浦实验学校与教师王秋红签订的聘用合同

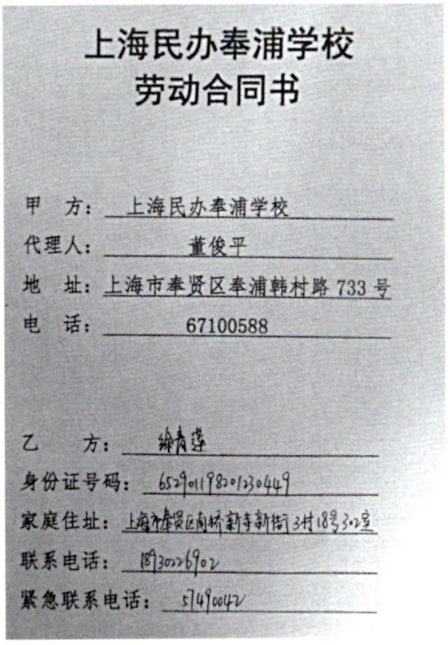
上海民办奉浦学校
劳动合同书

甲　方：上海民办奉浦学校

代理人：董俊平

地　址：上海市奉贤区奉浦韩村路733号

电　话：67100588

乙　方：徐青莲

身份证号码：652901198201230449

家庭住址：上海市奉贤区南桥新寺新街3村18号302室

联系电话：18930226902

紧急联系电话：57490042

2014年，民办奉浦学校与教师徐青莲的劳动合同书

3．职称评定公开

教职工职称评定实行学校网上公布名额，评定的条件及评定的范围，使每名教职工对职称评定有知晓权，增加透明度。职称评定，由学校建立初评委，在听取和征求各方面教师意见基础上，对教师职称进行初评，形成上报材料，由上级评委评定。自1998年9月上海民办协和实验学校开办以来，全校已先后开展多次职称评定工作。一批在教学一线工作肯钻研，能创新的中青年教师的技术职称得到晋升。2016年全校有中高级职称教师14人，其中高级教师5人。

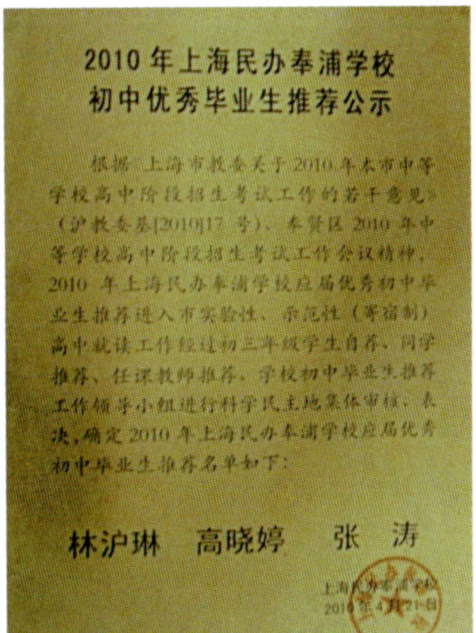
2010年上海民办奉浦学校
初中优秀毕业生推荐公示

根据《上海市教委关于2010年本市中等学校高中阶段招生考试工作的若干意见》（沪教委基[2010]17号）、奉贤区2010年中等学校高中阶段招生考试工作会议精神，2010年上海民办奉浦学校应届优秀初中毕业生推荐进入市实验性、示范性（寄宿制）高中就读工作经过初三年级学生自荐、同学推荐、任课教师推荐、学校初中毕业生推荐工作领导小组进行科学民主地集体审核、表决，确定2010年上海民办奉浦学校应届优秀初中毕业生推荐名单如下：

林沪琳　高晓婷　张涛

上海民办奉浦学校
2010年4月21日

2010年上海民办奉浦学校初中优秀毕业生推荐公示

4．推优评优公开

上海帕丁顿双语学校历年来做好教师、学生、班级的推优评优工作，调动师生奋发向上，追求进步的积极性。推优评优工作实行条件公开，评比先进的数量公开。通过全校自下而上的层层推荐，在听取学校各方面意见的基础上，由学校行政会议（评优领导小组）表决决定，并进行公示。2002—2016年，全校先后评出各类先进优秀教师181人次，优秀学生50多人次，优秀班级200多个次。

5．**奖金、福利、津贴分配公开**

学校所发奖金、福利、津贴分配涉及每个教职工的切身利益，实行公开发放是调动教职工工作积极性的重要举措。自1998年9月开学以来，学校实行同工同酬、绩效工资及各类奖励制度，都向全体教职工公开，并制订一系列实施细则，形成激励教职工积极认真做好各个岗位工作，又便于可操作的文件。2004—2016年，全校人员经费总支出11947.87万元，占学校总经费20340.85万元的58.74%。

6．**招生收费公开**

1998年9月开学前学校招生范围局限于奉浦地区。2000年，市教委批准上海民办协和实验学校可以在全市范围内招收学生的意见，招生范围扩大。民办学生学费收取标准如何定，加上部分学生实行住宿制，收费的标准涉及面广，政策性强。学校成立收费领导小组，根据各个学年学校实际，由学校行政会议提出初步标准，报学校董事会审查，提请区（县）物价部门核准，向社会公开。对学费以外学生校服等费用，学校除选择质量好、价格较廉的企业制作外，还召开学生家长会议，通报有关收费的原由，得到学生家长和社会理解。

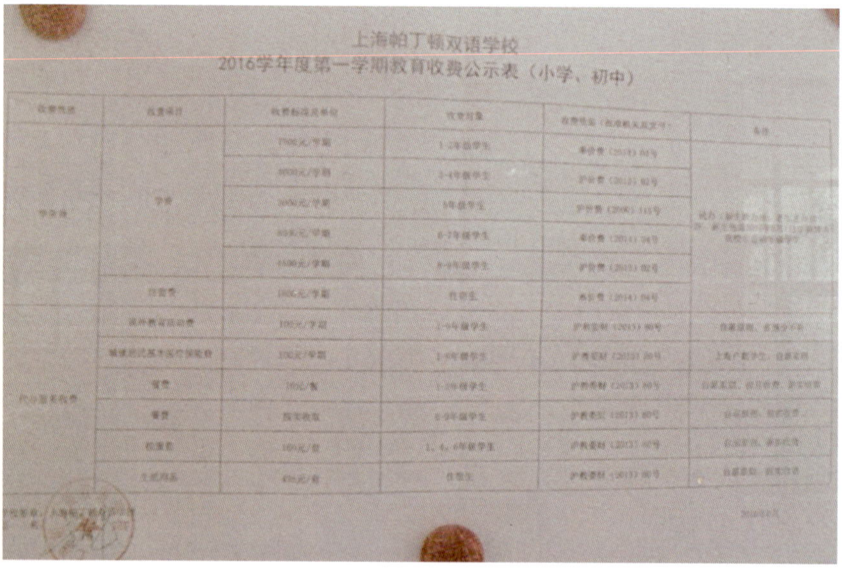
上海帕丁顿双语学校
2016学年度第一学期教育收费公示表（小学、初中）

2016年上海帕丁顿双语学校教育收费公示表

7．**财务收支公开**

从上海民办协和实验学校到几次易名的上海帕丁顿双语学校，学校性质由民办（公助）转为民办学校。财务收入以收取民办学生学费、区（县）财政下拨经费、社会捐助为主要来源。学校支出除教职工工资与福利等待遇外，学校每年的设施维修保养、设备添置资金占有较大的比例。学校建立财务预算、决算制度，审计制度，财务管理制度，收费管理制度，物资采购制度和现金、存款、收据管理制度，规定采购审批范围、采购招标办法，实行招标采购监督，使财务收支账目公开增加透明度，易于教职工知晓。

8．**重大活动经费公开**

1998年9月以来，学校举办开学典礼，校园运动会、艺术节及外出学习考察参观等活动，做到先有预算计划，活动期间精打细算不超支出，事后按实结算。学校还规定并公开资金使用审批权限：2万元以上由行政办公会议审批，1万元以上由校长办公会议审批；1000元以上不满1万元由分管校长审批。

二、校务公开方式

校园网视频播出，重要内容滚动播放。公示栏张贴，保留一定的时间。确保师生对重大校务知情权、推动学校民主管理。印发文件，做到上送下达，不留死角。会议宣传，以教职工代表大会或教职工全体会议传达。涉及学生的收费政策召开学生家长会议，实行面对面沟通，取得学生家长和社会的理解和支持。

三、校务公开监督

1998年起为加强校务公开的民主管理与民主监督，学校建立由校长任组长的校务公开领导小组，由党支部书记任组长的校务公开监督小组。每学期通过听取教职工及党群组织，包括学生家长在内的各方面意见，采纳涉及教育教学安全管理，食堂管理等上百条合理化建议，妥善处理违纪的个别师生，改进学校工作。2006年起，学校采用家长学校平台，请学生家长到校参观检查、座谈等方式直接听取意见，同时建立与规范教师家访制度，上门听取意见与提议，接受社会对校务工作的监督。2016年11月上中旬，学校就办学愿景在小学部、初中部54名教师中用无记名方式征求意见，对学校工作予以正面肯定的13个方面，对学校工作提出工资发放方式，学校岗位设置，学校环境设施等4个方便合理建议。年末，向小学部学生家长发匿名问卷239份，对学校工作满意或比较满意的意见42条，希望改进意见4条，满意与比较满意的占46条意见的95%。

第三节 学校顾问聘任制

一、顾问聘任

2008年4月至2015年12月，奉浦学校先后聘请8名市内名校长、名教师为学校顾问。

2005—2008年奉浦学校聘请顾问情况表

表4-3-1

姓名	职务	聘请时间
王小平	上海世界外国语小学校长	2005年12月
章绍岩	上海师范大学附属一中学校校长	2005年12月
郎建中	上海北郊中学校长	2005年12月
于 漪(女)	上海市教师学会会长、市特级教师	2006年4月
张思中	上海市英语教学名师	2006年4月
季洪旭	奉贤中学校长	2006年4月
金建中	上海邵光标小学校长	2008年4月
徐 鹄	上海小学写作协会会长	2008年4月

二、顾问活动

2005—2008年，学校8名顾问坚持为学校发展，制订和完善教育教学计划出谋划策，为学校引入先进的教育教学理念。

为师生作专题报告。2006年4月，上海世界外国语小学校长王小平为全校学生作“让学生学会做人”专题报告。是年6月，上海市教师学会会长、上海市特级教师于漪(女)为全校老师作“教师的责任”专题讲座。2008年8月，邵光标小学校长金建中为全校教师作“一个增强教师发展的内容和激情”报告。各个顾问经常深入各年级教室，开展听课指导活动，推动年轻教师迅速提高教育教学能力。

第四节 结对联盟 互访交流 到校指导

一、结对联盟

2000年6月18日，协和学校和日本国青森大学结为姐妹学校，进行教育教

2012年5月，奉浦学校与加拿大多伦多五湖学院共同参与加拿大国际高中文凭课程项目签字仪式

学工作互动交流。2010年，奉浦学校根据《国家中长期教育改革和发展规划纲要》《上海市教育国际化工程“十二五”行动计划》中关于“鼓励各级各类学校开展多种形式的国际交流与合作，探索多种形式利用国外优质资源”的精神，建立模式为“A+X”的奉浦教育资源联盟。“A”为上海民办奉浦学校，主要成员单位上海交通大学、国际创新教育联盟、澳大利亚哥伦比亚学校、加拿大多伦多五湖学院、美国美中经贸教委会常春腾国际教育、美国贝卡鲁尔高中、奉贤区教师进修学院、奉贤区致远高级中学。先后与澳大利亚哥伦比亚学校开设以英语雅思教育为主旨的“高中英语特长班”、与加拿大多伦多五湖学院组建“中加高中课程改革实验班”。2011年8月，奉浦学校与奉贤中学结对联办超常儿童实验班，9月1日正式开学。2014年9月，奉浦学校小学、初中阶段学生参加上海弘文学校教育资源联盟，高中阶段则参加奉贤中学教育集团。是年12月，奉浦学校校区成立上海交通大学教育集团现代教育示范园区。

二、互访交流

1999年4月，协和学校接待中国香港特别行政区校长代表团，向客人全面介绍学校规划和发展情况。是年12月，学校接待菲律宾师生30余人来校访问、学习、交流。2000年3月，协和学校接待来访的德国某大学校长就教育教学进行交流介绍。2004年7月，奉浦学校选派在上海市教学比武中获一等奖的教师丁永花(女)去美国学习

“协和”给我们留下了美好的印象

——香港校长代表团访问协和学校侧记

“哇，学校这么大，绿化这么好！”4月2日上午，香港汇知集团下属的4所私立中学伯裘书院、伯裘女子中学、柏雨中学、赛马会毅智中学的校长、主任、教员一行14人友好访问了我区的协和实验学校，也许是来自香港这个弹丸之地的缘故，客人们对协和学校漂亮、宽敞的校园不由地连连称赞。

客人们参观了协和学校的教学楼、实验楼、食堂、宿舍等。在看到橱窗里贴满了学生活泼生动、栩栩如生的剪纸作品时，客人们惊讶地问：“这是孩子们自己剪的吗？”得到肯定的回答后，他们连连点头。在书法教室里，客人们停留了很长时间，饶有兴趣地观看学生们练习书法，并不断询问艺术教育和课外活动的开展情况，看得出来，客人们对协和学校提出的多元发展的教学目标十分感兴趣，他们说：“协和给我们留下了美好的印象”。

在交流中，客人们详细了解了协和学校的机构设置、教育教学管理、科研和日常管理的情况，在英语、计算机教学面问得特别仔细，方还探讨了民间办体制、课程设置和生行为管理等方面问题。客人们说，陆学校教师的教学本功扎实，教科研卓有成效，值得香学习，双方可以取长补短。

协和学校是一所涵盖中小学12年纪的民办寄宿制学校，现有班级个，学生1000多名。学校正在积极索民间办学、体制激励、发展学生性、实施素质教育的办学模式，在素教育和生活服务方面形成了特色，教教学连年取得好成绩，去年参加高考线率63%。

协和学校丰忠汉校长高兴地说，港的民间办学十分发达，这样的学术流活动为协和学校这所民办学校的发提供了宝贵的经验。

（本报记者　徐建军）

1999年4月2日《奉贤报》关于香港特别行政区校长代表团访问上海协和实验学校的报道

深造。2007年10月，奉浦学校师生与参加世界夏季特奥会的运动员举行联欢活动，为客人进行百人参加的武术表演。2008年1月8日，奉浦学校迎接韩国教育界人士到学校考察。2011年4月，奉浦学校董事会组织学校中层以上干部去金苹果学校取经学习。2012年5日，奉浦学校试办高中国际班——中加国际教学班，加拿大多伦多五湖学院领导到校参加教学班签字仪式，并探讨高中国际班的计划与发展规划。2015年4月，上海交通大学教育集团现代化教育示范园区落成典礼在上海帕丁顿双语学校举行。

三、到校指导

1998年12月，上海市教育委员会主任张伟江一行40人到协和学校进行考察指导。1999年3月，协和学校举办教学节活动，邀请全县中学、小学校长到校指导教学活动。是年9月，市协和民办教育中心到协和学校检查工作，在肯定学校成绩的基础上，提出改进教学的9条建议。2000年6月15日，县教育局局长蒋辉蘽考察协和学校，提出加强班子团结、优化分配方案，形成民办学校师资特色的指导意见。2002年3月，上海市特级教师、全国模范班主任黄静华(女)应邀在协和学校作“无悔的选择”的专题报告。是年9月，上海协和教育中心专家到校帮助制订学校三年发展规划。2007年12月，上海普教研究所所长胡兴宏到奉浦学校作“关于课堂教学的研究”专题报告，并对学校教师进行教学科研的辅导。是年，学校聘请区青少年活动中心教师金田则到校指导学校科技创造，教师何南友与学生共同研制的一种组合式钥匙扣等11个科技发明项目被上海市教育委员会、上海市知识产权局认定为发明专利。2013年8月，教育部中学校长培训中心副主任、华东师范大学副教授刘莉莉(女)博士应邀到校讲课。是年10月13日，国家级艺术大师、上海立达学院艺术设计与传媒学院院长教授李斌为奉浦学校高一、高二学生250余人作“景德镇陶瓷文化”讲座，增强学生艺体文化的兴趣与爱好，充分调动学生多方面学习积极性。2015年，在全校录取的68名本科生中，依靠学校特色教育和学生自身特长而考入本科艺术类的学生37名，占54.4%。2016年，在校3名外籍教师在小学英语教学中发挥骨干和指导作用。

第五章　党群组织

1998年10月，中共奉贤县西渡镇委员会批准成立中共上海民办协和实验学校支部委员会，设支委3名，时有党员22名。1999年，支部关系隶属于中共上海奉浦工业区工作委员会。几度易名的学校党支部重视组织建设和思想建设。1998—2016年，按照党章规定，在中青年教师队伍中发展党员21人。根据上级党组织统一安排，进行支部委员会换届选举，充实调整支委班子成员。党支部坚持“三会一课”（党员大会、支委会、党小组会、党课）制度，加强党员自身学习，开展思想教育活动，充分发挥共产党员在教育教学工作中的先锋模范作用。期间2名共产党员被上海市人民政府授予“上海市劳动模范”称号。全校受到区（县）教育系统表彰的教职员工中，党员占70%以上。学校党支部重视文明学校创建工作，制订与完善学校文明建设的规章制度，在全校师生中开展“文明教室、文明班级、文明宿舍”“文明礼仪我知晓、文明创建我参与”等活动。2003年始，学校连续7次被评为奉贤区文明单位。

1998年11月起，学校先后建立学校工会、教职工代表大会、共青团、妇联、学生会、少先队、红十字会等群众团体，充分发挥各群众团体开展各项工作的组织作用与骨干作用。

第一节　中共学校基层组织

1998年10月，经中共奉贤县西渡镇委员会批准，成立中共上海市民办协和实验学校支部委员会。嗣后，随着学校名称的更改，党支部名称也随之改变。

一、组织沿革

1．中共上海市民办协和实验学校支部委员会

1998年10月8日，中共上海市民办协和实验学校支部委员会经中共奉贤县西渡镇委员会批准成立，时有党员22人。至2003年8月，先后有3人任党支部书记。

历任书记 夏明德 1998年9月—2000年4月

马伯相 2000年4月—2001年8月

张遴贤 2001年8月—2003年8月

2．中共上海市奉贤区教师进修学院附属奉浦学校支部委员会

2003年8月，上海市教育科学研究院奉浦实验学校由上海奉浦经济发展实业总公司接管，学校党支部更名为中共上海市奉贤区教师进修学院附属奉浦学校支部委员会，时有党员27人。至2005年8月，先后有2人任党支部书记。

中共西渡镇委员会（通 知 ）

西委字[1998]第43号

关于建立中共上海市民办协和实验学校支部委员会的
通 知

各村、企事业单位党支部（总支）：

为健全上海市民办协和实验学校党组织建设，加强党对学校的领导，经党委研究，报县委组织部同意，建立中共上海市民办协和实验学校支部委员会。

中共上海市民办协和实验学校党支部委员会由夏明德、朱锋、沈靖华三人组成。夏明德同志任党支部书记，朱锋、沈靖华同志任党支部委员。

特此通知

中共奉贤县西渡镇委员会

一九九八年十月八日

西渡镇委员会办公室印 一九九八年十月八日

签发：张弛 核稿：吴召忠 校对：杨志军 份数：80

1998年10月，中共奉贤县西渡镇委员会关于建立上海市民办协和实验学校党支部的批复

历任书记 杨连明 2003年8月—2005年5月

徐 建 2005年5月—2005年8月

3．中共上海民办奉浦学校支部委员会

2005年8月，学校改名为上海民办奉浦学校，学校党支部也随之更名为中共上海民办奉浦学校支部委员会，时有党员24人。至2014年4月，先后有2人任党支部书记。

历任书记 徐 建 2005年8月—2009年8月

戚盛伟 2009年8月—2014年4月

4．中共上海帕丁顿双语学校支部委员会

2015年9月，中共上海民办奉浦学校支部委员会更名为中共上海帕丁顿双语学校支部委员会，时有党员20人。2016年有党员21人，籍贯分别为江苏4人、安徽3人、重庆1人、江西2人、山东1人、河南2人、湖北1人、吉林2人及奉贤5人。

书 记 顾行健 2014年4月至今

二、组织建设

1. 党员发展

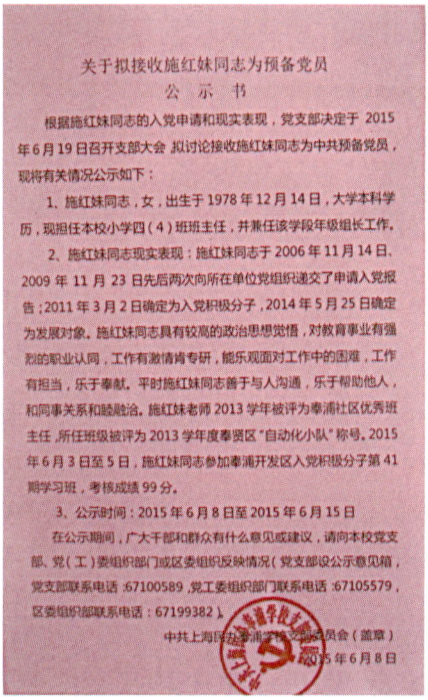

关于拟接收施红妹同志为预备党员
公示书

根据施红妹同志的入党申请和现实表现，党支部决定于 2015 年6月19日召开支部大会 拟讨论接收施红妹同志为中共预备党员，现将有关情况公示如下：

1、施红妹同志，女，出生于1978年12月14日，大学本科学历，现担任本校小学四（4）班班主任，并兼任该学段年级组长工作。

2、施红妹同志现实表现：施红妹同志于2006年11月14日、2009年11月23日先后两次向所在单位党组织递交了申请入党报告；2011年3月2日确定为入党积极分子，2014年5月25日确定为发展对象。施红妹同志具有较高的政治思想觉悟，对教育事业有强烈的职业认同，工作有激情肯专研，能乐观面对工作中的困难，工作有担当，乐于奉献。平时施红妹同志善于与人沟通，乐于帮助他人，和同事关系和睦融洽。施红妹老师2013学年被评为奉浦社区优秀班主任，所任班级被评为2013学年度奉贤区"自动化小队"称号。2015年6月3日至5日，施红妹同志参加奉浦开发区入党积极分子第41期学习班，考核成绩99分。

3、公示时间：2015年6月8日至2015年6月15日

在公示期间，广大干部和群众有什么意见或建议，请向本校党支部、党（工）委组织部门或区委组织反映情况（党支部设公示意见箱，党支部联系电话：67100589，党工委组织部门联系电话：67105579，区委组织部联系电话：67199382）。

中共上海民办奉浦学校支部委员会（盖章）
2015年6月8日

学校发展党员公示书

1998年10月8日，中共上海市奉贤县西渡镇委员会批准成立上海民办协和实验学校支部委员会，任命夏明德兼任书记，时有正式党员18人，预备党员6人。1999年年初，按照党章规定，党支部在加强对入党积极分子考察，组织入党积极分子参加党小组活动，根据"成熟一个、发展一个"的原则，吸收1名教师入党。是年起，定期组织入党积极分子学习党章。在群众中进行满意度测评调查，建立发展党员公示制。2000年起，注重在中青年、高学历教职员工中发展党员，不论学校支部班子有所变动，高标准高质量发展党员的原则不变。1999—2016年，全校发展党员21人，其中女性17人。

1999—2016年上海帕丁顿双语学校党员发展情况表

表5-1-1　　　　单位：人

年份	发展人数	其中		年份	发展人数	其中	
		男	女			男	女
合计	21	4	17	2009	2	0	2
1998	1	1	0	2011	2	0	2
1999	1	1	0	2012	2	0	2
2002	1	1	0	2013	3	0	3
2004	1	0	1	2014	1	0	1
2005	1	0	1	2015	1	0	1
2006	2	0	2	2016	1	0	1
2007	2	1	1				

2. 党支部换届选举

1999年3月26日，上海民办协和实验学校进行第一次支部委员会换届选举。选举产生由3名委员组成的新一届支部委员会，支部委员会设书记1人，委员2人。2000年4月至2005年3月，上级党委根据学校工作需要，先后任命马伯

相、张遴贤、杨连明、徐建任党支部书记，调整部分支部委员。2006年3月，经中共上海市工业综合开发区工作委员会批准，奉浦学校支部进行换届改选，全面实行“两推一选”（党内推荐、党外推荐支部委员候选人，报上级党组织批准后，在党内选举），设书记1人，委员4人。2014年5月，学校党支部换届，设支委4人，其中书记1人，副书记1人。顾行健为书记，曹春华(女)为副书记。2016年，帕丁顿学校支部委员3人，顾行健为书记。

1998—2016年上海帕丁顿双语学校党支部委员会成员情况表

表5-1-2

姓名	职务	任职时间	姓名	职务	任职时间
夏明德	书记	1998.9—2000.4	朱　锋	委员	1998.10—2000.4
马伯相	书记	2000.4—2001.8	沈靖华	委员	1998.10—2005.5
张遴贤	书记	2001.8—2003.8	江仁章	委员	2005.5—2009.8
杨连明	书记	2003.8—2005.5	唐　燕(女)	委员	2005.5—2009.8
徐　建	书记	2005.5—2009.8	姚仁兴	委员	2006.5—2009.8
戚盛伟	书记	2009.8—2014.4	诸海萍(女)	委员	2015.8至今
顾行健	书记	2014.4至今	吴小燕(女)	委员	2015.8至今
李永卫	副书记	2005.5—2014.4			
曹春华(女)	副书记	2014.5—2015.8			

三、思想建设

1. 加强自身学习

学校历届党支部坚持党的“三会一课”（党员大会、支委会、党小组会、党课）制度。1999年，根据上级党委统一部署，以党章要求，结合教育教学工作在党员中开展“让党放心、让人民高兴”的自查活动，自查率和评议合格率100%。2000年，组织党员学习毛泽东、邓小平等老一辈革命家的著作或论述，开展“三讲”（讲学习、讲政治、讲正气）教育，党员干部自觉接受党内外群众评议，改变领导作风和工作方法，推动学校各方面建设。2003年，在党员中开展“三个代表”重要思想学习活动，建立党内层层联系（书记联系委员、委员联系党员、党员联系群众）的制度。2014年，在党员中开展群众路线教育实践活动，按照党中央提出的“照镜子、正衣冠、洗洗澡、治治病”的总要求，学习《党的群众路线教育实践活动学习文件选编》，对照党章，廉政准则和中央“八项规定”，认真查找党员队伍中存在的“四风”问题，自我净化、自我完善、自我革新、自我提高。2015年12月，学校党支部结合党支部民主生活会，党员组织生活会，召

2014 年 12 月 25 日，民办奉浦学校党支部组织党员开展“学党章党规、学系列讲话，做合格党员”活动

开党员大会等，开展党员民主评议活动，通过自评、互评和发放测评表等方式评议党员，全校 20 名党员合格率 100%，25% 的党员评为优秀党员。同时发放书记测评表，加强党内民主监督。2016 年，党支部采用支部大会和党小组会，开展“两学一做”（学党章党规、学习近平总书记系列讲话、做合格党员）活动，提高党员的大局意识，增加党支部的战斗力、凝聚力。

2．**发挥模范作用**

1998 年 9 月，针对学校教师队伍中新人多，教育教学工作制度新的情况，党支部要求党员带头克服各种困难，发挥模范带头作用，在工作中自觉接受群众与社会考评。2009 年，学校党支部在党员中开展党风廉政建设教育，学校党支部与奉贤区教育局党委签订党风廉政建设责任书。2010 年，学校党支部向党员提出“五带头”（带头学习提高、积极参与学习型党组织建设；带头在教育教学工作中爱岗敬业，开拓创新、无私奉献；带头服务师生，树立群众观念，帮助师生家长克服实际困难；带头遵纪守法，自觉遵守党的纪律、社会公德、职业道德和家庭美德；带头弘扬正气，开展亮党员身份活动）。全体党员向党支部递交“一个党员，一面旗帜”的承诺书。2013 年 3 月，学校党支部向区教育局党委递交“在建设‘三型’校园中提高党员‘四自’能力”特色项目申请，提高党员的宗旨意识、服务意识，

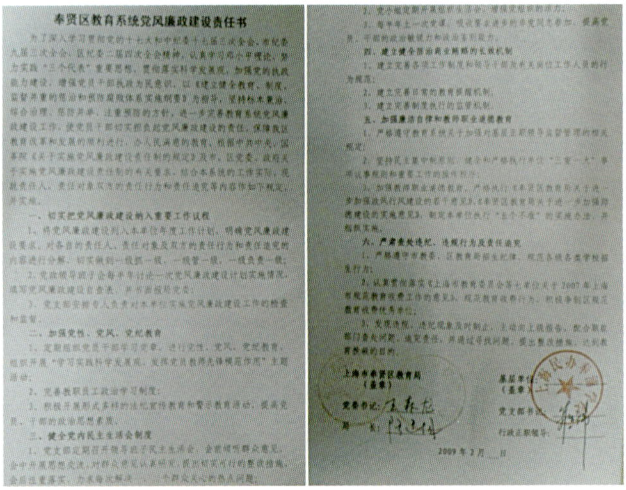

奉贤区教育系统党风廉政建设责任书

2009 年 2 月，民办奉浦学校党支部与区教育局党委签订党风廉政建设责任书

做到表率作用。2014年，党支部组织党员学习“社会主义核心价值观”，开展向捐献骨髓、奉献社会、为党争光的王益权先进事迹学习活动。1999—2016年，有30余名党员评为优秀教师、优秀班主任、我心中最美教师；10人次教师受到区级以上表彰奖励。以共产党员为骨干参加的“聪明学习，智慧教学”课题被列为市级课题项目。学校获得区级以上荣誉称号12项。2005—2016年，学校党支部发挥党员在教育教学改革中的带头作用，申请区级以上课题35个，其中市级课题5个。教师参加课题研究的38人次中，有共产党员15人次，占课题组人员的40%。

2015年6月25日，上海帕丁顿双语学校党支部组织党员参加中国共产党建党94周年暨“争当奉浦先锋”主动竞赛誓师大会

上海民办奉浦学校党支部党务公开栏

四、文明校园创建

1998年9月，学校开学后，把制订和贯彻落实“校训、校风、教风、学风”作为文明学校创建的重要举措。1999年，学校制订一系列创建文明学校的规章制度，开展创建“文明教室，文明宿舍、文明班组”和“文明从我做起”活动。2000年，在全校师生中开展“八荣八耻”（以热爱祖国为荣、以危害祖国为耻；以服务人民为荣、以背离人民为耻；以崇尚科学为荣、以愚昧无知为耻；以辛勤劳动为荣、以好逸恶劳为耻；以团结互助为荣、以损人利己为耻；以诚实守信为荣、以见利忘义为耻；以遵纪守法为荣、以违法乱纪为耻；以艰苦奋斗为荣、以骄奢淫逸为耻）思想教育活动，引导师生积极参与文明创建工作。2005年，针对学校存在的暂时困境，学校提出“校荣我荣、校耻我辱”“我与学校共成长”

民办奉浦学校在创建文明校园活动中的“环保秀”文艺表演

的发展理念，成立由校长、党支部书记为组长的文明创建领导小组，开展“文明礼仪我知晓，文明创建我参与”活动。在教师中倡导发扬文明高尚精神、文明娱乐、文明驾车新风尚。在高年级学生中组织“小黄伞”爱心服务、“绿箱子”环保宣传、“环保时装秀”等志愿服务活动。学校制订“教职工安全文明校园岗位工作细则”，落实文明创建措施。2007年，奉浦学校在“敬奉贤人、见贤思齐、共创上海文明城区”工作中，开展文明天使交友活动，全校735名学生给家长写一封信，与家庭成员共同参与文明创建。2009年1月16日，为帮助校内部分困难学生欢度新年，开展篮天下的至爱——手拉手共享温馨新年捐款活动，全校师生共捐款1.3万元。2010年1月20日，学校向学生家长分送告学生家长书，开展学生寒假生活评定暨“文明和谐家庭”申请评选活动，115户学生家庭递交了申请书。是年10月，学校举办“小手牵大手、共养好习惯”文明迎世博系列活动，全校评出迎世博礼仪少年62名。2011年，学校组织学生参与社区文明践行活动评选，高中年级155名学生自觉参与社区的上街扫垃圾、搀扶老人过马路、铲除黑广告等社会公益事业。2011年，学校开展文明创建从净化校园环境做起的活动，收到社会、学生家长对创建文明校园各种合理化建议百余条。2012年，学校发动全校师生开展为患白血病的王恒栋捐款8万余元。2014年，学校制作“社会主义核心价值观”PPT，在学校视频网

2015年1月27日，民办上海奉浦学校党支部、行政领导慰问困难教师

上滚动播放，推动文明创建工作常态化。学校与家长学校联合举办“好家训，好家风”传承征文活动，收到好家风小故事征文79篇，使学校文明创建与社会对接。学校还开展健康文明的校园读书、艺术、体育、科技活动，陶冶师生文明素质，学校先后被评为上海市安全文明学校。2003—2004年、2013—2014年两次被授予奉贤区文明单位。2014年，经上海市社会组织管理局验收，评为上海市AAAAA级社会组织。2016年，发动全校师生在“蓝天下至爱”活动中捐款2.38万元。

2010年2月，奉浦学校被评为2008—2009年度上海市安全文明校园

第二节　群众团体

一、工　会

1. 组织机构

1998年11月4日，召开上海民办协和实验学校第一次工会会员会议，选举产生由5人组成的工会委员会。工会委员会设主席1人，副主席1人，委员3人，翁连云为主席，宋建伯为副主席，李爱兵、沈晓红(女)、曹春华(女)为委员，岑备为经审员。

2001年4月，召开上海民办协和实验学校第二次工会代表会议，翁连云代表上届工会作工作报告。会议选举产生由4人组成的工会委员会。工会委员会设主席1人，委员3人，翁连云为主席。

2004年5月，召开上海市奉贤区教师进修学院附属奉浦学校第三次工会会员会议。会议选举产生由5人组成的工会委员会。工会委员会设主席1人，委员4人，盛伟宾为主席。

2006年5月26日，召开上海民办奉浦学校第四次工会会员会议，盛伟宾代表上届工会作工作报告。会议选举产生由5人组成的工会委员会。工会委员会设主席1人，委员4人，王益权为主席。

2009年4月12日，召开上海民办奉浦学校第五次工会会员会议，王益权代表上届工会作工作报告。会议选举产生由5人组成的工会委员会。工会委员会设主席1人，委员4人，王益权为主席。

2012年4月9日，召开上海民办奉浦学校第六次工会会员会议，由王益权代表上届工会作工作报告。会议选举产生由4人组成的工会委员会。工会委员会设主席1人，委员3人，李永卫为主席。

2015年10月23日，召开上海帕丁顿双语学校第一次（连续计算为第七次）教职工代表会议，出席教职工代表31名。李永卫代表上届工会作工作报告。会议选举产生由4人组成的工会委员会。工会委员会设主席1人，委员3人，顾行健为主席。

1998—2016年帕丁顿双语学校工会委员会成员情况表

表5-2-1

届次名称	委员数	主席	副主席	委员
上海民办协和实验学校第一次工会代表会议	5	翁连云	宋建伯	曹春华(女)、沈靖华、李爱兵
上海民办协和实验学校第二次工会代表大会	4	翁连云	—	曹春华(女)、沈靖华、李爱兵
上海市奉贤区教师进修学院附属奉浦学校第三次工会代表会议	5	盛伟宾	—	江仁章、刘明坤、沈靖华、张琴花(女)
上海民办奉浦学校第四次工会代表会议	5	王益权	—	江仁章、何翠娟(女)、吴玉莉(女)、李　宏
上海民办奉浦学校第五次工会代表会议	5	王益权	—	江仁章、何翠娟(女)、吴玉莉(女)、李　宏
上海民办奉浦学校第六次工会代表会议	4	李永卫	—	何翠娟(女)、吴玉莉(女)、李　宏
上海帕丁顿双语学校第一次（连续计算为第七次）工会代表会议	4	顾行健	—	施红妹(女)、程　涛、郎军红(女)

2. 主要活动

加强自身学习　1998年11月，学校工会成立后，坚持组织工会会员学习《中华人民共和国工会法》，结合学习《中华人民共和国教育法》，发挥工会会员在学校教育教学中，开展教育科技创新，参与“聪明学习、智慧教学”课题项目实践活动，发挥骨干作用。2008年，结合爱国主义教育学习活动，在迎世博600天行动中，工会提出“迎世博、讲文明、除陋习、树新风”从我做起学习活动，

2007 年 3 月，民办奉浦学校工会高中组被评为 2005—2006 年度奉贤区文明班组

制订“办公室文明公约”，使文明工会小组创建成为加强学习的重要内容。2011 年，工会组织工会会员参与创办《奉浦学校简报》在校报上发表学习体会文章。教职工代表还以“五提倡”“五表率”为行动准则，率先践行学校师德标准。2015 年，学校改为纯民办学校后，诸海萍(女)等教师职工代表安心自己的岗位，在全校优秀教师评比中，工会会员受到表彰占 80%。

参与民主管理学校 学校工会始终组织历届工会会员及教职工代表认真听取与审议学校发展计划，积极提出改善教学条件和管理学校的合理化建议上百条。认真贯彻学校提出的各种改革方案，参与民主管理与民主监督。2004 年前后，在学校工作出现曲折困难的情况下，许多工会会员主动挑起克服困境的担子，开展“进一言、献一计”的“金点子”活动，支持学校领导制订完善学校的规章制度，工会会员都率先贯彻执行。

2007 年 3 月，民办奉浦学校初中组被评为 2006 年度奉贤区教育系统文明组室

维护教职工合法权益 工会坚持组织教职工进行一年一度的体检工作，开展“蓝天下至爱”捐款活动。2007 年，教职工代表与工会会员参加为陶静(女)老师女儿的捐款、为灾区人民捐款捐物价值上万元。工会在学校食堂旁边开设咖啡吧，为每名教职工提供每月 100 元的费用。2010 年，工会建立奉浦学校劳动争议调解小组，制订上海民办奉浦学校劳动争议工作规则 4 章 19 条，经教职工代表大会审议后在全校贯彻执行。工会还

2006 年，民办奉浦学校工会获暑期教工休养工作先进单位

组织工会会员签订工作合同，监督合同的执行情况，维护教职工合法权益。2011—2016年，学校坚持对家庭困难的教职工，工会坚持做到“六必访”，开展经常性的送温暖活动。

3. 教职工代表会议

根据《中共中央关于教育体制改革的决定》精神，1998年9月，上海民办协和实验学校建立教职工代表大会（以下简称“教代会”）制度。制订教代会制度，分为总则、职责和权利、代表产生方法、组织制度、附则5个部分。2003年12月，召开奉贤区教师进修学院附属奉浦学校第一届教职工代表大会。至2010年先后选举产生3届教代会代表，充分发挥教代会作用，坚持对学校实行民主管理和民主监督。

代表产生　教代会代表人数按照占教职工总人数的一定比例分配到全校各学部（年级），根据代表条例，由教职工直接选举产生。2010年选举产生教职工代表31名。

教代会主席团　历届教代会选举产生大会主席团，主持教代会闭会期间工作。主席团一般由7～9人组成，其中教师人数应过半数，主席团成员实行常任制。在教代会闭会期间，由学校工会委员会主持教代会日常工作。

教代会活动　通过听取教职工意见和建议、吸纳教职工代表提案，在教代会会议期间行使民主管理工作、民主监督工作的职能。每年教代会参与制订与审议学校建设规划，重大改革方案，年度财务预算及执行情况，学校福利费管理使用原则和办法，教师考核办法与奖惩规定等，参与民主评议领导干部岗位职责执行和廉洁自律情况，推动学校各方面工作有序展开。

二、妇女联合会

1. 组织机构

1998年12月，召开上海民办协和实验学校第一次妇女代表会议。会议选举产生由3名执委组成的妇女联合会。2015年10月23日，上海帕丁顿双语学校妇女代表会议召开。选举产生由3名执委组成的学校妇联机构，施红妹(女)为主席，郎军红(女)、么凤娟(女)为委员。

2. 主要活动

学校历届妇联主席原则上由学校工会女工委员兼任。由于女教职工在全校教职工中占70%，活动大多数结合工会活动同时进行。活动内容以关爱女性、维护女教职工合法权益为主。每逢“三八”国际妇女节，学校妇联则单独组织学习或纪念活动。在学校建设发展中，学校党政领导，注重发挥妇联的作用，涌现一批优秀女教师。2007年，奉浦学校初中英语组被奉贤区教育局妇女工作委员会、区教育工会女职工委员会评为2006年巾帼文明示范岗。

2015年3月，民办奉浦学校高一年级组获2013—2014年度教育系统巾帼文明岗

三、青年团

1．组织机构

1998年9月，全校有共青团员246名，经上级团委批准，是年11月召开共青团上海协和实验学校首次团员代表会议。会议选举产生由7名委员组成的团委，周林锋为书记。2010年，全校设学生团支部15个，团员226人，教师团支部1个，团员33人。以后，学校团委及团支部由于毕业升学等原因变动较多，按团章规定进行补充与调整。2014年，全校团委下设团总支2个，有团员300余人。2016年，上海帕丁顿双语学校有团员324人，其中教师团员41人，学生团员283人，下设16个团支部，团委书记诸海萍(女)。

2．主要活动

1999年，学校团委及所属团支部组织要求入团的学生进行分期分批以团章为主要内容的学习培训，陆续发展团员，对新入团团员举行入团宣誓仪式。2003年起，学校团委关心支持学生会组织的学生社团活动，充分挖掘和发挥团员青年在文艺、科技、体育活动中的骨干带头作用。2006年3月，团委组织25

民办奉浦学校团委组织新团员在爱国主义教育基地李主一烈士墓前举行入团宣誓仪式

名团干部参观中共奉贤县委旧址，缅怀先烈重温党史，表示要当好党的后备人才。2008年6月，学校团委组织团员参加“书信传递关爱”活动，向四川汶川受地震灾害的同龄人写慰问信200余封。是年，团委干部实行公开竞选，竞选人员填写竞选申请，并发表竞选宣言，经过票选产生团委组成人员，并予以公示。2009年，继续开展优秀团员评选活动，经层层推荐选拔，全校评出品学兼优团员12名。

2010年，民办奉浦学校共青团开展向国旗敬礼为世博添彩活动

2010年5月，学校团委组织有15个选择题、10个判断题、3个问答题组成的环保知识测试，收到测试答卷43份，平均得分良好。是月，团委举办“青春闪耀五四、奉献精彩世博”征文评选活动，评出第一、二、三名征文各1篇。举办“生命、感恩”纪念母亲节演讲比赛，经选拔有13名团员在全校团员大会上演讲。开展“与爸爸、妈妈通家信”优秀作品评选，40多篇作品榜上有名。2011年，学校团委坚持运用团校平台，组织团员青年上团校学习培训，举行结业考试。全年2期团校学员90多名，30多名青年加入共青团组织。不少团员担任学生会、学生社团的骨干。2014年5月，教师张建团结带领团员青年参加各项公益活动，以身作则、认真负责，被区教育系统团工委评为优秀团干部。

民办奉浦学校团委、少先队组织的学雷锋活动志愿者服务队举行授旗仪式

2010年3月，民办奉浦学校团组织被评为2009年度上海市工业综合开发区优秀团组织

四、学生联合会

1. 组织机构

1998年11月，上海民办协和实验学校建立学生会。经选拔，首届学生会有主席，副主席及学习、宣传、文艺、劳动、纪律、体育部部长，副部长及各部干事。在初中年级以上班级的学生中吸收学生会会员。由于每年学生毕业、升学，学生会干部通过自主报名(个人申请)、组织推荐、公开竞选、综合考察等选拔程序，产生学生会干事27人，其中主席1人，副主席2人，部长、副部长各6人，各部干部12人。学生会干事以学校政教处名义公示。在学生会会议上，当选的学生会干部均作简要就职宣言。学生会主席为范佳敏(女)。2012年，民办奉浦学校学生会机构与人员进行调整，设主席1人，副主席2人，下设学习、文艺、宣传、纪律、体育、义工、社团部共19人组成。学生会主席为吴凌超。2016年，上海帕丁顿双语学校学生会会员900余名，占初中以上学生人数的90%，学生会设学习、文艺、宣传、纪律等部，配备学生会干部18人。

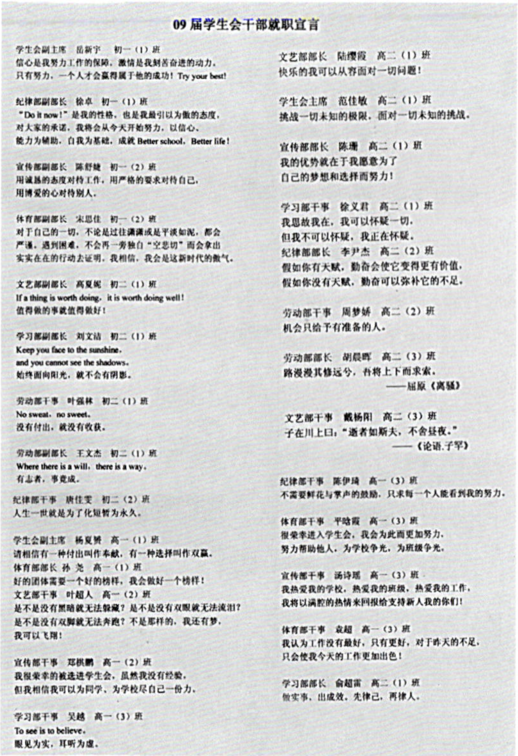

09届学生会干部就职宣言

学生会副主席　岳新宇　初一（1）班
信心是我努力工作的保障，激情是我刻苦奋进的动力，
只有努力，一个人才会赢得属于他的成功！Try your best!

纪律部副部长　徐卓　初一（1）班
"Do it now!"是我的性格，也是我最引以为傲的态度，
对大家的承诺，我将会从今天开始努力，以信心、
能力为辅助，自我为基础，成就 Better school，Better life!

宣传部副部长　陈舒婕　初一（2）班
用诚恳的态度对待工作，用严格的要求对待自己，
用博爱的心对待别人。

体育部副部长　宋思佳　初一（2）班
对于自己的一切，不论是过往满谦或是平淡如泥，都会
严谨，遇到困难，不会再一旁独白"空悲切"而会拿出
实实在在的行动去证明，我相信，我会是这新时代的傲气。

文艺部副部长　高夏妮　初二（1）班
If a thing is worth doing，it is worth doing well!
值得做的事就值得做好！

学习部副部长　刘文洁　初二（1）班
Keep you face to the sunshine，
and you cannot see the shadows.
始终面向阳光，就不会有阴影。

劳动部干事　叶强林　初二（1）班
No sweat，no sweet.
没有付出，就没有收获。

劳动部副部长　王文杰　初二（1）班
Where there is a will，there is a way.
有志者，事竟成。

纪律部干事　唐佳雯　初二（2）班
人生一世就是为了化短暂为永久。

学生会副主席　杨夏赟　高一（1）班
请相信有一种付出叫作奉献，有一种选择叫作双赢。
体育部部长　孙尧　高一（1）班
好的团体需要一个好的榜样，我会做好一个榜样！
文艺部干事　叶超人　高一（2）班
是不是没有黑暗就无法躲藏？是不是没有双眼就无法流泪？
是不是没有双脚就无法奔跑？不是那样的，我还有梦，
我可以飞翔！

宣传部干事　郑棋鹏　高一（2）班
我很荣幸的被选进学生会，虽然我没有经验，
但我相信我可以为同学、为学校尽自己一份力。

学习部干事　吴越　高一（3）班
To see is to believe.
眼见为实，耳听为虚。

文艺部部长　陆缨霞　高二（1）班
快乐的我可以从容面对一切问题！

学生会主席　范佳敏　高二（1）班
挑战一切未知的极限，面对一切未知的挑战。

宣传部部长　陈珊　高二（1）班
我的优势就在于我愿意为了
自己的梦想和选择而努力！

学习部干事　徐文君　高二（1）班
我思故我在，我可以怀疑一切，
但我不可以怀疑，我正在怀疑。
纪律部部长　李尹杰　高二（2）班
假如你有天赋，勤奋会使它变得更有价值，
假如你没有天赋，勤奋可以弥补它的不足。

劳动部干事　周梦娇　高二（2）班
机会只给予有准备的人。

劳动部部长　胡晨晖　高二（3）班
路漫漫其修远兮，吾将上下而求索。
——屈原《离骚》

文艺部干事　戴杨阳　高二（3）班
子在川上曰："逝者如斯夫，不舍昼夜。"
——《论语.子罕》

纪律部干事　陈伊琦　高一（3）班
不需要鲜花与掌声的鼓励，只求每一个人能看到我的努力。

体育部干事　平晗霞　高一（3）班
很荣幸进入学生会，我会为此而更加努力，
努力帮助他人，为学校争光，为班级争光。

宣传部干事　汤诗瑶　高一（3）班
我热爱我的学校，热爱我的班级，热爱我的工作，
我将以满腔的热情来回报给支持新人我的你们！

体育部干事　袁超　高一（3）班
我认为工作没有最好，只有更好，对于昨天的不足，
只会使我今天的工作更加出色！

学习部部长　俞超雷　高二（1）班
做实事，出成效，先律己，再律人。

2009年9月，民办奉浦学校学生会干部就职宣言

2016年，上海帕丁顿双语学校学生会成员（左起）
第一排：晋孟罡
第二排：许芮菡、王劲杰、潘在芸
第三排：汪瑾、陈诗浩、鲍雅静、施闻迪、沈雯琦
第四排：顾情缘、瞿李、金家浩、蒋沈凯、龚维瀚、朱佳靓、王万宏、杨燕、姚安琪

2. 主要活动

2009年，民办奉浦学校学生会小报

学生会是在学校党政团队领导下自愿参加、自我教育、自我服务的学生群众团体。承担组织学生会会员开展形式多样的学习、文艺、宣传、体育、义工、社团活动及执行学生会纪律的职能。学生会建立后，积极组织会员参加学校的各类征文活动，组织小记者会员培训，黑板报展评，协助学校举办全校性重大会议活动，开展学生礼仪检查，做好学校周值班工作检查，组织校园歌手大赛。同时发起成立文化社团，定期进行活动。根据学生会成员毕业离校的特点及时发展新会员，通过竞选，选举产生学生会组织机构。2010年，在全校开展最优绿箱子评选，全校11个班级评为最优绿箱子班，其中小学3个班、初中4个班、高中4个班。

五、少年先锋队、儿童团

1. 组织机构

1998年11月，上海协和实验学校建立中国共产主义少年先锋队（简称少先队），队员250人。同时在小学一年级学生中建立儿童团。发展少先队员以小学二年级以上小学生为主，每年都有计划发展。在小学二年级至初中预备班学生中，少先队人数占学生人数的90%。进入初中学习的少先队员，按队章规定陆续

2012年民办奉浦学校小三（3）班学生朱睿祺竞选少先队干部的竞选宣言

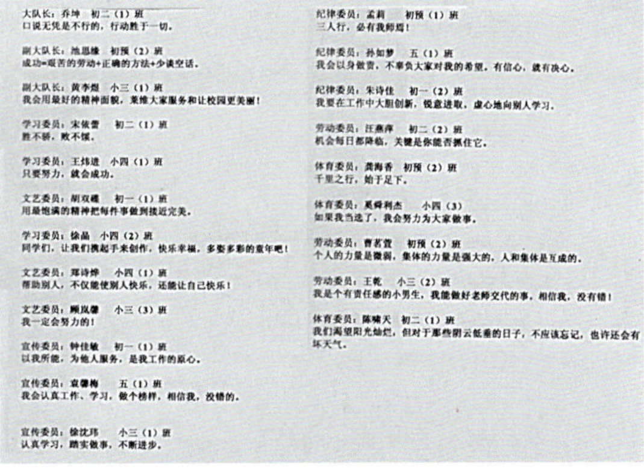
大队长：乔坤 初二（1）班
口说无凭是不行的，行动胜于一切。

副大队长：池思缘 初预（2）班
成功=艰苦的劳动+正确的方法+少谈空话。

副大队长：黄李煜 小三（1）班
我会用最好的精神面貌，来维大家服务和让校园更美丽！

学习委员：宋依雷 初二（1）班
胜不骄，败不馁。

学习委员：王炜进 小四（1）班
只要努力，就会成功。

文艺委员：胡双巍 初一（1）班
用最饱满的精神把每件事做到接近完美。

学习委员：徐晶 小四（2）班
同学们，让我们携起手来创作，快乐幸福，多姿多彩的童年吧！

文艺委员：郑诗烨 小四（1）班
帮助别人，不仅能使别人快乐，还能让自己快乐！

文艺委员：顾岚馨 小三（3）班
我一定会努力的！

宣传委员：钟佳敏 初一（1）班
以我所能，为他人服务，是我工作的原心。

宣传委员：袁馨梅 五（1）班
我会认真工作、学习，做个榜样，相信我，没错的。

宣传委员：徐沈玮 小三（1）班
认真学习，踏实做事，不断进步。

纪律委员：孟莉 初预（1）班
三人行，必有我师焉！

纪律委员：孙如梦 五（1）班
我会以身做责，不辜负大家对我的希望，有信心，就有决心。

纪律委员：朱诗佳 初一（2）班
我要在工作中大胆创新，锐意进取，虚心地向别人学习。

劳动委员：汪燕萍 初二（2）班
机会每日都降临，关键是你能否抓住它。

体育委员：龚海香 初预（2）班
千里之行，始于足下。

体育委员：奚舜利杰 小四（3）
如果我当选了，我会努力为大家做事。

劳动委员：曹茗萱 初预（2）班
个人的力量是微弱，集体的力量是强大的，人和集体是互成的。

劳动委员：王乾 小三（2）班
我是个有责任感的小男生，我能做好老师交代的事，相信我，没有错！

体育委员：陈啸天 初二（1）班
我们渴望阳光灿烂，但对于那些阴云低垂的日子，不应该忘记，也许还会有坏天气。

2009年民办奉浦学校少先队大队干部就职宣言

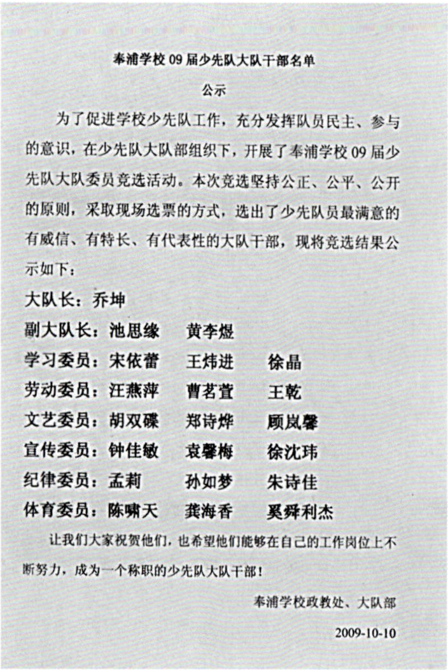

奉浦学校09届少先队大队干部名单

公示

为了促进学校少先队工作，充分发挥队员民主、参与的意识，在少先队大队部组织下，开展了奉浦学校09届少先队大队委员竞选活动。本次竞选坚持公正、公平、公开的原则，采取现场选票的方式，选出了少先队员最满意的有威信、有特长、有代表性的大队干部，现将竞选结果公示如下：

大队长：乔坤

副大队长：池思缘　黄李煜

学习委员：宋依蕾　王炜进　徐晶

劳动委员：汪燕萍　曹茗萱　王乾

文艺委员：胡双碟　郑诗烨　顾岚馨

宣传委员：钟佳敏　袁馨梅　徐沈玮

纪律委员：孟莉　孙如梦　朱诗佳

体育委员：陈啸天　龚海香　奚舜利杰

让我们大家祝贺他们，也希望他们能够在自己的工作岗位上不断努力，成为一个称职的少先队大队干部！

奉浦学校政教处、大队部

2009-10-10

2009年10月，奉浦学校少先队大队干部竞选结果公示

举行退队仪式。少先队在全校设大队，年级设中队，班级设小队，并分别选举产生少先队干部。2009年10月，上海民办奉浦学校有少先队员468人，通过“小苗苗入团”的儿童团员125人。是年，少先队大队干部根据公开、公正、公平原则，通过中队民主选举产生大队干部候选人，竞选演讲，现场投票方式，选出有威信、有特长、有代表性大队干部21人，设大队长1人，副大队长2人，委员18人。由学校政教处、少先队大队部向全校公示。当选大队干部向全体少先队员发表就职宣言。2012年，少先队大队部由大队长1人，副大队长2人、学习、劳动、文艺、宣传、纪律、体育委员各4人共27人组成。另设红领巾广播员2人、小记者2人。2016年，上海帕丁顿双语学校有少先队员500多人，儿童团员90多人。全校少先队设1个大队部，有大队委员27人。少先队设大队辅导员，先后分别为：谢党（1998.11—2005.8）、诸海萍(女)(2005.8—2009.8)、汤玲玲(女)(2009.8—2014.8)、李平(女)(2014.8—2016.8)、李若男(女)(2016.7至今)。

上海帕丁顿双语学校少先队2016届大队部成员。前排左起：蔡匀、陈芊聿、许圣、陈朝红、章荣俊、董晨曦、徐致柔、蒋宇晨、郑志毅、兰婷婷、沈施瀚、蔡海涛；后排左起：陈欣雨、曹欣怡、茅彦欣、吴研、徐锦东、郑志伟、孙亦涵、吴亦晨、刘思宇、郎曼妮、王文文

2．主要活动

组织少先队队员学习少先队队章，发挥少先队员先锋模范作用。2001年12月，为参加2001年上海市第三届学生艺术节中小学生优秀节目调演，上海协和实验学校组织管弦乐队积极准备，参演的管乐合奏曲目获二等奖。2002年10月，学校少先队组成的乐队参加2002年上海市布谷鸟学生音乐节中小学乐队比赛，演出的西洋乐合奏“安妮波尔卡，快速波乐卡”获一等奖。2004年，奉浦学校少先队、儿童团员参加2004年上海市“和我一起改变世界”《儿童权利公约》宣传海报设计大赛，被上海市妇女联合会、中国儿童发展中心评为优秀组织奖。2007年5月，奉浦学校初一（1）班少先队中队，在学习生活中处处起表率作用，德智体得到全面发展，被共青团奉贤区委、区教育局、少先队奉贤区工委授予红旗中队荣誉称号。2008年6月，为鼓励汶川地震少年儿童树立克服困难、树立信心，全校少先队员、共青团员投入“书信传递关爱”活动，给同龄人写信750余封。2009年1月，全校小学、初中二年级20个班级的少先队员、儿童团员700多名在蓝天下的至爱——手拉手、共享温馨新年捐款活动中纷纷捐出零花钱与压岁钱计9396元。是年3月，奉浦学校小学二年级至初二年级少先队员468名及同学共501名，向西渡小学患白血病儿童捐款2607.1元。6月1日，举办少先队红领巾跳蚤书市义卖捐款活动，义卖所得3374元，全部上缴学校。2010年，学校少先队大队部组织开展“少先队调研征文”活动，两次获奉贤区征文评比三等奖。

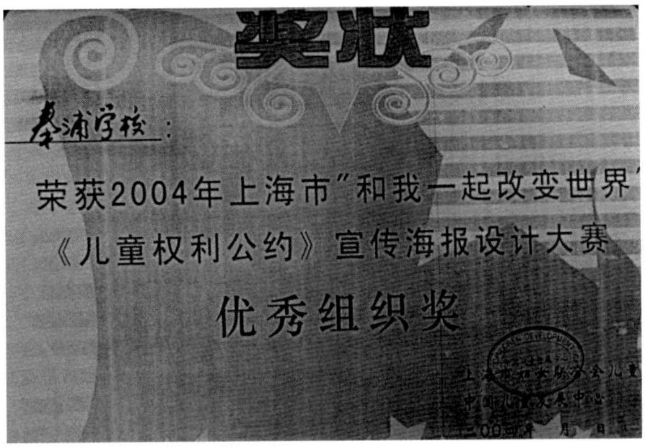

2004年奉浦学校少先队获上海市“和我一起改变世界”《儿童权利公约》宣传海报设计大赛优秀组织奖证书

蓝天下的至爱——手拉手，共享温馨新年

各班捐款清单

班级	捐款额（单位：元）	备注
一(1)班	775.00	捐款用途： 1、向四川都江堰中兴学校、柳街小学分别捐献人民币两仟元。 2、向本校学生捐助： 500元： 小二（1）朱亦玄、黄李煜 小三（3）金嘉灵 小五（2）池思缘、顾琰 高一（1）陆缨霞 高三（3）朱玲 400元： 小三（3）徐　婷 初二（1）朱古力 初一（3）张　吉 高三（1）陶雪诗怡 高二（1）方晶 300元： 小五（2）汤志强 初预（2）张静静 初三（2）张艺辉 高一（3）金玉慧 高燕 高二（1）季晨雷 高二（2）沈庄一、邱佳敏 人民币总计柒仟玖佰元。 3、其余款额玖佰玖拾元伍角暂存学校红十字捐款账户中，用于今后的各类善举活动。
一(2)班	231.00	
一(3)班	1400.00	
一(4)班	345.00	
二(1)班	524.10	
二(2)班	855.00	
二(3)班	623.00	
三(1)班	396.00	
三(2)班	530.00	
三(3)班	425.00	
四(1)班	510.00	
五(1)班	510.00	
五(2)班	412.00	
初预(1)班	388.50	
初预(2)班	280.00	
初一(1)班	233.00	
初一(2)班	232.00	
初一(3)班	280.00	
初二(1)班	247.00	
初二(2)班	200.00	
初三(1)班	200.00	
初三(2)班	290.00	
高一(1)班	330.70	
高一(2)班	400.00	
高一(3)班	365.00	
高二(1)班	474.5	
高二(2)班	532.00	
高三(1)班	270.00	
高三(2)班	300.00	
高三(3)班	300.00	
无名氏	31.70	
总计	12890.5	

2009年，民办奉浦学校蓝天下的至爱捐款情况

民办奉浦学校爱心志愿者队伍开展义卖活动

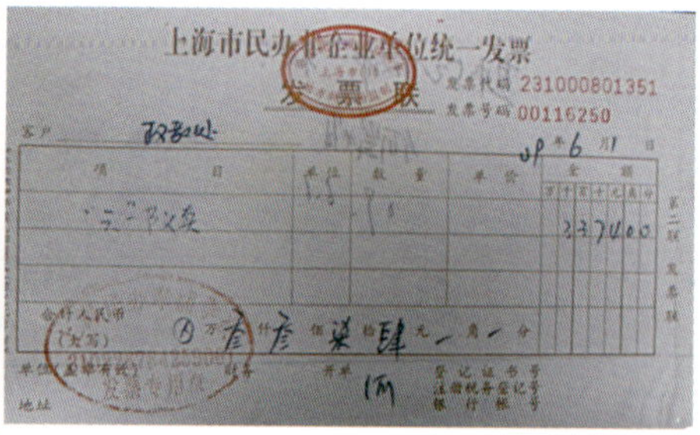

2009年6月，民办奉浦学校学生“六一”儿童节义卖所得款上缴学校的收据

2011—2012年，组织少先队员与儿童团员参加重阳节敬老“红领巾心向党”活动竞赛，开展“成长的脚印”“走进艺术的海洋”“雷锋精神与我同行”黑板报展评，举办“美丽的上海、我的家”采访活动。2013年，学校少先队派出代表队参加“红领巾心向党”全国少先队知识竞赛，获优秀辅导奖，大队部被共青团奉贤区委、少先队奉贤区工委授予“奉贤区红旗大队”称号。2016年，上海帕丁顿双语学校坚持在优秀少先队员中每周挑选男女学生各1名为国旗升旗手，并公示升旗手的事迹，激励少先队员学有榜样，奋发向上。

民办奉浦学校团委、少先队组织团员、少先队员开展敬老活动

六、学校红十字会

1. 机构　宗旨

1998年9月，成立上海协和实验学校红十字会。嗣后数次更改校名，红十字会从未停止活动。上海帕丁顿双语学校红十字会主要工作内容有：知识传播（国际红十字运动基本知识普及培训；探索《国际人道法》师资培训；探索《国际人道法》项目交流与展示活动；探索《国际人道法》系列宣传活动）、救护培训（现场初级急救知识与技能普及培训；现场初级急救技能师资培训；“十二五”

2009年6月1日，民办奉浦学校举行红十字会会员入会仪式

彩票公益金计划红十字学校健康安全辅导员培训）、预防艾滋病宣传（“预防艾滋”教育主持人培训，“预防艾滋·反对歧视”知识与理论普及宣传，“12·1”世界艾滋病日大型主题宣传活动）、红十字青少年交流交往（红十字青少年夏令营）、红十字青少年文化建设（“红十字精神伴我成长“红十字青少年文化节）、学校红十字工作理论探讨、上海市红十字会青少年系列文化阵地建设。

2．**主要活动**

上海帕丁顿双语学校红十字会产生理事会，设会长、副会长、秘书长、副秘书长、理事若干人组成。历任校长兼任会长，学校有关领导任副会长，日常工作由秘书长主持。1998年以来，学校召开过6次会员代表大会，选举产生学校历届红十字理事会成员。

按照国际红十字会运动“人道、公正、中立、志愿服务、独立、统一、普及7项基本原则与人道、博爱、奉献的红十字精神；保护人的生命和健康，发扬人道主义精神，促进和平进步事业”要求，学校红十字会每年发展新会员；开展红十字志愿服务、红十字运动基本知识传播及国际人道法活动；预防艾滋病、无偿献血及造血干细胞捐献宣传；青少年交流活动；现场初级急救知识与技能培训；红十字会人道救助、收缴会费等工作。1998年以来，会员人数占三年级以上学生人数的98%以上。2009年5月，在“手拉手，共享美好明

民办奉浦学校红十字会捐款活动

天”捐款活动中，全校红十字会员捐款6216元。2010年，经验收学校被评为上海市红十字会合格学校。2012年1月，教师王益权捐献造血干细胞配对成功。学校还制订各种突发事件的应急预案并实行演练，在师生中开展包扎抢救技能培训和模拟逃生知识教育。在奉贤区第五届中学生民防运动会上学校代表队获民防团体总分第二名，包扎抢救、定向越野、模拟逃生等项目取得好成绩。2016年5月，帕丁顿学校红十字会开展“爱心汇聚，花开贤城博爱月”主题活动，发展红十字会新会员112名，举行新会员入会仪式，按照“人道、博爱、奉献”的红十字会精神，筹集善款6083元，并向区红十字会缴纳青少年会员、成年会员费2312元。组织七年级学生开展“三角巾急救包扎技能”培训，在学校操场进行防灾减灾逃生演练。学校红十字会与政教处等配合，开展每周健康广播活动，进行自护、自救安全、远离毒品、健康生活、艾滋病防治、无烟校园等教育。

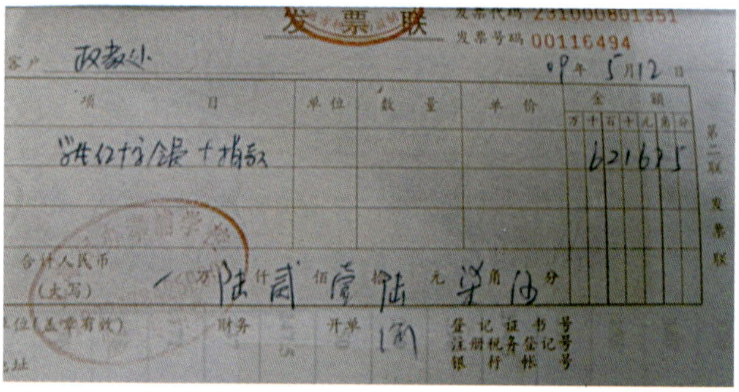

2009年5月，民办奉浦学校上缴学生红十字会会员、捐款收据

2013年，学校组织学生开展急救技能培训

第六章　教职员工

学校自创办至2015年8月，学校教师主要由公办教师、民办教师和外聘教师组成。2015年8月，学校公办教师与公办学生析出，单列公办上海市奉贤区奉浦学校。自此，上海帕丁顿双语学校为纯民办学校，学校教师均为民办性质。

学校坚持公、民办教师同工同酬，这对稳定师资队伍发挥了积极作用。1998年8月至2010年2月，学校教师待遇总体略高于一般公办学校。2010年2月后开始实行绩效工资，帕丁顿双语学校教师的工资福利待遇与全区公办学校统一。2015年8月后，帕丁顿双语学校教师的分配方案总体上与公办学校持平。

学校坚持对在岗教师的培训，其形式包括“开设专题讲座”“团队带教”“职初教师带教”“高一层次带教”“青年教师讲习班”“课堂教学展示活动”“出国、出省培训”等，还包括具有校本特色的“课堂教学改进计划”等。校本培训对提升教师的专业能力，形成“四有”师资队伍发挥积极作用。

学校坚持对教师的师德教育，宣传执行奉贤区教育局提出的“五不准”“五提倡”“五表率”(附)，拟定《奉浦学校师德规范十条》，开展“师爱、师风、师强”教师演讲活动。加强师德考核和表彰，对形成风正气清的教师队伍，实现学校的整体目标发挥重要作用。学校严格对教师进行评价与考核，制定《教师业务学期综合考评奖励条例》《班主任工作考核奖励办法》《年级团队合作考核奖励办法》《职初教师考核办法》，发挥重要的激励与导向作用。

学校成立职称评审小组，由历任校长任组长，完成历年来对职初教师转正评定工作。一级教师与高级教师的评审与上报上级职称办审定的工作。

由于是寄宿制学校，在职工的使用上除教辅、后勤人员外，还聘用部分宿管人员，所以职工队伍较一般公办学校为多。学校加强管理与考核，使这支队伍为学校的后勤服务工作起到安全保障作用。

第一节 教 师

一、教师来源

1998年9月至2015年8月，教师的基本来源分为调配和招聘两类。调配是由奉贤区（县）教育局从全区（县）各学校中抽调教师，或由学校从应届大学毕业生中选聘教师。调配教师的编制性质均属公办。招聘类教师又分为两类，一类是到社会上招聘在职教师或新毕业的外地籍应届大学毕业生，这类人员一般定性为民办教师；另一类是招聘退休教师进校任教，这类人员一般定性为外聘教师。

学校创办时，全校教师65人（含员工8人），其中42人由奉贤县教育局从全县各学校中抽调，23人从应届大学毕业生中选聘。当时学校教师（或员工）均属公办性质。教育局额定学校公办教师（含员工）编制为65人，不得再行扩大。2003年9月教师进修学院接管学校，带入公办编制教师18人，公办教师（含员工）扩大至75人。2006年教育局再度核定公办教师编制为70人，并规定只出不进。

随着学校班级与生源的增加，1999年始，陆续开始招聘民办教师与外聘退休教师，各年数额均有不同。2015年8月，公办教师全数从学校析出，进入公办上海市奉贤区奉浦学校。民办教师留上海帕丁顿双语学校任教。2016年8月，上海帕丁顿双语学校教师102人，都属民办性质。

二、教师结构

1998年9月至2015年9月，学校教师基本上由公办教师、民办教师与外聘教师三部分构成。随着学校办学规模的变化，教师的结构也随之发生变化。

2015年9月，公办教师全数析出，上海帕丁顿双语学校的教师全为民办或外聘性质。2016年全校教师102人，其中男教师20人，女教师82人。从学历上分，研究生14人，本科生88人；从职称上分，高级职称5人，中级职称9人，其他职称88人。

1. **公办教师**

为支持民办教育事业的发展，在学校创办之初，因学校兼收公办学生，原奉贤县教育局以民办（公助）的方式在教师（含员工）的编制上给予大力支持。1998年，公办教师编制65人，直至2003年，除个别人员调离外，教师队伍较稳定。

2003年，教师进修学院托管带入18名公办编制教师。2005年，解除托管，调离部分公办教师。2006年，教育局额定学校公办编制不得超过70人，并只准出，不准进。

公办教师在民办学校工作，在师资培训、职称评定、工资福利等方面均享有公办教师的权益。这支队伍在该校发展和教育教学改革的进程中始终成为学校的主力军。1998—2015年，先后有128名公办教师在上海帕丁顿双语学校任教。

附：公办教师名录

沈爱玉(女)	刘明坤	沈靖华	沈利德	曹建军	王胜利
冯志华	朱　峰	俞　铮	郁玉芳(女)	宋建伯	唐继英(女)
高决心	沈晓红(女)	陈小红(女)	刘德根	周时青	吴新华
王益权	何新莲(女)	孙美红(女)	曹春华(女)	李爱兵	胡荣海
詹　强	谢华芳(女)	顾　微(女)	苏卫芳(女)	夏庆华(女)	瞿燕群(女)
寿引莲(女)	陈桂杰(女)	吴玉莉(女)	罗　燕(女)	金海芹(女)	陶　静(女)
顾叶丽(女)	李永卫	阮　颖(女)	李　宏	宋玉英(女)	周林峰
朱绍忠	倪美红(女)	吴栋梅(女)	石　瑛(女)	陆　竞(女)	夏春妹(女)
池　敏(女)	凌　玲(女)	高春妹(女)	钱康利(女)	阮骏燕(女)	施静华(女)
黄小媚(女)	谢　党	陆建国	盛国英(女)	洪梅华(女)	赵　坤(女)
张建新	张秀英(女)	姚仁兴	孙凤仙(女)	徐　英(女)	何南友
姚友兴	周向勤(女)	胡荣海	吴新华	汪六弟	瞿　锋
谢芳华(女)	邢光伟	冯　斌	唐　敏(女)	汤　铭	钱彩群(女)
焦　莹(女)	江仁章	范小莲(女)	何新莲(女)	陈　岚(女)	何　芳(女)
马欢权	潘海鸥(女)	邵引龙	汤　慎	陈　红(女)	何翠娟(女)
王晓蕾(女)	柳肖云(女)	余　琳(女)	陈春红(女)	汪林英(女)	张　莉(女)
丁　梅(女)	朱爱民	何　岚(女)	唐继英(女)	周桂花(女)	唐燕燕(女)
吴　玲(女)	阮慧华(女)	张黎花(女)	杨卫平	王秋红(女)	吴　莹(女)
钱　红(女)	徐志云(女)	吴光蔓(女)	张　玲(女)	韩　建	洪　莲(女)
唐国华	李　敏(女)	翁丹香(女)	叶　丹(女)	汤玲玲(女)	张舒晔(女)
鞠宝龙	张春辉	夏红波	王　英(女)	姚美玉(女)	杨　龙
丁永花(女)	杨春燕(女)	杨忠莲(女)	钟菊红(女)	钱玉红(女)	张琴花(女)
周　威(女)					

2. 民办教师

随着学校办学规模的不断扩大，原有的公办教师已不足以承担学校的全部教学任务。1999年始，学校开始招聘民办教师。2005年之前民办教师在师资培训、职称评定、工资福利上与公办教师比较有所差异。由此优秀的民办教师难以留住。2005年9月始，学校对民办教师实行与公办教师同工同酬，此后优秀民办教师得以留住，并呈壮大趋势。民办教师大部分为外地高学历的在编教师转入。此后，民办教师在职称评定、师资培训、工资报酬等方面均与公办教师享有同等权益。2011年始，学校为民办教师办理年金，以提高退休后的待遇，同时也为学校振兴发挥重大作用。1998—2016年，先后在上海帕丁顿双语学校工作的民办教师151人。

附：民办教师名录

蒋义素(女)	周华星(女)	任其兵	黄艳红(女)	诸海萍(女)	林 莹(女)
王树松	丁 瑛(女)	臧桂玲(女)	吴小燕(女)	汤春燕(女)	么凤娟(女)
刘 佳(女)	郑 妹(女)	唐丽丽(女)	张建丽(女)	刘超红(女)	徐青莲(女)
吴海波(女)	鞠斌斌	赵 丽(女)	施红妹(女)	刁晓红(女)	杨 华
毛 平(女)	翁丽娜(女)	沈晓玲(女)	程 涛	张 婷(女)	张荔婧(女)
靖若晴(女)	王 飞	武秀丽(女)	巴 欢(女)	刘晓敏(女)	孔维佳(女)
杜 星(女)	黄瑞霞(女)	刘圣荣	李佳燕(女)	赵艳艳(女)	李 平(女)
刘 玲(女)	陈晶晶(女)	金晓芹(女)	朱 骏	张伟国	尹 晶(女)
朱晓君(女)	姜凯夫	蔡秋香(女)	葛淑华(女)	刘瑜会(女)	李艳玉(女)
邹 炜(女)	张文明	曹晶晶(女)	严佳慧(女)	张丽君(女)	李若男(女)
李茵茵(女)	汪 宏	陈雯佳(女)	孙晓琼(女)	张 楚(女)	陈燕茹(女)
曾均婷(女)	郝玉婷(女)	徐依凡(女)	李素丽(女)	金 丹(女)	陈艳艳(女)
高嘉旖(女)	方晓燕(女)	史 佳(女)	张 燕(女)	段华华(女)	王晓蓓(女)
张静静(女)	孔 迪(女)	王 婷(女)	王萌萌(女)	汪文晋(女)	王文静(女)
连 峥(女)	许晓杭(女)	君甜甜(女)	翁晓岚(女)	杨 琴(女)	狄张磊(女)
李 平(女)	李坤峰(女)	朱杰宇(女)	武云红(女)	曾 莉(女)	毛楚楚(女)
禾 慧(女)	舒 畅(女)	阚 媛(女)	周 媛(女)	张先宏(女)	朱佳佳(女)
陆丽丽(女)	胡 辉(女)	李志强	董俊平	王志伟	陆桂英(女)
张 臻	殷崇德	唐超群(女)	周 华	王春艳(女)	曾倩倩(女)

张　媛(女)	费文华	庄　燕(女)	韩秀蓉(女)	罗　媛(女)	朱琳娜(女)
刘　阳(女)	范丽萍(女)	王春艳(女)	王魁颖(女)	郝凌云(女)	马　华(女)
邱樱莹(女)	陆爱群(女)	范永恩	王天玲(女)	冯月霞(女)	曹阿娟(女)
顾俊杰	谢　杰	贺萌萌(女)	闻晓燕(女)	曹　琳(女)	邹　伟(女)
姚慧吉(女)	汪　蕾(女)	周　雯(女)	钱　娜(女)	许娟娟(女)	刘明敏(女)
程其标(女)	宋海丽(女)	姚　远(女)	李　吉	刘迎春(女)	侯素英(女)
郭翠莲(女)					

3．外聘教师

为满足师资的需求，弥补缺额或教师病、产假，学校按因需聘用外聘教师。外聘教师不在编制内。一般为区内退休教师或外地在职教师。外聘教师的工酬以课时工资计算，福利与在编教师相同。外聘教师占教师总比例不高。但有些外聘教师教育教学能力很强，被学校长期聘用，如陶宝娣(女)教师等。1998—2016年，先后在上海帕丁顿双语学校任教的外聘教师23人。

附：外聘教师名录

库月平(女)	蒋秀芳(女)	徐琍萍(女)	戚盛彪	曹善明	陈翠莲(女)
沈靖华	相梅英(女)	龚晓燕(女)	沈忠勤	章　丽(女)	金志锋
刘　平(女)	程春影(女)	戚盛伟	方玲英(女)	陶宝娣(女)	余丽萍(女)
邢同成	王立群(女)	王毅心	汪宝法	张　珏(女)	

4．外聘外籍教师

1998年10月，上海民办协和实验学校首次聘用英国籍女教师1人，由创意宝贝与学校签订1年的合同，在小学部讲授口语课。1999—2002年6月，又先后聘用外籍教师4人。2006年2月，民办奉浦学校再次聘用外籍教师讲授小学外语口语课。2010年8月，学校与莱尚培训学校合作，由莱尚培训学校出面聘

2012年5月6日，外籍教师与民办奉浦学校学生进行英语口语交流活动

用有5年以上经历的美籍老师2人，分别为莫尔姆·莱弗凡达和默莱及·捷克白。是月，学校与澳大利亚哥伦比亚学院、上海奉贤中学试办高中英语特长班，由澳大利亚哥伦比亚学院委托澳大利亚籍女教师1人，任雅思课程与民办奉浦学校小学口语课。是年12月，上海市外国专家局为学校颁发聘用外籍教师资格证。2012年，民办奉浦学校与加拿大多伦多五湖学院合作试办高中国际课程班，由五湖学院派遣外籍教师任教。2015年，上海帕丁顿双语学校制订《上海帕丁顿双语学校外籍教师管理制度》，规范外籍教师管理。2016年8月，上海帕丁顿双语学校举办小学国际班，聘外籍教师3人。至2016年，先后有16人次的外籍教师来学校任教，分别来自英国、澳大利亚、美国、爱尔兰等国家。

上海帕丁顿双语学校外籍教师管理制度

为保证我校聘请的外籍教师能更好地服务于教育、教学工作，依据国家相关法律法规，联系我校实际，特制定本规定。

一、外籍教师来校任教，必须与学校签订聘用合同，学校依照合同严格进行管理。外籍教师必须遵守学校的各项教育、教学及管理制度，自觉履行合同规定的各项义务。

二、学校负责向外籍教师介绍我国的基本情况和我国的教育方针、政策、法律、法令及有关规定，帮助其了解中国。

三、外籍教师必须遵守我国的法律、法规，尊重中国人民的文化传统和风俗习惯，不从事与教师身份不相符的政治、经济、文化活动。任职期间不得传教，不得散发宗教宣传品，不得发展教徒。

四、学校国际教育交流部，全面负责外籍教师管理工作，并为外籍教师配备一名政治素质好、业务能力强、具有较强责任心的英语教师作为合作教师。协助外籍教师开展教学；指导外籍教师学习汉语；帮助其解决学习、工作、生活中的实际困难。主动关心他们的业余生活；创造条件切实保障外籍教师的人身安全。

五、外籍教师应当勤快敬业，每学期均要制定出详细的教学计划，注意探讨研究教学方法。在教学中，必须严格按学校规定的教学大纲和教学计划授课，必须依照学校提供的课表按时上课，不迟到、不早退、不缺课，不随意调课。并按学校提供的教材从事教学工作，对组织教学讨论等非教材的内容及为方便教学临时补充的音像制品、书刊等教学辅助材料，应征得外语教研组长及主管教学的校长同意后，方可使用。应当为人师表，衣着整洁，树立良好的教师形象。

六、学校支持外籍教师参与学校组织的各项教育、教学活动和教师、学生组织的文化及娱乐活动。但外籍教师不得从事与教学无关的社会工作，如采访、经商、咨询服务以及与其身份不相符的其它活动。未经学校同意，外籍教师不得兼任与学校无关的其他劳务。确因学校工作需要，需外出讲课或交流，一般应安排在非工作日进行，并应事先向教务处主管领导报告，并征得学校国际教育交流部同意后，方可外出讲课或交流。聘用期间不得以任何形式向社会和学生作涉及我国政治思想、社会状况、经济和科技秘密、特殊的生物资源以及其它违反规定的调查。特殊需要者，须经学校报有关部门批准后，方可进行。

七、学校每学期组织有关人员对外籍教师的教学工作进行检查、考核、评估。外籍教师在教学或其它工作中做出显著成绩的，学校将予以表彰奖励，并向上级主管部门申请奖励。

八、外籍教师因事、因病请假时，须提前办理手续，请假程序为本人提出书面申请（或医院诊断 证明），教务处主管领导加注意见，征得主管教学校长同意。假满后应向教务处办理销假手续，教务处及时将请假情况报校务办备案。如遇突发事件或不可抗拒因素无法按时回归时，需向主管领导报告并在回归后补假。因事、因病耽误的课程，要及时补上。

九、外籍教师外出旅游时，应提前三天办理请假手续，并告知外出时间、路线、到达地点及返校时间。旅游途中如遇到自己无法自行解决的困难和问题，应及时与学校取得联系。

十、外籍教师在宿舍住宿的，必须遵纪守法，遵守学校各项规章制度，爱护宿舍公共设施，维护宿舍正常秩序，创造安全文明生活环境。不得随便留宿他人。宿舍内严禁使用电炉、热得快等大功率电器和酒精炉、煤气炉、火柴等明火用具；严禁私自回接电线、改装电路、安装插座、灯头；不得将易燃、易爆、剧毒等危险品带入楼内。宿舍内不得传播、复制、观看、贩卖反动、淫秽书刊和声像制品；严禁酗酒、赌博、打架斗殴、聚众喧哗；不得在宿舍举办舞会以及其他不健康的活动。外籍教师在宾馆住宿的，需严格遵守宾馆的各项规章制度。

十一、尊重外籍教师的风俗习惯和宗教信仰，适当照顾外籍教师的生活特点。外籍教师除在我国法定节假日及中小学寒、暑假可以休假外，圣诞节也可以休假两天。

2015年上海帕丁顿双语学校制订的外籍教师管理制度

2012—2013 年上海帕丁顿双语学校聘用外籍教师情况表

表 6-1-1

姓 Last Name	名 First Name	中文译名 Chinese Name	职位 Title	学位 Degree
BOUKHART	ANGEL RADOUANE	安吉尔拉多安	教师	教育学学士
MEIN	THOMAS DOUGLAS WALTER	梅思·托马斯·道格拉斯·沃特尔	教师	教育学历史与文学学士
KILLENS	MELANIE JEAN	琪琳·梅兰妮·简	教师	教育学与儿童家庭学学士
CHESHIER	HANNAH KATHARINE	切希尔·汉娜·卡特琳	教师	教育学与电影艺术学学士
YOUNG	COLLEEN ZITA	扬·科林·梓塔	教师	教育学与数学学士

2016 年上海帕丁顿双语学校聘用外籍教师情况表

表 6-1-2

姓 Last Name	名 First Name	中文译名 Chinese Name	职位 Title	学位 Degree	国家 Nation
Gary	James	吉姆	Mister	BSEd	America 美国
Power	Martin	马丁	Teacher	BA in History and German	Ireland 爱尔兰
Knott	Adam	亚当	Teacher	Bachelor of Science	America 美国

5. 退休教师

由于学校办学时间不长，退休教师及员工人数不多，一般都为公办教师。学校工会组织负责退休教师定期回校参加活动，学校根据区教育局退管委员会的工作精神，每年给退休教师发放福利费，组织体检及外出旅游等活动。至 2016 年，帕丁顿双语学校退休教师 6 人。

2012 年 10 月，民办奉浦学校召开重阳节退休教师座谈会

附：退休教师职工名录

刘明坤　陈桂杰(女)　盛伟宾　姚美玉(女)　沈利德　沈靖华

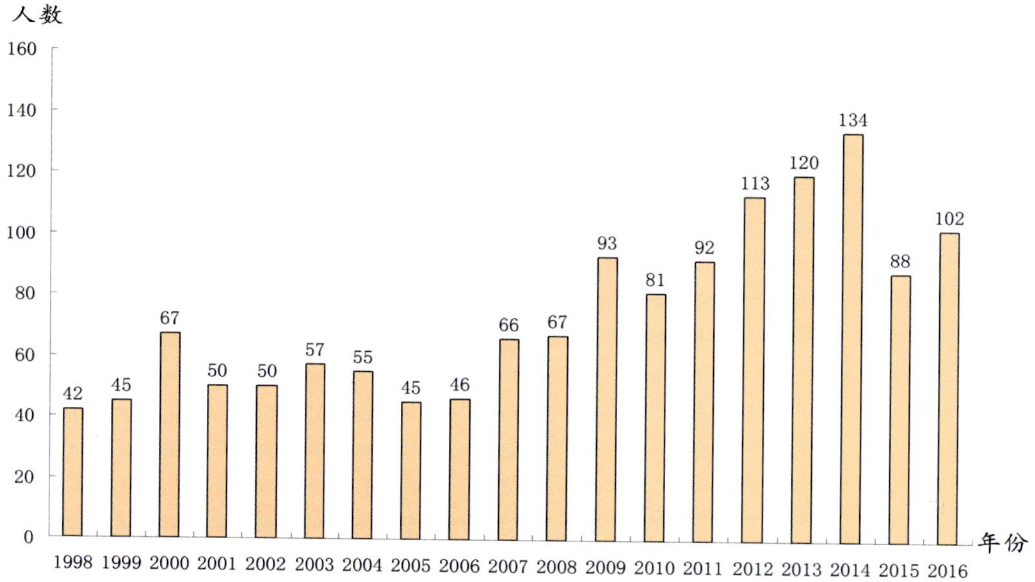

1998—2016年上海帕丁顿双语学校专任教师人数示意图

说明：1．1998—2015数据摘自《奉贤统计年鉴》；2．专任教师不包括外聘退休教师

三、教师培训与待遇

1．师资培训

自1998年9月学校开办至2016年，学校采用多种形式对教师进行不断的教育教学业务培训。

教师教育教学理论学习 营造学习型组织，关注教师教育教学理论水平的提升是师资业务培训的首要任务。学校曾为教师购置郑金洲教授主编的《上课的变革》《备课的变革》《听课的变革》丛书，组织学习交流，引导教师深刻理解课堂教学的变革现状。组织全校教师学习的理论基础书籍有江苏杨思中学的《先学后教，当堂训练》，上海市课改办编制的《上海市二期课改探索与实践——来自课改研究基地学习的报告》《读懂中国》系列丛书，斯宾塞·约翰逊的《谁动了我的奶酪》，雷夫·艾斯奎斯的《56号教室》，美国米勒的《QBQ问题背后的问题》，美国著名教师罗恩·克拉克的《优秀是教出来的》等教育教学理论书籍。这些校本培训教材犹如源头活水，对教师教学行为优化起到良好的引领作用。

开设专题讲座 专题讲座可以在较短的时间内为教师提供海量信息，引发教师的思维碰撞。学校多次邀请上海市教育教学专家到校作讲座。1999年始，先后所作的报告讲座有国家教委脑潜能开发组上海组组长陈根宝的“脑科学与课堂教学”的报告；市教委教研室英语学科组组长陈少敏的“英语实验教材教学”的报告；市教委教研室数学教研组袁霞(女)的“奉献——教师的天职”的报告；上海市世界外国语小学校长王小平的“学做现代人”的报告；上海市教委课程教材部江铭初的“关于中小学拓展课程建设和实施的思考”；上海市名校长邵光标小学校长金建中的“让有效教研唤醒教师发展的内需与激情”的报告；上海市教科院普教所胡兴宏的“关于课堂教学研究”的报告；教育中小学校长培训中心刘莉莉(女)教授的“办一所好学校——文化引领与学校特色”的报告等。2005年起，学校校长戚盛伟开设的专题讲座有“创造性思维能力培养”“高效率教学概要”“脑的功能——将脑研究成果应用于课堂实践”“行为主义的学习动机理论”“元认知知识”“教学反思的价值与意义”“获取知识的高效率策略”等。

“团队带教”模式 学校针对教师流动性大，新教师多的特点，为迅速提升师德师能，学校形成“团队带教”运作模式。“团队带教”包括“师徒带教”“资源联盟学校优秀教师带教”“教研组带教”等多种形式。“师徒带教”又分“职初教师带教”与“高一层次带教”两类。学校对招聘到的新大学毕业生实行“职初教师”带教培训方式带教。拟定“学年职初教师带教计划”，确定带教教师与被带教教师名单，召开带教工作座谈会，明确带教教师与被带教教师的职责要求。一般新教师由两位成熟教师带教，1名负责学科带教，1名负责班主任工作带教。

职初教师带教 这是一项长期的校本研修项目。项目实施以来，奉浦学校在各方面都取得长足发展。在教学质量上，各部、各年级都有不同程度的进步。小学部各年级的教学质量已不逊于南桥镇的各所兄弟学校，初中毕业班的中考成绩一年上一个台阶，进入区前十名的行列，在全区范围内，也是教学质量提高较快的学校之一。在教师的专业发展上，职初教师迅速成长，2011—2016年，有近30名新教师在校上岗，通过参加各类培训，都已基本胜任学校安排的教学工作，特别是参加本项培训二三年后，大部分的职初教师的课堂教学有了质的飞跃，如翁丹香(女)、周华星(女)、诸海萍(女)等老师，她们在区的1、3、5年期的考核中获课堂教学优秀奖，在区域联盟及区范围内进行教学展示，受到相关专家的首肯，特别像诸海萍(女)老师应教研员的要求，在区内进行数次教学展示。而业已成熟的骨干教师也在不断的反思、改进和创新中体验着自己的成功，引领大批的青年教师投身于教学改革之中，积极参加到“智慧教学，聪明学习”这一上海市民办学校特色项目的创建活动中。学校科研室在教师们记载的“课堂教学改进”案例中挑选一部分，编撰《奉浦学校“智慧教学”案例集》，激励、引导教师们继续探索减负增效的策略和途径，让“建设智慧型校园”的理想成为现实。

“高一层次带教” 这是指高级教师对一级教师的带教，一级教师对二级教师的带教。新教师经过1年期的培训一般可晋升为二级教师，但还不是成熟型教师，所以学校有必要实行高一层次的带教，继续师徒结对，帮助1年期教师迅速成长。5年期教师一般可晋升为一级教师。为帮助一级教师不断提升教科研水平与实际教学能力，拓展视野，逐步形成自身的教学风格，学校还创设高级教师带教一级教师的带教平台。

“师徒带教” 这是有层次性的，对各级各类教师的专业发展发挥了正效应。

资源联盟学校教师带教源于2009年，当时教育局为促进区域内学校的均衡发展，由区域内发展阶段领先的学校与其他学校形成联盟体。由1所好学校带领一批学校共同进步。奉浦学校的资源联盟体的盟主学校为育秀学校。学校新教师1年实习期内必须参加育秀组织的新教师培训，与他们学校的带教教师签署带教协议，并由他校教师作学校培训合格鉴定。

在2009年前，学校为帮助新教师成长也先后与解放路小学、实验小学、实验中学等学校签署过带教新教师的协议。“借他山之石攻玉”也在师训工作中发挥有效作用。

出国出省培训 主要是外语学科。奉贤区为提高区内学校外语教学水平，缩小与市中心区的差距，多年暑假组织外语教师到南京集训1个月。学校有4名外语教师参加过此类培训。选派2名外语教师出国培训。

青年教师讲习班 青年教师是学校一支不可或缺的生力军。同时，面对复杂的教育教学现状，青年教师也有着各种困惑。为破解这个难点，学校特开设“青年教师讲习班”。

讲习班以学校入职5年以内的青年教师为主要培训对象，以主讲教师作讲解传授主题讲座、学员交流为主要培训形式，学校颁发相关学分。

学校先后开设20余个主要讲座，如“教育效应及其在教育教学实践中的运用”“行为主义教育理论及其运用”“认知心理学教育理论及其运用”“社会心理学教育理论及其运用”“教师的角色定位及其领导作风”“当代教师的几个最主要的忌讳”“学习策略与思维策略是如何形成的”“教学反思的价值与意义”“教育的政策与法规”“教学常规的应知应会”“学科教学中‘三维目标’的制定与实现”“作业辅导与减负增效”“学业质量绿色评价指标校本检测”“教师备课的现状分析与基本格式要求”“学业测试中双向细目表的编制及质量分析”“学校教育科研实践操作指导”“班主任教师的主要职责和必须掌握的几个‘会’”“班主任工作基本规范”“班级活动设计与组织”“温馨教室建设”“与家长沟通的艺术”等。

课堂教学展示活动　学校每学期举行课堂教学展示活动，为教师成长搭建舞台。通过优秀教师展示课、青年教师亮相课、骨干教师比武课等，提升教师教学行为。在活动中，教师们参与备课、教学设计、听课和评课等活动，共同讨论、分享经验与成果，优势互补，达到“共赢”的目的。

校本研修特色项目——课堂教学改进计划　2008年始，为提升全体教师课堂教学的执行力和反思意识，学校开展“课堂教学改进计划”项目实践。此项目对教师业务能力与专业发展发生过重大影响，成为校本研修的特色项目。

附：奉浦学校校本研修特色项目“为了智慧型校园的理想”

奉浦学校教师课堂教学改进计划和实施记载

——奉浦学校校本研修特色项目

培训目标

1. 通过培训，让教师对自己的课堂教学行为作一个全面的反思，分析自己的优势与不足，明确自己发展的目标与方向。

2. 让广大教主动转变教学观念，更新教学方法与手段，改变自身的教学行为，提高课堂教学的技能与技巧，最终实现提高课堂教学质效的目标。

3. 让教师养成主动反思的习惯，通过不断反思自己和他人的教学行为，促使教师学习新的教学理论，提炼基于自身实践的成功做法与经验，积累案例，上升为理论，指导今后的教学工作，不断探索，最终成为一名研究型的教师。

培训形式

1. 制定目标和措施。教师对自己在教学上的主要优势和不足，做一个全面的分析，在此基础上，制订学年度课堂教学改进目标和措施。

2. 组织学习。学校组织、教研组组织与个人自学相结合，学习有关课堂教学的理论和实践资料，帮助教师提高理论素养，丰富教学实践经验，以改善和提高教师的课堂教学水平。

3. 案例记载。教师根据自己所提出的目标和措施，撰写能体现自己“课堂教学改进”的案例（每学期不少于4篇），把自己在课堂教学中的收获记录下来（新教师也可以记录在听课中的收获），及时改进自己的教学活动。

4．学期小结。每学期写一篇课堂教学改进小结，每隔一段时间及时反思自己的课堂教学，对照所提出的目标，总结自己做到了哪些，哪些还没做到位，在后一段时间里如何去做，或调整自己的目标和措施。

5．反馈。记载手册被学期收交一次，平时做抽查。校长室和有关部门根据教师的记载情况和教学实际，教学比较分析，对教师的课题教学状况作一个调查判断，肯定优点，指出不足，对教师的教学工作提出建议。

培训过程

1．学年初，学校下发《奉浦学校奉浦学校教师课堂教学改进计划和实施记载》手册，教师完成其中的“课堂教学主要优势分析”“课堂教学主要不足分析”和“学年度课堂教学改进目标和改进措施”模块。

2．学校、教研组制订学习计划，推荐或下发相关学习资料，由教研组具体落实，进行学习交流，并组织相关的教学实践活动，并由教研组长（或教导处、教研员）填写“日常课堂教学评价记载”（每学期至少一次）。

3．教师撰写体现“课堂教学改进”的案例。

2014年4月，上海民办奉浦学校编辑、中华书局出版《为了智慧型校园的理想》一书

《为了智慧型校园的理想》目录摘录

4．期末完成“课堂教学改进学期小结”，并上交至学校相关部门。

5．由学校相关部门（校长室、教导处）进行检查、评价、反馈。

考核管理

1．收交《奉浦学校奉浦学校教师课堂教学改进计划和实施记载》手册，检查记载情况，完成“量”的考核。

2．将《奉浦学校奉浦学校教师课堂教学改进计划和实施记载》手册上记载的“目标和措施”与教师实际的工作态度和效果做比较，完成“质”的考核。

3．其他的教师个人专业发展的成果考核（如区级及以上的公开课教学、发表文章、研究课题等等）。

4．以上各项考核结果，都纳入教师年度考核和学年度考核中，作为“师德”“师能”考核的依据之一。

2．教师待遇

1998年学校创立后，作为奉贤境域内唯一的民办学校，学校董事会在教师的待遇问题上的总体思路是优于一般公办学校。1998—2005年，一般公办学校尚未实行绩效工资，而帕丁顿双语学校（奉浦学校）已实行班主任岗位、领导干部岗位津贴，还实行课时工资。公办教师除享受区域内统一待遇外，还享受本校的津贴与课时工资，但民办教师的工资待遇与公办教师有差距，致使部分优秀民办教师流失。2005年后，学校确定公办教师与民办教师同工同酬的方针，稳定民办教师的队伍。2005—2009年，学校提高福利水平与加大考核奖励的力度。参照公办的考核奖励水平后，增加考核奖励总额每年人均约5000元，增加福利每年人均约5000元。2010年2月，全区学校根据市人事局的绩效工资方案，实行基本工资、绩效工资和奖励工资组成的教师工资分配方案，民办学校内的公办教师也不得突破此方案。2010年，民办奉浦学校根据市教委关于建立教师年金的要求，为民办教师购买养老金，教师每月出资300元，学校董事会每月出资600元，民办教师退休养老有了保障，起到了稳定教师队伍。2010年2月至2015年8月，学校公民办教师待遇与一般公办学校相同。

外聘教师享受与民办教师、公办教师同等的福利待遇，工资以课时工资计算。他们的收入低于公、民办教师。

1998年，以全年计算，教师年均报酬1.26万元。2009年老师年均报酬突破

5万元。2014年教师年均报酬达到8.34万元。2016年教师年均报酬为10.65万元，比1998年增长7.45倍。

1998—2016年上海帕丁顿双语学校部分教师年均报酬情况表

表6-1-2　　　　单位：元

年份	年均报酬	说明	年份	年均报酬	说明
1998	12553.00	公办民办教师年均	2010	70322.00	公办民办教师年均
2000	14301.60	公办民办教师年均	2011	74316.00	公办民办教师年均
2001	18737.00	公办民办教师年均	2012	75595.05	公办民办教师年均
2003	22050.00	公办民办教师年均	2013	76961.96	公办民办教师年均
2204	23069.63	公办民办教师年均	2014	83440.66	公办民办教师年均
2006	35588.00	公办民办教师年均	2015	93729.30	民办教师年均
2007	46854.55	公办民办教师年均	2016	106543.30	民办教师年均
2009	55777.76	公办民办教师年均			

说明：1. 1998、2001年为全区（县）教师年均报酬数据；2. 教师报酬中含基本工资、津贴、年金

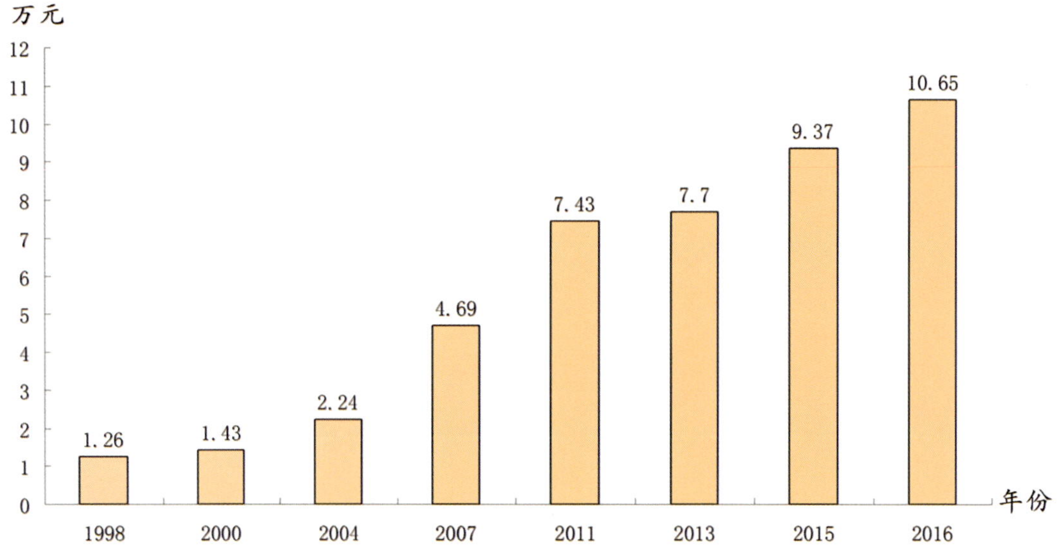

1998—2016年上海帕丁顿双语学校教师年均报酬增长示意图

说明：1. 教师报酬中含基本工资、津贴、资金；2. 2015年前为公办民办教师工资，2015年为民办教师工资

四、考核与职称评定

1. 教师考核

对教师评价是学校管理的重要项目，发挥重大的激励与引导作用，可保证学校各项工作目标的达成。学校开办至2016年，曾拟定过一系列的考核奖励办法。包括《师德考核办法》《学期综合考核》《班主任工作考核奖励办法》《年级团队合作考核奖励办法》《职初教师考核办法》等。在学校发展的不同历史时期，教师考核的制定与选择各有不同，也决定着学校的发展变化。

（1）《教师业务学期综合考评奖励条例》

该条例制订于2005年8月，自是月起执行。为提高广大教师的师德师能，调动他们的劳动积极性，焕发其创造才能，提高对学校发展的认同感，学校制定本条例。

该条例侧重于对教师工作态度与绩效的质与量的考核，融常规性工作与发展性要求于一体，运用评价促进教师根据自身已有条件不断攀升，并对他们的成长与对学校的贡献予以褒奖。

条例由指标体系、考核步骤与奖励方法两部分组成。

指标体系分6项一级指标，即师德表现、学识水平、德育工作、教学工作、教科研工作与工作负荷。每个一级指标下设2～7个二级指标。囊括教师的全部工作与学校的主要目标任务。每项二级指标赋予相应分值。

考核步骤为自评、互评、学校考评小组考评、统计反馈4步。

自评——教师期末交本学期工作述职报告，对照考核指标作自我评价。

互评——教师对同组室成员的述职进行认定或修正，对照考核指标对其他教师作出定性定量评价。

学校考评小组考评——考评小组成员由2处1室以上领导组成，校长为组长、组室负责人与代表各1位参与本组校级考评，考评人员在听取各项工作负责同志汇报后作无记名评分。

统计与反馈——考评成绩统计由学校人事干部负责。互评与学校考评各占30%与70%。

奖励方法　对照教师学期综合考核指标，按相关程序累计积分评定每位教师实得分值。每学期确定每分值奖金额，折合成奖金分发给教师。教师学期综合考评的结果，作为学年度考核及年终奖发放、晋升职务、评选先进的重要依据。

（2）《奉浦学校团队合作竞争发展目标》

2007年，为促进学校形成团队合作氛围，加速学校整体目标的实现，设立该项考核，对学校发展发挥激励作用。

该考核项目有德育发展目标与学业水平发展目标两部分组成，以年级组为考核单位。

德育发展目标有5条，包括班级组的战斗团队的形成；学生自主管理制度的健全；每月德育常规工作的成绩；校各项活动的参与度与获奖情况；年内安全情况。

学业发展水平分基本目标与理想目标两部分，都是根据年级原有水平与对照校现有水平为起点考察进度与速度。基本目标为应达目标，理想目标为高速度目标，按年份对年级明确下达各学科的要求。

考核奖励办法 德育工作由政教处负责考核；学业水平发展情况由教导处负责考核；校长室审核呈报材料根据目标达成度给予奖励。年级总奖励额度按学生数每生发放若干，达成德育目标后，按学业发展水平两级目标的不同情况发放不同的奖金；各人在年级达成目标中的不同作用，发放不同的奖金。

（3）《班主任工作考核奖励办法》

学校对班主任考核分为每月1次的考核与学期考核两项。月班主任百分考核由政教主任负责。月百分考核指标包括班级纪律、宿舍管理、卫生检查、广播操、眼保健操、班级活动等各项常规指标。各相关检查部门，按日按实打分记录，政教处根据记录，汇总考核表，给每位班主任评出考核等级。每月班主任的津贴发放金额由等级决定。一般从300元/月～600元/月不等。

学期班主任考核由考核办法、考核内容、奖励办法3部分组成。

考核办法 建立由分管领导、政教主任、团委书记、年级组长组成的考核小组；学校制订工作考核登记表，由班主任对照自评；班主任自评报告在高中、初中、小学各部班主任考评会上交流；考评组根据平时检查与月考情况，在全面听取各方面意见后给予考核评分；考核小组的考核结果报校长室审批，根据成绩给予奖励。

考核内容 按时上交各种表格及计划总结，每学期至少完成1篇德育论文或案例。准时参加班主任例会，认真完成学校布置的各项工作。参加学校常规教育“百分竞赛”活动情况。与任课教师沟通情况，班级风气，召开学习经验交流会情况，班级学业水平。参与学校各项活动，广播操、眼保健操情况。班级制度督促检查，有无严重违纪现象。主题班会、主题教育，发动组织实施情况。树立班级先进典型情况。爱护公物，班级设备设施完好情况。参与社会活动情况。

奖励办法　根据班主任考核内容及工作实绩，评定分A、B、C3等考核奖。每学期期末发放（注：2010年后列入绩效工资奖励部分）

（4）《学校师德考核办法》

师德考核根据教育局提出的“五不准”要求，要求每位教师每学期写出1份师德表现的小结。结合学期教师综合考核。在小组交流时，每位教师给组内其他同志打上师德表现分。根据教育局的标准，师德表现分优秀、良好、合格、不合格4等，优秀比率在25%，年度行政奖励者必须在优良之列，不合格者停职或降级。师德考评由学校党支部负责。2011年学校参加教育局师德考核档案制试点，为每1位教师建立个人师德档案，档案手册每人1本，记录3年内容。

2．职称评定

其主要有职初教师转正评定、一级教师职称评定和高级教师职称评定。

（1）职初教师转正评定

大学本科毕业，获得教师资格证书，在教师工作岗位上实习满1年者可由职初教师（实习期教师）转正为二级教师。

职初教师转正考核工作由学校教导处负责。教导处负责人根据区（县）教育局有关文件精神，安排职初教师接受培训进修。职初教师要填写培训进修班记录手册，期满1年后，带教教师将其1年内表现与实际能力作出鉴定，并递交学校职称评审小组评审。学校职称评审小组组织听课，视其情况最后确定是否给予转正。如期转正者报教育局备案，并及时调正其工资等待遇。

1998—2016年，学校转正职初教师48人次。

（2）一级教师职称评定

中学一级教师或小学高级教师为中级教师职称。教育局根据学校的性质确定各校中高级职称的比例。如比例尚未达到则可下达给予学校上报申请中高级职称的指标。学校根据区（县）教育局下达的指标数，对提出职称评定要求的教师进行初步评审。

学校组成由校长为组长的学校职称评审小组，成员为学校各学科的优秀高职称的教师，数额为5、7、9单数。

中教一级申报的基本条件为在二级教师工作满5年，师德评定在合格以上且通过计算机与英语合格考试。

申报一级职称教师须根据一级教师的要求，如实填写本人在各方面的表现与实绩，按时递交学校职称评审小组。学校评审小组在充分阅读材料后，组织听课活动，结合其平时表现，根据教育局职改办的表格要求，对各位申报者作出评定意见，确定其师德表现、课堂教学能力、科研能力的分值，并按分值由高到低排出各位申报者在校内的名次，上报教育局职改办。

职改办将各位材料分发给区（县）学科组评审小组评审，最后上报区职称评审委员会评审。通过者张榜公布，次月调整工资等待遇。

1998—2016年，学校通过一级教师评审的有25人。

（3）高级教师职称评定

高级教师申报的基本条件为一级教师岗位上工作满5年，师德评定在合格以上，且通过计算机与高级教师合格考试。申报高级教师还需要呈交本人的教育论文、课题报告至上海市职改论文鉴定机构鉴定。论文鉴定必须在C级以上才可有资格参与评审。

申报高级职称教师，须根据高级教师要求如实填写本人在各方面的表现与实绩。按时递交给学校职称评审小组。学校评审小组成员认真阅读材料后对其工作实绩与表现作出评价打分。按分值由高到低，排出申报者在校内参评者中的名次。

区职改办安排区学科评审小组成员到校听课，并对申报者课堂教学能力评价记分。

区学科评审小组在审阅受评者材料与学校考核意见后，结合其平时教育教学实况作出评价并打分。区职称评审委员会作出审定意见，并报市备案。高级教师职称由市职称评审委员会发证认定。1998—2016年，学校通过高级教师职称评审有9人。

附：职初（见习期）教师考核办法

见习期教师的考核时间一般为1年。2012年之前，考核由见习期教师聘用学校与区级考核两级完成。2012年之后除聘用学校与区级考核外，外加基地学校考核。

考核内容

以《上海市中小学见习教师规范化培训手册》为考核依据，全面、科学、准确地检查评价见习教师培训任务完成情况，进行相应量化考评，并出具详细培训鉴定。

考核项目包括职业感悟与师德修养；课堂教学实践；班级工作与育德体验；科研与专业发展；综合素养；工作学习表现；综合评价7项。

考核办法

1.基地学校考核。基地学校成立考核小组，组织见习期教师自评，指导教师与基地学校评价，将结果交区教育培训管理中心。

2.见习教师聘用学校考核。聘用校组织见习教师自评，学科与班主任工作指导教师与学校评价，将结果交区教育培训管理中心。

3.区级考核。选聘学科专家组成评委，对见习教师全面考评。包括区级培训学习情况；备课能力（120分内完成）；课堂教学能力（借班上课）；区级综合评价百分记录。

考核总分值计算。见习教师考核总分，为基地学校考核、聘用学校考核、区级考核三者的具体成绩的综合，其占比例为20%、10%、70%。85分以上为优秀，80分以上为良，60分以上合格，60分以下不合格。优秀占比例15%。

五、师德建设

1. 师德教育

1998年9月，上海民办协和实验学校开办后，把师德教育作为师资思想建设的重要内容，制订具体的学习培训计划。坚持每周组织教师进行2小时师德师风教育。提出师德修养的6个要求：爱国守法、爱岗敬业、关爱学生、教书育人、为人师表、终生学习。2000年3月，学校组织教师参加“祖国宝岛台湾在我心中”的千人签名活动。2002年3月，邀请全国模范班主任黄静华(女)为全校教师作题为“无悔的选择”专题报告。2005—2006年，学校先后聘请上海市名教师、名校长6人为顾问。2006年6月，由上海市特级教师、上海市教师学会会长于漪(女)，用她几十年执教的经验，现身说法向全校教师作“教师的责任”的专题报告。2007年8月，请县教育局原局长蒋辉藁作“中国传统和教师的人文修养”专题课。根据教育局提出的师德修养中的“五不准”“五提倡”“五表率”作为教师师德的标准。在教师中开展自查自评活动。学校还建立学生、家长、社会评价网络，开展“我心中的好教师”征文活动，并开展由9名教师参加的“我是一名光荣的人民教师”演讲，以及开展《谈师德形象》征文活动。2012年11月，学校举办“道德讲堂”专题活动，由3名教师从4个方面讲述师德修养的体会。各年级开展“做学生满意的教师”演讲会，使师德标准人人知晓，付诸行动。学校在教育局提出的“五不准”的师德要求的基础上还提出“五个发扬”（发扬敬业奉献、无偿补缺补差；发扬宽容仁爱精神，善待学生，友爱同事；发扬自尊自爱精神，遵纪守法，清正廉洁；发扬文明高尚精神，加强学习，文明娱乐；发扬公民自律精神，遵守交规，文明驾车）。

在进行正面的师德教育中，学校还建立师德修养责任追究制和“师德一票否决制”。2009年，学校修订《奉浦学校师德规范九条》，把师德考核和学年考核、职称评聘挂钩。学校还开展“师爱——师德之核，师风——师德之魂”的教师演讲、师德论文评比、师德案例分析、出版师德论文集、宣传师德“五表率”先进人物的事迹。师德修养培训教育进一步具体化、规范化、常态化。学校在师德建设方面做到有计划有目标有措施，制定切实可行的奉浦学校师德计划。目标是全面提高学校教师思想政治素质和职业道德水平，打造一支学生信任、家长放心、社会满意的师资队伍。制订了奉浦学校师德建设“五不准”细则，细化每个“不准”的要求，并经教代会通过，使之成为每个教师在行为规范考核中的刚性指标。2012年，学校重新制订了《奉浦学校师德规范九条》，完善了考核机制，由党支部制订考核标准，由教师本人写出小结，由学生家长、主管部门进行测评，由各组处室负责人进行汇总，校师德领导小组给予评价，本人签字。考核制度健全，操作程序到位，师德考核有成效。

2012年12月14日，民办奉浦学校承办“道德讲堂”，倡导“敬奉贤人，见贤思齐”的师德教育

针对校内学生年级跨度大，生源地域广，年龄差异和习俗不同，文化素质不一，住宿生多的特点，全校教师采用中医“四法”（望、闻、问、切），从学生晨检、

衣着、身体状况、情绪变化、个人卫生等方面进行24小时常态化全程关爱。学校制作“社会主义核心价值观”“厚德载物有几个法”的PPT在学校电子屏幕上滚动播放，在教师中进一步提倡“学贤人、做贤师”活动。学校提出：德字为先，课题引领，提升师德教育的实效性。校区级重点课题《民族魂·现代人》研究核心是道德教育与师德教育紧密结合。道德素质的教育从“立身、处世、为人、处事”4个方面着手，在师德建设中利用课题本身的研究资源，教育师生首先要“立身”：自强不息、知耻更过、竞争勇进、挑战传统。教育师生“为人”：宽厚仁爱、律己宽人、尊师孝亲、合作乐群。“处世”：报效祖国、放眼全球。“处事”：节俭崇简、诚信守纪、笃学不倦、乐学新知、惜时务实。课题的4个一级指标细化成17个子目标，全校各学段师生共同摘抄名人名言，编写具有较深刻教育意义的小故事，收集优秀的教育案例，整个课题研究的过程也正是师德教育的过程，在最终结题时，既是一本实用的校本德育课程，也是师德建设的一个成果。至2016年，学校两次被评为奉贤区师德先进集体，63人次被奉浦社区以上领导部门授予“优秀班主任”“优秀教师”称号。每年都有师德计划与师德总结。

民办奉浦学校小学数学教研组被奉贤区教育局党委评为师德师风建设“五表率”专业发展表率班组

附：民办奉浦学校教师“五不准”“五提倡”“五表率”内容

五不准：不准从事有偿家教；不准向学生、家长索要钱物、推销商品、擅自向学生收费；不准有体罚、变相体罚及其他侮辱学生的行为；不准参与赌博；不准酒后驾车。

五提倡：提倡学习修身；提倡专业发展；提倡关爱学生；提供合作奉献；提倡热心公益。

五表率：(1) 学习修身作表率。长期工作在教育教学第一线，牢固树立终身学习的理念，政治理论素养和专业发展素质强；能够学以致用，岗位成长，成为引领校园学习之风的典型示范；注重立德立身立行，乐观开朗、积极向上。(2) 专业发展作表率。长期工作在教育教学第一线，在专业思想、专业知识、专业能力等方面表现突出，在教育教学过程中注重科学性、艺术性、针对性和实效性，教育教学风格富有特色，成绩显著；在实施素质教育中起到示范、带动作用。近两年来所承担的学科教学成绩不低于区域平均水平；在区级以上（含区级）教学评比中获等级第奖；在区级以上（念区级）专业刊物发表2篇以上学术论文，或作为主要研究者承担过区级以上（含区级）课题研究。(3) 关爱学生作表率。尊重学生人格，公正对待、关心爱护学生，师生关系平等和谐，把学生身心健康、快乐成长放在第一位，让学生轻松愉快学习，促进学生全面发展；有较强的“学科德育”意识，善于培养学生正确的世界观、人生观、价值观和良好的品德，善于做好学生素质养成教育、安全法制教育、心理健康教育。师德事迹突出、感人，富有时代感。(4) 合作奉献作表率。具有强烈的事业心和责任感，模范履行岗位职责；乐于助人，发扬奉献精神，有较强的团队协作精神；维护学校荣誉，善于整合教育力理，积极推动和谐校园建设。(5) 热心公益作表率。认真履行社会道德义务，积极投身以“做贤人、建贤城、扬贤风”为主题的全国文明城区创建等活动，积极参加志愿者服务，家庭美德、社会公德在单位和所居住社区具有示范表率作用。

2. 师德规范

年级组、教研组的组室文化是成员的行为规范体系，是生存方式与状态。形成团队合作竞争的组室文化，对完成学校整体任务，起着至关重要的作用，也是师德、师风建设的重要落脚点。奉浦学校平行班级少，年级跨度大，强调上下级的团结，各学段教师间的协作，班主任与任课教师的通力协作，依靠集体的力量增加教育的合力显得尤为重要。为此学校专门制定“奉浦学校团队合作竞争目标达成奖的实施意见”，从组织、制度、考核、经费上予以保证，树立校荣我荣、组活我活的合作理念。出现许多备课资源共享、凝聚全组教师的智慧、公开演示课、各学段间老师的相互讨教、不同科目老师间的默契配合等。这些事例不仅使师资力量得到加强，也促进人际和谐关系的建立。

用教师的专业发展，促进教师的道德建设。为建设高素质的师资队伍，学校提出“师爱是核、师风是魂、师能是本”的核心理念。没有高素质的师资队伍，学校无法根本改变落后面貌，而师德的提高与师能的发展是相辅相成的，学校整体目标的实现与教师个体的发展是融为一体的。

附：上海民办奉浦学校师德规范9条

为贯彻落实区教育局2008年第2号文件，依据《中华人民共和国教师法》和上海市拟订的《上海市教师师德规范》，特制定《上海民办奉浦学校教师道德规范》，经教代会讨论审定。

(1) 教师应参加政治学习和业务进修，不断提高自身的思想道德和科学文化素质，提高教书育人的本领。政治学习和业务进修原则上不能请假。

(2) 教师应积极参与学校教育教学的各项改革，更新教育观念，努力掌握现代化的教育方法与教学手段，提升教育教学的质量。

(3) 教师应认真备课，精心设计教案，指导学生全面交流，准确地掌握所学的知识，教龄在5年之内的教师必需备详案。

(4) 教师应以发展的眼光看待学生，在课堂提问、作业评定、试卷批阅、评语撰写、家庭访问等教育工作中，对学生作出客观全面公正的评价，尊重学生、关爱特殊学生，对学习有困难的学生进行无偿课外辅导，严禁有偿家教。

(5) 教师应严格遵守学校的教学管理制度，严禁上课迟到、早退和拖堂，不得随意调课，杜绝教学事故。教师在教育工作中应使用规范的职业用语，不得侮辱学生人格、变相体罚学生。

(6) 教师在学生家长交流中不得收受礼品和现金等，在家校联系工作中不得将应承担的教育责任推给家长，在接待家长时热情有礼、文明相待。

(7) 教师严禁赌博，严禁酒后驾车，违者按照学校“师德实施细则”处理。

(8) 教师应注意自己的仪表举止，在校内要求衣着整洁、仪表端庄、打扮得体。

(9) 教辅后勤应尽心尽职于自己的岗位，杜绝安全事故，严格遵守有关法纪法规，确保学校正常开展各项教育教学活动。

3. 师德考核

学校制定严格的师德考核制度，用制度约束全校教职工的行为规范，用制度体现学校管理的规范。

由政教处主任、教导处主任、总务处主任、年级组长、教研组长、门卫保安、监控中心、值日老师、生活老师负责考核。月底由各学部负责人统计，报党支部审核，校长审批，财务处发放师德考核津贴。学年末政教处统计每人师德津贴总额，数额低于全校平均数的教师不得评优、评先，不得参加职称评定。

考核内容以“五提倡”“五表率”和奉浦学校师德规范为标准，有下列情况者予以扣分：工作期间未请假私自离开教学区，迟到、早退超过15分钟以旷职论处。有事办理请假手续。未请假不参加升旗仪式、政治学习、业务学习（含集体备课）。不服从领导或不接受分配的任务，无理与领导顶撞造成不良影响。随便打电话向家长告状或叫家长到校，与家长发生冲突。没收学生的物品、撕学生的课本、作业本。办公期间用电脑打游戏、吃零食或伏在办公桌上睡觉。办公桌上摆放无序或不干净，不按时或不认真做好办公室卫生值日工作。不按时放学，不负责整队送学生进餐厅。校园内吸烟，饮酒后进课堂。校园内乱扔废纸、杂物。校园内骑自行车、摩托车、汽车未进停车处。私自叫学生停课或罚站在教室外，停考、私自调课。不能严守课堂规则，不讲普通话或板书潦草，不按时上下课或带茶杯、手机进课堂，坐着上课、随便离开课堂、停课处理学生纠纷。无教案上课或不按教案上课。作业批改不及时、不认真。不按时做好办公室的清洁工作。监考迟到、早退、中途出场、看书报杂志、打手机阅卷等。考试成绩退步趋势达5分（含5分）的任课老师不得享受师德考核津贴。因工作失职致使学生出走（含旁听生），人为造成学生退学，退款由教师自己承担。歧视、讽刺、挖苦学生，体罚学生（或变相体罚），情节严重，造成不良影响，年度考核不合格，新教师不得转正。学生、学生家长对任课老师的测评，结果满意率低于80%。有赌博、嫖娼或违反婚姻法等违法行为。接受家长钱物（或请吃）或利用家长办私事；向家长索取钱物，搞有偿家教。叫异性学生进宿舍谈话。出卷、阅卷、统计分数作弊者。乱订复习资料，乱收费。对其他违反教师行为规范者，视情节大小处理。

4. 表彰奖励

建立师德考核奖励基金，每年每人在绩效奖励中提取1000元作为师德奖励基金，奖励严守师德规范的教师。

2007年初，学校经教代会审议并通过“关于实施奉浦学校团队合作竞争目标达成奖的意见”，组织实施以后，极大地增强了教师的目标意识与主体意识。该文件规定受奖对象为考试科目的教师、班主任与年级组长，保证此类岗位人员的责与利的统一。为激励全体教师在各自岗位上都能为实施学校的整体目标而不懈努力，增设如下奖项。

（1）高尚师德奖

凡在教师岗位上识大体、顾大局、勇挑重担、无私奉献、不计个人利益、模范履行“五不准”“五发扬”，表现突出者，可获此奖。

（2）教育教学论文奖

教师在各级各类期刊杂志上发表教育教学论文，或市、区各项立项的课题论文，可获此奖。

上海帕丁顿双语学校2015年教学节活动成果展示——教学论文案例集

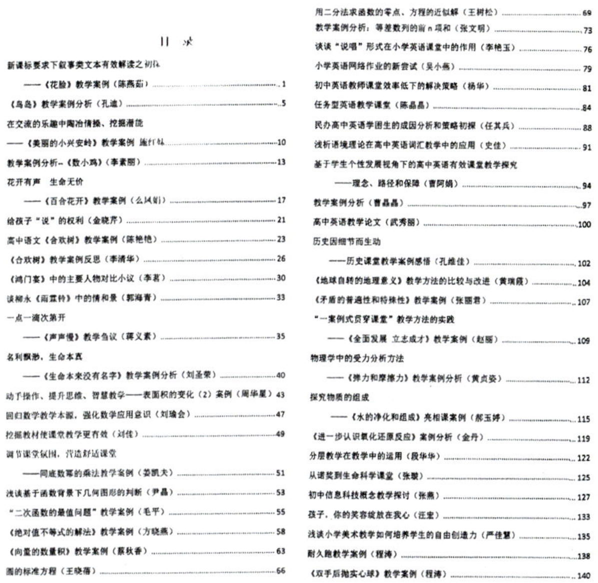

目 录

2015年上海帕丁顿双语学校教学节活动成果——教学论文案例集目录

（3）教育教学评比奖

教师在区级以上教育教学评比中获得荣誉称号或在学科评比获等第奖者，可获此奖。

（4）学生竞赛指导奖

凡在学校基础学科、艺体学科、科技教育及其他竞赛活动中指导学生，并参与国家、市、区竞赛获等第奖或荣誉称号的，可获此奖。

（5）教研组建设奖

凡获得区级优秀教研组及以上荣誉称号的教研组全体成员，可获此奖。

（6）带教奖

为学校教师队伍的成长，认真负责地履行带教任务，毫无保留，悉心指导带教对象，促进带教对象在教育教学能力迅速提高，取得显著成绩的带教者，可获此奖。

（7）特别贡献奖

在学校管理、教育、教学、科研、宣传、兴趣活动辅导、后勤服务、医保、心理辅导、安全保卫等方面做出特殊贡献者，经行政会议提名，校长审核，可获此奖。

上述奖项，每学期期末一次性执行。校长室在每学期期末通知相关人员上交有关证明、证书与原件，验证后按实际情况计发奖金。如发现弄虚作假现象，除不计发奖金外，还将进行严肃处理。经校教代会审议通过后，于2009年2月起开始执行。

附：奉浦学校师德承诺书

教师是科学文化知识的传承者，教师的思想政治素质和职业道德水平直接关系到学校教育工作的成效，关系学校全体学生的健康成长。师者为师亦为范，学高为师，德高为范。走上三尺讲台，教书育人；走下三尺讲台，为人师表。师德是一种文明精神的体现，是一种文化品位的凸现，我们必须始终严格履行教师职业道德规范，热爱教师职业，严谨治学的工作态度；要有严以律己，为人师表的道德形象。为此我们应该自觉加强职业道德建设，树立良好的师德风尚，规范教育行为、改善行业风气，为创建奉浦学校教师的新形象、新风貌做出应有的贡献。谨向学校领导、学生家长、全体学生及社会做出庄严的承诺：热爱教育事业，认真履行教师职责，依法执教，以德育人，以德修身；规范从教行为、严以律己、有令必行、有禁必止，不做有偿家教，义务为学生补缺补差，不向学生家长推销商品、索取财物或谋取私利，洁身自好，不做有损教师形象的事；刻苦钻研业务，改进教学方法，提高教育水平，服从大局，团结同事，与学校同心同德，为改变学校面貌，达

2014年，民办奉浦学校通过考核，奖励一批师德先进教师

到办学的预期目标而努力工作；热爱学生、尊重学生人格、关心学生成长，杜绝体罚、变相体罚与侮辱学生人格的行为；遵守社会公德，积极参与社会公益活动，自觉抑制不良风气，不赌博、不酒后驾车。以上承诺，我将用自己的赤诚之心去履行、去实践，自觉接受上级领导和社会各方的监督，做崇高师德的实践者，素质教育的力行者，学生成长的引领者，为谱写奉浦学校的美好明天竭尽我之所能。

第二节　员　工

一、员工来源

学校员工从岗位上可分为职员与工人，职员担任图书管理、后勤管理、实验室管理、财务管理等工作，工人为宿舍、后勤、食堂等操作人员。学校员工从编制上可分为三种，一种为在编公办人员，是由教育局调配的。第二种是在编的民办人员，是由学校招聘的人员。第三种为学校招聘的临时工。1998年9月教育局从全区（县）各学校抽调的65名教职员中含8名公办职员编制，后因学校发展需要又逐年招聘民办职工与临时工。2016年，上海帕丁顿双语学校有民办职员14人，临时工2人。2015年9月公办教职工全数析出。此后，学校职工悉数为民办职工与临时工。

二、员工待遇

公办职工的待遇，一般都参照教育局有关公办教职工的待遇进行分配。2010年1月实行绩效工资之前，公办职工除按月发放公办的职务工资外，也参加学校考核，享受教师的70%的奖金与100%的福利待遇。有编制的民办职工待遇参照同等级的公办职工执行，享受教师70%的奖金与100%的福利待遇。临时工的工资标准以上海市最低工资为起点，按照技术级别与临时工工龄的长短及劳动表现，逐次提升工资。享受学校50%的福利待遇与学期末的考核奖。2010年1月起，实行绩效工资。公办职工的分配方案按教育局的规定执行，奖励金额按教师平均的70%执行，岗位工资与工作量工资按有规定执行。民办职工参照公办职工执行后按工资总额的90%执行。临时工仍依照原方案。

三、员工考核奖励

公办职工与民办职工，由学校考核小组统一考核，方法与教师相同。考核内容简化为德、识、能、绩、勤5个方面，等第分4档，分值为10、8、6、4分。临时工考核分别由总务主任、政教主任负责。对自己部门内的临时工进行打分，然后计算奖励额度，汇总后上报校长室审核发放奖金。

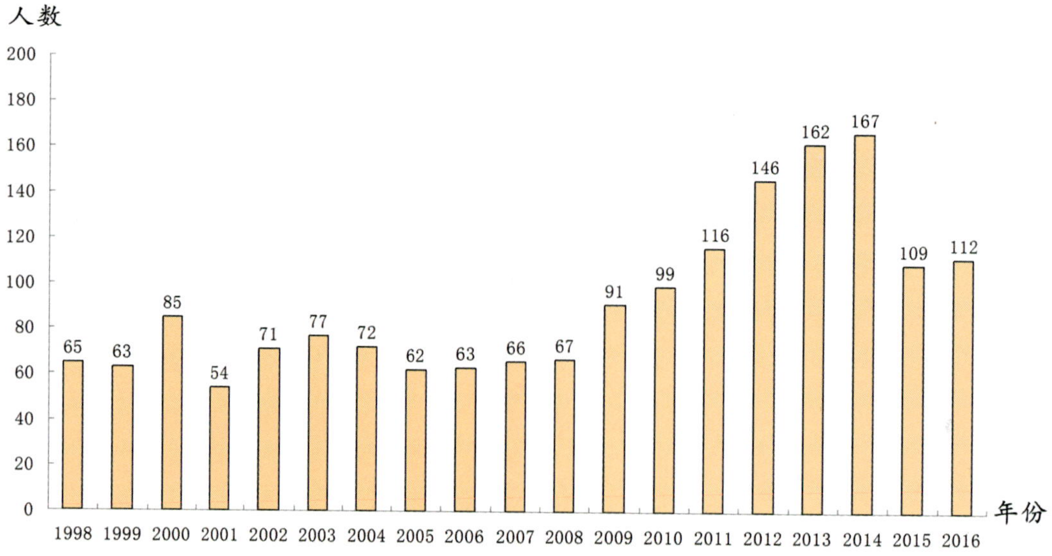

1998—2016年上海帕丁顿双语学校教职工人数示意图

说明：1998—2015年数据摘自《奉贤统计年鉴》。2016年数据由学校提供

第七章　课程　教学

1998年9月，学校创办时实施的是国家规定的课程与部分学校自定的活动课程。2005年后，在市教科院有关教研员指导下形成《提供适合学生发展的学习经历——上海民办奉浦学校课程方案》。此方案后获市学校课程方案二等奖。同时提出"适人、适时、适度"的适合教育的学校办学理念。在此办学理念的指导下，学校努力形成具有校本特色的若干课程，如"扎根民族魂，学做现代人"的校本德育课程、特色外语课程、特色艺体科技课程、数学思维训练课程、生活作文与诗文颂吟语文特色课程。在课程实施中建立伙伴式团队文化，实现学校课程的统整。通过课程评价，促进学生自主成长，促进教师专业发展，促进学校整体教学水平与教学质量的提升。2006年始，学校以"科研兴校"为立校之本。至2012年，小学毕业考成绩跃居全区第3名，中考成绩由2004年的23名上升至第7名，高中140名考生本科录取83人、专科录取43人，总录取率达90%。2009年，完成"民族魂·现代人合作竞争团队建设实践研究"德育课题与"聪明学习的案例开发的实践研究"的教育策略研究两大课题。2010年1月，被评为区教学科研示范学校。至2014年完成市规划课题1项、市条线课程1项、区条线课题1项、区重点课题2项、区一般课题21项。2015年4月，被评为区教科研工作示范校。

在教学管理方面，学校除加强备课、上课、批改作业、辅导、考核5常规管理外，还根据学校发展需要，建立常模对照加强对质量的监控。在教学改革方面，以"聪明学习"为行动纲领，以学生学习方式转变与教师教学行为改变为指向，实施综合性实践研究，取得根本性的突破，成为教学质量先进校。2012年4月，小学、初中"走班制""高中英语特长班""智优初中学生实验班"都曾取得过一定实效。

第一节　课程建设与教学

一、课程方案

上海二期课程始于1997年，近乎建校之初。第二期课程改革是在一期课改

(1986—1997年）的基础上开展的。这一课程改革确立课程是为学生提供学习经历并获得学习经验的观念。在课程结构上，一期课改提出了“三大板块”，即必修课、选修课与活动课。二期课改在此基础上提出基础型课程、拓展型课程和研究型课程的课程板块结构。为此在课程来源上又划分为国家课程、地方课程与校本课程。

在民办协和实验学校期间，学校基本上实施的是国家规定课程与部分活动课程。2005年起，学校开展全校性的课程改革大讨论，并逐步形成富有特色的校本课程。校本课程经过两年余的自上而下、自下而上的探究，在市教科院教学研究所相关同志的指导下形成《提供适合学生发展的学习经历——上海民办奉浦学校课程方案》。该方案获上海市学校课程方案评选二等奖。

二、办学理念

上海帕丁顿双语学校是一所跨度大、公民办兼收的学校，造成生源的基础性学力水平差异很大。针对这样一种现况，学校提出的办学理念是：倡导适合教育，其核心价值就是提供适合不同学生的可供其可持续发展的学习经历。一切成功的教育都是顺应时势，顺应人的自身发展规律的教育，教育的功能既为社会生产合格的人才，又要为人的“全面发展”与“整体性幸福”承担责任。所以学校要提供一个适合于每一个人成长的“适人、适时、适度”的适合教育，服务于社会与人的成长。

三、课程理念

1. 面向教育现象，草根式民主共建理念

草根式民主共建理念主张国家赋予学校课程决策的自主性，给学校以弹性空间，结合学生特点和学校具体环境。一方面面对鲜活的教育现场与过程，应以生为本，面对个别差异，全力解决学校环境出现的教育问题，迅速响应社会及知识的变迁，赋予学生和家长参与课程决策的机会，设置适切而有意义的课程，促进学生个体现实的健康发展，未来的就业生存能力，以及终身发展的需要；另一方面面向全体教师，赋予他们课程开发的权利和责任。从某种意义上说，课程改革的成败，关键在于教师。教师是课程的研究者和最后的裁决者。校本课程作为三级课程的一个重要组成部分，是促进教师专业化发展的平台。要给予教师赋权增

能，提高教学积极性，同时通过参与课程开发，也促使教师对课程本质特征、意图有透彻的理解，确保教学质量的提高。

2．情境化知识建构理念

知识是理性与非理性的统一，学校的知识不能局限于学科知识，还要考虑知识的境遇化与个性化。学校课程更应立足于境遇文化的母体，发扬社区文化优势，共建特色的学校文化，以利于为学生的学习设置知识建构的环境，让他们调动自身的潜能、体验、感悟，与外界相互作用重新构建，形成情境化知识建构。

3．学校机构重组理念

校本课程的主要场所是学校。学校不仅是课程管理实施机构，还是课程开发的再生产场所。教导处、教研组、备课组等机构不仅是课程落实的组织，更是课程开发、管理、生产的重要机构。立足校本，转换机能，重组机构是落实新课改的重要一环。

四、培养目标与课程目标

1．培养目标

让全体学生形成既有民族精神又有现代人要素的人格品质；学业成就值必须高于一般公办学校；个性得到充分的自由的发展。

2．课程目标

学校课程改革的总体目标就是要在相对短的时期内形成与提升学校办学效益与办学质量相适应的课程体系，从而保证学校声誉在短时期内得到提升。

3．具体目标

(1) 完成“根扎民族魂、学做现代人”贯穿十二年的校本德育课程体系。(2) 完成小学、初中、高中各学段的基础课程、拓展课程与特色课程的统整。(3) 促进课改成功的教师教学观念与行动的转变，学生学习态度与方式的转变。

五、课程结构与课程设置

1998年9月，学校创办开学后，经过历年来教育教学的改革创新，在实践中逐步形成民办学校“基础扎实，特色艳明”的课程结构。小学、初中、高中学部普遍设置丰富多样各具特色探究型、拓展型、基础型课程。至2016年，不受学校体制改变而改变。

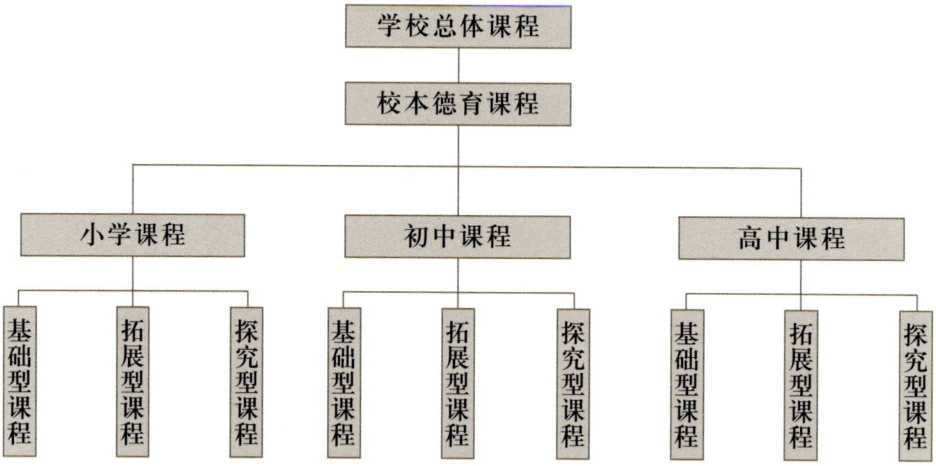

上海帕丁顿双语学校“基础扎实、特色鲜明”课程结构图

2012年5月7日，民办奉浦学校与加拿大多伦多五湖学院共同参与加拿大国际高中文凭课程项目签字仪式（右起顾行建、王丹花、五湖学院负责人）

1．高中课程设置

设置基础型课程13科，拓展型课程9科，研究型课程每周2～3课时，高一、高二每周39课时，高三每周40课时。

学校高中课程计划表

表 7-1-1

课程科目			周课时			附注
			高一	高二	高三	
基础型课程	语文		4	4	6	
	数学		4	4	6	
	英语		4	4	6	
	物理		3	3	1	
	化学		2	2	1	
	生物		1	2	1	
	政治		2	2	3	
	历史		3		6*	6* 为加一史地选修
	地理			3	6*	
	信息		2			
	劳技		1～2	1～2		
	体育		3	3	2	
	艺术		1	1		
	小计		30	29	32	
拓展型课程	学科类	阅读	1	1	1	
		古诗文	1	1	1	
		张思中英语	1	1	1	
		其他	1	2	1	
		美术	2*	2*	1*	带 * 号属于选修其一
	活动类	技能	1*	1*	1*	
		其他	1*	1*		
	专题教育		1	1	1	
	社会实践		每学年2周			
研究型课程			2	2	3	
小计			9	10	8	
总计			39	39	40	

2．初中课程设置

设置基础型课程17科，拓展型课程8科，基础型课程每周2课时。其中，初中预备班至初二每周37课时，初三每周38课时。

学校初中课程计划表

表7-1-2

课程科目			周课时				附注
			初预	初一	初二	初三	
基础型课程	语文		4	4	4	5	
	数学		5	5	5	6	
	英语		4	4	4	5	
	思品		1	1	2	2	
	科学		2	3	/	/	
	物理		/	/	2	3	
	化学		/	/	/	3	
	生物		/	/	3	/	
	社会		/	/	/	1	
	历史		/	2	2	/	
	地理		2	2	/	/	
	艺术		/	/	2	2	
	音乐		1	1	/	/	
	美术		1	1	/	/	
	体育		3	3	3	2	
	劳技		2	1	1	/	
	信息		2	/	/	/	
	小计		27	27	28	30	
拓展型课程	学科类	张思中英语	2	2	2	1	
		阅读	1	1	1	1	
		古诗文	1	1	1	1	
		科技	1	1	2	2	
	活动类	技能	2*	2*			带＊号属于选修其一
		其他	2*	2*			
	专题教育		1	1	1	1	
	社会实践		每学年安排2周				
研究型课程			2	2	2	2	
小计			10	10	9	8	
合计			37	37	37	38	

3．小学课程设置

设置基础型课程10科，拓展型课9科，研究型课程每周1课时。其中小一、小二每周35课时，小三至小五每周36课时。

学校小学课程计划表

表7-1-3

课程科目			周课时				
			小一	小二	小三	小四	小五
基础型课程		语文	8	8	5	5	5
		数学	3	3	4	5	5
		英语	3	3	4	5	5
		自然	2	2	2	2	2
		音乐	2	2	2	2	2
		美术	2	2	2	1	1
		体育	3	3	3	3	3
		品德	2	2	2	3	3
		劳技				1	1
		信息			2		
		小计	25	25	26	27	27
拓展型课程	学科类	阅读	1	1	1	1	1
		古诗文	1	1	1	1	1
		书法	/	1	1	1	2
		张思中英语	3	2	2	1	1
	活动类	武术	1	1	1	1	/
		乐器	2	/	/	/	/
		其他	/	2	2	2	2
专题教育			1	1	1	1	1
社会实践			每学年安排2周				
研究型课程			1	1	1	1	1
小计			10	10	10	9	9
总计			35	35	36	36	36

六、校本特色课程

1．“根扎民族魂，学做现代人”德育校本课程

学业成就的高低首先在于学生的自我定位与自身的价值取向，从小铸入中华民族的优良文化传统，又具有直面世界的目光与眼界，这是面对竞争社会所必备的人格要素。有个这样的道德根基，社会的责任感、历史的使命感才会产生巨大

的学习动力。因而构建校本德育课程是形成校本课程的主要特征之一。学校在设定学校德育总目标后，设定各年级段的德育目标及操作方案。

2．特色外语校本课程

现行的《牛津》英语课程是国家规定的基础教学课程，奉浦学校学生的基础性差异大，为提高外语教学质量，适合各种学生的不同层次发展，学校聘请享受国务院专家特殊津贴奖的张思中老师作学校顾问，在12个不同学段中全面推行张思中教法，并补充使用张思中教材。期望从小学起始年级起到毕业时外语达初中二年级水平，初中从起始年级起至毕业时外语达高中二年级水平，高中生由于原有基础薄弱，也补充张思中教材，使其迅速跟上上海市高中生的整体平均水平。

各年级外语课程框架：（1）小学。小学阶段外语教学的基本目标是自2006年起始年级的学生（民办班）到毕业时，其外语水平一般达到初二水平，即通过上海市民考2级水平。一年级增设3节张思中儿童英语第一册；二年级增设3节张思中儿童英语第二册；三年级增设4～5节张思中儿童英语第三册；四年级增设4～5节张思中英语教程第一册；五年级增设4～5节张思中英语教程第二册。同时，尝试《思品》《自然》《美术》《音乐》《体育》《劳技》等学科的双语教学。（2）初中。初中阶段外语教学的基本目标是自2006年起始学生（民办班）到毕业时，其外语水平一般达到高中二年级水平，即通过上海市民考3级水平。2006届初预年级增设4节张思中英语教程第一册；2006届初一年级增设4节张思中英语教程第二册；2006届初二年级增设4节张思中英语教程第三册；2006届初三年级增设4节张思中英语教程第四册。同时，尝试《历史》《地理》《音乐》《体育》部分拓展性课程的双语教学，开设空中英语、英语沙龙等活动。（3）高中。高一年级增设张思中英语1～3册。高二年级增设张思中英语4册。高三年级增设《张思中英语强化读本》。

3．艺、体、科技特色课程

小学。钢琴：2006届新招学生，报名录取者保证培训至三级水平。美术、写字：2006届新招学生，除参加钢琴班外的学生自愿参加。其他年级学生可选修工艺课、美术、写字、钢琴、民乐、围棋等课程。小学中国武术特色教学和种植课程等。初中。除开设基础性艺术教育课程外，学校还开设美术、书法、声乐、民乐等课程。初中年级全面开设无线电通讯课程，形成全校性的特色拓展课程。开拓“IT”和“TI”拓展性课程，全面提高学生对现代科学的感性认识、运用信

民办奉浦学校开设中国功夫特色课程

息技术能力与发展数形转换的思维能力。开设工艺制作课程，包括陶艺、绳艺、布艺、木艺等。高中。高一高二分别开设素描、色彩、速写等课程。部分学生参加专项艺术培训与专项体育培训，培养艺体特长生参加相应的高等学校招生考试。加强数学“基础知识”与“基本能力”训练，编制适应学校学生的数学教学目标体系与训练习题体系。加强理化生教学内容的浅易化，生活化进程，加强教学的基础性，趣味性。开设拓展性活动课程包括摄影、动漫制作、异国文化、电脑维修、生活技能、科技之光、时事瞭望、古宝鉴赏等课程，让课程走近生活、走近现代，为学生开启另一扇智慧之窗。

民办奉浦学校为足球俱乐部小队员上足球理论课

4．小学、初中数学思维训练课程

小学。现代小学数学思维训练1～2册（一年级）。现代小学数学思维训练3～4册（二年级）。现代小学数学思维训练5～6册（三年级）。现代小学数学思维训练7～8册（四年级）。现代小学数学思维训练9～10册（五年级）。初中。初中数学竞赛辅导与练习80讲，1～40讲（初预年级）。初中数学竞赛辅导与练习80讲，41～80讲（初一年级）。初中数学竞赛辅导与练习120讲，1～60讲（初二年级）。初中数学竞赛辅导与练习120讲，61～120讲（初二年级）。

5．生活中作文与诗文颂吟语文特色课程

小学。低年级的看图作文（口头作文）；中年级的观察作文（口头+书面）；

高年级的生活作文（在对生活内容的观察、思考、理解后捕捉写作素材，形成有立意的从实际生活出发的生活作文）。小学1～5年级诗文颂吟1～5册。初中。开设校本初中生拓展诗文颂吟课程1～5册。开设从精读→泛读→观察→立意→表述教学链的生活作文拓展课程。

老师对学生进行写作特别指导

七、课程实施

1. 实现教师由单环学习向双环学习转变，逐步完成校本课程研发与推行

学校课程改革方案能否顺利实施与教师对课程方案的理解、认同程度，以及自身的专业发展水平有密切的联系。首要的是改变教师的心智模式，事实上，教师能否通过学习改变自己的心智模式是其能否深刻学习的关键。有学者区分两种学习——单环学习和双环学习。单环学习是指在不改变原有思维模式或观念结构的情况下，对环境或事件进行反思，修正其中矛盾，产生正确行动，但所做的修正行为并没有超出固有的思维框架。双环学习要深挖潜藏在矛盾下面的深层问题，使自己过去不明朗的思维清晰化，改变思维的结构，因此这种学习会为教师带来质的变化。学校课程改革意味着应该促进教师由单环学习向双环学习的迈进。课程领导需及时了解教师所面对的困难，为教师引入新的理念，为教师提供发展新的思维模式的支架，为教师专业发展提供所需的学习机会，包括外出学习、参加校本课程开发等。

学校的校本课程开发的主体是教师，学校教师是最熟悉教学现场的人。在调动广大教师参加课程改革的同时，提升教师的课程意识与理念，为他们完成校本课程开发提供基础。学校的任务就是对个体心理和特征给予充分关注的同时，为相关教师提出编撰校本课程的任务，在物质上给予支持与奖励，并提供自由学习和试谈的机会。只有当教师真正参与课程改革的实践，才能保证课程改革的成功，才能为教师在课程改革的过程中提供专业发展的最有力的动力。

2．**建立伙伴式团队文化，实现学校课程统整**

学校课程发展与课程统整有密切的关系，课程发展的两大主轴，即课程发展趋势与课程统整。在学校课程方案的实施过程中，必须加强课程的统整工作。一是要探讨“学校本位”的课程统整的理论依据；二是要探讨进行学校本位的课程统整的方法，包括学科内部的统整、学科间的统整、德育课程与其他学科间的统整、年级与年级间的统整、学段与学段间的统整以及文科间的统整、理科间的统整和文理科的统整。而实现学校课程统整的先决条件是建立伙伴式的团队文化。任何一项课程改革的推行，都不可能依靠教师的孤军奋战。营造教师间协作文化势在必行。不只是同学科内教研组间的教师需要互相协作、相互交流、积累改革的经验、交流改革的感知，还要在不同学科不同教研组间的教师建立起相互合作、相互交流的伙伴关系，这样才能使每一个参与改革的教师都不会再感到无助，才能在相互间的交流合作中实现课程的统整与专业的共同成长。

3．**建立共同愿景，构建学习型组织**

学校的共同愿景（Shared Vision）应该是学校所有成员，包括学校行政人员、教师、学生及家长对学校教育共同的期望，共同努力达成的教育理想图像。摆脱学校现实的困境，把学校最终打造成一所精品学校，建立起乐学、好奇的小学课程，基础扎实的初中课程与基础加特长的高中课程，应该成为全员的追求目标，而达成这一目标的最重要的途径就是通过课程改革，激发全员参加课改的热情，这是课程改革成功保证。而学校共同愿景是学校行事活动、课程教学、教辅措施、空间规划、学情布置的重要依据，更是学校整体课程不可或缺的目标。

实现学校共同愿景构建学习型组织是重要前提，学校课程领导就是通过建立学习型学校，改变学校的文化氛围，形成一个积极进取的“专业学习社区”。推进学校学习型组织的形成主要可通过如下途径实现：（1）课程领导者的模范带头，带动学习氛围。模范带头的重要作用就是帮助组织走出由于职业等原因所造成的“舒适地带”，注入新的能力和活力，经历超越自我的学习过程。课程领导者可以通过“主题讲座”、示范课等形式使一些默守陈规者的心智模式发生改变。（2）赋权增能，提供平台。赋权可分心理面向、行为面向和政治面向。在心理上要感受外在环境的支持，行动上要参与课改的所有活动，并与同事一起对课程事务进行慎思、决策和评估。在政治上要感受到培养高素质的下一代的光荣感和责任感，而不是期待行政的命令。由此引发下面的工作平台：新教师、青年教师的带教；教研组内的主题研究与相互观课、评课；教师完成《课堂教学改进计划》内规定的改进计划内容；教师论坛；为每一个教师的专业发展作出系统的整体规划。(3) 促进个体和群体之间的转换。在构建学习型学校的过程中，要重视个体性学习和社会性学习的互惠互助，个体的学习受到自己所处的群体的文化背景的影响，而个体学习的成果在某种程度上也成为这个群体的学习成果，促进整个群体学习的发展，学习通过“互惠螺旋”上升的策略，实现知识管理、知识建构、知识分享、知识创造。

八、课程评价

1．学生自主成长评价制度

根据学校学生现状，在不改变社会主导的考试等终结性评估手段的同时，要更好地利用好《上海市学生成长指导手册》。不只是对学生学习成绩及表现作测定，而更重要的是在评估之后对学生提出改进的建议，不只是重视学生的外显行为，还要评估学生学习兴趣以及在学习中的投入程度，实现形成性评估与终结性评估的统一。发展促进以学生为主体的元认知评估是促进学生学业成就的最理想的途径，学校在《上海市学生成长指导手册》的基础上，做进一步的强调，课程领导者要帮助教师协调各类评估方式间的平衡，最后实现评价的导向作用与激励作用。

2．教师专业发展评价体系

不同的管理范式，会出现不同的评估工具，从而产生不同评估结果。在奉浦学校时期拟定的《奉浦学校教师学期综合考核指标》，为每一个教师在每一学期内教学行为和其背后的教学理念的“尺子”。而《奉浦学校教师课堂教学改进计划》则是为每位教师提供实录个人教学行为的反思的成果。前者是终结性的他人评价，后者是形成性的过程评价。让两者结合起来，就可形成一个连续的周期性的评价，促进教师在新的课程理念的引导下，自觉地对自己的教学行为与教学信息作反思，以改善自己的教学效能。

3．学校课程良性发展评价机制

学校课程不是一成不变的。每年在课程改革领导小组等的组织下，学校要对课程本身作一系统评估。这个评估不仅仅是考虑实施成效，而更重要的是对日后的课程计划作修正，从而更周密更仔细更有效地考虑课程目标的设置、课程内容的组织以及学校资源的调拨，从而保证学校课程的承继性、序列性，并在实践中不断革新、不断完善。

九、课程管理

1. 课改工作领导小组

2006年学校成立学校课程改革领导小组。加强对课改工作的领导，统一领导和组织全校课程改革工作，校教科室为常设机构。课程改革领导小组的组织形式要与学校的常规组织机构教导处、政教处、教研组、年级组融合整合，把课程改革工作与日常的教育教学管理工作有机结合在一起，定期研究课改进程与成效。

2. 课程改革专款基金

课程改革专款基金由课程改革领导小组支配，保障课改的顺利开展。

十、校本课程

在课程方案实施过程中，重点形成5方面校本特色课程。

1. 德育校本课程

根据扎根“民族魂·学做现代人”德育校本课程为学校德育的纲领性课程，由校长戚盛伟总体设计，2006年底形成初步构想，2007年夏立为区重点课题，2010年结题。

2. 张思中英语课程

学校特聘享受国务院专家特殊津贴奖的张思中老师作学校顾问。学校根据不同年级的需求购置不同的张思中教材。结合国家课程与学校实际情况整体实施，使民办学校学生外语水平得到有效提升。

2009年，民办奉浦学校向特色教育中得奖的小小画家颁奖

3. 艺、体、科技特色课程

主要在小学与高中阶段。为使小学生掌握一种乐器技能，在每周一节音乐课与夜自修时开设自编乐理教程与自编电子琴教程。学生在乐器课程训练之后，普遍提高乐理水平与琴键的运用能力，学优者有

的达到了8～10级水平。

高中因大部分学生参加艺术类高考，所以必须参加专项美术培训，包括素描、色彩、速写。因此学校开设专门的美术培训课，选用自编的美术教程。

体育特色课程主要是小学的中国武术。武术教程由体育教师张俊杰编写。由专业人士拍摄全套艺术动作，并作文章说明。小学部广播操改用自编武术操，并组成校武术队，购置服装100余套，并在重大活动中表演。

科技类校本课程主要在少年宫科技组与区科委专利局指导下，进行科技创新活动，向学生普及创新思想与思维方法，进行科技创新实验，在何南友老师指导下学校曾有11项科技发明获专利。

4．数学思维训练课程

2007年，学校特聘上海黄浦区邵光标小学校长特级教师金建中任顾问。金老师多次到校听课评课，介绍数学教研动态与全国、市区各项活动情况，同时介绍中科院心理研究所研发的《小学现代数学》。学校在金建中指导下，引入《杭州现代小学数学思维训练》教程，经三年实践，与民办奉浦学校学生与教学实际情况相结合，形成《奉浦学校小学数学思维训练》校本教材。并获得区百佳校本课程奖。

2008年，南汇区第一中学邀请民办奉浦学校参与其上海市教科研规划项目——培养智优学生应用数学方法研究成果的实践运用。该研究旨在以数学思想方法应用为导向，培养学生创新创造综合应用能力。该教程分初中预科年级与初一年级80讲与初二、初三年级120讲两册教程，依据二期课改，了解掌握基本数学思想方法与应用，使学生乐学、勤学、会学。教程在实践中几经修改，学校也参与其全过程。

5．小学生作文与初中古诗文颂吟语文特色课程

2007年初，学校特聘上海市特级教师小学语文教材编写组成员徐鹄指导语文教学。为克服小学生习作的困难与背记范文代替习作的弊端，特开设生活中作文的课题研究参加上海小学写作会，并有意于教材的编制，开创小学作文教学的新局面。

初中生拓展古诗文颂吟课程1～5册，由初中语文教师唐继英(女)编制，自开设此课程后，学生在多届上海市古诗文创作与颂吟比赛中多人多次获奖。

十一、教学效果

为比较客观地反映学校的实际教学效果，下面分别统计历年小学毕业考成绩汇总表、历年初中毕业生中考与历年高中毕业生高考成绩及历年高考录取率。

1998—2006 学年，全区不实行小学统一的毕业考，期间全区各校的教学质量监控主要是采取抽考检测的办法，以后仍保留抽考，同时实行全区统一的毕业考。表格反映了当时协和学校的教学质量的实际情况。

1. 小学教学效果

1998—2006 学年，全区不实行小学统一毕业考。期间全区各校的教学质量监控主要是采取抽考检测的办法。2007 年，学校除仍保留抽考外，同时实行全区统一的毕业考。

“协和”致力于学生潜能的开发

记者见闻

我县第一所民办协和实验学校半年多来究竟如何，这是全县人民共同关注的话题。日前，县教育局在此举行现场观摩会，来自国家教育部、教科院、教育协会等专家和全县各级各类学校 120 多位校长和教导主任们进行了现场观摩，并给予普遍好评。

游戏式的小学一年级英语公开课正在进行，小学生坐在教室内的地毯上、头上带着各种动物面具，边游戏边回答问题，课堂气氛十分活跃。前来听课的校长们也不时发出阵阵笑声。初、高中的课堂教学充分利用现代化音像教学手段，激发学生学习兴趣。

在数学、外语教学研究方面颇有建树的夏明德校长对记者说：“每个学生都是天才，关键是如何去开发他们的潜能。因此，开发潜能教育就是我们的办学宗旨。”“协和”注重学生创造能力和心理素质的培养，努力在数学、外语、电脑方面办出特色。

记者还从《数学园地》、《英语天地》等校刊中了解到学生思维的质与量有所上升，小学一年级学生能唱 20 首外语歌，住宿学生的宿舍整洁有序，自理能力明显高于在父母身边的孩子。教育不是一朝一夕的事，但显而易见，“协和”已有了一个良好的开端。　（本报记者　景　凤）

2000 年 4 月 1 日，《奉贤报》对上海民办协和实验学校的报道

学校小学部在区域内公、民办学生兼收。总的情况民办生优于公办生（本学区属奉浦地区的弱势群体），因公办生可参加中考，所以对后续初中部参加中考的影响较大。2008 年前总体成绩处全区中等或中等偏下水平。自 2008 年学校倡导“聪明学习”之后，学生成绩上升明显，至 2012 年达到高峰，成绩居全区第三名，并多次获区课程教学奖。2015—2016 学年，上海帕丁顿双语学校小学部学生成绩达到 A 级。

1998—2008 学年上海帕丁顿双语学校小学调研抽考成绩情况表

表 7-1-4

学年	调研抽考名称	成绩
2000 学年	五年级（语、数、艺术、自然）综合卷	区平均持平
2002 学年	四年级语文	超区平均
2004 学年	四年级语文	第 9 名
	四年级英语	第 8 名
2005 学年	五年级语、数、英	第 8 名
2006 学年	三年级语文	第 18 名
	三年级数学	第 10 名
2007 学年	三年级数学	第 7 名

说明：全区小学共 31 所

2007—2015学年上海帕丁顿双语学校小学毕业考试情况表

表7-1-5

学年	语文	区名次	数学	区名次	外语	区名次	三门总分	区名次
2007学年	82.24	20	88.61	17	87.44	14	258.29	16
2008学年	82.88	17	92.00	11	82.53	29	257.41	18
2009学年	84.61	17	92.76	8	87.66	18	265.03	12
2010学年	85.45	13	94.12	1	91.29	8	270.86	5
2011学年	84.15	10	89.98	7	94.93	5	269.06	7
2012学年	81.93	11	92.02	1	93.86	4	267.81	3
2013学年	86.49	4	92.15	2	91.88	5	270.53	4
2014学年	84.61	11	89.27	1	89.60	5	263.48	6
2015学年		A		A		A	A	
2016学年		A		A		B	A	

2. 初中教学效果

帕丁顿双语学校历年中考成绩的起伏很大。1998年招生的第一届初中生在2001年毕业，成绩在全区居中下水平。2003年教师进修学院的民办初中部划入奉浦学校共3届学生，5个班。优秀学生的划入，使奉浦学校在2005年、2006年、2007年初中部学生成绩跃居全区前列。至2008—2009年原奉浦学校小学部的本地学生学业基础很差，造成了两年成绩下滑。后在“聪明学习”教学策略的指导下，2010年成绩迅速反弹，2012年达到高峰，名列全区第七，并获全区课程教学奖。2016年，上海帕丁顿双语学校的中考成绩在全区38所学校中列第11位。

2001—2016学年上海帕丁顿双语学校中考成绩情况表

表7-1-6

年份	实考人数(人)	语文	数学	英语	物理	化学	总分	区名次
2001	63	71.35	69.98	71.83	72.49	75.10	360.75	20
2002	59	70.28	71.53	69.65	63.34	65.26	340.12	18
2003	26	66.73	64.38	73.46	79.10	81.10	364.77	20
2004	27	75.93	43.52	50.26	53.00	59.67	316.85	23
2005	80	81.93	97.97	94.00	44.66	31.55	350.07	8
2006	82	114.20	109.60	114.54	67.29	42.96	448.50	5
2007	48	103.85	110.96	97.49	65.08	42.46	419.84	10
2008	27	116.24	120.52	97.24	68.30	47.30	529.50	18
2009	42	114.20	123.90	99.60	71.40	46.80	455.90	26
2010	45	117.10	116.20	121.10	67.80	43.50	465.80	14
2011	50	119.10	122.00	118.30	68.70	48.20	476.30	11
2012	45	123.60	120.60	117.70	73.00	47.30	482.10	7
2013	43	119.00	121.50	114.10	71.60	46.60	472.90	11

续表 7-1-6

年份	实考人数(人)	语文	数学	英语	物理	化学	总分	区名次
2014	31	117.60	116.70	99.20	64.80	47.50	445.80	20
2015	55	115.80	111.10	109.0	65.00	40.10	440.90	13
2016	15	114.60	108.90	96.80	66.00	42.60	439.00	11

说明：2001—2016年，全区参考学校在28～32所

3．高中教学效果

学校创办第一年即1998年，8月招收的第一批高中生的基础仅次于当时区内的两所重点校，居全区9所高中的第三名。但由于错失良机，第二年始生源质量急剧下降。2000年起，生源学业基础成绩一直处在全市的最低水平（民办校可自定降分录取），高考成绩及高考录取率一路下滑。2005年起，学校开始加强艺体、科技特色教育，所以2008年始，高中毕业生中录取艺术类本科的学生，以及总录取率明显上升。2009年始上海市高考录取率大幅调整，全市录取率在85%左右，学校高中部在"聪明学习"教学策略引领下，因材施教，自2011年起总录取率始终保持在80%～90%，多次获区教学课程奖。2016年，上海帕丁顿双语学校高考总录取率100%，其中本科录取率85.5%。

2001—2016学年上海帕丁顿双语学校高考主要学科成绩情况表

表 7-1-7

年份	语文	数学		英语	历史
		文科	理科		
2001	94.34	82.45	87.63	82.39	93.57
2002	80.61	53.35	77.10	58.97	71.94
2003	79.76	37.53	58.69	60.56	93.22
2004	83.12	51.26	65.81	57.47	88.36
2005	81.42	46.58	78.50	56.87	86.90
2006	81.77	70.89	62.05	56.77	90.74
2007	81.14	54.70	63.50	53.83	76.63
2008	81.91	47.39	57.26	48.88	76.43
2009	88.89	61.66	76.52	65.58	81.31
2010	82.64	61.03	61.05	56.90	81.35
2011	86.16	79.33	76.93	69.78	84.48
2012	87.64	62.20	63.96	68.86	87.13
2013	90.26	83.62	68.46	69.56	91.48
2014	87.16	70.43	72.04	70.51	91.00
2015	84.40	71.90	49.00	64.81	88.38
2016	87.01	74.33		55.90	89.01

2001—2016 学年上海帕丁顿双语学校高考录取情况表

表 7-1-8

年份	参考人数（人）	本科		专科		总录取率（%）
		录取人数(人)	录取率（%）	录取人数(人)	录取率（%）	
2001	173	28	16.18	70	40.46	56.64
2002	132	11	8.33	27	20.45	28.79
2003	139	19	13.67	25	17.99	31.65
2004	125	16	12.80	28	22.40	35.20
2005	152	17	11.18	34	22.37	33.55
2006	66	14	21.21	4	6.06	27.27
2007	36	9	25.00	3	8.33	33.33
2008	113	36	31.86	26	23.01	54.87
2009	147	55	37.41	29	19.72	57.14
2010	103	33	32.04	37	35.92	67.96
2011	132	72	54.55	44	33.33	87.88
2012	140	83	59.29	43	30.71	90.00
2013	176	96	54.55	47	26.70	81.25
2014	125	72	57.60	41	32.81	90.40
2015	134	77	57.46	39	29.10	86.57
2016	109	92	85.50	17	100	100

第二节　教育科研

一、发展与成果

建校初，学校没有教学科研室，也没有教学科研负责人。学校虽有科研活动，有教师撰写科研性质的论文，但总体呈个别散落之态。直至2004年，才有政教处参与的市级条线课题研究，题为“寄宿制学校教师心理健康的标准”。2006年始，学校以“科研兴校”作为立校之本，号召全员参加科研活动，以科研推动全体教师探索教育教学规律，提高绩效，响应者甚众。

学校校长注力在教学、教育两方面规划学校整体的科研项目。自2006—2008年完成《“民族魂·现代人”合作竞争团队建设实践研究》的德育课题与《聪明学习的案例开发的实践研究》两大课题。以科研为引领，构建以“民族魂·现代人”为核心理念的学校德育体系与以“聪明学习，智慧教学”为核心理念的学校教学工作体系。形成学校在操作层面上的德育工作与教学工作的“一双翅翼”，为学校的腾飞、超越发挥巨大的作用。2009年，学校成立教育科研室，任命唐继英(女)为教育科研室主任。在学校两个主题的引领下，各教研组、教师分别确立了课题，并参与区级科研课题立项。至2014年，立项的市规划课题1项，市条线课题1项，区级重点课题2项，区级一般课题21项。

学校于2010年1月，被评为区教学科研优秀学校。2015年4月，被评为区教学科研工作示范校。

2006—2016年上海帕丁顿双语学校区级以上课题情况表

表7-2-1

编号	课题名称	课题申请人	级别	立项时间	结题时间
01	《“民族魂·现代人”竞争合作团队建设实践研究》	戚盛伟	区级重点课题	2006.3	2008.10
02	《初中语文教学中学生健康人格培养的策略研究》	唐继英(女)	区级一般课题	2006.3	2008.10
03	《引导小学生生活化作文的教学方法的实践研究》	蔡国英(女)	区级一般课题	2006.3	2008.10
04	《中学数学“先行组织”教学模式的实践与策略研究》	高决心	区级一般课题	2006.3	2008.10
05	《关于初中思想政治课“合作学习”模式的实践研究》	钱　红(女)	区级一般课题	2006.3	2008.10
06	《初中英语课堂教学中形成性评价实践研究》	王　虹(女)	区级一般课题	2006.3	2008.10
0833	《“聪明学习”实践案例的开发与研究》	戚盛伟	市级规划课题	2008.3	2010.10
08084	《在初中拓展课程中培养智优学生运用数学方法的实践研究》	陈春红(女)	区级一般课题	2008.3	2010.10
0885	《初中现行牛津英语教材再开发的研究与实践》	吴　莹(女)	区级一般课题	2008.3	2010.12
09	《中学生化学科教学中提高学案使用实效性的实践研究》	瞿　锋	区级一般课题	2009.3	2012.12
09106	《在语文教学中落实生命教育的实践研究》	幺凤娟(女)	区级一般课题	2009.3	2012.12
16-165	《发挥家长学校功能，提高家长育子水平的探索与实践》	江仁章	市级条线课题	2011.3	2012.12
ZD11028	《基于“聪明学习”的优化教师教学行为的实践研究》	唐继英(女)	区级重点课题	2011.3	2013.5
YB11328	《初中生“美好人生早规划”课程开发与实施研究》	周文红(女)	区级一般课题	2011.3	2012.12
YB11329	《高中数学作业纠错环节中师生、生生互动的实践探索》	马欢权	区级一般课题	2011.3	2012.12

续表 7-2-1

编号	课题名称	课题申请人	级别	立项时间	结题时间
YB11330	《初中牛津英语“校本练习优化的探索与实践”》	吴　莹（女）	区级一般课题	2011.3	2012.12
YB13252	《初中数学“学出问题来”教学策略的实践研究》	夏红波	区级一般课题	2013.3	2015.3
YB13253	《优化小学低年级语文课堂教学口头评价的策略研究》	张建丽（女）	区级一般课题	2013.3	2015.3
YB13254	《对话理论指导下的语文阅读教学的实践研究》	许娟娟（女）	区级一般课题	2013.3	2015.3
YB13255	《高中语文各类文体教学范式的案例研究》	池　敏（女）	区级一般课题	2013.3	2015.3
YB13256	《“生活中的作文”课题成果推广的研究和实践》	翁丹香（女）	区级一般课题	2013.3	2015.3
YB13257	《高中信息科技学科中运用“短视频”帮助学生有效预习的实践研究》	诸海萍（女）	区级一般课题	2013.3	2015.3
YB13258	《高中史学方法系统性课堂教学探究》	黄艳红（女）	区级一般课题	2013.3	2015.3
YB13259	《艺术拓展课教学过程中技与趣的相融的实践研究》	刘明敏（女）	区级一般课题	2013.3	2015.3
YB13260	《提高高中英语课堂交流能力的实践研究》	邢光伟	区级一般课题	2013.3	2015.3

二、重点课题

1．“民族魂·现代人”竞争合作团队建设

2005 年，学校董事会聘奉贤区已退休的名校长戚盛伟接任学校校长。他凭着几十年教育管理经验和对教育事业的激情，立足于校情，为学校精准把脉，提出“适合”教育办学理念，构建以“民族魂·现代人”为核心理念的学校德育体系，和以“聪明学习，智慧教学”为核心理念的学校教学工作体系，带领全体师生开展“聪明学习、智慧教育”的教学实践研究，以及《“民族魂·现代人”竞争合作团队建设》育人实践研究。几年的研究结出硕果，学校逐渐走出低谷。

《民族魂·现代人竞争合作团队建设的实践研究》旨在学校育人目标和育人方法上的研究和操作。研究活动从 2006 年区级立为重点课题起步，确立以“立身、处世、为人、处事”为 4 大德育培养目标，以及下设的 17 个子目标的研究，奠定开展此项研究的基础。

2007年调整研究策略，重点在教师团体竞争合作研究和课题目标操作体系、管理机制、评价机制作深入研究，制订出适合学校实际的《奉浦学校“民族魂·现代人”德育目标操作、评价方案》，强调以班主任为首的班级组团队协作，和以年级组为核心，联动教导处、政教处、各学段组内教师团队协作良好格局，提升年级组竞争与合作效能，促进教师评价机制的完善。其间为提升研究成效,学校先后邀请市特级教师于漪(女)做题为“信心·风气·队伍”报告，学校顾问王小平的“做有国际意识的人”讲座，戚盛伟的“构建奉浦学校‘民族魂·现代人’新德育目标体系”“学习动机理论概要”“正视差异倡导适合 提高质效”“高效率教学概要”“生命教育须还教育以生命性”等的系列专题讲座。通过学习讨论，收获颇丰，许多教师研究论文频频获奖，教师阮慧华(女)的“创设良好心理环境，建设竞争合作团队”获上海市郊德育论文评比二等奖。教师靖珍(女)的“高中语文阅读与学生健全人格养育的教学模式探索”发表于安徽大学学报。教师柳肖云(女)“让学生成为班级的主人”获区“班主任专业发展”论文评比二等奖。

《学生个人自我管理手册》也在这个研究阶段编制而出，形成学生自主管理为主、老师、父母辅助成长模式。

2008年进入课题的深化研究阶段，融汇“两纲”教育的推进工作，深化德育课题研究，激发学生在人格与学业两方面的极大发展。凭藉教师职业特有的敏感，学校抓住期间蕴含的教育契机，开展各类主题的教育活动。在临近结题阶段，还作研究开题前曾做的调查问卷，并作专项对比报告；完成小学、初中、高中三个学段《学生成长指导手册》校本德育课程的编纂；最后以结题报告完美完成此课题的研究活动。

此研究的成果：(1) 形成《奉浦学校“民族魂·现代人”德育体系的育人目标》，形成比较完整的德育目标的构架，这是具有一定的创新价值的突破；(2) 形成小学、初中、高中各自不同的操作序列、活动载体与评价体系。这为学校落实德育目标，实施德育教育奠定基本保证；(3) 形成学科德育教育纲要，形成每学年1册《学科德育教育案例集》；(4) 编纂了分高中、初中、小学3册的《奉浦学校学生成长指导手册》，作为校本德育课程，落实实施，帮助学生达到德育目标的内化；(5) 促进学生道德水准和学业水平的全面提升；最后就是教师的育人意识获得增强，以人为本的现代教育的基本价值成为教师们的共识，把教育与人的幸福、人的自由、人的尊严、人的终极价值联系起来，以现代人的精神培养现代人，以全面发展的视野培养全面发展的人，加强道德教育的必要性得到肯定，教师育人的能力在实践活动中也得到很大提升。

2."聪明学习、智慧教学"实践案例

2012年6月21日，在上海市晋元高级中学举办的"上海市中小学创造自己的高效教学经验"颁奖大会上，民办奉浦学校高效的教学经验成果《"聪明学习"教学案例的开发与研究》，荣膺上海市一等奖。

这次评选活动，全市共有220个"教学经验成果"参加评选，全市共评出一等奖10项，学校的成果就是其中之一，获得这次评选活动的最高奖项，这也是奉贤区获得的唯一的一个奖。

学校的《"聪明学习"实践案例的开发与研究》课题，于2008年5月，被正式批准为上海市规划课题。2011年5月撰写结题报告，顺利结题。2011年6月，再次整理材料，参加上海市第四届教科研成果评选活动，获三等奖。2013年10月，其子课题"基于'聪明学习'的教师智慧教学的实践研究"被评为奉贤区第十届教科研成果评选一等奖；其成果——"'优化教师教学行为'的情报综述"被上海市普教所评为"情报综述"评比二等奖，并在《上海情报研究》杂志上发表。2013年11月，张春辉主编的《色彩静物技法突破》一书由上海人民美术出版社出版；2014年4月，戚盛伟主编的《为了智慧校园的理想》一书由中西书局正式出版。

其间，学校还形成3本《聪明学习　智慧教学》案例集，共包含90个教师智慧教学的典型案例。2009年1月，《奉贤教育》"学校专栏"共发表本校15位教师的案例，另外有13篇论文分别发表于《长三角教育》《新教育论坛》《现代教学》《中国高等教育研究》等刊物。

在这4年的实践研究中，学校围绕"聪明学习 智慧教学"理念，从学校实际出发，有效发挥专业团队的引领作用，为教师的专业成长建立有效的支持系统策略。借助《课堂教学改进案例》的有效载体，全校教师进行"草根式"的研究，实践"知识有停靠点""情感有激发点""思维有展开点""行为有反思点"教学策略，开发大量的课堂教学改进案例，激发教师课堂教学研究的能动性，从根本上改变教学方式，实践智慧教学。在"智慧教学"策略的引领下，学生的学习方式发生根本变化。学校校本课程的开设更是如虎添翼，提高学生学习的内驱力和主动性，学习成绩和学习能力大幅提升。

2011学年和2012学年，学校连续被评为奉贤区课程教学奖二等奖和三等奖，小学五年级两年的毕业考试分别为全区第7名和第3名，初三两年的中考分别为全区第11名和第7名，高三高考两年本科上线率分别是87%和90%。学生参加各级各类竞赛获奖层次高，获奖奖项多。学校在区域范围内的影响力不断扩大。

本课题研究得到市专家胡兴宏、刘海虎、刘定一、金建中、徐鹄等教师到校指导。2008年，学校召开奉贤区“聪明学习——为了建设智慧型校园的理想”现场会，市人大常委会教科文卫副主任委员夏秀蓉(女)、区教育局局长等出席；2009年3月19日，召开奉贤区《“聪明学习”——探索有效教学的途径》现场会，市专家胡兴宏、刘定一、金建中、徐鹄和区教育局领导参加。两次现场会分别得到领导的高度赞扬。教育局领导多次在市级、区级现场会及工作会议上给予褒奖。

第三节　生源变迁与师生获奖

一、生源变迁

生源的变化反映学校办学的社会认同度。学校开办之初，小学只招8个班，初中招收6个班，高中招收4个班，学生总人数为765名，生源数相对较少。随着逐年招生年级的增加，学校人数也显上升趋势，但自2000年后学生数又呈下降趋势，直至2002年学校社会认同感坠入低谷。2003年年初，奉贤区教师进修学院接管民办协和学校，更名为奉贤区教师进修学校奉浦实验学校。那年，进修学院将原来自已办的二届初中学生计180余名并入奉浦学校，小学、初中招生又呈迅猛上升之势。之后又逐年回落，2005年再度落入低谷。自2006年后，学校办学质量逐年上升，社会声誉不断改善，小学、初中、高中招生呈回热之势。2007年突破千名，直至2014年每年平均增加数在百余名。2014年，全校学生人数1556名。2015年4月，民办奉浦学校改为上海帕丁顿双语学校。是年8月，公办学生析出后，学校改为民企民办学校。民办学生人数仍超过千人。2016年，全校学生1212人，其中外省市学生601人，占49.59%

1998—2016年上海帕丁顿双语学校学生情况表

表 7-3-1

年份	合计		小学		初中		高中	
	班级(个)	人数(人)	班级(个)	人数(人)	班级(个)	人数(人)	班级(个)	人数(人)
1998	18	765	8	292	6	270	4	203
1999	72	897	8	220	9	348	7	329
2000	29	1048	11	288	7	251	11	509
2001	27	996	11	325	5	186	11	485
2002	24	916	9	285	4	133	11	498
2003	26	1013	9	310	9	299	8	404
2004	26	783	8	207	13	381	5	195
2005	24	863	7	239	10	311	7	313
2006	24	868	9	285	8	193	7	390
2007	30	1042	10	305	8	228	12	509
2008	34	1150	13	386	9	234	12	530
2009	35	1198	13	406	10	241	12	551
2010	37	1303	16	515	8	212	13	581
2011	40	1365	17	543	10	284	13	538
2012	46	1441	18	551	12	367	16	523
2013	43	1505	19	631	12	387	12	487
2014	48	1556	20	687	13	401	15	468
2015	32	1014	14	466	6	131	12	417
2016	37	1212	17	554	6	147	14	511

说明：1. 1998—2015年全校班级、学生人数摘自《奉贤统计年鉴》；2. 2016年班级、学生人数由学校提供

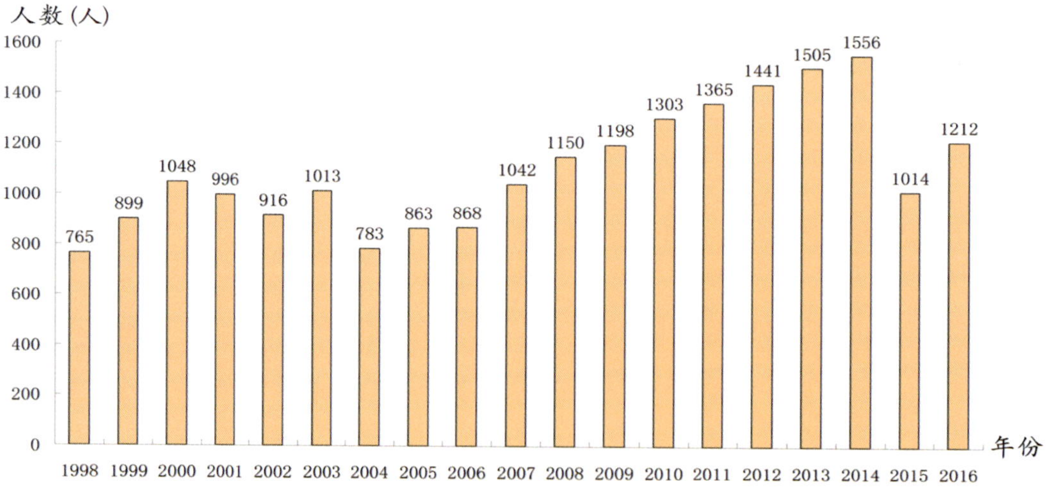

1998—2016年上海帕丁顿双语学校学生人数示意图

说明：1.1998—2014年为公办、民办学生数，2015—2016年为民办学生数；2.1998—2015年数据摘自《奉贤统计年鉴》，2016年数据由学校提供

1．**小学部学生**

1998年9月学校创办后，小学部学生人数基本稳定在200人以上。2004年为207人，2014年上升到687人，为历史最高年。2015年8月，上海帕丁顿双语学校改为纯民办学校后，小学学生人数以外来民工子女为主。2016年，小学学生554人，占全校学生的45.71%。

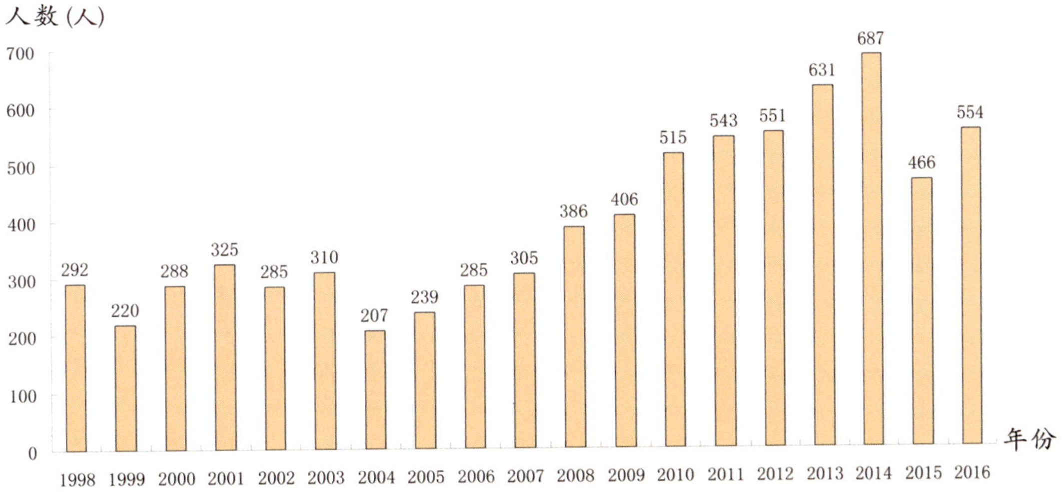

1998—2016年上海帕丁顿双语学校小学部学生人数示意图

说明：1.1998—2014年为公办、民办学生数，2015—2016年为民办学生数；2.1998—2015年数据摘自《奉贤统计年鉴》，2016年数据由学校提供

2．**初中部学生**

1998年9月学校创办后，初中学生生源历年来人数比小学部、高中部学生少。1998—2014年，公办、民办学生在同时招收条件下，人数在200～300人。2015年8月，上海帕丁顿双语学校改为纯民办后，初中学生人数减少。2015—2016年各设6个班。2016年，初中学生147人，占全校学生的12.13%。

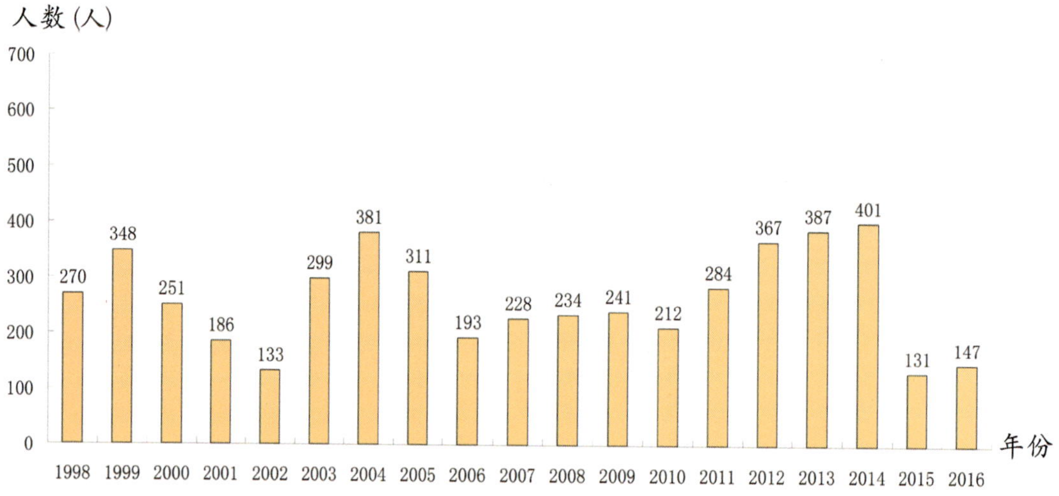

1998—2016年上海帕丁顿双语学校初中部学生人数示意图

说明：1.1998—2014年为公办、民办学生数，2015—2016年为民办学生数；2.1998—2015年数据摘自《奉贤统计年鉴》，2016年数据由学校提供

3. 高中部学生

1998年9月，学校创办开学，由于学校特色教育和社会需求，学生人数占历年学生人数的40%左右。2000年，高中学生509人，占全校学生总数48.57%。2010年高中学生581人，占全校学生44.42%。2015年，上海帕丁顿双语学校改为纯民办学校后，民办高中学生仍占有重要地位。2016年，高中学生511人，占全校学生42.16%。

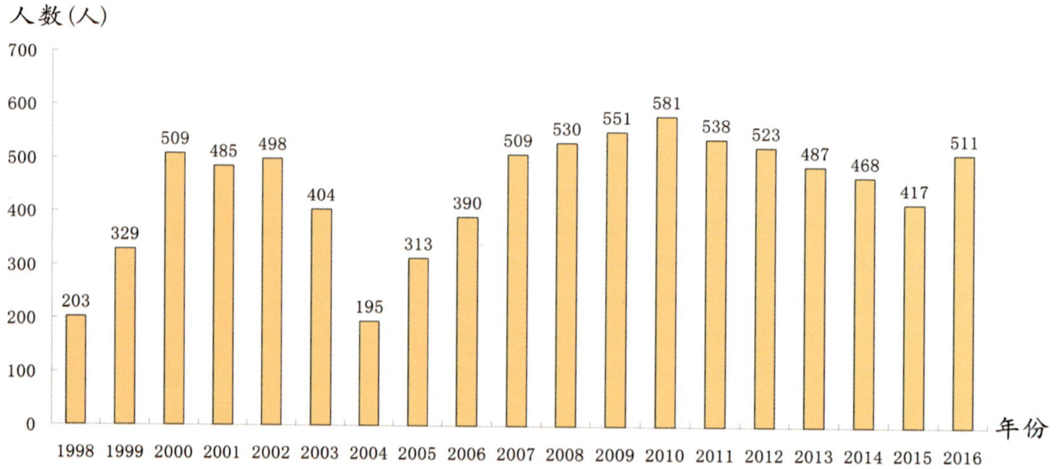

1998—2016年上海帕丁顿双语学校高中部学生人数示意图

说明：1.1998—2014年为公办、民办学生数，2015—2016年为民办学生数；2.1998—2015年数据摘自《奉贤统计年鉴》，2016年数据由学校提供

二、师生获奖

1998年9月学校创办后，学校坚持正确的办学理念，在教学教育中推行“适合教育”，创新校本课程，实践“聪明学习、智慧教学”。2003—2016年，受到区教育系统奖励的师生170多人次。

2003—2016年上海帕丁顿双语学校部分年份教学评比获奖情况表

表7-3-1

年份	姓名	奖项	获奖等第	发证单位
2003	丁永花(女)	上海市英语学科中青年教师教学评比	一等奖	市教研室
2008	阮慧华(女)	上海市心理辅导课教学评比	一等奖	市教研室
2008	池　敏(女)	奉贤区中青年语文教师比武	二等奖	区教育局
2009	诸海萍(女)	区第十五届教学节中青年教师教学评比“中学信息科技”	二等奖	区教育局
2009	丁　梅(女)	区第十五届教学节中青年教师教学评比“中学数学”	二等奖	区教研中心
2010	诸海萍(女)	区“中学信息科技教学”评比	一等奖	区教研中心
		上海市“中学信息科技”中青年教师教学评比	二等奖	市教研室
2015	张春辉	第七届上海市中小学美术教师基本功大赛	一等奖	市教育学会美术专业委员会
		第六届上海市中小学美术教师基本功大赛	一等奖	市教育学会美术专业委员会
2016	李若男(女) 李　平(女)	DQ杯第二届少儿Q舞大赛	教师指导奖	上海市学生活动管理中心
2016	么凤娟(女)	上海市古诗文大赛	优秀个人	上海市教育委员会
2016	杨　华	奉贤区自动化小队竞赛	自动化小队称号	奉贤区教育局
2016	杨　华 孙晓琼(女)	亚洲学生第23届奥林匹克英语演讲大赛（中国区）	优秀教师指导奖	大赛（中国区）组委会
2016	靖若晴(女) 施红妹(女)	2016年奉贤区青少年健康教育主题活动	优秀指导教师	奉贤区教育局等

2007—2016年上海帕丁顿双语学校教师主要论文情况表

表7-3-2

年份	姓名	名称	发表刊物或奖第	发证单位
2007	靖　珍(女)	高中语文阅读与学生健全人格养育的教学模式探索	《安徽大学学报》	安徽大学学报社
2007	柳肖云(女)	让学生成为班级的主人	德育论文评比二等奖	区教育局
2008	翁丹香(女)	全国中小学德育教育成果评比论文	一等奖	评比组委会
2008	潘海鸥(女)	区初中探究型课程教师教学设计评比	二等奖	区教育局
2008	唐燕燕(女)	语文教学中探究学习主体意识培养实践研究	《区第八届教科研获奖成果论文集》	区教育局
2008	唐继英(女)等15人	教学案例	《奉贤教育》2009.1	奉贤教育社
2009	朱爱民	奉贤区中学业余足球发展现状	二等奖	奉贤教育社
2009	郁玉芳(女)	区政治教师教学论文评比	二等奖	区教育局
2009	周文红(女)	区信息科技学科教学论文评比《培养学生能力策略研究》	二等奖	区教育局
2009	吴　莹(女)	初中现行牛津英语教材再开发	《现代教学》	现代教学社
2009	柳肖云(女)	春风化雨 水到渠成	《奉贤教育》	奉贤教育社
2009	柳肖云(女)	让审美成为阅读教学不落的太阳	《现代教学》	现代教学社
2009	朱爱民	学校与社区体育互动发展研究	《中国高等教育研究》	《中国高等教育研究》
2009	范丽萍(女)	例折乘法公式的解题技巧	《中学生报》	《中学生报》
2010	周文红(女)	上海市拓展型课程“时装秀”教学论文评比	一等奖	市教科所
2010	倪美红(女)	体育教学中如何培养寄宿制高中女生的自锻能力	学校体育发表	区教研中心
2010	倪美红(女)	多学段学校如何有效培养学生自主锻炼能力	论文评比区一等奖	区教研中心
2011	何南友	第二届“赛复创智杯”上海市青少年科技创意设计大赛	优秀组织奖	市科技竞赛组委
2011	吴光斐(女)	永远的追求	《英语测试报》16期	《英语测试报》
2011	余　琳(女)	巧设新教学理念的课堂实践	《英语测试报》	《英语测试报》
2011	瞿　锋	生命科学运用适切学习训练提高学力	三等奖	区教育局
2011	张琴花(女)	区中小学心理健康论文评比	三等奖	区教育局
2012	戚盛伟 唐继英(女)	上海市“创造自己高效率教学”教科研论文	市一等奖	市普教所
2012	戚盛伟 唐继英(女)	聪明学习实践案例的开发与研究	市三等奖	市教科院

续表 7-3-2

年份	姓名	名称	发表刊物或奖第	发证单位
2012	张春辉	概念——我们追求的建筑教学案例	市教科研室课程展示案	市教科研室
2012	许娟娟(女)	“校训指引我成长”征文赛	一等奖	区教育工会
2013	翁丹香(女)	小学中低年级学生语文训练模式探索	二等奖	区教研中心
2013	唐继英(女) 幺凤娟(女)	优化教学行为的情报综述	市二等奖	市普教所
2013	夏红波	初中数学教学论文评比	二等奖	区教研中心
2014	张　媛(女)	环保教案设计	一等奖	区教育局
2014	陈春红(女)	提高初中学生数学交流表达能力的实践研究	《奉贤教育》160 期	《奉贤教育》
2014	夏红波	一堂教学复习课引发的思考	《奉贤教育》160 期	《奉贤教育》
2014	黄艳红(女)	区“中国梦”诗歌大赛	二等奖	区委宣传部
2016	许娟娟(女)	“萌芽杯”课题研究	一等奖	民办中小学协会

2008—2016 年学生主要获奖情况表

表 7-3-3

年份	姓名	项目	获奖等第	发证单位
1999	高三（2）班	“共铸明天的辉煌”主题班会	优秀奖	奉贤区主题班会组委
1999	周悦、张晶(女)	奉贤县“海文杯”英语竞赛	三等奖	县英语竞赛组委
1999	赵洁(女)、潘军辉	奉贤县“东华杯”化学竞赛	二等奖	县化学竞赛组委
1999	陈亮、张晶(女)	上海市中学生化学论文评比	优秀奖	市中学生化学竞赛组委
1999	陈亮、张晶(女)	奉贤县中学生化学论文评比	一等奖	县化学竞赛组委
1999	陈　杰	奉贤县地理论文比赛	二等奖	县地理竞赛组委
1999	高三（3）班	上海市中学先进班级评比	三好先进班级	市先进班级组委
2006	徐　丹(女)	奉贤区英语听力竞赛	二等奖	区英语听力竞赛
2008	王　超	奉贤区中小学生科学创想英语擂台赛	三等奖	区英语竞赛组委
2008	韩潇鋆	区青少年车模技能竞赛	一等奖	区竞赛组委
2008	沈羽翀	安全 2008 中国结竞赛	一等奖	中国结竞赛组委
2008	孙逸婕(女)	区 2008 水仙雕刻技能竞赛	一等奖	区竞赛组委
2008	刘雨桐(女)	第十二届全国青少年作家杯作品大赛	全国金奖	作家杯组委
2008	吴鸣晗(女)等 2 人	市“中环杯”竞赛奉贤赛区	一等奖	市竞赛组委
2008	陈啸天	市“虹桥友谊商城”英语故事演讲	二等奖	市演讲组委
2008	陈啸天	区“奥运同行”英语演讲赛	二等奖	区演讲组委
2008	沈　瑜(女)	区创想英语擂台赛	二等奖	区演讲组委
2009	朱文琪(女)	市“小学生优秀作文征文活动”	一等奖	市征文活动组委

续表 7-3-3

年份	姓名	项目	获奖等第	发证单位
2009	顾岚馨(女)等2人	市“小学生优秀作文征文活动”	二等奖	市征文活动组委
2009	朱文琪(女)	市“七彩杯”现场作文赛	特等奖	市征文活动组委
2009	褚晨悦等3人	市“七彩杯”现场作文赛	一等奖	市征文活动组委
2009	魏庆朋	市“大白兔”杯写作活动	二等奖	市征文活动组委
2009	岳新宇(女)	“恒源祥”全国中学生作文上海赛区	一等奖	上海赛区组委
2009	金丹婷(女)等4人	“恒源祥”全国中学生作文上海赛区	二等奖	上海赛区组委
2009	陈震宇	上海市第二届古诗词创作大赛	一等奖	市大赛组委
2009	奉浦学校	上海市青少年创造发明设计竞赛	团体一等奖	市大赛组委
2009	马鑫海等2人	市青少年创造发明设计	一等奖	市大赛组委
2009	黄叶俊等2人	市动漫比赛	一等奖	市大赛组委
2009	张楚瑶(女)等2人	区青少年车辆模型竞赛	一等奖	区竞赛组委
2010	夏艳玲(女)	区第三届中小学生“小科学家”创想英语擂台赛（小学组）	二等奖	区擂台赛组委
2010	严鸿飞	上海市第三届古诗词创作大赛	一等奖	市大赛组委
2010	岳新宇(女)	上海市第三届古诗词创作大赛	二等奖	市大赛组委
2010	韩雷等2人	区青少年船模比赛	一等奖	区比赛组委
2010	龚海香(女)等2人	奉贤区2010年中学生布艺、木工竞赛	一等奖	区比赛组委
2010	吴君怡(女)	“颂祖国·迎世博”上海市中小学生电影节网上影坛百字评比赛	一等奖	市评比组委
2010	陆缨霞(女)等3人	“颂祖国·迎世博”上海市中小学生电影节影评征文评比	二等奖	市影评征文组委
2010	岳新宇(女)	区“外研杯”作文赛	二等奖	区比赛组委
2010	阳海婷(女)	2010年奉贤区第六届小学生英语竞赛	一等奖	区比赛组委
2010	奚紫莹(女)等3人	全国第九届希望杯比赛	全国三等奖	全国希望杯组委
2010	陈舒婕(女)等23人	区第九届希望杯比赛	获区一、二、三等奖	区希望杯组委
2010	何维康	区十一届中环杯比赛	一等奖	区比赛组委
2010	李强等9人	区十一届中环杯竞赛	二、三等奖	区比赛组委
2010	韩潇鋆等3人	上海市中学生应用数学	二等奖	市竞赛组委
2011	邵菲尔(女)	上海市中学生作文大赛	一等奖	市竞赛组委
2011	殷俊莹(女)	上海市中学生作文大赛	二等奖	市竞赛组委
2011	八（1）班学生	奉贤区《初中探究型课程学生小课题成果》评比	一等奖	区教育局

续表 7-3-3

年份	姓名	项目	获奖等第	发证单位
2011	刘　涛	2011 年上海市中小学常见植物识别竞赛	三等奖	市竞赛组委
2011	徐淑雯(女)	第二十三届上海市优秀发明选拔赛	铜奖	市竞赛组委
2011	夏雪妍(女)	区水仙花雕刻比赛	一等奖	区比赛组委
2011	俞国庆等 2 人	2011 奉贤区中学劳动技术学科竞赛手工布艺	一等奖	区比赛组委
2012	范思航	第十一届中环杯比赛	一等奖	区比赛组委
2012	顾　家(女)	全国中学生作文大赛	二等奖	全国比赛组委
2012	殷俊莹(女)	区古诗文阅读大赛	一等奖	区比赛组委
2012	袁何斌	区古诗文阅读大赛	二等奖	区比赛组委
2012	岳新宇(女)	古诗文创作大赛	二等奖	市比赛组委
2012	徐如意(女)	二十三届希望杯全国数学邀请决赛	三等奖	国家级比赛组委
2012	徐如意(女)	二十三届希望杯全国数学邀请决赛	一等奖	区比赛组委
2012	朱聪聪	二十三届希望杯全国数学邀请决赛	三等奖	国家级比赛组委
2012	宋文侠	二十三届希望杯全国数学邀请决赛	一等奖	区比赛组委
2012	叶倩彦(女)	二十三届希望杯全国数学邀请决赛	三等奖	国家级比赛组委
2012	邵煜轩	二十三届希望杯全国数学邀请决赛	一等奖	区比赛组委
2012	岳新宇(女)	二十三届希望杯全国数学邀请决赛	一等奖	区比赛组委
2012	宋思佳(女)、姚一凡	第五届上海市中小学生“小科学家”创想英语擂台赛活动	最佳写作奖	市比赛组委
2012	岳新宇(女)	第五届上海市中小学生“小科学家”创想英语擂台赛活动	最佳翻译奖	市比赛组委
2012	徐　卓(女)	第五届上海市中小学生“小科学家”创想英语擂台赛活动	最佳口语奖	市比赛组委
2012	汤诗瑶(女)	区高中生作文竞赛	二等奖	区比赛组委
2012	张佳奇(女)	高三数学竞赛	三等奖	区比赛组委
2012	阙春勇	高二物理竞赛	三等奖	区比赛组委
2012	吴　禛	第二届“赛复创智杯”上海市青少年科技创意设计大赛	二等奖	市比赛组委
2012	吴静惟(女)	区水仙艺术造型评比《心心相印》	一等奖	区比赛组委
2012	张子伟	区中学生劳技手工布艺	一等奖	区比赛组委
2012	周　慧(女)	奉贤区作文大赛（初中组）	一等奖	区比赛组委
2012	殷俊莹(女)	奉贤区作文大赛（初中组）	一等奖	区比赛组委
2012	陆文婷(女)	区作文竞赛（高中组）	一等奖	教研室
2012	张博凡	“119”消防日，创意金点子	一等奖	区比赛组委
2013	朱亚婷(女)等 4 人	全国“希望杯”小学数学邀请赛	全国三等奖	希望杯数学邀请赛上海工作站

续表 7-3-3

年份	姓名	项目	获奖等第	发证单位
2013	奚紫莹(女)等 33 人	全国"希望杯"小学数学邀请赛	区一、二、三等奖	希望杯数学邀请赛上海工作站
2013	袁何斌	市科普英语竞赛	市三等奖	市科技艺术教育中心
2013	合唱团学生	奉贤区合唱比赛	二等奖	区比赛组委
2013	王尹方、周慧(女)	奉贤区作文大赛	二等奖	区比赛组委
2013	学校代表队	上海市阳光大联赛"武术操"比赛	二等奖	上海市阳光大联赛
2014	唐羽扬(女)	市"文慧杯"汉语言文字比赛	特等奖	上海文萃教育
2014	邵煜轩、陈阳、金嘉雯(女)等	全国希望杯竞赛	三等奖	全国竞赛组委
2014	袁何斌	市第 13 届科普英语比赛	区一等奖	市比赛组委
2014	张雨晴	第 13 届科普英语比赛	市三等奖	市比赛组委
2015	黄新怡(女)	第十六届 CTVE 创桥杯全国学生能全历奇英语国际大赛上海赛区决赛一等奖二年级组	三等奖	市大赛组委
2015	汪　洲	第十六届 CTVE 创桥杯全国学生能全历奇英语国际大赛上海赛区决赛一等奖一年级组	优胜奖	市大赛组委
2015	李　娴(女)	第十六届 CTVE 创桥杯全国学生能全历奇英语国际大赛上海赛区决赛一等奖一年级组	三等奖	市大赛组委
2016	沈施瀚	"美丽汉字"征文活动车五年级组	二等奖	上海中文自修社
2016	张一弋	"美丽汉字"征文活动车五年级组	三等奖	上海中文自修社
2016	廖逸枫	"美丽汉字"征文活动	三等奖	市活动组委会
2016	李毅轩	"美丽汉字"征文三年级	三等奖	市活动组委会
2016	黄劭涵	"美丽汉字"征文三年级	二等奖	市活动组委会
2016	靖若晴(女，教师)李安琪(女)、李怡萱(女)、叶欣怡(女)、李毅轩	2016 年上海市青少年健康教育主题活动小学组小品比赛	三等奖	市比赛组委会
2016	魏梓涵、蔡匀、张心怡(女)、沈依卓(女)、李毅轩、李安琪(女)	"舞动中国梦"Q 达人、DQ 杯第二届少儿 Q 舞大赛	三等奖	市比赛组委会

续表 7-3-3

年份	姓名	项目	获奖等第	发证单位
2016	李安琪(女)、李怡萱(女)、叶欣怡(女)、汪雨涵(女)、李争廷	奉贤区 2016 年“健康成长、放飞梦想”健康教育主题活动小品比赛	特等奖	区比赛组委会
2016	邓　乐	2016 年“雏鹰杯”上海市少年课外活动大赛	小学组一等奖	区大赛组委会
2016	邵国芮	奉贤区第二届学生活动节“童声唱童谣，共筑中国梦”健康教育主题活动小品比赛	二等奖	区比赛组委会
2016	一、二年级集体	奉紧区第二届学生活动节“童声唱童谣，共筑中国梦”健康教育主题活动小品比赛	特等奖	区比赛组委会
2016	严湘凝(女)	2015 年奉贤区优秀少先队员评比	优秀少先队员	区少年活动中心
2016	兰婷婷(女)、沈施瀚	2015 年奉贤区优秀少先队员评比	优秀少先队员	区少年活动中心
2016	四 (1) 新月中队	2015 年奉贤区优秀少先队评比	快乐中队	区少年活动中心
2016	四 (3) 向阳中队	2015 年奉贤区优秀少先队评比	快乐中队	区少年活动中心
2016	倪悦嘉(女)	奉贤区“老师您好，我的好老师”征文评比	优秀征文	区教育局
2016	刘霖楠(女)	“红领巾国学达人”上海市古诗文阅读大赛	优秀奖	区工会大赛组委
2016	刘霖楠(女)	第十六届剑桥杯全国学生能全历奇英语国际大赛上海赛区决赛	七年级组三等奖	市赛区组委会
2016	万婧彤(女)	第十六届剑桥杯全国学生能全历奇英语国际大赛上海赛区决赛	六年级组优胜奖	市赛区组委会
2016	屠晓宇(女)	第十四届奉贤区古诗文阅读大赛	优秀奖	区大赛组委会
2016	陈伯佃	奉贤区三好学生评比	三好学生	区教育局

第四节　教学管理

教学管理包括小学、初中、高中统一的教学常规管理制度，也包括各学部特殊的管理制度，如幼小衔接管理制度、高中美术特色班管理制度等。

一、教学常规管理制度

教学常规管理制度主要根据教学过程的主要环节与教学活动的内容而拟定。19年办学过程中基本不变。

1．教学计划管理

教学计划主要包括学校教学工作计划、教研组（备课组）工作计划、教师个人教学计划等。

学校教学工作计划每学期开学之前由教导主任或分管校长向全体教师传达。计划依据学校工作计划中的教学工作目标、统筹协调，对各年级、各学科教学提出明确的要求和相应的检查措施，对各项主要的教学工作作出具体安排，作为各教研组和任课教师制定教学工作计划的依据。

教研组（备课组）教学计划应依据学校教学工作计划，结合本学科特点，对本学期各项教研工作作出具体安排，经全组教师讨论通过后，于开学初1周内交教导处审定存档。教研组长（备课组长）为计划执行的具体负责人。

个人教学计划由各任课教师制定，在开学后1周内完成。各任课教师在制定计划时要充分理解学校教学工作计划的总体精神，熟悉课程标准，明确本学科、本学期总的教学任务，明确教材各章节在教材中所处的地位，以及各章节之间的相互联系，充分估计到完成教学任务可能遇到的问题和困难，拟定教学进度，提出教学中应注意的问题和改进措施。

以上各项计划分学期制订，计划制订后，一式两份，一份交学校教导处存档，一份由计划执行人保存。学校应采取切实有效的措施，对计划实施情况进行定期检查，确保计划落实到位。学期结束时各责任部门和学科教师应及时对照计划，结合教学实际进行反思，并写出书面总结。

2．备课管理

教师备课时要根据课程标准，学情分析，确定教学设计、教法和教学手段，并要充分考虑教学中可能遇到的问题，如何应变处理等。坚持做到“三备”：即备课程标准、备教材教法、备学情学法，教学环节要完整合理。加强集体备课，落实16字备课制度：“集体备课、资源共享、个人加减、课后反思。”在个人自备的基础上进行集体备课，每周至少1次，做到“四定”，即定时间、定地点、定内容、定中心发言人。为防止“集体备课”的异化现象，每次集体备课之前由备课组长检查所有教师本次教案，然后在集体备课通案的基础上再形成个人风格的教案。个人教案应针对所教班级的具体情况，做到既有基本要求，又有拓展内容，既有共性，又突出个性，体现个人教学风格。每单元授课前应拟定单元教学方案，掌握教学具体要求，划分课时，确定课时教学主要内容。力求钻透“五点”即重点、难点、知识点、能力点和德育点。编写课时教案。教案要分课时编写。教案应包括教学目标、教学过程、教学方法、重点、难点、课后反思等内容。课件选用写入教案。复习课、练习课、习题讲评课也要有教案。5年内新教师不得用旧教案。老教师用旧教案必须得补充修改。

3．上课管理

上课是完成教学目标，保证教学质量的核心环节。教师上课的基本要求：严格按课表上课，未经教导处同意，不得随意调课，更不准随便缺课。上课不得迟到早退，不得中途离开教室，不得拖堂。教师在预备铃响时应站在教室门口，目视学生做好上课准备，同时清点学生人数，弄清学生缺席情况，对非正常缺席学生应及时报告学校教导处。上课开始和结束，师生应相互问候致礼。教学活动要紧扣教学目标，面向全体学生，对学习基础不同的学生体现不同层次要求，采用不同的教学方法，以适应他们的学习需求。反对满堂灌，倡导探究式、合作式、讨论式教学，强化师生互动、生生互动。课堂练习设计要典型精确，防止盲目多练、老师包办，真正做到精讲多练。上课教师需用普通话，语言精确、生动，声音响亮；板书清楚、布局合理、字迹工整。教态亲切、衣着得体。上课时关闭手机。教师不得中途离开教室，不得提前下课或拖堂。教师应尊重学生人格，严禁体罚和变相体罚、羞辱学生。不得把学生赶出教室，同时应严格要求学生遵守课堂纪律，课堂内发生的问题不能及时处理的，任课老师应在课后处理好。重视教学卫生，注意纠正学生坐、写姿势，随堂教师负责督促学生认真做好眼保健操。体育教师应在上课铃前2分钟到操场集合队伍。实验课、音乐课、美术课要确保师生准时到专用教室。活动课纳入课堂教学，活动形式要灵活多样，以学生活动为主，但教师不得离岗。

4．作业管理

作业布置和检查是学生巩固所学知识和教师反馈教学信息、改进教学的重要手段。布置作业要有明确的目的性和针对性，以利于巩固所学的知识。一般课堂作业难易程度以多数学生学习水平为基础，让大多数学生在课堂内能完成。课外作业可根据学生实际，因人而异分选做题与必做题，坚决杜绝惩罚性作业，随意作业，大量机械重复作业。小学一、二年级原则上不布置课外作业，三至五年级每天不超过1小时；初中生课外作业量每天不超过1.5小时；高中不超过2小时。

5. 实验管理

严格按照课程标准做好教学中的演示实验与学生分组实验，学生实验报告教师要及时批阅。认真做好初三、高三毕业班的物理、化学、生物等学科实验。学校要积极创造条件开放实验室，逐步培养学生自行设计实验的能力。学校要认真组织学生实验能力考核，并计入学生学业成绩。

6. 辅导管理

辅导要贯彻因材施教的原则，既要课内辅导，又要课外辅导，既要集体辅导又要个别辅导。集体辅导要有计划。认真分析所教班级学生的特点实施有针对性的辅导。个别辅导要特别关注困难学生与学有余力的学生。学困生辅导要有的放矢地查漏补缺；学有余力的学生可布置提高性作业，推荐课外补充读物。

7. 考试管理

各学科平时考核及月考可由备课组长教研组长负责。期中、期末考试由学校统一组织命题、组考、制卷、阅卷。试题难易度要适中，基本要求中等或较高难度之比为8∶1∶1。命题平均分期望值一般为小学85～90分，初中80～85分，高中70～75分。阅读实行流水阅卷，要严格按标准答案和评分标准批阅，坚决反对弄虚作假。认真上好考试后质量分析课，分析课应有教案，督促学生做好考后答题订正。考试后，教导处、备课组、任课老师都要认真做好质量分析，科学地进行数据统计，找出教学中的成绩与存在的问题，提出改进教学的工作意见，并逐级上报质量分析报告。教导处的分析报告应在全体教师大会上公布。学期期末成绩评定应按5∶3∶2进行，即期末考试成绩占50%，期中考试成绩30%，平时成绩（含小考、提问作业、实验及平时表现等）占20%。

二、高中美术特色班管理制度

为贯彻“适合教育”的办学理念，针对学校高中学生原有学力基础的特点，办好高中美术特色班意义重大。为巩固和发展美术教育成果，特拟定以下管理考核条例。

1. **课程管理**

学校教师应转变教学观念，增强课程执行力，提高对学校美术特色教学的认识，积极支持和配合美术课程的开设。以拓展型（或研究型）课程为载体，落实美术教育课程设置，高一年级第一学期2节/周、第二学期4节/周，高二年级4节/周，高三年级6节/周。编制校本美术教材，完善美术校本课程体系。参照学校课程管理的评价体系，建立美术教育评价指标。

2. **过程管理**

高中各年级组长、班主任积极参与美术特色班学生的组织管理。班主任协助培训班做好特色班学生的日常管理，加强学生的思想行为教育，随时进行家访，定期召开家长会，如遇学生有旷课、迟到、早退等现象，及时与家长联系。加强美术班教学质量管理，促进美术专业和学科成绩同步提高。建立美术培训班学员学习档案，全程跟踪学生文化学习和专业训练状况，科学地协调文化学习与专业训练的时间，有效克服学科成绩和专业成绩顾此失彼的现象，提高学生高校录取率。利用美术班办学的有利条件，班主任配合培训班实行封闭式管理，克服松散无序现象，加强安全教育，减少事故隐患。

3. **考核管理**

美术特色管理考核工作纳入学校教师考核评价体系，实行单项与整体相结合的奖励制度。每学期根据班级学生在美术班的参与率、巩固率、提高率及相关老师的实际表现，进行分项考核。

第五节　教学改革

一、教学方法改革

1. **“聪明学习，智慧教学”教学改革**

2008年，学校在上海市二期课改的大背景下，提出“聪明学习，智慧教学”的教学改革要求。新课程提出“以学生为本”的理念，呼唤从根本上改变学生被动的、接受式的学习方法，要学会主动地、探究性、创造性地学习。“聪明学习”理念的提出正是把研究视角定位在学生“学”的状态上，旨在“聪明地学，学成聪明”。所以“聪明学习，智慧教学”项目既是研究项目，也是实践项目，是二期课改校本实施的产物。这一项目2007年秋开始，2008年夏立项为市级课题，2011年夏结课题。2012年获上海市学校教学科研项目二等奖。而迄今仍在实践中。

“聪明学习，智慧教学”是一项以学生学习方式转变与教师教学行为改变为指向的综合性实践研究，其基本内涵有两个方面。一是聪明学习的内涵。学习有笨学与聪明学之别。笨学学得很累，负担重，效果却不好；而聪明学学得轻松，有兴趣，能获得高效。所谓聪明学习，第一就是指在很强烈的直接兴趣与内在动机驱动下的学习行为；第二是指能充分运用与把握学习策略，包括基本学习策略、支持性学习策略与元认知自我调节策略的学习行为；第三是指注重包括独立性、自主性、批判性、求异求同，发散聚合等思维品质的发展与成熟的学习行为。简单可概括为：具有深厚兴趣，把握学习策略，发展思维品质。二是智慧教学的内涵。学生的学习行为方式不是一个孤立的存在。聪明地学，必然涉及教师的教学智慧。没有科学的教学方法，聪明学习就很难实现。

“智慧教学”是立足于学生原有学力与认知水平，重视新旧知识联系，把握可教育时刻，有效促进学生发展的教学行为；善于激发学生兴趣，调动积极情绪，产生进一步学习强烈要求的教学行为；能充分利用课堂独立价值——公共空间，并在这空间里充分激发学生思维活动，展开思维过程，产生思维碰撞，师生相互心灵交流，生成新知的教学行为；能在教学过程中自觉地将教学活动本身作为认知对象，不断反思，不断改进与完善的教学行为。简单可概括为：知识的停靠点，情感的激发点，思维的展开点，行为的反思点。

聪明学习的实施包括创设“聪明学习”的教育环境，确立学生自主评价的机制，学习方法（学习理论基础）的传授与交流等，从课堂教学内到课堂教学外的学习的各种环节去实施。

智慧教学的实施包括智慧教学的气氛创设，智慧型教师的校本培养，良好的合作团队建设，与形成适合智慧型教师的评价机制等方面组织实施。两次区域内举行的大型活动，在奉贤区内产生积极影响，亦影响于学校全体学生与教师。

在“聪明学习，智慧教学”教学策略的指导下，在奉浦学校时的教学改革几乎涉及到教学的各个环节。特别是学生的预习、课内学习、课外练习与教师的备课、上课、作业布置各大环节。

2.“学习包”教学改革

所谓“学习包”，就是教师为帮助学生做好教学前的课前准备，而为学生提供的学习材料与思考的问题。有的"学习包"也包含了课后的练习材料。"学习包"项目的理论支持是源于教育家奥苏贝尔的"先行组织者"的教学策略。他认为这是能促进有意义学习的发生和保持的最有效策略。利用适当的引导性材料对当前所学新内容加以定向与引导。这类引导性材料与当前所学新内容之间在包容性、概括性和抽象性等方面应符合"认知同化理论"的要求，即便于建立新、旧知识之间的联系，从而能对新学习的内容起固定、吸收作用。这种引导性材料就称为"组织者"。由于这种组织者通常是在介绍当前学习内容之前用语言文字表述，用适当媒体呈现出来，目的是通过它们的先行表述或呈现帮助学习者确立有意义学习的心向。所以又被称为"先行组织者"。这种教学策略与学校提出的智慧教学原则的第一点"知识的停靠点"是完全一致的。为达到这一教学目的，学校自2008年起开始组织各学科各年级的教师编写"学习包"。

"学习包"工作由校长亲自拟定工作计划，在全体教职工大会上宣讲该项目的理论依据，工作的价值与意义，强调教师在付出辛勤劳动的同时，也将收获可喜的成果，强调项目是落实"智慧教学"的一部分，同时也是教师自身成长专业发展的需要。学校"学习包"工作将列入教师学期考核内容，作出成绩就及时给予奖励。

宣传动员之后是落实工作。学校在多次教研组长工作例会上，强调把此项工作落实到教研组的每学期的工作计划之内。

"学习包"教学自2008年5月到2010年5月，历时两年。由于全体教师的主动参与，特别是主要学科教师的主动参与，小学部编纂语、数、外3门学科5个年级计15份"学习包"。初中部完成语、数、外3门学科4个年级12份"学习包"及物理、化学3分"学习包"共15份。高中完成语、数、外、物理、化学、历史、地理、生物、政治9门学科3个年级21份"学习包"。全校共完成51份"学习包"。

3．课堂教学改进

2009年2月，学校在学期工作计划中提出《课堂教学改进计划》的项目任务，要求每位教师每学期完成《奉浦学校课程教学改进计划》所规定的任务。《奉浦学校课程教学改革计划》是在"聪明学习，智慧教学"教学策略指导下的一项具体任务。《计划》要求每位教师每学期从自己全学期中的备课教案内，抽选4个教案写改进计划。即在原教案的基础上写出改进的新教案，目的在于加强教师的反思精神。《改进计划》订成1个小册子，可用两学期。第一部分为个人的三年发展目标。第二部分为分析个人教学的优点与缺点。第三部分为改进教案。《改进计划》分发给每位教师，规定4个教案中必须有两份教案侧重于三维目标中思想情感价值观方面的内容。以加强德育在教学中的渗透。《改进计划》于每学期期末收交校长室，由校长与分管教学副校长分别对每位教师的改进教案作评价。记入考核的内容，由于领导的重视，这项工作获得教师高度重视与支持，在外力的作用下也产生一定的教师改进教案的内驱力。

为提高教师课堂教学的执行力，赋予课堂教学的生命力。推进《改进计划》工作，2009年9—10月，学校对教师的课堂教学现状作了1次全面的校本调研。共聘请教育局、督导室、教育学会、进修学院有关专家23人对全校教师进行听课、调研分析。调研对象涉及小学、初中、高中22门学科，77人次，发现大量存在于教学现场的鲜活的经验或问题。并作出了《加强校本课堂调研，促进课堂教学改进》的调研报告。报告分“教师在区内教学水平属向”“优势与不足”“发展建议”三方面作出书面分析，这项工作为《改进计划》工作的深化，产生积极的影响。

附：校本课堂调研报告（摘编）

加强校本课堂调研，促进课堂教学改”——校本课堂调研报告

一、想法

校本调研实际上是校本管理的一种载体，是学校内涵建设、自主发展的一种做法。

首先，它能弥补学校领导及管理部门处于第一线的教学实况不可能零距离接触，对教学现场不可能全程、全息掌握的缺陷。为真实了解常态下教师的教与学生的学究竟是什么状况提供依据，从而做出相对正确的判断与评价，提高管理的有效性。

其次，通过调查—评析—反馈—整改等环节有机整合，使每位教师在《校本课程调研》过程中能得到感悟、提高，实现“面向一线、崇尚实践、以评促改、以教定研、推进发展”的价值取向，从而推进学校、教师、学生的优质发展。

二、做法

聘请有关专家23人参与这次调研工作，其中有原教育局局长蒋辉藻、督导

室副主任李逢五、进修学院教研员及其他学校一些专家。调研对象共涉及到小学、初中、高中语数英等22门学科，77人次，除返聘老师外做到了听课对象全覆盖。听课时间主要分布在本学期四到七周。

课堂调研以学校“智慧教学”的理念为评价指南。听课形式为“推门课”，就是事先不与被听老师打招呼，以专家自行安排的时间来校听随堂课。除了听课，专家还关注学生课堂内的习得情况（许多专家当堂课结束后与学生进行了交流），查看备课、检查作业情况等。听课后，专家与所有教师一一作交流，提出他们的见解。与校方也作反馈，对突出问题校方马上与教研组和个人进行联系，及时提醒、解决。专家还就“教师在区内的教学水平属向”“这堂课的优势不足”“发展建议”三方面作书面分析。

三、调研情况分析

1．区内水平属向分析

表 7-5-1

等级	优	良	中上	中	中下	下
人数	5	21	13	25	9	4
百分率 %	6.4	27.2	16.8	32.4	11.68	5.1

教师的整体教学水平属向为上：中：下=2：3：1。

2．专家肯定方面

饱满的教学情感。教师教学很投入，有激情，感情饱满，也很风趣，有感染力，时时鼓励学生积极地学、主动地学，师生情感融洽，课堂气氛热烈、民主、和谐，学生被深深地吸引。

清晰的教学目标。根据学生的水平安排内容，目标清晰，内容集中，重点突出，教学要求明确，学生始终在明确、具体的教学目标引导下，展开有效教学。

环环紧扣教学过程。设计的各教学环节有层次，逻辑性强，有过渡，教学内容随着环节的深入使学生渐渐得到认知、体验、感悟，学生在教师的指导下有节奏地学习，学生学得自信，教师教得踏实。

“温故知新”把握教育时刻。教师在教学设计时充分关注学生已有的知识经验和认知水平，导入以旧引新，知识的呈现直接、简洁，从现有学生实际出发，通过“温故知新”有效地降低学生学习新知识的难度，符合学生的认知特点。

关注细节，提高成效。教学过程中，教师具有教学敏感性，能预设学生存在的错情，及时发现并反馈学生在学习活动中出现的问题，并采取相应措施。由于教师善于关注教学细节，因此教学难点化解巧妙，教学效果明显。

3．主要不足之处

课前准备、备课存在较大问题。77堂课反馈存在问题有20人次，占比例26%。有些在专家要求查看备课时拿不出备课，有些是备课与上课两张皮，专家说“上课的实际操作与备课有差距”“教师要认真研读教材，不仅做到本上有案，还要做到心中有案、有人”。更多的是备课马虎，没有认真地研究教材教法、研究学生。引用专家的一些话来说：“在备课环节上要多下些功夫，除了熟悉教材，还要研究怎样做，教学难点的处理不细致，也不科学。”“对教材内容不熟悉，只是表面理解，甚至讲课有错误，学校的智慧教学理念无法体现，建议老师在走进课堂时做充分准备。”“缺乏对教材的钻研和理解，缺乏对《课标》的认识与正确理解，上课表现出随意、不严谨，不利于学生良好学习习惯的养成，所举例不符合《课标》，也不符合学生的认知能力，课堂有效性差。”“对新教材的理解还没有初步框架，希认真备课、研究教材，确立每节课的主题、重点、难点，上课主次分明。”评讲试卷也要认真备课，一位专家说“由于课前准备不充分，试卷分析了，但针对问题没有安排相应配套的东西操练，导致同样的错误，学生今后还会重犯。”

缺少思维展开点。学校智慧教学的理念告诉我们要利用课堂这个空间，充分激发学生思维活动，展开思维过程，产生思维碰撞，师生相互心灵交流，形成教学高潮。然而从专家的评价来看，这方面的肯定很少，但有一定量的批评：“不能很好地引导学生做思维分析，喜欢按照自己预设的思路去教学，发散性思维的训练点拨都不到位。”“课堂教学沉闷，始终是教师一言堂，教师讲学生听，教师做学生模仿，学生是被动的，甚至不知道我在学什么做什么，不明白为什么这样做。”“许多可以形成思维的地方被老师忽略了，就事论事、就题论题，不举一反三，没有变式训练。”“知识呈现方式单一，学生思考时间太短，师生互动变为教师与学生之间的对话。”“教师课堂教学形式单一，比较注重结论教学，缺少学生思维过程的展示，给予学生自主学习、自主探索学习方法的时间与空间不够，太多教师包办。”

精讲多练，分层教学也是要引起重视的问题。“举例不妥当，问题设计太大，学生无法回答，有些简单的问题被老师复杂化，讲得太烦、太复杂，甚至讲不清，影响了学生听课情绪。”（以己昏昏，怎能使人昭昭）“概念的形成要考虑学生的认知规律和情感需要，要帮助学生梳理知识，以简练的语言、典型的例题突出重点、突破难点。”“你听懂了吗的意识强烈，我讲明白了吗的意识薄弱。”“课堂提问要注意分层，让各个层次的学生都有发展空间”“作业布置也要设计，要考虑各类学生能力，分层布置、分层评价。”

四、思考

此次调研，使我们从一个方面了解了目前学校师资大致情况，也比较具体地知道了每位教师课堂教学的实况，由于是“推门课”，随机性强，真实性也强（当然也不否定有偶然性）。

针对调研情况，我们思考如下：

1．师资队伍的建设仍是我校头等大事

“名校”“精品校”的实现愿景对师资提出很高要求，然而从这次调查情况来看，整体师资水平在区内只能算中等状态，优良率还低，优秀的更少，而中下水平占到了17%，这里有教师的能力问题，有青年教师多的问题，更有态度问题。首先还是要加强师德教育，最近总理向全国教师提出了“充满爱心、努力钻研、以身作则”三点希望，我们认为落实在行动上就是尽心尽职地备课、上课、批改作业、辅导学生，责任心有了，态度也上去了，工作质量问题自然而然也能解决了，建议加大师德考核力度。其次青年教师的培养仍要常抓不懈。本学期已经做了不少工作，如参加新教师的培训、青年骨干教师研训班，校内外的带教关系建立，与外校建立教研联动工作的牵线搭桥等。但还要在建立长效机制，落到实处，在有效性方面加大管理力度，另外培养青年教师的目标要清晰。这次调研中，专家已发现了几位可造之材，学校可以对这些老师重点培养，形成青年教师的骨干力量。目前在青年教师中起带头作用，不久挑起教学的大梁。

2．“智慧教学”的理念更要深入人心

我们感到学校“智慧教学”的理念，很代表现代二期课改的思想，教师们人手一份，但从此次听课的反应来看教师理解理念、实施理念的水平很不平衡。专家给的评语中甚至出现“学校的智慧教学理念无法体现”的评价。理念中四个方面的落实情况也不平衡。

所以要进一步加大宣传力度、学习力度。一是教研组的研讨课要围绕这个中心来进行，二是学校组织落实“智慧教学”的示范课活动，三是继续写好课堂改进计划，四是教师本人要加强反思。虽然备课强调要有三分之一的反思，但很多不得要领，有许多是后面加上去的。建议青年教师做“教海拾贝”工作。

2010年9月，为深化此项工作，在“智慧教学”基础上，鉴于师德与师能相辅相成关系的认识，学校提出“三带、四动、五生成”的课堂教学原则。所谓“三带”就是：爱心带进课堂、激情带进课堂、方法带进课堂；所谓“四动”就是：问题驱动、学生主动、教师引动、多元互动；所谓“五生成”就是：问题生成、情景生成、情感生成、能力生成、知识生成。

在这些课堂教学要点与课堂教学原则的引导下，学校教师加强同行间的教学研究与个人的教学反思，不断提升课堂教学的执行力。《课堂教师改进计划》这个项目实质是教师校本培育的舞台与契机。

4．“校本练习”教学改革

“校本练习”项目是教学环节中“作业”这一环节的重大改革，是继“预习”环节改革，校本“学习包”编制基础上，研制属于符合学校实际的练习体系的一项教改活动。

起因是作业过程、是知识习得的重要环节，但在片面追求升学率的影响下，市场上教辅材料，特别是练习册充塞于市，良莠不齐。而教师在布置作业的量与质上都比较随意。对所提供的作业资料基本上采用“拿来主义”的策略，缺乏系统性、针对性。盲目选择重复题型，在迂回于多本教辅材料中搞“题海战术”，再次，课外作业统一，缺乏个性化和层次性而造成优生“吃不饱”，学困生“吃不了”，多数学生“不爱吃”的局面。为了改变这种现状，学校于2010年8月提出“校本练习”的改革要求。

为开展此项改革，学校于开学初的全体教师大会上正式提出编撰“校本练习”的号召。强调有否“校本练习”是学校实力的一个重要标志。全校从小学到高中各学科各年级都要在两年时间内完成编撰工作。并提出编撰原则：即“本土性”“简约性”“高效性”“分层性”12字方针。“本土性”体现校本的特点，才能切合学校的实际；“简约性”才能减轻学生负担，提高学习的兴趣；“高效性”就是要求作业有质量，能落到各个知识点与相应的能力发展水平。

“分层性”就是保证优等生与后进生都能在自己的原有发展水平上获得进一步的发展。

嗣后，由分管教学副校长负责召开教研组长会议布置落实此项工作，作为各教研组近年内的一项重要任务。

在教研组长带领下，全校各学科教师结合自身的教学情况与学生实际水平，分别研制“校本练习”。有些教师还把这个编制过程列为自己的教学科研课题，如吴莹老师的“初中牛津英语‘校本练习优化’的探索与实践”、马欢权老师的“高中数学作业纠错环节中师生、生生互动的实践探索”等列入当年区级课题。

“校本练习”于2012年5月基本完成，包括12个年级22门学科诸多的资料，使奉浦学子从茫茫无际的“题海”中解救出来，取得良好的学习、巩固教学要求的目的，提高了教学质量，也培养锻炼教师，促进教师的专业成长。

二、教学组织形式改革

1．小学、初中“走班制”

根据“适合教育”的理念，鉴于人是具有独立性、自主性与差异性的本体的科学界定，于2006学年至2012学年，学校实施小学、初中“走班制”的教学组织形式改革的尝试。学校利用寄宿制的特点，在辅导环节上，实行“走班制”。即打破原班级编制，按学生各学科发展的不同水平，编入不同班级授课，实行走班。主要学科包括数学与英语。年级分布于一年级至八年级。对学业水平高，接受能力强的学生开设数学拓展思维训练课程、新世纪英语课程等，拓展思路，增加知识量；对学习能力差，学业基础薄弱的学生，在“走班”时主要解答学习中的困难，指导作业，落实双基（基础知识、基础能力）。这样操作，对不同教育对象施以不同的教育，收到实效，提高学校整体教学质量。

2．高中英语特长班

为体现民办学校可供选择性的存在价值，走高中教育国际化的发展途经，学校于2010年8月起试办高中外语特长班，共两届。后因举办国际高中班而停止。

高中英语特长班项目是教育部中国教育国际交流协会确定的教育改革试点项目，目的在于加强教育的国际交流，有利于培养外语人才。全国有多个城市搞试点，而上海地区未设班，学校得知信息后，由董事长亲率成员与国际教育交流协会领导接洽，于2010年4月获得批准的信函。2010年5月报区教育局同意，并接受区教育局行政主管部门领导与监督。

高中英语特长班的办班宗旨是为一部分初中毕业生打算在读完高中后出国作准备的。他们可参加高考，也可不参加高考，直接选送至澳大利亚、英国、美国学习。所以，课程内容除国内规定的高中课程外，增加英语雅思课程每周六节，相应删减物理、化学等选修课程。目标定位在高中毕业时达雅思5级。

为保证生源质量，经教育局批准，区招生办认可，决定在全区初中毕业生中参加市中考的学生中择优录取，计划单列报名号。

为吸引更多学生报名，上海民办奉浦学校决定与上海市奉贤中学（市实验性示范性高中）联合举办。学生高中三年在奉贤中学学习，享有市重点高中优质师资的待遇，教学由奉贤中学统一管理，教育工作由奉浦学校配置班主任与奉贤中学政教处共同管理。

收费标准为全年15000元，由奉贤区物价局核准后实施。

高中英语特长班，共举办两届，第一届自2010年进奉贤中学就读至2013年6月毕业。第二届自2011年9月进奉贤中学就读至2014年6月毕业。其中，部分在高中获得雅思5级成绩，更多学生仍选择国内高考。

2015年4月，上海帕丁顿双语学校国际交流体验中心开学，设上海交通大学教育集团示范教育基地和英语、美国、澳大利亚高中课程中心，提高学生学习质量。

A16

不出国也能“留学”

上海帕丁顿双语学校国际交流体验中心开学典礼仪式掠影

2016年9月6日《上海晨报》刊载上海帕丁顿双语学校国际交流中心开学典礼仪式的报道

3．**智优学生初中实验班**

2004年，上海民办奉浦学校初中毕业生仅27名，成绩在全区排序为23（共31所学校）。2005年初中毕业生80名，成绩跃居全区第8名，2006年毕业生82

名，成绩上升至全区第5名。最重要的原因是2003年区进修学校接管后，将其原校的民办初中班并入奉浦学校，共两届4个班，均为全区优秀生。此后初中生源又恢复为原校小学部升入的学生，成绩迅速下滑。为使学校初中部重振雄风，学校曾于2011年与2012年连续办过两届智优学生初中实验班。办智优初中学生实验班出于为异质学生提供公平教育，也为提升学校初中部教学质量，最终更是为学校的崛起所作的努力。

2011年初，学校争取到奉贤中学的支持，共商联合办班之事。5月签署《奉贤中学与奉浦学校建立资源联盟关系的协议》，决定在2011年7月中考后，在全区范围内招收本市户籍的智优学生。学校拟定并颁发“智优初中学生实验班招生简章》，其中规定凡本市户籍，奉贤地区的小学毕业生都可报名，择优录取，凡学习成绩在初中毕业时列入奉贤区200名之内的学生，免去初中4年民办学校所有的学费。奉贤中学对此班学生提供高中课程提前渗透的支持，并为此班开设《新概念英语》（奉贤中学教师执教），并开放图书馆。招生简章还规定奉贤中学对该班学生在今后招生中提供一切可提供的自主招生的便利。

奉浦学校还为该班拟定特殊的《课程计划》，除常规课程外增加高中实验课程，初中数学思维训练课程，语文现代汉语课程，新概念英语课程等，包括开拓视野的外出参观等活动。奉浦学校校长亲自执教《现代汉语》课程。

由于奉贤中学的声望与社会影响力，再则农村学校的学生可进入南桥地区学习的优惠条件，经两校共同严格选拔，2011年7月，共招收到40名智优学生。该班在历次区初中统考中，始终名列全区100多个平行班中1～5名的好成绩。

2012年7月，用同样方法又招生1个班，学生45名。该班在历次区初中统一考试中，成绩都名列前茅。

三、现代教学技术运用

1998年创办时，由协和教育集团投资，购入50台电脑，建立学校电脑房。当时，电脑房主要提供教学的需求。

2006年，学校为每名在岗教师配置联想笔记本电脑，主要供教师备课及查阅资料。就当时而言，这一项现代教学技术应用还是走在全区学校前列。

2007年夏，学校更新两个电脑房电脑计50台，全为联想最新型号。

2008年春，教育局为学校配置30个教室的多媒体设备，包括实物投影仪与数字投影设备与屏幕。

学校开展校本培训，让每名在岗教师都学会多媒体的操作要领，并将现代教学技术运用列入教师学期综合考核项目之中。至2008年夏，课堂多媒体的应用在全校普遍展开。

2008年，奉贤区教师进修学院建立区教育网站，民办奉浦学校建立网站，取消原百度实名网站，将自己网站纳入区教育网。

2009年春，教育局调入6套教室多媒体给奉浦学校，学校每个教室都配置多媒体设备。

2010年，高中物理实验需要D.P.S实验设置，先由学校购置2套，后在教育局大力支持下，在学校建立高中物理D.P.S实验室供全区使用，投资50余万元。学校的网络建设起动于2007年，请网络公司安装网络设置。分设内线与外线。

2010年，区教育局对各校网络建设进行验收，学校被评为网络建设合格校，网站内容获教育系统二等奖，发挥网络加强校校联系的功能。

2012年，为开设国际高中班，在董事会安排下，对学校网站进行一次全面提升。

四、教学质量监控

教学质量的监控包括形成性质量监控与结果性质量监控。

形成性质量监控包括听课评课、备课检查、作业检查、学生座谈会。结果性质量监控包括期中期末考试成绩的常模参照、月考等。

1. 形成性质量监控

领导听、评课。学校作为对教师教学执行力的常态监控与指导，领导的听课、评课是最有效的手段。学校规定校长、分管教学副校长，每学期听课不得少于30节。教导主任、副主任每学期听课不得少于40节。领导听课包括课堂教学的目标设计、过程实施、效果鉴定等方面对被听对象进行评价是认定教师教学水平属向的重要手段。而评课则是领导对教师听课后的反馈意见。小结课堂教学的得与失，则是对教师的指导，帮助教师成长，也利于教学质量的提升。领导听课、评课工作是教学质量监控的常规工作。质量监控措施在帕丁顿双语学校19年历程中，凡处质量上升时期均得到好的落实，反之则有所懈怠。

对教师上课的评价包括以下6个方面：(1) 教学目标：教学目标要求做到符合课程标准，符合学生实际。(2) 学习条件准备：教师精神状态良好，教态亲切自然，衣着得体，学习活动所需资源（相关知识、与社会生活联系、教学手段等级）充分。(3) 学生活动：学生参与活动态度积极，能提出有意义的问题或发表个人见解，课堂气氛活跃，生生互动，师生互动活跃、有序。(4) 教师指导：教师创设的问题情景具有启发性，能引起学生的兴趣；关注全体学生，及时进行有针对性的集体或个别辅导，采用多种评价方式，调控教学进程及随机情况。(5) 教学效果：教学任务中的问题基本解决，绝大多数学生能完成学习任务；有些学生能灵活解决学习中问题，及时发现新问题，学生能体验到学习成功的愉悦。(6) 教学基本功：准确运用普通话教学，教学语言简练、生动，富有感染力，板书规范，演示正确，合理使用教具及多媒体设备；能有效处理偶发事件。

备课检查。备课检查采用定期普查或不定期抽查两种方式，以保证全部教师认真做好教案，这是教育质量监督的重要手段。定期检查一般在期中考试与期末考试之前，期中考试前的检查由各教研组组长负责执行，检查结果要实行定性评价，查后在末一节处注明检查结果，并盖教导处专用章。期末考试由各教研组，将各位教师备课情况进行研究定性评价，评价结果计入教师学期综合考核的教学常规分值栏。不定期抽查是针对某些存在问题的教师进行监督检查，定期指令纠正。备课检查主要看教案撰写是否分课时；是否延用旧教案而不作修改；教案内容是否充实；教学设计是否恰当；重点、难点是否突出；有没有课后反思或改进意见。在每学期期末教学工作总结时，则公布检查结果，在大会上予以表扬或批评。

作业检查。作业检查的重点为作业布置适量、有效，作业批阅要及时，做到“有发必收，有收必批，有批必评，有评必改”。

作业检查分定期检查与不定期检查两种方式。定期检查为教研组每月检查1次作业布置与批改情况；教导处每学期期中与期末两次检查作业，并给予定性评价与等级，计入学期教师综合考核教学常规栏，并将结果公布。学校每学年组织不少于1次的各年级各学科优秀作业展评，以榜样带动好学风、好教风。

上海市奉贤区奉浦学校教师作业批改评价表

学科：__________ 任课教师：__________ 检查日期：__________

<table>
<tr><td rowspan="4">基本情况</td><td>年级（班级）</td><td>检查形式</td><td>作业形式</td><td>数量</td><td>批改率</td></tr>
<tr><td></td><td></td><td></td><td></td><td></td></tr>
<tr><td></td><td></td><td></td><td></td><td></td></tr>
<tr><td></td><td></td><td></td><td></td><td></td></tr>
<tr><td>评价内容</td><td>批改范围</td><td>作业量</td><td>作业设计</td><td>批改情况</td><td>学生情况</td></tr>
<tr><td rowspan="2">参考标准</td><td>优（9-10）</td><td>良（8-9）</td><td>中（6-8）</td><td colspan="2">差（6分以下）</td></tr>
<tr><td>作业内容符合教学进度；作业量、难易度适宜；作业设计针对性强、分层清晰；作业全部批改并及时、准确、规范，有面批；学生订正及时，书写工整，格式规范</td><td>作业内容符合教学进度；作业量、难易度较适宜；作业设计针对性较强、分层较清晰；作业全部批改并及时、准确、规范，有面批；学生订正较及时，书写较工整，格式较规范</td><td>作业内容基本符合教学进度；作业量、难易度不够适宜；作业设计针对性不够强、分层不够清晰；作业大部分批改，较及时、准确、规范，有面批；部分学生订正不及时，书写不够工整，格式不够规范</td><td colspan="2">作业内容不符合教学进度；作业量、难易度不适宜；作业设计针对性不强，无分层作业；作业部分批改；学生订正不及时，书写不工整，格式不规范</td></tr>
<tr><td>总体评价 得分</td><td></td><td></td><td></td><td colspan="2"></td></tr>
<tr><td>总体评价 等第</td><td></td><td></td><td></td><td colspan="2"></td></tr>
<tr><td>评价意见</td><td colspan="5"></td></tr>
</table>

评价人：__________

评价日期：__________

学生座谈会。教师教学行为的对象是学生，学生对教师的评价可能是最真实的。所以向学生搜集教师教学工作的信息，对总结教师的工作经验成绩，提出教师改进工作的建议方法是很直接的手段与方法。学校历年来重视从学生处反馈教师教学工作的第一手资料。这种做法起到了发挥良好的监督指导作用。

学生座谈会由教师自身召开座谈会与教导处定期召开座谈会两种。

学校要求教师每学期召开1～2次学生座谈会，听取学生对自身工作的评价，做好记录，提出改进的措施。

学校教导处每学期期中考试与期末考试前分别召开各年级的学生座谈会。参加座谈会的学生为各班优秀生、中等生、学困生的代表，鼓励他们大胆发言，作记录，会后反馈给各位教师。座谈会期间还要求学生根据调查表给各位任课教师各方面表现作等级评价。教导处将座谈会对各位教师的评价纳入教师学期综合评价的内容。

2. 结果性质量监控

成绩常模参照。由于学校的年级跨度大，每年级的平行班不会太多，有些时候1个年级的某门学科就由1名教师完成。为正确有效评价教师的教学效果，学校采用常模参照就是将其他学校的同一次考试成绩作为参照物，进行比较来确定本校教师教学效果的优劣的做法。如第一次考试为X=70分，比参照校低5分，而第二次考试X=70分，但与参照校比分数相同，那末仍可确定教师的教学效果提高5分是显著进步。这种比照有很强的说服力，也能为大部分教师所接受。2005年起，学校小学部先将奉贤实验小学作为对照校，后几年参与南桥地区10所小学的联合考试的成绩作为对照校。初中部先将实验中学作为对照校，后又参与南桥地区8所初中的联合考试，作为对照校。高中部先将奉贤中等专业学校的综合高中班作为对照校，后又参与区普通高中联合考试。

期中期末考试采用成绩常模参照考评对教师的工作产生很强的监督作用与激励作用，为学校教学质量的逐年提升发挥重要作用。

月考。由于实行常模参照，期中考试期末考试的试卷是由其他学校或教学机构教师命题，本校教师的命题机会就少。为给学校教师的命题机会，也为不间断地增加学生学习的动力，学校采用月考的方法，作为质量监督的手段。

月考一般每学期进行两次，由各教研组负责命题阅卷与质量分析。难度一般高于期中期末的水平，以帮助学生克服骄气，看到自己学习上的不足。各教研组汇总本组各年级的成绩，并分析试题题型、难度、效度、信度。教导处在各教研组分析的基础上，再进行全校性的综合分析，提出日后要改进的薄弱环节，并报校长室。

第八章　学生教育管理

上海帕丁顿双语学校始终重视学生的教育管理工作。学校设置政教处，并配备专职人员具体负责学生德育工作。19年间，学校坚持升国旗制度，先后组织学生开展“八荣八耻”“社会主义核心价值观”的教育，组织高一学生开展军事训练，举办“祖国宝岛台湾在我心中”千人签名和学先辈学先进唱红歌活动，进行爱国主义教育。采用文明礼仪教育、主题班会、养成教育、社会实践活动等方式，推动行为规范教育逐步深入，使学生从小学会做人，立身、处事，迈好人生第一步。

学校加强学生的学习、生活、卫生、安全等方面的管理，制订和不断完善学生教育管理的各项制度，不断探索与坚持家校结合管理模式，促进学生管理的制度化、规范化、科学化、社会化，保障学生身心健康，德智体全面发展。

第一节　道德素质教育

一、升旗仪式教育

1998年9月起，学校坚持举行每周一升中华人民共和国国旗、奏中华人民共和国国歌的仪式。并根据《中华人民共和国国旗法》的规定，制订协和学校升降国旗的10条具体规定，明确“中华人民共和国国旗是中华人民共和国的象征和标志，全校师生都应尊重和爱护国旗，维护国旗的尊严”“学校把升旗制度纳入常规管理，对学生参加升国旗的出勤、列队状况、精神面貌等进行考评，并作为评比文明班级

民办奉浦学校坚持举行升国旗仪式

的重要条件”。学校每周从优秀学生中挑选出护旗手、升旗手，并向全校公示。学校还将升旗程序作出细化要求（出旗；升旗；奏国歌；唱国歌；国旗下讲话），以此从小培养学生“国旗在我心中”“祖国在我心中”的爱国情怀。1998—2015年，上海帕丁顿双语学校校名曾几度更改，升国旗制度坚持不变。

二、荣辱观、核心价值观教育

2000年，学校根据各年级学生的接受程度，在学生中进行以爱国为核心内容的“八荣八耻”荣辱观教育，作为爱国主义教育的具体要求。2005年，针对学校出现的困难曲折，学校在师生中提出“校荣我荣、校耻我辱”的口号。全校1000余名师生迎难而上，改革奋进，逐步走出人心涣散、教育质量下降的困境。2006年，学校提出“根扎民族魂，学做现代人”的爱国教育思路，在教学大楼制作民族魂红墙、丝绸之路油画等弘扬民族文化的作品，把中国古文化与当代爱国主义教育相结合。2015年，帕丁顿双语学校在学生中进行社会主义核心价值观教育，把社会主义核心价值观（富强、民主、文明、和谐、自由、平等、公正、法治、爱国、敬业、诚信、友爱）的内容，运用张贴、宣讲、交流等方式在学生中学习落实，并作为学校讲德堂讲座的主要内容。学校重视爱国主义教育环境建设，在新教学楼走廊悬挂中华人民共和国国旗和世界各国国旗，教育引导学生热爱祖国、胸怀世界。学校利用中华民族传统节日，举办“梨花风起正清明”“圆圆月饼寄深情”“九九重阳浓

上海帕丁顿双语学校关于“八荣八耻”的宣传

2014年12月，民办奉浦学校举办践行社会主义核心价值观宣传讲座

浓孝心”活动，弘扬中华民族优良美德。

三、国防教育

1998年9月起，学校把高一学生中开展军训作为必修课，把国防教育与爱国主义教育相结合。学生军训列入政教处的岗位职责。学生军训，除训练军队队列、军容风纪、培养学生组织纪律性外，把政治训练作为军训重要内容。政治训练内容以国防教育为主，回顾中国近代曾沦为半殖民地史实，了解中国人民在反侵略战争中前仆后继、英勇不屈的斗争精神，理解“落后要挨打”的真理，激励学生培养基本的军事知识与技能，树立正确的国防观和富国必须强兵，爱国必须强军的思想，为今后适龄应征参军保家卫国打下思想基础。1998—2016年，参加必修课军训的高一学生1300余人，多次被评为军训先进连队，不少高中学生参加征兵体检。

民办奉浦学校组织学生军训，开展国防教育

四、爱台湾千人签名活动

2000年3月10日，学校结合爱国主义教育，根据小学、初中、高中学生的认知程度，上好讲祖国历史、讲台湾历史之课，让学生坚定台湾是中华人民共和国不可分割的一部分的信念。举办“祖国宝岛台湾在我心中”的千人签名活动，全校29个班级1033名学生与全校90余名教职员工在横幅布上签下各自姓名。

五、学先辈学先进唱红歌活动

1998年9月至2016年，学校举办的学先辈唱红歌活动持续不断，先后举办的13届学校文化艺术节和一年一度的元旦联欢晚会以及中国共产党的“七一”建党纪念日、国庆节、“五四”青年节、“六一”儿童节的庆典活动，歌颂党、歌颂祖国，学先辈、唱红歌成为主要内容。2008年，学校自编包括10多篇爱国主义故事的《学生成长指导手册》，全校学生人手1份，作为课外教育读物。2009年5月，民办奉浦学校专门举办由全校师生参加的“红五月歌会”活动，全校1198名小学、初中、高中学生分别参加班级、年级及全校歌会活动。演唱抗日战争、解放战争及解放以后尤其是改革开放以来的红歌50余首。2016年，学校举办元旦文艺联欢会，歌颂党和祖国的红歌等节目占全部节目三分之一。每年清明节，学校坚持组织学生去爱国主义教育基地烈士陵园、东方绿舟等开展活动，举办学习先烈征文比赛。2012年98篇征文入选优秀征文。学校还组织学习先进人物先进事迹，发扬上海市劳动模范王新其热衷于教育事业回报社会、不忘初心、坚定前行，上海市劳动模范王益权老师无偿捐献干细胞的奉献精神。

第二节 行为规范教育

一、文明礼仪教育

1998年9月，学校根据学生来自全国各地，接受教育程度不同，家庭背景差异等特点，制订学生素质基本要求10条（公——以公为先，爱国报国；义——见利思义，不失人格；仁——团体协作，助人为乐；信——真诚无妄，守信知报；礼——尊师敬长，谦恭礼让；律——严于律己，守法遵纪；智——追求真知，勤奋学习；美——注重仪表，情趣高尚；毅——力行坚毅，自强自立；俭——热爱劳动，戒奢尚俭）。2001年，组织初中年级学生收集文明礼仪的名人名言活动，编写校园文明礼仪歌曲，开展“行为规范知多少”德育知识竞赛，每月由班主任、全班同学评选1名表现优秀的同学和1名进步显著的同学为文明礼仪标兵，激励学生讲文明、讲礼仪、同进步。2005年，成立以班委干部组成的文明礼仪评价小组，建立和完善学生文明礼仪电子档案和自我评价制度，文明礼仪作为升学、评优、推优的依据之一。

民办奉浦学校“感动奉浦校园十大小贤人”事迹介绍栏

学校结合世界禁毒日、艾滋病防治日，举办“珍爱生命，远离毒品”“我们在成长”“女学生自重自爱”等专题教育，在“世界环境日”“世界水日”组织学生参加环保“绿箱子”“环保时装表演”“节约水资源”等活动，培养文明礼仪好习惯。2005年，学校在初中、高中学生中开展“熟、知、背”名人名言100条，寻找身边的礼仪榜样活动，各班级、年级分别设礼仪荣誉栏，每周每月有表扬。2006年，学校顾问——上海世界外国语小学校长王一平为学生专门讲授“让学生学会做人”的报告，推动文明礼仪教育。2008年5月，结合“上海市迎世博600天行动计划”，奉浦学校制订“迎世博盛会，做礼仪少年”活动方案，开展“垃圾不落地，校园更美丽”签名活动，全校1150多名学生在“我承诺”单上签名。2010年，学校制订《小学生日常行为规范》20条，把4个尊敬（尊敬国旗国徽，尊敬父母，尊敬老师，尊老爱幼）放在行为规范之首。同时制订《中学生日常行为规范》5个方面（自尊自爱、注重仪表；诚实守信、礼貌待人；遵规守纪、勤奋学习；勤劳俭朴、孝敬父母；严于律己、遵守公德）40条。至2015年，在文明礼仪荣誉栏上千余人次得到表扬。

二、主题班会

1998年9月起，学校运用主题班会活动，加强学生的行为规范教育，小学部学生从一年级至五年级分别举办“我上学了”“自己的事情自己做”“我长大了”“10岁烛光晚会”“我要毕业了”系列主题班会。班会主题分别为“14岁生日晚会”“我最敬佩的人”“20年后的我——我的理想是什么”“认识自我，走向成功—成功教育”；高中学生则推出“我上高中了”“17岁的思索”“面临挑战，我准备好了”等主题，对不同学年的学生提出不同的学习目标与要求，教育学生一步一个脚印成长。各年级结合主题班会开展“温馨教室”活动，注重学习环境布置、制订班级公约、开展“我心中好老师”征文演讲，进行“行为规范示范班”“流动红旗”评比，营造良好的学习氛围。

三、学生养成教育

1998年9月，学校参照兄弟学校的经验制订校规，培育有利学生健康成长的校风。学校先后制订《小学生守则》《小学生日常行为规范》《中学生守则》《学生一日守则》，为学生履行校规促进良好校风的形成产生导向作用。2003年起，全校以班级为单位，开展"让每个学生都有进步"活动，及时发现学生遵守校规的亮点予以表扬、鼓励，对特殊学生形成互帮互学共同进步的校风。2006年起，学校以班级为单位，开展学生好习惯培养活动，制订做人（自尊自强、诚实可信、认真负责），做事（遵规守则、讲究效率、友善合作），学习（主动勤奋、独立思考、学用结合）3个方面养成标准，并对小学、初中、高中学生做人做事好习惯考评提出21条不同要求。对遵守校规校风好的学生，通过校刊、广播、学校网站等方式进行宣传。2010年，学校开展"好习惯"养成教育活动，把"好习惯班班比""好习惯月月见""好习惯人人爱"列为行为规范教育的平台。2012年，学校把历年形成并修改的校规、校风标准汇编装订成册，下发各年级贯彻执行。2015年，帕丁顿双语学校进一步细化校规校纪教育，每个班级制订各自的管理教育制度，推动学生德、智、体、美全面发展。2016年，学校进一步规范学生养成教育，教学成绩同步提高，高考学生录取率93%。

开展小学生争章活动。2010年，奉浦学校针对小学生多为独生子女，家庭呵护备至而养成的娇惯特点，开展行为规范争章活动。根据小学生不同年级进行分类争章安排：一年级学生设必修的自理章（自己的事情自己做，自己的学习自己管，自己的责任自己担），好朋友章（交好朋友，为小朋友做好事，自制贺卡送好朋友），苗苗章（争当儿童团员）；二年级必修孝敬章（孝敬父母，给父母做能做的事，知父母生日），星星火炬章，做到六知（知队名、知红领巾、知队旗、知队礼、知呼号、知宣誓内容），六会（会戴红领巾、会行礼、会呼号、会队歌、会写入队申请、会宣誓），五要（要学一位英勇少年、要养成好习惯、要为班级做一件好事、要改正一个缺点、要争取一点进步），四自（自己的活动自己搞、自己的事情自己做、自己的伙伴自己帮、自己的进步自己争）；三年级学生必修手拉手章（关心同学手拉手），自锻章（坚持锻炼，强健身体），礼仪章（学礼仪争做文明好少年）；四年级学生必

上海帕丁顿双语学校投资举办方——上海申生投资有限公司董事长王新其（右一）对学生进行成长教育

修家务章（学做家务，做小帮手），环保章（保护环境尽责任，做绿色小卫士）；五年级学生必修自动章（自主自动学做小主人），信息章（知天下事，做小灵通），并分别设选修章。通过争章活动，小学生普遍达到自学、自理、自护、自强、自律。学校成立社团联合会，下设学生科学活动中心，学生艺术中心，青少年体育俱乐部。中心下设学生社团，有小学生合唱团、文学社、书法社、美术社、计算机社、舞蹈社、机器人社、植物栽培社、科技制作社、足球社、篮球社、棋牌社、英语社、数学社、时事社、武术社、鼓号队、课本剧社等，丰富课外活动内容。

四、学生生活准则教育

学校坚持开展学生生活准则的教育活动，注重学生生活实践教育。通过教育活动，引导学生明理善行，礼貌待人，爱护公物，爱护环境，刻苦学习，不怕困难，勤俭节约。在日常生活中学会做人、学会理解、学会善待自然。以“自尊自爱、注重仪表、诚实守信、礼貌待人、遵纪守法、勤奋学习、勤劳俭朴、孝敬父母、严于律己、遵守公德”的生活准则，强化学生的德育教育，促使学校“校风、教风、学风”建设上新台阶。增强学生的道德观念，区别善恶的能力和道德选择与行为评价能力。通过开展学生准则教育活动，加强规范了学生的思想道德建设，也推动了学校精神文明建设，形成“文明、诚信、守纪、和谐”的育人氛围，使学生成为诚实、守信、礼貌待人和身心和谐发展的文明学生。学校在2010年被评为区“行为规范”三星级学校。

小学生日常行为规范　（三字歌）

升国旗 要敬礼 唱国歌 要肃立
尊长辈 爱幼小 孝父母 遵教导
会使用 文明语 遇外宾 要知礼
帮残疾 乐助人 不打架 不骂人
要诚实 不说谎 损公物 要赔偿
捡东西 要上交 借东西 要归还
不挑吃 不挑穿 惜粮物 节水电
爱整洁 常洗澡 勤刷牙 习惯好
不旷课 不迟到 对老师 有礼貌
上课时 用品齐 敢发言 多动脑
做作业 写工整 按时完 卷面净
广播操 要做好 炼身体 争达标
保视力 做眼操 三个一 要做到
集合时 快静齐 做值日 要积极

上海民办奉浦学校制订的小学生日常行为规范

第三节　特色教育

一、“温馨教室”建设

1998年，学校创办以来，坚持实施班级经营与发展的“二三四三”的温馨教室建设规划，即小低年级的二年规划，小高年级的三年规划，初中部的四年规划和高中部的三年规划，并制定每学期的阶段计划，注重计划和规划相结合，构建校园人文环境。开展“温馨教室”建设系列活动，成为增进班级团队的凝聚力、竞争力，促进学生行为规范，构建和谐校园的有效载体。学校注重物化环境布置，包括反映班级文化建设核心思想的标语口号、班级公约、奖惩制度，设置宣传板报、图书角等。结合师德建设，开展和谐师生教育活动周，如开展“我心中的好老师”征文，演讲比赛等。

“温馨教室”建设实施各班级团队考核，并采用每周1次的值周点评，值周班长就1周各班行规情况，在周二升旗仪式时作综述，表扬先进，鞭策后进，而后进行每月1次“行为示范班”流动红旗的评选。评选结果挂学校德育天地之“行规示范班”栏目。

二、“果行懿德”德育校本教育

2005年始，学校以“‘民族魂·现代人’竞争合作团队建设实践研究课题”为引领，以校训“果行懿德”为内涵，编辑德育校本教育教材。根据学段不同，汇编小学部、初中部、高中部3套德育校本教材。教材围绕立身、处世、为人、处事4方面展开，设置17个子目标，包含道德行为和自主意识范畴，从中华美德和现代人格要素的视角，审定德育教育，民族精神教育的具体目标，分别以格言、名人名言、小故事等，有针对性地对学生进行道德教育。

学校制订《“民族魂·现代人”德育目标操作，评价方案》，提出教师以“全员育人”的理念，通过课堂基础学科教学，对学生进行“两纲”（生命教育为纲、爱国主义教育为纲）教育。在教学中，将“知识与技能”“过程与方法”“情感态度与价值观”等德育教育目标和内容，落实在备课、听课、评课等各个环节，采用灵活多样的教学方法，让学生在潜移默化中受到感染和启迪，达到“润物细无声”的境地，收到事半功倍的教育效果。

三、绿色环保教育

学校是传播文化的特定学习场所。1998年，学校开办后重视学生知识的获得、价值观行为的养成。校园环境对学生潜移默化的影响是巨大的。通过校园的环境、生活和管理，传递可持续发展的思想。学生通过了解校园环境问题产生和改善，理解人与环境的关系，提升环保素养。学校在2000年组织的“绿箱子”活动，学生参与，教师指导，曾得到区环保部门的好评。学校组织学生参加“环保时装园”活动，倡导低碳、绿色环保生活，了解人与自然和谐生存。学生参与学校节约水资源、节约用电等科技小创作、小发明，获各类等第奖项。2009年，由区教育局与环保部门根据国家对学校的“绿色校园评价指标”的验收，学校获“奉贤区绿色学校”称号。

四、学困生教育

这是学校贯彻党的教育方针中需要特别加强的工作，面向全校学生，让每一个学生都有进步，始终贯彻在学生教育管理中。学校特别制定学困生转化的具体帮教措施。校党支部发动全校党员教师认养1～2名特困生，引导干部、年级组长、各课组长等都与学习困难学生签下教养协议，从思想上、学习上、生活上全面关心这类学生。对学困生增加感情投资，用爱心哺育他们，用耐心教导他们。及时抓住学困生的闪光点，鼓励他们进步，采取倾斜政策，偏爱厚爱学困生。根据这类学生的特点“一把钥匙开一把锁”，帮教老师与班主任共同家庭访问，建立“学困生转化档案”，目标明确，责任到人，年终进行专项考核。根据学生转化情况进行考核表彰，真正“让每一个学生都有进步”落到实处。

五、心理健康教育

学校重视学生的心理健康教育，提出“认识自我，纳悦自我，学会交往，友谊长存，快乐学习，充满自信”24字的心理健康标准。在执行标准的过程中体验快乐，做情绪的主人，养成爱心无限、乐于奉献的思想修为。学校专门配备心理学教师，开设心理讲座，建有心理辅导室、谈心活动室，帮助学生纠正学习障碍、矫正行为偏差、开发潜力、培养特长、提高素质。心理教师传授适当的技能来纠正问题学生的行为，帮助学生走出困境。正确认识自己、评价自我、完善自我。通过心理教师的专业指导，学生学会悦纳自己、与人分享。学校德育处常年开展心理辅导示范课，多次受到专家的好评。2010年学校被评为“奉贤区心理教育健康学校”。

第四节 社会实践活动

一、参观学习交流

1998年10月，学校组织全校学生千余名由老师带领参观上海植物园、上海万人体育馆，并观摩在上海举办的第八届世界中学生运动会。通过考察参观访问，让学生从上海变化看中国，培养爱国爱家乡的思想。1999年4月，学校举办“小眼睛看大上海”社会考察学习活动，先后参观东方明珠塔、上海大剧院、上海浦东金桥出口加工区、浦东新区孙桥现代农业园区，亲身感受国家改革开放的窗口——上海的发展成就。2007年，在“特奥会”期间，学校组织学生与驻奉浦的特奥运动员举行联欢活动。2008年暑假，学校举办“奥运今夏数我最行”学生干部技能拓展培训，“手牵手心连心，迎奥运共成长”暑期主题夏令营，“遨游书海，快乐成长”读书活动，“塔尔社”社团的“巴黎圣母院”获奉贤区一等奖，学校团委获优秀组织奖。是年10月，学校组织100余名学生组成武术队，为参加北京世界特奥会的各国运动员进行武术表演，展示中国武术魅力。2009年，学校组织6～8年级学生收集我国首次载人飞行圆满成功的有关资料与为中国航天事业做出巨大贡献的科学家的事迹，开展“航天精神伴我行”演讲比赛，举办“航天给奉贤插上翅膀”科幻画比赛，“航天模型制作”“登月球设计”“航天器设计制作”活动，进行“明日科技之星”评选，增强学生科技创新意识。2010年，学校组织学生干部50余人去上海世博会展示中心参观，每名学生干部写下自己对世博的感慨留言。每年寒暑假，学校都要求学生积极参加家务劳动与“在家我是小主人”“环线带我访家乡”“我做一天居委干部”“文明出行始于足下”社会实践活动。2013年，学校组织初中年级300名学生，分成30个学生小队，与全国30个省、市、自治区挂钩，一对一的收集各省市自治区地理、自然、文化、风俗与56个民族的服饰，各民族特色节日资料上百件，达到不出上海看全国的社会实践活动的目的。学校还先后组织学生与来校访问学习的德国、菲律宾学生进行文化艺术等方面的交流，增进中外学生的友谊。学校对学生每年社会实践活动进行针对性的安排：小学部必修课程：一二年级春秋游各1天；三年级民防自护体验2天，秋游1天，参观当地高科技企业1次；四、五年级春游或秋游1次，学军学农3天，参观高科技企业1次。初中部必修课程，优秀剧目和电影观摩4

民办奉浦学校组织学生参加学农等社会实践活动

次，春秋游2天。其中，初二学生民防救护体验3天。高中部必修课程，新生暑期军训7天，东方绿舟军训3天，春游或秋游1天，农村社会实践10天，高考后社会考察3～5天。学校还组织各年级学生的教育基地活动，雏鹰假日小队活动，校内公益劳动，社会公益活动，考察了解社会等选修课，增加学生社会知识面。

二、爱心奉献活动

自1998年9月，学校创办后的19年中，学校发动全校师生坚持每年参加“蓝天下的至爱”向红十字会捐款活动，还先后两次发动全校学生向西渡小学、奉浦学校患病困难学生的爱心奉献捐款活动。2008年，四川汶川地震发生后，学校共青团、学生会、少先队发动全校学生以个人或班级的名义向灾区同龄人写1封慰问信，鼓励灾区同龄人树立战胜困难的信心与决心。学校“绿箱子社团“等参加环境保护义务活动，组织青少年志愿服务队慰问孤独老人，为他们送上温暖。2012年，学校还组织学生向父母写1封信的活动，弘扬孝敬长辈的民俗传统。许多学生在“我心中的好老师”征文中纷纷参加活动，向老师抒发尊敬之情。

第五节　学生管理

上海帕丁顿双语学校为加强学校管理和学生管理，先后制订和修改完善9个方面150多项规章制度，为学校各方面工作起到推动和保障作用。本节就学生管理的有关制度作简要阐述。

一、管理制度

1. 日常管理制度

帕丁顿双语学校日常管理制度主要有“小学生日常行为规范”，是根据国家正式颁发的《小学生守则》制定，共设20条，目的是加强对小学生的文明礼貌教育和行为训练。学校还为小学生日常行为规范教育编写三字歌，促使小学生从小养成良好的行为习惯。2010年，“中学生日常行为规范”是根据中学生的成长特点制订，共设5个方面（自尊自爱、注重仪表；诚实守信、礼貌待人；遵规守纪、勤奋学习；勤劳俭朴、孝敬父母；严于律己、遵守公德）共40条，规定的内容体现学校在社会变革和发展中对中学生提出的新要求，有利于学习进步与健康成长。“学生一日常规”是对学生每天学习生活的具体安排，分为进校、早操、上课、作业常规、自修课、课间眼保健操、课外活动、放学、晚自修10个方面58条，对学生一天学习作规律性安排，促进学生学习有序进行。

学生文明礼仪要求

一、礼貌用语

1. 与人交谈（特别是长者），对别人表示尊敬，就用尊称“您”，对长辈、老人应称“老伯伯”“老太太”等。忌语“老头子”“老太婆”等或直呼其名；

2. 当你要求别人帮助时，应使用商量的、表示客气的词语“请”、“劳驾”等。忌语：“喂”、“哎”等。

3. 当别人帮助了自己、方便了自己时要用道谢的词语：“谢谢”或“多谢了”。忌：无动于衷。

4. 当自己增添了别人麻烦或妨碍了别人时，要主动说“对不起”或“请原谅”。忌：强词夺理。

5. 当别人不小心妨碍了你或你帮助了别人而受到感谢时，要说“没关系”、“不要紧”或“别客气”。忌：冷若冰霜。

6. 早晨或路上见面时，要问候“您早”或“您好”；相聚分别时说声“再见”。忌：不打招呼，懒于开口；转过头绕着走或装做没看见。

二、尊敬师长礼仪

7. 尊重老师的劳动，上课专心听讲，上好每一堂课。

8. 在路上遇见老师，要主动向老师问好。

9. 进出门口、上下楼梯，遇到老师，要让老师先走。

10. 要虚心听从师长教导，不顶撞，不强词夺理；对老师有意见要用正确方式善意提出，不在背后乱发议论，不在背后叫老师名字，更不能给老师取绰号。

11. 认真对待老师的批改，不得随意涂改老师的评语或分数；认真订正做错的作业；发现发现老师批改错误，应主动或诚恳地与老师交换意见。

12. 尊敬学校的全体教职工，尊敬自己小学时代、初中时代的老师。

三、同学之间礼仪

13. 同学之间相互要以利他主义、尊重别人为原则。

14. 同学之间相互尊重，不可伤害别人的自尊心，特别是不能嘲笑同学的失败或生理上的缺陷。

15. 同学之间应和睦相处，不吵骂、不打架、不侮辱人格，不取不叫绰号。

16. 早晨到校遇到同学要相互问早、问好；进入课堂，抹自己课桌椅时，不要忘记给邻座揩一揩。

17. 同学在做练习时，不干扰、不捣乱，不在走廊上奔跑，不大声喧哗，保持宁静的学习环境。

18. 当自己在学习中碰到困难向别人请教时，态度要诚恳，发问时要说“请”、“麻烦”等词儿。

民办奉浦学校制订的“学生文明礼仪要求”

2. 住校学生常规

上海帕丁顿双语学校生源除来自奉贤地区外，50%左右来自全国各地在奉就业人员的子女，其中要求住校的学生比较多，而且涉及到小学到高中年级的男女学生。为满足住校学生需求，1998—2000年，先后建学生宿舍楼3幢万余平方米。为加强住校生管理，学校学习兄弟学校住校生管理经验，制订完善帕丁顿双语学校住校生常规。住校学生常规主要分为“学生宿舍内务、卫生管理制度”“学生宿舍安全管理制度”。在学生宿舍内务、卫生管理中，每间寝室设寝长1名，负责日常工作。明确规定建立轮流的值日生制度，每个宿舍设寝长，负责全寝室工作。同时对每名学生提出5点要求。在学生宿舍安全管理中，作出以安全保卫为重点的10条规定，保证学生宿舍整洁、卫生、安全。

3．**学生请假、接送制度**

学生请假制度是保证学校正常放学秩序，营造良好的育人环境，顾及学生的特殊需要，根据兄弟学校的经验而制订。学生请假制度分为9条，规范学生有事请假的规定。同时对住校学生周末请假作出4条规定，保证住校学生离校回家安全。

4．**初中毕业生推优制度**

2011年，学校根据奉贤区教育局"关于认真做好奉贤区2011年推荐优秀应届毕业生进入市实验性、示范性中职校国家级示范专业就读工作的通知"精神，学校建立推优工作领导小组，制订推优具体方案，通过向全校初三学生集中宣讲、班级评议推荐、政教处协同年级组召开学生和教师座谈会评议，报学校形成推荐决议，在校园网上张榜公示，体现公正公开的要求。2011—2015年全校初中毕业推优学生10余名。

5．**三好学生、优秀学生干部评选公示制度**

对三好（思想品德好、学习好、身体好）学生，优秀学生干部（德才兼备、品学兼优、具备三好学生的各项条件；热爱为同学和他人服务，有一定的组织能力，骨干作用强，在师生中有较高的威信，积极参加学校教育改革和各项集体活动，主动配合老师开展管理工作，语言表达能力强，善于调动学生积极性，在学校和班级工作中大胆创新，成绩突出）的评选，实行学期中初评学年末总评，三好学生控制在班级人数10%以内，优秀学生干部每班1人。1998—2015学年，全校评出三好学生1800余名，优秀学生干部500余名。

6．**贫困学生帮扶制度**

1998年9月，学校根据上级有关政策和上海市教育委员会规定，制订《贫困学生申请补助条件试行办法》，列出贫困学生申请补助的6个条件（国家法令规定的抚恤对象；市（区）劳动部门登记在册困难职工、社会救济，优抚对象子女，确认遇特殊灾害（事故）家庭、父母享受最低生活保障金、因病因故困难家庭的子女），学校对申请困难补助的学生，按程序办理审批手续。学校关心弱势学生，建立弱势学生档案，分门别类对症帮助。学校党政领导与共产党员与弱势学生落实结对工作。2013年有3名因家庭困难而面临失学的高中学生帮助完成高中学业。

7．学生心理咨询制度

健全学生心理咨询制度，建立以班主任和专、兼职心理辅导老师为骨干的心理咨询队伍。提出心理咨询必须遵循的原则，规定心理工作者的职责及保密制度。为学生提供心理健康服务。

8．违纪学生处分制度

对学生的处分坚持以思想教育为主、行政处分为辅的方针，欢迎学生改正错误。对受校纪处分不服，对教师教学中不符《中华人民共和国教师法》规定等事项，学生可以申诉，学校必须调查处理，保障学生合法权利、权益。

二、管理工作

1．值班员制度

1998年9月，学校开始实行学校领导值班制度，制订学校领导值日细则5项7点要求。学校领导值日为值班工作起到表率与示范。2005年学校建立集值勤管理、劳动服务、文明示范于一体的值班周制度，培养学生的劳动观念、集体主义观念，实行自我服务、自我管理。值周班人员由学生骨干组成，主要职能是参与对全校学生日常行为规范的管理。学校明确值周班的培训、岗位、着装、纪律、劳动、安全、评价、示范的具体要求，每学期展开“优秀值周班”“优秀值周班长”评选工作，推动值周班各项工作有序进行。

2．学生宿舍管理员（寝长）

1998年9月，学校建立专（兼）职的学生宿舍管理员。学生宿舍管理员由热爱学生工作认真、品行端正、身体健康、善于管理的中年人员组成，经过学校培训上岗，与学校签订劳动合同，确保合法权益。学生宿舍管理员每年由学校进行考核，实行择优组建，保持队伍稳定性，有利管理水平的提高。2016年，全校有学生宿舍管理员22名。学生宿舍实行寝长制度，在同寝室的学生中推选产生。寝长负责团结帮助同学搞好寝室内务、卫生、安全、起居作息等工作。学校组织寝室开展流动红旗评比活动。

3．学生自我管理组织

1998年年末，学校建立共青团、学生会、少先队等群众性的组织。2003年起，陆续组建学生自愿参加的兴趣文化社团，在组织同学实行自我教育管理方面发挥积极作用。

4. 家校联合管理

1998年9月，学校建立家长学校，建立教师家访制度，做好家访记录。学校以班级为单位定期召开学生家长会议，通报学生在校学习生活情况，让学生家长及时了解掌握子女表现，配合学校加强教育管理。在每学年寒暑假期间，开展返校日活动，开展假期学生自我评价与社会评价活动，培训学生自我管理的自觉性，参与社会义务活动的主动性。2010年寒假，学校向每个学生家长发告学生家长书，提示家长关心学生假期生活。2012年暑假，学校开设网络在线调查平台，制作"奉浦学校学生暑假生活在线调查"等3张表，规定学生每半个月上网登录，教师及时掌握活动动态予以健康指导。

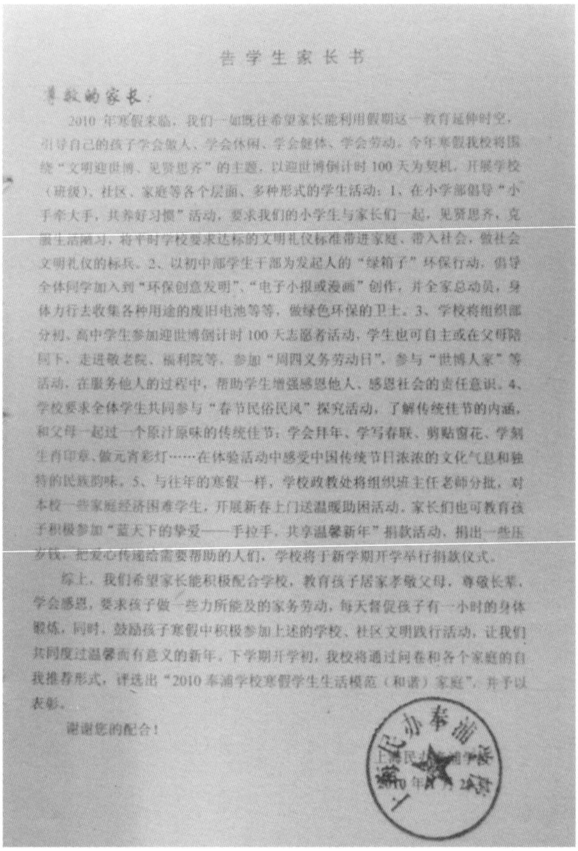
告学生家长书

尊敬的家长：

2010年寒假来临，我们一如既往希望家长能利用假期这一教育延伸时空，引导自己的孩子学会做人、学会休闲、学会健体、学会劳动。今年寒假我校将围绕"文明迎世博、见贤思齐"的主题，以迎世博倒计时100天为契机，开展学校（班级）、社区、家庭等各个层面、多种形式的学生活动：1、在小学部倡导"小手牵大手，共养好习惯"活动，要求我们的小学生与家长们一起，见贤思齐，克服生活陋习，将平时学校要求达标的文明礼仪标准带进家庭、带入社会，做社会文明礼仪的标兵。2、以初中部学生干部为发起人的"绿箱子"环保行动，倡导全体同学加入到"环保创意发明"、"电子小报或漫画"创作，并全家总动员，身体力行去收集各种用途的废旧电池等等，做绿色环保的卫士。3、学校将组织部分初、高中学生参加迎世博倒计时100天志愿者活动，学生也可自主或在父母陪同下，走进敬老院、福利院等，参加"周四义务劳动日"，参与"世博人家"等活动，在服务他人的过程中，帮助学生增强感恩他人、感恩社会的责任意识。4、学校要求全体学生共同参与"春节民俗民风"探究活动，了解传统佳节的内涵，和父母一起过一个原汁原味的传统佳节：学会拜年、学写春联、剪贴窗花、学刻生肖印章、做元宵彩灯……在体验活动中感受中国传统节日浓浓的文化气息和独特的民族韵味。5、与往年的寒假一样，学校政教处将组织班主任老师分批，对本校一些家庭经济困难学生，开展新春上门送温暖助困活动。家长们也可教育孩子积极参加"蓝天下的挚爱——手拉手，共享温馨新年"捐款活动，捐出一些压岁钱，把爱心传递给需要帮助的人们，学校将于新学期开学举行捐款仪式。

综上，我们希望家长能积极配合学校，教育孩子居家孝敬父母，尊敬长辈，学会感恩，要求孩子做一些力所能及的家务劳动，每天督促孩子有一小时的身体锻炼，同时，鼓励孩子寒假中积极参加上述的学校、社区文明践行活动，让我们共同度过温馨而有意义的新年。下学期开学初，我校将通过问卷和各个家庭的自我推荐形式，评选出"2010奉浦学校寒假学生生活模范（和谐）家庭"，并予以表彰。

谢谢您的配合！

2010年，学校向学生家长发告学生家长书

学校还组织培养好家风好家训活动，举办由学生及学生家长共同参与的好家训小故事征文活动，加强家校联合管理力度。学校建立的家长学校，定期组织家长学习日活动，举办家长开放日，开展家长走进学校走进课堂，体验子女在学校的学习生活。开展"优秀家长"评选，颁发"优秀家长"证书，完善家校结合的教育模式，提高教育效果。

第九章　综合管理

学校重视学校安全管理，建立学校安全责任制度，确定校长、班主任为全校与班级的第一安全责任人，每年分别与区（县）教育局、学校校长签订安全保卫责任书，建立和不断完善学校安全保卫制度。在师生中开展多种形式的安全教育、各种应急预案演练、开展平安学校创建。2008—2009年，学校被上海市社会治安综合治理领导小组评为上海市安全文明学校。

学校加强后勤保障管理，坚持对食堂工作人员定期进行体检，加强思想教育，增强服务意识，制订和完善一系列食堂管理制度，加强食堂硬件设施建设，设备更新添置、保养。2010年，学校食堂被评为上海市（6T实务）示范食堂。严格学校财务、财产的管理工作，遵守国家财务管理规定，加强学校经费收支预决算及审计工作，实行公开收费，合理收费。坚持民主管理学校物资采购、校舍维修实行公开招标投标方法。1998—2016年，学校经费收支贯彻“统筹安排、量力而行、保障重点、略有节余”原则，经费收入2.32亿元，支出2.35亿元。2015年，学校事业费收入1311万元，占学校总收入68%，学校投资举办方拨款办校经费494万元，占学校经费27%。

学校建立档案室，人事、会计档案管理工作做到专人负责，完善制度，档案管理进一步加强。

第一节　安全保卫管理

学校安全是学校教育教学顺利开展，学生身心健康成长的重要环境。1998年9月，学校开学之后，学校把校园安全保卫管理作为重大议事日程运作。

一、安全责任制度

1. 安全责任人

学校安全保卫工作实行校长负责制，校长为学校安全的第一责任人，同时成立校园安全管理工作领导小组，由1名校级领导干部具体分工负责，把安全工作列为学校行政会议重要议事日程，分工明确、职责到人。学校明确各年级的班主任为班级安全第一负责人，对班级的学生安全、教育教学安全、教室内设施设备安全负责。

2．安全责任书

2001年起，学校校长与奉贤区教育局签订《上海市奉贤区教育系统校园安全工作责任书》。责任书明确要健全校园安全管理工作制度；履行校园安全管理工作职责；明确校园安全管理工作责任追究制共3个方面25条规定。学校各班主任与校长签订《奉浦学校班主任班级安全责任书》，责任书提出9项具体规定，并把安全工作列为考评教师、推优评优的重要内容。2015年全校签订安全责任书37份。2016年，坚持签订学校安全责任书制度不变。

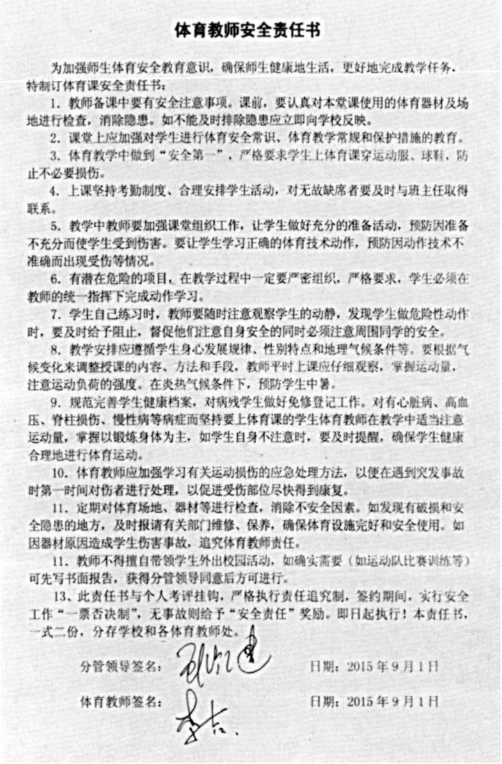

体育教师安全责任书

为加强师生体育安全教育意识，确保师生健康地生活，更好地完成教学任务，特制订体育课安全责任书：

1. 教师备课中要有安全注意事项。课前，要认真对本堂课使用的体育器材及场地进行检查，消除隐患。如不能及时排除隐患应立即向学校反映。

2. 课堂上应加强对学生进行体育安全常识、体育教学常规和保护措施的教育。

3. 体育教学中做到"安全第一"，严格要求学生上体育课穿运动服、球鞋，防止不必要损伤。

4. 上课坚持考勤制度、合理安排学生活动，对无故缺席者要及时与班主任取得联系。

5. 教学中教师要加强课堂组织工作，让学生做好充分的准备活动，预防因准备不充分而使学生受到伤害。要让学生学习正确的体育技术动作，预防因动作技术不准确而出现受伤等情况。

6. 有潜在危险的项目，在教学过程中一定要严密组织，严格要求，学生必须在教师的统一指挥下完成动作学习。

7. 学生自己练习时，教师要随时注意观察学生的动静，发现学生做危险性动作时，要及时给予阻止，督促他们注意自身安全的同时必须注意周围同学的安全。

8. 教学安排应遵循学生身心发展规律、性别特点和地理气候条件等。要根据气候变化来调整授课的内容、方法和手段，教师平时上课应仔细观察，掌握运动量，注意运动负荷的强度。在炎热气候条件下，预防学生中暑。

9. 规范完善学生健康档案，对病残学生做好免修登记工作。对有心脏病、高血压、脊柱损伤、慢性病等病症而坚持要上体育课的学生体育教师在教学中适当注意运动量，掌握以锻炼身体为主，如学生自身不注意时，要及时提醒，确保学生健康合理地进行体育运动。

10. 体育教师应加强学习有关运动损伤的应急处理方法，以便在遇到突发事故时第一时间对伤者进行处理，以促进受伤部位尽快得到康复。

11. 定期对体育场地、器材等进行检查，消除不安全因素。如发现有破损和安全隐患的地方，及时报请有关部门维修、保养，确保体育设施完好和安全使用。如因器材原因造成学生伤害事故，追究体育教师责任。

11. 教师不得擅自带领学生外出校园活动，如确实需要（如运动队比赛训练等）可先写书面报告，获得分管领导同意后方可进行。

13、此责任书与个人考评挂钩，严格执行责任追究制，签约期间，实行安全工作"一票否决制"，无事故则给予"安全责任"奖励。即日起执行！本责任书，一式二份，分存学校和各体育教师处。

分管领导签名： 日期：2015年9月1日

体育教师签名： 日期：2015年9月1日

2015年上海帕丁顿双语学校体育教师安全责任书

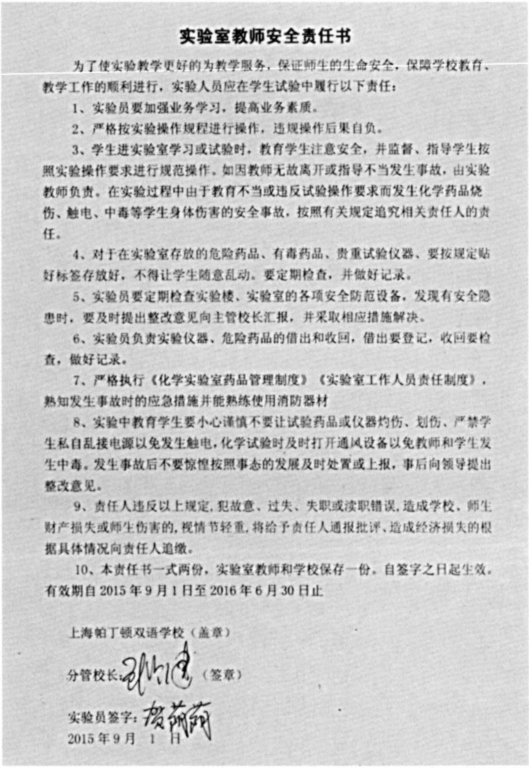

实验室教师安全责任书

为了使实验教学更好的为教学服务，保证师生的生命安全，保障学校教育、教学工作的顺利进行，实验人员应在学生试验中履行以下责任：

1、实验员要加强业务学习，提高业务素质。

2、严格按实验操作规程进行操作，违规操作后果自负。

3、学生进实验室学习或试验时，教育学生注意安全，并监督、指导学生按照实验操作要求进行规范操作。如因教师无故离开或指导不当发生事故，由实验教师负责。在实验过程中由于教育不当或违反试验操作要求而发生化学药品烧伤、触电、中毒等学生身体伤害的安全事故，按照有关规定追究相关责任人的责任。

4、对于在实验室存放的危险药品、有毒药品、贵重试验仪器、要按规定贴好标签存放好，不得让学生随意乱动。要定期检查，并做好记录。

5、实验员要定期检查实验楼、实验室的各项安全防范设备，发现有安全隐患时，要及时提出整改意见向主管校长汇报，并采取相应措施解决。

6、实验员负责实验仪器、危险药品的借出和收回，借出要登记，收回要检查，做好记录。

7、严格执行《化学实验室药品管理制度》《实验室工作人员责任制度》，熟知发生事故时的应急措施并能熟练使用消防器材

8、实验中教育学生要小心谨慎不要让试验药品或仪器灼伤、划伤、严禁学生私自乱接电源以免发生触电，化学试验时及时打开通风设备以免教师和学生发生中毒。发生事故后不要惊惶按照事态的发展及时处置或上报，事后向领导提出整改意见。

9、责任人违反以上规定，犯故意、过失、失职或渎职错误，造成学校、师生财产损失或师生伤害的，视情节轻重，将给予责任人通报批评、造成经济损失的根据具体情况向责任人追缴。

10、本责任书一式两份，实验室教师和学校保存一份。自签字之日起生效。有效期自2015年9月1日至2016年6月30日止

上海帕丁顿双语学校（盖章）

分管校长：（签章）

实验员签字：

2015年9月 1 日

2015年上海帕丁顿双语学校实验室教师安全责任书

3．治安防范体系

2006年，学校建立110报警中心，并以此为枢纽，逐步完善人防、物防、技防为一体的校园治安防范体系。2007年起加强防范体系检查工作。2016年，全校设报警探头200余个，分布在学校重要场所。另设110紧急报警按纽，在学校

重点专用教室安装防盗栅，防盗铁门，在电脑房等专用教室配齐消防灭火器，全校消防灭火装置全覆盖。在校内设立安全标语牌，悬挂安全为主题的图片和美术作品，增设安全宣传栏，开展安全知识竞赛，推动治安防范体系巩固、完整。

二、安全保卫制度

1998年，为做好学校安全保卫工作，学校先后制订18项安全管理制度。建立门卫制度，选择政治上可靠、安保意识强、工作认真负责的中年人员担任门卫工作。2000年起，学校从社会上招聘热心教育、关爱学生，有一定管理能力的中年人员，组成学校男女学生宿舍管理员队伍，辅导学生的安全、生活等方面的工作，增强住宿学生安全感。自此，宿管员工作也成为学校安全工作的一支重要队伍。2001年起，学校陆续制订与完善学校领导值班7项制度、值日细则，学校值周班制度及值周班管理要求、值周班管理对班主任、值周班长的要求。学生在校安全管理规定（住宿学生安全、纪律规定，走读生安全、纪律要求）。为保证实验室教学安全，学校制订实验室管理制度，制订实验室安全操作常识，危险品和剧毒药品领用办法，安全守则、安全防护制度，化学准备室工作制度，体育安全制度等，均做出明确具体规定。2006年制订校园网安全管理条例。2012年，学校把安全工作的各项制度整理成文，作为学校汇编资料的重要内容之一。2016年，帕丁顿双语学校在现有制度基础上，经过总结修改补充，进一步完善安全工作的各项规章制度。19年来，安全保卫制度的贯彻执行成为考核各部门、班级、教师的重要内容。

三、安全教育

1. 日常安全教育

1998年9月，学校创办后，坚持“预防为主、防治结合、加强教育、群防群治”安全保卫工作方针。规定学校开学前、学期中、放假前对师生进行安全保卫工作检查，落实“一日安全常规”。坚持每学期开学第一个月为“安全教育月”制度。2006年起，学校坚持安全教育与法制宣传教育相结合，做到“四落实”（落实计划、落实课时、落实人员、落实教材）、“四注重”（注重法制教育“四落实”、注重学科教学渗透教育、注重形式多样的专题教育、注重青少年法制实践活动），形成安全教育、法制教育常态化。学校多次邀请消防、公安等方面专家到学校进行现场讲解和演示，增强师生安全防范意识和应对能力。日常安全教育实行明确分工，学部负责安全意识教育、交通安全和社会治安安全教育；政教处负责校内外安全、防震安全、自然灾害安全教育；总务处负责防消安全、预防触电、溺水和煤气中毒安全、校舍安全常态化教育；校医负责食品卫生、传染病预防教育、禁烟禁毒教育；班主任与各任课教师配合，坚持每周进行一次安全教育的制度。同时对学生进行心理健康安全教育。2007年，针对校史上学校发生的学生殴打门卫及伤害事故，学校把处分犯错学生和伤害事故处理与安全教育相结合，提高安全教育的成效。2009年9月，在应对禽流感工作中，学校分别落实防治的多项具体措施，确保师生健康安全。是年，为巩固市安全学校的验收成果，学校提出“四全”（安全教育全员化、安全教育全天候、安全教育宣传全方位、安全教育责任全落实）目标责任制。学校安全工作领导小组成员安全目标分工明确，政教处与各年级班主任及其他相关人员签订安全协议30余份。2012年7月，学校修订、完善安全管理制度体系，从组织领导、安全教育、安全管理等方面提出具体的安全工作目标与要求，使学校实验室安全管理、体育活动安全、交通安全、课外集体活动安全、饮食卫生安全、消防安全、住宿学生安全管理工作、学校周边环境安全、节假日安全、门卫制度等逐项细化，成为学校安全管理教育的抓手。2016年9月，帕丁顿双语学校修订历年来系列安全防范制度，汇编成册，印发全校坚持执行。

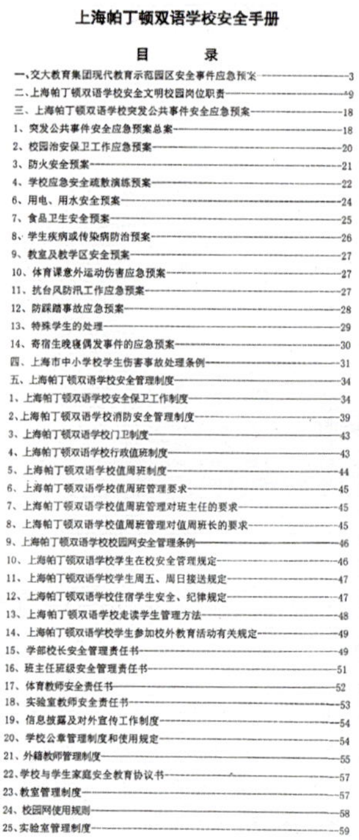
上海帕丁顿双语学校安全手册

目　　录

2016年9月，上海帕丁顿双语学校把学校安全工作制度修订汇编后成册

2．预案应急演练

2005年，学校根据安全保卫工作的新形势、新特点，总结社会上正反两方面的经验，制订学校突发性事故应急预案（伤害事故应急预案、消防火灾事故应急预案、停水停电应急预案、群体性食物中毒事故应急预案、突发传染性、流行性疾病应急预案、自然灾害应急预案及学生违纪事件、学生突发疾病处理流程、寄宿生晚寝偶发事件的应急预案等）、学校停电紧急疏散演练方案、学校校园安全稳定事件应急预案，建立由校长任组长的学校应急领导小组，下设8个工作小组，由学校领导成员及骨干教师任工作组负责人，具体分为宿舍管理工作组，建立小学工作组、初中工作组、高中部3个工作组和流行性疾病防控工作组，教育教学设施安全工作组，同时完善教师对各类事故的首见责任制。2012年3个应急预案和应急演练修改后，每学期组织师生进行模拟操作和实用演练，提高应急能力。2016年，帕丁顿双语学校修订完善14个突发事件应急演练方案，细化预防与应急的各项具体措施。

附：奉浦学校停电紧急疏散演练方案

一、指导思想

通过停电紧急疏散方案演练，让全体师生在发生停电、火灾、灾害性天气、地震等紧急情况时能够逃生自救，迅速、有序、安全地撤离疏散，最大限度地减少财产损失和人员伤亡，提高师生的安全意识和逃生能力。

二、事故假设：晚自修时间发生突然停电事件。

三、时间：　　年　月（具体时间待定）

四、地点：学校教学楼、运动场（早操场地）

五、对象：在校全体师生及安排的相关人员

六、分工：见后

七、形式：停电疏散演练

八、疏散线路：按照早上出操时出场顺序，先一楼、后二楼、再三楼、最后四楼，各班级应严格按照规定顺序，路径从教学楼疏散到运动场。

九、演练程序（见附表）

2012年奉浦学校停电紧急疏散演练方案

表 9-1-1

时间	事项
	各班主任利用下午第四节课或课间时间，对学生讲解如何在室内快速、有序成立队形及撤离时的注意事项，并进行撤离演练
20：00	发生突然停电事件（电工拉闸）各班主任迅速至各自班级稳定学生
20：03	楼道和楼层负责人及时到各楼梯口值班，维持秩序，负责学生疏散安全
20：05	演练总指挥宣布进行疏散，通知师生实施紧急疏散
20：05	听到紧急疏散指令后，各班主任组织本班学生迅速、有序地按规定顺序路径向外撤离，跑到指定安全区（外操场或篮球场），所有师生必须撤离到指定地点
20：06	在各班老师指挥下，有序地进行疏散（手提广播告诫：请大家不要慌张，不要拥挤抢道）
20：15	学生疏散结束，楼道负责人检查楼层各教室是否有人员滞留，确认无人时马上离开，并向情况上报指挥室（广播室）
20：20	各班级疏散到外操场指定的安全区后，按广播操队形整队，体育委员和班主任清点人数并向楼层负责人汇报，各楼层负责人向演练总指挥（广播室）汇报人数（××年级应到××人，实到××人，报告完毕）
20：24	安全逃生演练总指挥进行总结讲话，宣布本次安全逃生演练结束
20：25	警报解除，电工送电，各班级按秩序退场回教室

奉浦学校突发事件应急领导小组：

组长：顾行健　副组长：王益权

成员：曹善明、周时青、曹春华(女)、李永卫、刘平(女)、沈靖华、王胜利、曹建军、沈利德、姚仁兴、柳肖云(女)、王秋红(女)

应急事件八大工作组负责人：

宿管工作组：王胜利　小学工作组：王秋红(女)　初中工作组：柳肖云(女)

高一工作组：曹建军　高二工作组：沈利德　高三工作组：姚仁兴

流行性疾病防控工作组：刘平(女)　教育教学设施工作组：沈靖华

四、平安学校创建

1999学年，学校把安全教育列为教育的主要内容之一。学校评选学校文明组室，把安全工作列为考核内容。学校被评为2003—2004年奉贤区文明单位，校园安全工作列为学校文明创建的重点工作。2005年，学校发生伤害事故，全校上下举一反三，认真吸取教训，完善学校各项安全制度，全面发动开展平安学校创建工作。2008—2009年，经上海市社会治安综合治理委员会学校周边治安治理领导小组验收，学校被评为上海市安全文明校园。2010年5月5日，根据外省市兄弟

民办奉浦学校坚持对学生进行安全文明教育

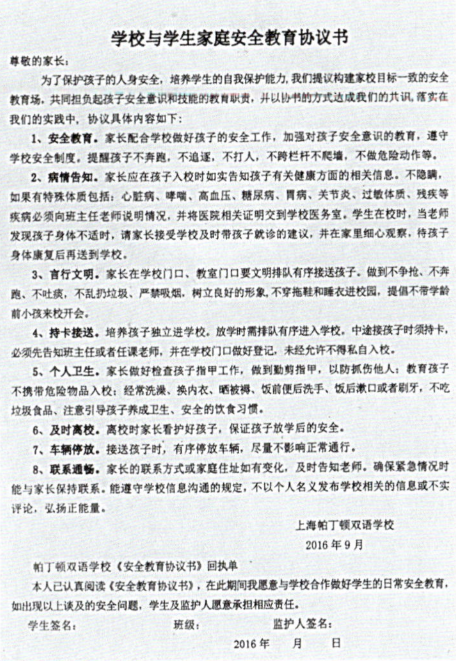

学校与学生家庭安全教育协议书

尊敬的家长：

为了保护孩子的人身安全，培养学生的自我保护能力，我们提议构建家校目标一致的安全教育场，共同担负起孩子安全意识和技能的教育职责，并以协书的方式达成我们的共识，落实在我们的实践中，协议具体内容如下：

1、**安全教育。**家长配合学校做好孩子的安全工作，加强对孩子安全意识的教育，遵守学校安全制度，提醒孩子不奔跑，不追逐，不打人，不跨栏杆不爬墙，不做危险动作等。

2、**病情告知。**家长应在孩子入校时如实告知孩子有关健康方面的相关信息。不隐瞒，如果有特殊体质包括：心脏病、哮喘、高血压、糖尿病、胃病、关节炎、过敏体质、残疾等疾病必须向班主任老师说明情况，并将医院相关证明交到学校医务室。学生在校时，当老师发现孩子身体不适时，请家长接受学校及时带孩子就诊的建议，并在家里细心观察，待孩子身体康复后再送到学校。

3、**言行文明。**家长在学校门口、教室门口要文明排队有序接送孩子。做到不争抢、不奔跑、不吐痰，不乱扔垃圾、严禁吸烟，树立良好的形象，不穿拖鞋和睡衣进校园，提倡不带学龄前小孩来校开会。

4、**持卡接送。**培养孩子独立进学校。放学时需排队有序进入学校。中途接孩子时须持卡，必须先告知班主任或者任课老师，并在学校门口做好登记，未经允许不得私自入校。

5、**个人卫生。**家长做好检查孩子指甲工作，做到勤剪指甲，以防抓伤他人；教育孩子不携带危险物品入校；经常洗澡、换内衣、晒被褥、饭前便后洗手、饭后漱口或者刷牙，不吃垃圾食品、注意引导孩子养成卫生、安全的饮食习惯。

6、**及时离校。**离校时家长看护好孩子，保证孩子放学后的安全。

7、**车辆停放。**接送孩子时，有序停放车辆，尽量不影响正常通行。

8、**联系通畅。**家长的联系方式或家庭住址如有变化，及时告知老师。确保紧急情况时能与家长保持联系。能遵守学校信息沟通的规定，不以个人名义发布学校相关的信息或不实评论，弘扬正能量。

上海帕丁顿双语学校

2016 年 9 月

帕丁顿双语学校《安全教育协议书》回执单

本人已认真阅读《安全教育协议书》，在此期间我愿意与学校合作做好学生的日常安全教育，如出现以上谈及的安全问题，学生及监护人愿意承担相应责任。

学生签名：　　　　班级：　　　　监护人签名：

2016 年　　月　　日

2016年上海帕丁顿双语学校与学生家庭安全教育协议书

学校发生的校园伤害案件，全校开展“安全教育进课堂”教育活动，加强对门卫人员的安全意识、岗位职责教育，进一步巩固门卫制度。学校与奉浦社区居委、奉浦派出所开展治安联防，增加学校关键部位的技防设施。安全学校创建逐步规范、常态化。2014年，在评选学校优秀班主任活动中，有13名各年（班）级班主任通过安全教育考核，评为学校优秀班主任。2015年上海帕丁顿双语学校公办、民办分设，一个校园内虽然两所学校共处，不少设施设备共用，两校领导在创建安全学校工作上互相协调，安全工作不放松，执行安全制度不走样，食堂用餐、体育场所活动安排不冲突，为安全工作增加保险系数。2016年，学校进一步开展平安学校创建系列活动，学校与学生家庭签订安全教育协议书，巩固平安校园创建成果。

第二节　后勤保障管理

一、食堂管理

1. 食堂人员管理

1998年9月，学校招收食堂人员，坚持从身体体检合格、政治思想作风好、热爱食堂工作的人员中挑选。此后学校坚持对食堂人员实行每年体检制度，聘用身体合格人员。对食堂工作人员经常进行食堂管理规章制度、服务态度、食堂卫生与炊事人员个人卫生习惯养成制度教育，明确要求食堂工作人员树立全心全意为师生服务的思想，牢固树立搞好食品卫生安全重要性认识，学校对食堂人员坚持实行1年1次签订工作合同，明确学校与食堂人员的权利与义务，落实食堂人员“两到位”（服务思想到位、卫生安全到位）、“两合格”（身体合格、工作合格），对食堂管理人员实行考核。作为继续聘用的依据之一。1998—2016年，食堂管理人员10余人次受到表扬奖励。

2．食堂管理制度

1998年9月，学校制订《食堂卫生制度》，建立《食堂卫生责任制》，落实《食堂管理员岗位职责》《炊事员岗位职责》《食堂工作人员守则》，规定每周五下午1时，对食堂管理人员进行卫生、防疫的教育。2002年，学校食堂迁移之后，总结前4年食堂管理经验教训，进一步修订食堂管理制度，实行严格食堂原料、质量检查与验收制度，坚持不合格原料不进厨房，不合格食品决不供应的原则，保证管理制度连续性和制度完善、创新。2005年，学校行政会议把食堂管理作为议事日程之一，认真听取食堂管理工作汇报。分管领导多次深入食堂检查各项制度的执行情况，找出薄弱环节，推动食堂管理制度的贯彻执行。2006—2011年，学校行政会议讨论食堂管理制度达10次，分管领导坚持每月下食堂检查制度。2012年，为加强食堂食品卫生安全，学校重新制订《上海民办奉浦学校食堂食品卫生安全应急预案》，提出7个方面20条具体规定，对发生食物中毒（或疑似食物中毒事故）提出7条相应应急的措施，在师生中进行演练。对一旦发生食物中毒事故，提出事故处理预案。学校贯彻执行《中华人民共和国卫生法》，坚持实行食堂采购原料到成品供应的“四不”制度（采购人员不买腐败变质的原料；保管员不收腐败变质的原料；加工员不用腐败变质的原料；炊事员不出售变质的食品），落实成品存取的“四隔离”（生与熟隔离；成品与半成品隔离；食品与杂物、药品隔离；食品与天然水隔离），用具、食具过“五关”（一洗、二刷、三冲、四消毒、五保洁）。2015—2016年，帕丁顿双语学校、奉浦学校分设，学校食堂用餐师生人数逐年增加，执行食堂管理各项制度不走样。

3．食堂硬件管理

食堂硬件建设是食堂管理的必要条件。1998年9月开办前，食堂硬件设施一步到位。师生就餐场所面积、厨房工作场所面积实现达标。2003年后食堂硬件设备不断更新。2012年，学校新建食堂面积3800余平方米，比1998年增加1倍。食堂设备陆续购置，满足师生用餐需要。2016年，学校厨房面积200多平方米，实行操作间、厨房间、打菜间、点心间分开，食堂生熟食品严格分开，有无毒桌椅642套，不锈钢餐具1000余套，高温消毒设备等10余套。食堂硬件设施设备采购实行招标，发现损坏及时维修保养，保持良好的状态。

二、财务（物）管理

1．财务人员

1998年9月，学校设财务科，配备助理会计师1人，有会计上岗证的出纳1人。此后，财务人员调动、配备均需具备会计任职资格。2016年，财务科编制2人，其中科长1人，财产专管员1人。主要职责是严格按照国家规定及上级有关部门批准的标准收取各种费用。并使用专用票据；对学校财产进行登记造表，按规定分类记账；财产专管员负责财产记账、领用登记、财产登记，执行校产损坏赔偿制度，不把校产用于担保和转让。

2．财务会计制度

1998年学校创办后，学校财务实行独立核算。根据《中华人民共和国会计法》有关规定，严格执行教育系统规定的财务会计制度。学校还从校情出发建立财务管理制度，现金、存款、收据管理制度。2005年起，不断完善财务审批制度。规定财务审批权限制度。财务会计制度逐步巩固完善。2012年，学校对财务管理作出进一步明确审批权限的规定，万元以上财务支出，须由相关科室提出申请，由分管校长签署意见，由校务会议审核；万元以下由分管校长签署意见，交校长审核决定的审批程序。2016年，学校坚持财务会计制度不走样。

3．财务预决算制度

（1）日常经费收支预决算。1998年，学校建立日常预决算制度，在学校民办公助期间，预算收入主要是民办学生学费，住宿费收入及国拨经费。每年学校预算经学校董事会审议同意后施行，每年决算1次，决算情况向董事会报告。2003年起，学校财务预算坚持以人为本，把教职工基本工资、津贴、社会保障经费列为预算的重点安排。预算收支贯彻“统筹安排、量力而行、保证重点、略有节余”原则。2003—2005年预算收入2380万元，支出2269万元，其中教职工报酬、福利费支出1641万元，占日常经费支出的72.3%。2005学年，为增添教学设备，把为每名教师配置1台手提电脑计划列入年度财务预算，全校58台电脑3万余元经费得以保证。2006年5月，把学校砂石跑道改为塑胶跑道、建设校园网、教室多媒体设施建设、太阳能热水供应设施列入预算，学校投资举办企业拨出专款441万元，保证预算资金按时到位。2009年，学校食堂更新餐厅设备成为预算的重要组成部分。2015年8月，学校改为纯民办性质后国家停拨教育经费，学校经费来源主要来自学生学费、住宿费收入，学校投资举办方注资。学校经费收支预算以保障教职工队伍稳定，教育教学的有序展开为重点，推动学校健康发展。1998—2015年，学校实际总收入2.12亿元，决算支出2.11亿元，实现预决算总体平衡，略有节余的目标。2016年，学校总收入1917.66万元，支出2220.28万元，不足部分由学校投资举办方弥补。（2）基础设施建设计划。学校办学之初，学校基础设施建设的投资由奉浦经济发展实业总公司根据学校建设实际需要预算，投入资金3500余万元。2009年，上海申生投资有限公司成为学校投资举办方后，学校基础设施建设投资由学校投资举办方预算投入。随着学校规模扩大和改善教育教学条件需要，2010年起，学校投资举办方不断加大基本建设投资力度。2011年，投入3600余万元兴建教师公寓。2012年预算投资建设的学校新食堂3800平方米，新教学大楼14000余平方米，分别投入资金2680余万元、9895万余元。2015年，建成建筑面积4826平方米的游泳球类馆，地面15层、地下1层、建筑面积26000平方米的国际教育交流中心。2016年，增建国际教育交流中心2部观光电梯，投入资金400万元。1998—2016年，学校投资举办方投入基础设施资金现值达4.8亿元。

4．财务审计制度

1998年，根据《中华人民共和国审计法》和教育部关于《教育系统内部审计工作规范》，结合上级主管部门的有关要求，学校董事会设立审计组，由董事长任组长，分管学校财务的学校领导任副组长，吸收党支部、学校工会负责人参与审计工作。审计内容为：学校预算、财务计划的执行情况；固定资产的管理和使用；建设、修缮工程项目；重要经济合同的签订和执行情况；教职工收益分配的合法性、合理性；各项资金筹集、分配、使用和管理是否取得好的经济效益和社会效益；财会人员履行法定职责和执行国家会计制度情况；学校内控制度、财会制度执行情况等10项内容。每年11月，对学校有关经济活动真实、合法、效益进行审计，形成审计报告送学校董事会，并建立审计档案。2009年起，学校审计工作接受学校监事会监督。2015年8月，帕丁顿双语学校改为纯民办性质学校后，学校设立监事会，由学校投资举办方董事长等担任监事会成员。2016

年，监事会参与学校财务审计监督，推动财务审计工作制度化、规范化。

5. **收费管理**

学校在民办公助阶段，经费主要来自民办学生学费、住宿费及公办国拨经费。学校收费严格执行区物价局、教育局关于收费项目、收费标准及调整收费权限的规定，不自立项目，不提高标准，实行收费公开规范。民办阶段经费主要来自学生学费、住宿费收入及投资举办企业的资金投入。

民办学生学费，其收费标准由上级有关部门审批后方可实施。收费标准通过各种渠道向社会与学生家长公开。其他收费如学生服装费等，由学校召开学生家长会议宣传，本着为学生服务、为学生家庭着想，尽可能减少收费的原则，收费标准经学生家长会议通过后执行。

1998—2016年上海帕丁顿双语学校民办学生学费收取情况表

表 9-2-1　　单位：元/学期

年份	小学	中学	高中（英语特长班）
1998	800	1200	2000
1999	800	1200	2000
2000	1500	2000	3000
2001	1500	2000	3000
2002	2000	2500	3000
2003	2000	2500	3000
2004	2000	2500	3000
2005	2500	3000	4000
2006	2500	3000	4000
2007	2500	3000	5000
2008	2500	3000	5000
2009	3000	3500	6000
2010	3000	3500	6000
2011	3000	3500	高中 6800、英语特长班 12000
2012	3000	3500	高中 6800、英语特长班 12000
2013	1 年级 4000、 2～5 年级 3000	6 年级 4500、 7～9 年级 3500	高一 8000、高二和高三 6800、 英语特长班 12000
2014	1～2 年级 4000、 3～5 年级 3000	6～7 年级 4500、 8～9 年级 3500	高一和高二 8000、高三 6800
2015	1 年级 7000、 2～3 年级 4000、 3～5 年级 3000	6 年级 8000、 7～8 年级 4500、 9 年级 3500	高一 10000，高二和高三 8000
2016	7000	8000	10000

说明：1. 2016 年小学、初中、高中新生收费标准为 7000 元、8000 元、10000 元；2. 2016 年小学、初中、高中住宿费每学期 1600 元

三、学校经费收支

学校经费保障是办好学校的物质基础。学校从1998年9月创办开学至2015年8月，为民办（公助）性质的学校。开办初，除奉贤县教育局调拨部分公办教师外，学校向社会招聘部分民办（退休）教师。学生主要招收奉浦地区居民子女与来奉创业办企业的民工子女。2000年后，市教育局同意学校面向全市招生，生源范围扩大，学校经费也日益增加。学校经费主要来源，一是入校就读的民办学生学费、住宿费；二是区（县）教育局对学校公办教师、学生的教育经费；三是学校投资举办方根据各学年学校经费开支实际拨入专款；四是少量社会资助款。1998年，学校经费以县教育局拨款为主，半年经费支出仅26.6万元，其中教育经费22.64万元，事业收入3.96万元。2000年，学校总支出569.11万元，其中学校事业费收入390.5万元，占全部经费支出68.5%，教育经费拨款177.72万元，占学校经费总支出的31%。2006年，全校经费总支出为1048万元。其中，事业费收入441.66万元，占学校经费总支出的42.08%，县拨教育经费229.58万元，占学校经费总支出的21.85%，经费缺口较大。是年学校投资举办方拨专款461.8万元，占学校经费总支出的44%，保证学校经费略有节余。2012年，学校经费总支出2246.56万元。其中，事业费收入1204.68万元，占学校经费总支出的53.66%，教育经费拨入864.96万元，占学校经费总支出的38.47%，企业拨入专款102.34万元，占学校经费总支出的4.5%。当年学校经费支大于收，亏71万元，由投资举办方承担。

1998—2016年，除学校投资举办方投入基础设施资金外，学校日常经费总收入2.32亿元。其中，历年事业费收入1.35亿元，占总收入58.29%，国拨教育经费7237万元，占总收入31.24%，学校投资举办方拨款2093.26万元，占总收入9.03%，其他收入358万元，占总收入1.55%。学校历年总支出2.35亿元。其中，事业费收入占总支出57.54%，国拨经费占总支出的30.84%，学校投资举办方占总支出8.92%。

2015年8月至2016年，学校改为纯民办性质后，学校不再享受国拨教育经费，学校经费收入全靠学校事业费收入和投资举办方拨款。两年学校总收入3845.24万元。其中，事业费收入2598.48万元，占全校经费总支出的67.58%，学校投资举办方拨款974.77万元，为学校创办以来拨款最多的2年，占学校总支出的25.35%，学校其他收入130.04万元，占总支出的3.38%。真正体现“以校养校，企业办校”的办学目标。

1998—2016学年上海帕丁顿双语学校经费收支情况表

表9-2-2　　单位：万元

学年	总收入	其中				总支出	其中		
		教育经费拨款	拨入专款	事业收入	其他收入		人员支出	公用支出	其他支出
1998	26.60	22.64	—	3.96	—	26.60	—	—	—
1999	555.17	135.15	0.75	283.14	136.13	542.22	541.47	—	—
2000	569.11	177.72	0.89	390.50	—	569.11	568.22	—	—
2001	656.89	190.25	0.88	465.66	—	656.90	656.02	—	—
2002	720.07	214.70	10.58	490.67	4.12	720.07	705.60	—	—
2003	562.43	229.75	1.17	326.24	5.27	561.91	561.25	—	—
2004	728.28	202.10	89.74	411.73	24.70	610.37	355.92	232.47	21.98
2005	614.70	198.27	7.29	372.18	36.86	614.85	367.06	212.57	35.22
2006	1198.53	229.58	461.89	441.66	65.40	1048.38	328.59	371.72	348.07
2007	1245.12	403.05	103.28	738.79	—	1106.94	389.88	448.87	268.19
2008	1495.46	550.10	265.14	652.68	28.04	1421.72	660.26	526.11	235.35
2009	1476.78	580.11	77.58	811.13	7.96	1615.23	1065.14	331.60	218.29
2010	1687.53	769.15	111.52	805.69	1.17	1681.01	1052.23	491.89	136.89
2011	1873.55	824.25	13.44	1033.78	2.08	1923.48	1252.83	552.23	118.42
2012	2173.74	864.96	102.34	1204.68	1.76	2246.56	1443.57	729.44	73.55
2013	2384.60	848.95	328.37	1206.02	1.26	2292.51	1311.55	678.21	302.75
2014	1350.14	—	40.25	1264.21	45.68	1694.01	1196.64	497.37	—
2015	1927.58	—	494.51	1311.22	121.85	1910.51	1201.15	744.88	15.37
2016	1917.66	—	480.26	1287.26	8.19	2220.28	1323.05	864.37	32.86

说明：① 2004—2005学校收支为计划预算数。② 支出项目：人员支出包括基本工资、津贴、奖金、社会保障经费、其他经费；公用支出包括办公费、印刷费、水电费、邮电费、交通费、差旅费、培训费、招待费、福利费、劳务费、维修费、专用材料费、办公设备购置费、专用设备购置费、图书资料购置费、其他经费；补助支出包括住房补贴、助学金、其他经费

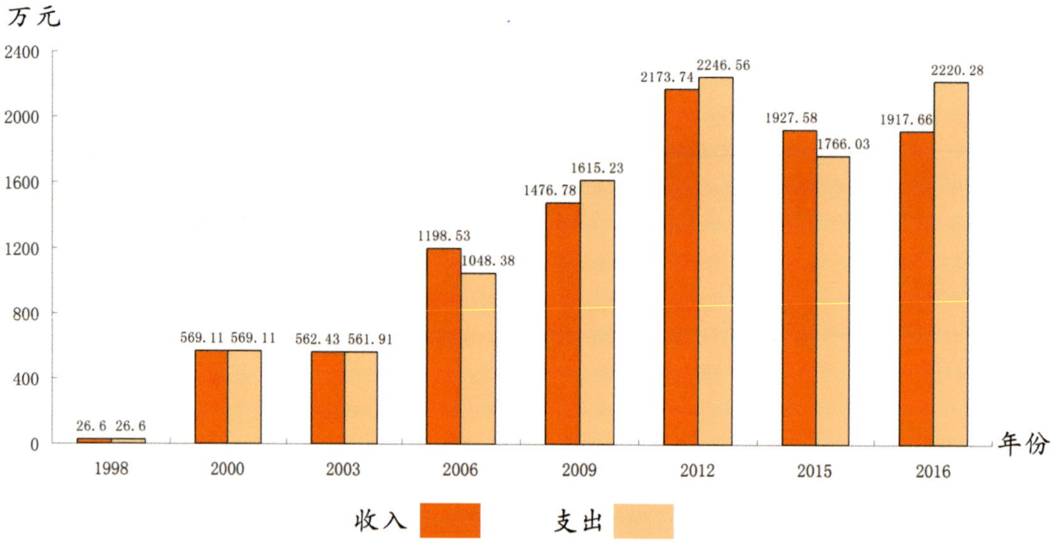

1998—2016学年上海帕丁顿双语学校部分年份经费收支示意图

说明：2015—2016年为纯民办学校

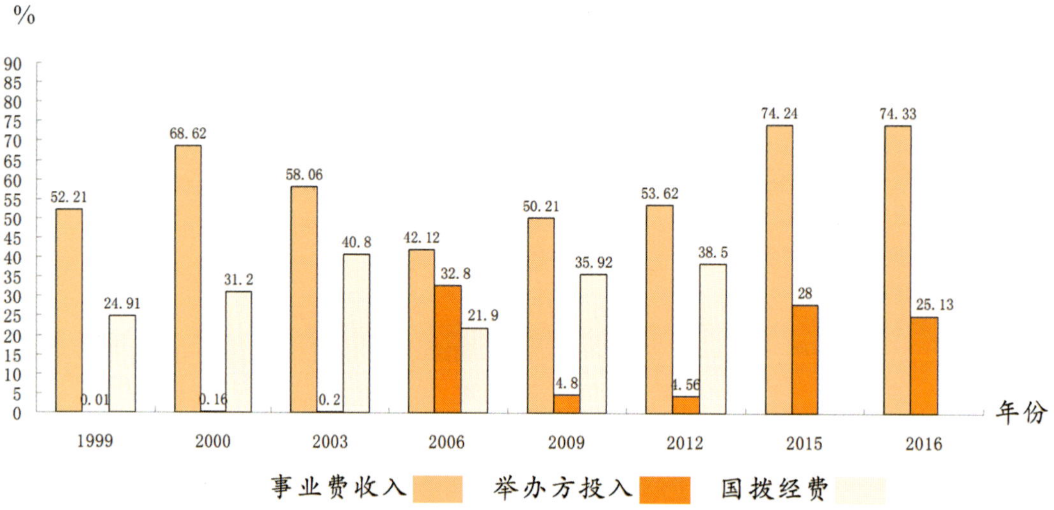

1999—2016学年上海帕丁顿双语学校事业费收入、
举办方投入、国拨经费占学校年度经费支出比重示意图

第三节　档案管理

一、档案室

1998年9月，学校档案室在原教学楼建立，建筑面积100多平方米。2011年，新教学大楼建成后，档案室设在国际教育教学大楼地下一层，占地100平方米，由校务办公室负责管理。档案室由兼管员1人。2015年上海帕丁顿双语学校公办、民办分设学校，民办学校的档案资料调走，在新教学大楼设学校档案室。原档案室为公办奉浦学校使用。档案室藏有学校、上海营巢房产开发有限公司档案万余册。

二、档案管理制度

1998年9月学校创办后，建立档案制度。学校档案室保管人事档案和会计档案，根据《中华人民共和国会计法》《会计档案管理办法》有关规定，学校人事档案由人事干部负责整理，把管辖范围内人员个人的简历、奖惩、职务调动、职称评定等内容存入档案以便查阅。会计凭证、账簿、报表以及其他会计资料由财会人员定期整理，在财会室保管1年后，由会计立卷造册交学校综合档案室。会计档案按规定期限保管，会计凭证、总账、明细账为15年，年度决算报表永久保存。会计室档案查阅，须经主管领导同意。档案管理人员变动，须办理交接手续。2015年，国际教育交流中心大楼竣工后，档案室移至大楼地下室。上海帕丁顿双语学校的公办部分析出后，民办上海帕丁顿双语学校档案室迁入教学大楼506室，由1名专职人员负责管理。并建立档案管理、查阅登记等系列制度。学校档案室有档案柜10个，存放各种档案5000余件。

第十章　设施　设备

1997年1月，上海奉浦经济发展实业总公司根据奉浦工业区域内居民和外来民工子女上学需求，以新颖、舒适、安全、有利开展教育教学为目标，投入资金3500余万元，兴建学校基础设施第一期工程，其中有教学大楼、宿舍楼、艺术楼、乒乓房、操场、浴室等设施，建筑总面积1.89万平方米，1998年7月竣工。1999年，协和学校副董事长胡卫以上海教育科学院民办教育中心的名义，投入资金300万元增建学生宿舍大楼。2005年12月，学校出资为教师配备手提电脑58台。2006年5月，学校操场由煤屑跑道改建为塑胶跑道，建设校园网、多媒体教室、宿舍太阳能热水供应设施。2010—2013年，学校投资举办方上海申生投资有限公司先后建设新教学大楼、学校食堂、游泳球类馆和国际教育交流中心、校园长廊，总建筑面积5.25万平方米。至2015年7月陆续竣工，其中物理、化学生物实验室、自然常识室、美术室、音乐教室、舞蹈房、阅览室、教室等181间。2016年为国际教育中心南墙外侧安装观光电梯2部。2016年，全校建筑总面积7.45万平方米。现值4.8亿元。

为改善教育教学条件，各种教学设备陆续添置。2016年，全校各种教学设备9427余台（件），其中教学用彩色电视机65台、多媒体集控设备45台、音箱（有源音箱、音响组合）106台、视频图象展示台45台、电子计算机422台、标准投影仪102台。至2016年，全校设备总投入4000余万元。设备现值1351.52万元。

第一节　学校设施

一、教学楼

1. 上海帕丁顿外国语幼儿园大楼

原为学校创办初期上海民办协和实验学校教学楼。1997年年初由上海奉浦工业区的开发主体上海奉浦经济发展实业总公司投资建设，1998年4月竣工。四层中庭式建筑，建筑面积7614.55平方米，始设教室26间，底层设化学实验室，二层设物理、电工实验室，三层设生物实验室，四层设电脑房。2012年9月，新教学大楼建成后迁出。2016年初，按照幼儿园教育的需要进行全面装修改建。是年9月，上海帕丁顿外国语幼儿园在该楼创办。有教室、教师办公室40间，实用面积2642.04平方米，其中一层9间实用面积716.12平方米，二层12间实用面积859.76平方米，三层11间实用面积455.12平方米，四层8间实用面积438.84平方米。

2016年上海帕丁顿外国语幼儿园教室办公室分布情况表

表10-1-1

层次	编号	实用面积（平方米）	层次	编号	实用面积（平方米）
一层	1	57.12	三层	22	57.12
	2	57.12		23	57.12
	3	20.74		24	20.74
	4	20.74		25	20.74
	5	60.48		26	60.48
	6	60.48		27	60.48
	7	74.52		28	74.52
	8	74.52		29	74.52
	9	190.40		30	43.20
二层	10	57.12		31	62.64
	11	57.12		32	37.80
	12	20.74	四层	33	57.96
	13	20.74		34	57.96
	14	60.48		35	57.96
	15	60.48		36	57.96
	16	74.52		37	57.96
	17	74.52		38	57.96
	18	290.40		39	74.52
	19	43.20		40	74.52
	20	62.64			
	21	37.80			

2. 上海帕丁顿双语学校教学楼

2011年，由上海申生投资有限公司投资建设。2012年9月，竣工投入使用。中庭式五层教学楼，建筑总面积1.41万平方米，楼内设教室34间，其中小学部教室20间，实用面积1615.32平方米；初中部教室4间，实用面积301.80平方米；高中部教室 10 间，实用面积 745.92 平方米。另设化学、物理、音乐等教学实验室等 15 间，实用面积 1925.34 平方米。

2016 年上海帕丁顿双语学校教室分布情况表

表 10-1-2

教室编号	班级	实用面积（平方米）	教室编号	班级	实用面积（平方米）
111	一（3）	78.00	411	五（1）	78.00
112	一（4）	78.00	412	五（2）	78.00
113	一（5）	78.00	413	五（3）	78.00
114	二（3）	78.00	305	九（1）	71.40
211	一（1）	78.00	414	七（1）	78.00
212	一（2）	78.00	415	七（2）	81.12
213	二（1）	78.00	419	八（1）	70.56
214	二（2）	78.00	420	高二（2）	70.56
215	三（1）	81.12	421	高二（3）	70.56
219	三（2）	70.56	511	高一（1）	78.00
220	三（3）	70.56	512	高一（2）	78.00
221	三（4）	70.56	513	高一（3）	78.00
311	六（1）	78.00	514	高一（4）	78.00
312	六（2）	78.00	515	高二（1）	81.12
313	四（1）	78.00	519	高三（1）	70.56
314	四（2）	78.00	520	高三（2）	70.56
315	四（3）	81.12	521	高三（3）	70.56

上海帕丁顿双语学校教学楼教师办公室

上海帕丁顿双语学校教室

2016年上海帕丁顿双语学校五层教学楼实验室情况表

表 10-1-3

教室编号	名称	面积（平方米）	教室编号	名称	面积（平方米）
合计	1925.34		303	自然室	142.80
119	扩展课程室	70.56	402	DIS 室	142.80
319	舞蹈房	141.12	403	物理室	142.80
321	书法教室	70.56	405	物理室	142.80
301	书法教室	139.86	502	生物室	142.80
401	多功能教室	139.86	503	化学室	142.80
501	音乐教室	139.86	505	化学室	142.80
302	科技室	142.80	115	小食堂	81.12

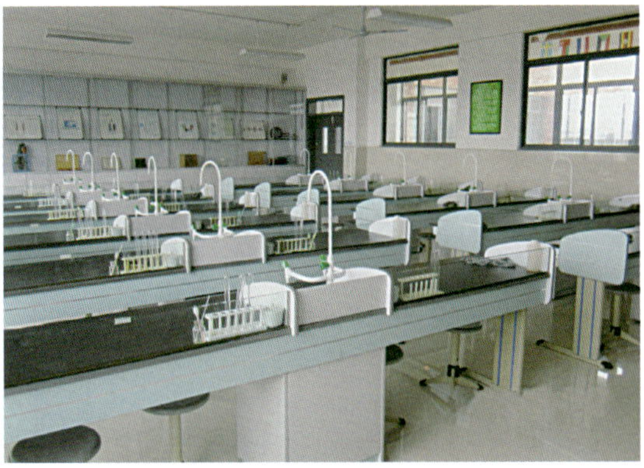

上海帕丁顿双语学校教学楼化学实验室

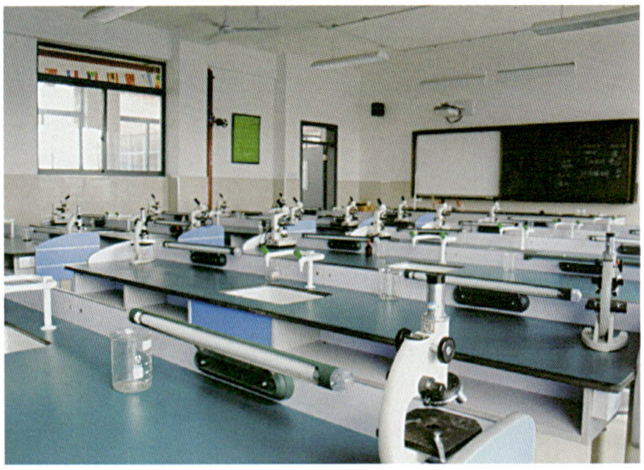

上海帕丁顿双语学校教学楼生物实验室

上海帕丁顿双语学校教学楼电子琴室

上海帕丁顿双语学校教学楼 DTS 室

3. 国际教育中心大楼

2013年，由上海申生投资有限公司投资建设。2015年，竣工投入使用，为地面15层、地下1层的高层建筑，建筑总面积2.6万平方米。设教室92间，实用面积7854.48平方米。2016年，上海申生投资有限公司投资400万元，在大楼南侧安装2部观光电梯。该大楼每个层面建筑面积1735.8平方米。

2016年上海帕丁顿双语学校国际教育交流中心大楼层面使用情况表

表10-1-4

层次	使用单位	层次	使用单位
1	上海交通大学教育集团	9	上海交大教育集团英语课程中心
2	金仕堡健身中心	10	上海交大教育集团美国高中课程中心
3	上海市奉贤区奉浦学校（公办）	11	上海交大教育集团美国高中课程中心
4	上海市奉贤区奉浦学校（公办）	12	上海交大教育集团美国高中课程中心
5	上海市奉贤区奉浦学校（公办）	13	上海交大教育集团国际教育学院澳大利亚高中课程中心国际预科课程中心
6	上海百练培训学校	15	上海营巢房产开发有限公司
7	中国平安保险（集团）股份有限公司	16	上海申生投资有限公司
8	中国平安保险（集团）股份有限公司	-1	档案室、仓库、后勤人员办公室

二、宿舍楼

1. 2号女生宿舍楼

1997年年初，由上海奉浦工业区开发主体奉浦经济发展实业总公司投资开发。1998年4月竣工。四层宿舍用房，建筑面积3854.98平方米，有宿舍85间，单间实用面积22.68平方米，总实用面积1927.8平方米。其中一层19间，实用面积430.92平方米，二层22间，实用面积498.96平方米，三层22间，实用面积498.96平方米，四层22间，实用面积498.96平方米，每间寄住学生6名。全部入住可寄住学生510名。

上海帕丁顿双语学校女生宿舍

2. 3号男生宿舍楼

2000年，由上海民办协和实验学校副董事长胡卫以上海教育科学研究院民办教育中心名义投资建设。2001年竣工使用（2003年由奉浦经济发展实业总公司结算接收)，建筑面积3062.86平方米，四层宿舍用房。有宿舍57间，实用面积1327.32平方米，单间实用面积22.68平方米。其中一层12间，实用面积272.16平方米，二层14间，实用面积328.86平方米，三层14间，实用面积328.86平方米，四层14间，实用面积328.86平方米。

上海帕丁顿双语学校男生宿舍

上海帕丁顿双语学校学生宿舍

3. 1号综合楼

1997年初，由上海奉浦工业区开发主体奉浦经济发展实业总公司投资建设，1998年4月竣工。位于校区西北角，西邻南桥镇陈桥路、北靠南桥镇韩村路，为四层综合用房，建筑总面积3854.98平方米。办校初期曾兼作宿舍、食堂等用房。3号宿舍楼建成后，部分用房为奉浦社区党工委、奉浦社区办事处租用。

4. 教师公寓

2010年，由上海申生投资有限公司投资建设，2011年竣工使用。公寓位于校区东北角，东靠奉贤区工业中专、西邻南桥镇韩村路为7层教师宿舍用房，建筑面积5208.91平方米，为外籍、市区及外省市在校任教老师提供使用。

上海帕丁顿双语学校教师公寓

三、食堂大楼

2011年，由上海申生投资有限公司投资建成，2012年9月竣工使用。位于校区西部，紧靠南桥镇陈桥路，3号宿舍楼与游泳球类馆中间，为二层餐用房，建筑总面积3829.34平方米，上层为就餐之用，下层为厨房、仓库用房，餐厅实用面积2300平方米，分为学生餐厅与教职员工餐厅，同时可容纳1000余人用餐。

四、游泳球类馆

上海帕丁顿双语学校游泳馆

2012年2月，由上海申生投资有限公司投资建设，2014年竣工使用。位于校区西部，学校食堂与国际教育中心大楼之间，为二层建筑，建筑面积4826平方米。内设标准大小游泳池各1座，分别适合成年人、少年儿童使用；乒乓、桌球、羽毛球、击剑等比赛场地。2015年，以此场所建立奉浦体育俱乐部。

五、校园长廊

2014年，上海申生投资有限公司在建设新教学大楼、国际教育中心及游泳球类馆同时，建设校园长廊。长廊使新教学大楼，国际教育中心，学生宿舍2号、3号楼与食堂，体育运动场互相串通。长廊全长380米、宽5米、高3米，建筑面积1900平方米。走廊南部为平顶，北部为篷帐式，成为雨天防雨，夏天乘凉休闲的通道。

六、浴　室

1998年建成，建筑面积240.77平方米。

七、门卫室

上海帕丁顿双语学校有2处门卫室，北门门卫室1998年与1号宿舍楼同时建成，南门门卫室于2013年与新教学大楼同时竣工。两处门卫建筑总面积111.09平方米。

八、操场　绿化

1998年7月，由奉浦经济发展实业总公司投资建设，设250米长的环形跑道，由煤屑铺设，环形跑道东侧有100米跑赛道。操场东部设单、双杠运动器械，北侧设3个篮球场，操场总面积2万平方米。2006年5月，煤屑跑道改为塑胶跑道，篮球场也铺设塑胶面。2013年夏，操场环道内草坪改为塑胶草坪。操场同时向西延位20米，操场东侧设停车坪，篮球场重新铺设塑胶面，移至操场西侧。

上海帕丁顿双语学校操场

学校重视校园绿化设施建设。1996年筹建学校时，把绿化设施建设列入学校总体规划。1998年4月，学校首批基础设施竣工，绿化设施基本同步完成。时全校绿化面积近2万平方米。2010年，学校评估验收时，人均绿化面积超35平方米。2011年，学校陆续新建教学大楼、食堂、球类馆、国际教育交流中心大楼，绿化设施做到统一规划合理安排。2016年，全校绿化面积人均保持在规定平方米范围内。

第二节　学校设备

1998年初，随着学校基础设施建设的陆续竣工，各种教学设备、医疗保健卫生设备、文化体育设备、交通通信设备、食堂用具、教室用品、宿舍生活设备等不断添置。至2016年，全校各类设备9427台（件、套），现值1351.52万元，其中超10万元以上的设备29台（件）。

一、教学设备

1998年9月开学前后，根据学校教学需要购置各类设备，以后随着教室迁址，教学设备不断更新换置，推动教学条件不断改善。2016年，全校更新教学设备1910台（件、套），投入资金716.27万元。

2016年上海帕丁顿双语学校主要教学设备情况表

表10-2-1

名称	单位	数量	金额（元）	名称	单位	数量	金额（元）
专用设备	台	4	337944.0	保鲜柜	只	6	10785.0
集中控制装置	台	12	13800.0	超纯水终端处理装置	台	4	268000.0
生物显微镜	台	27	16970.0	电扇	台	299	53964.0
多功能视频显示器	台	63	213826.5	计算机	台	98	312606.0
生理心理实验仪器及装置	台	1	108690.0	电子计算机	台	422	1740651.0
投影银幕	幅	55	31310.0	小型电子计算机	台	2	30100.0
标准投影仪	台	102	1097404.0	微型电子计算机	台	1	12000.0
照相机	架	3	20159.0	彩色打印机	台	7	61708.0
空气调节器（空调）	台	349	1554597.0	激光打印机	台	15	35192.0
彩色终端	台	132	164430.0	音箱	套	46	13460.0
电子白板	块	45	241200.0	有源音箱	套	57	18630.0
专用计算设备	台	1	76364.0	音响组合	套	3	25720.0
多媒体教学系统	台	1	345800.0	CAI多媒体视频系统	套	1	43000.0
计算机应用科技软件	台	1	11000.0	多媒体集控系统	套	45	64800.0
视频图象展示台	台	45	67500.0	诊察器械	台	1	16290.0
扩音机（功放）	台	8	17650.0	绿板	块	51	137158.0

二、文体卫生设备

1998年9月，学校开学前后，文体卫生设备陆续购置更新，不断满足全校师生文体活动、卫生工作需要。2016年，全校有文化体育卫生设备621台（件、套），资金总额187.42万元。

2016 年上海帕丁顿双语学校文体卫生主要设备情况表

表 10-2-2

名称	单位	数量	金额（元）	名称	单位	数量	金额（元）
专用设备	台	4	337944.0	书橱	只	110	66150.00
钢琴	架	56	83705.00	仪器橱	架	87	86770.00
电子琴	架	51	28900.00	货架	件	204	43730.00
足球、乒乓、羽毛球设备	套	8	12796.00	图书	册	40000	110438.00
篮球架	副	4	23900.00	雕塑	座	1	10600.00
跳高海绵垫体操跳垫	副	26	15802.00	投影教育学片	套	1	62000.00
单杠、双杠、跳马山羊	件	17	13151.00	粉笔书写板、黑白板	块	27	15160.00
肋木综合健身训练器	套	4	117750.00	阅览桌	只	121	59740.00
一般设备	套	4	937762.00	丛书年鉴年刊	册	1000	10454.00
综合性图书			175312.82				

上海帕丁顿双语学校体育俱乐部乒乓球馆

上海帕丁顿双语学校体育俱乐部羽毛球馆

上海帕丁顿双语学校体育俱乐部击剑馆

上海帕丁顿双语学校图书馆

三、教室设备

1998年9月开学前，学校根据实际工作需要添置教室设备，之后不断更新、升级。2016年，全校教室设备5755只（套），资金138.6万元。

2016年上海帕丁顿双语学校教室主要设备情况表

表10-2-3

名称	单位	数量	金额（元）	名称	单位	数量	金额（元）
桌椅	套	642	187050	微机工作台	只	65	17390
台桌	只	101	36360	绘画桌	只	40	7720
办公桌	只	228	143520	阅览椅	只	239	37685
一般讲台	只	12	14000	折叠椅	只	130	20800
演示讲台	只	42	42800	转椅实验凳	只	542	11670
单人课桌	只	320	27200	单人课椅	只	1387	72390
双方课桌	只	460	63814	方凳	只	539	13482
多人组合课桌椅	只	630	201600	各种沙发	只	14	29050
实验台	只	96	96000	衣柜、矮柜、铁皮柜	只	245	308481
实验准备台工作台	只	23	55000	档案柜	只	10	

四、交通通信设备

1998年9月学校创办后，交通通信设备陆续购置、安装、更新。2016年，学校有货、客车3辆，通信设备47台（辆），投入资金85.21万元。

2016年上海帕丁顿双语学校交通通信主要设备情况表

表10-2-4

名称	单位	数量	金额（元）	名称	单位	数量	金额（元）
封闭式小货车	辆	1	66600	通信配电设备	套	1	123000
客车	辆	1	397824	电话机	台	1	598
小轿车	辆	1	218726	两用电话机	台	1	987
网络控制设备	台	43	43790	无绳式电话机	台	1	598

五、宿舍食堂设备

1998年9月开学前，学校宿舍、食堂设备与教学设备同步购置，之后陆续更新（改造）。2016年，全校宿舍、食堂各种设备1094件，资金224.02万元。

2016年上海帕丁顿双语学校宿舍、食堂主要设备情况表

表10-2-5

名称	单位	数量	金额（元）	名称	单位	数量	金额（元）
家具	套	18	706952	双人床	只	312	199500
床	只	86	293040	桌、椅	只	642	187050
蒸饭箱	只	4	28300	水箱	只	1	12000
燃气炉灶	只	1	36000	洗地车（机）	辆	1	11600
保暖送饭车	辆	4	22000	清洗机	台	1	16800
洗衣机	台	17	21176	供水设备	套	4	697890
电热开水器	台	1	2100	保暖桶	只	2	5800

上海帕丁顿双语学校学生餐厅

上海帕丁顿双语学校教职工餐厅

上海帕丁顿双语学校餐饮楼食品加工房

上海帕丁顿双语学校餐饮楼食品消毒房设备

第十一章　校园文化　科技　体育

1998年9月，上海民办协和实验学校开学以后，坚持组织文化、科技、体育活动，形成艺体科技特色、丰富多样的校园文化氛围。以校旗、校徽、校服为代表，以校训、校风、教风、学风为引领，树立校训石碑、制作民族魂红墙、文武德艺浮雕、丝绸之路油彩画，开展多层次多形式文化艺术活动。1999—2016年，全校举办文化艺术节16届，参演节目500余个，参与师生2万余人次。2003—2016年，先后组织动漫、摄影等学生社团17个，丰富课余文化体育生活。开展读好书做“小贤人”评选活动，先后建立学校广播台、网站。创办校刊《果行园》，分层次开展师生作品展20多次，展出作品上千件，全校教师50多人次在区级以刊物上登载论文33篇，其中获区级以上奖励17篇。有2名学生作文分别参加全国性比赛，分获金奖、二等奖。学校创办家长学校，加强与学生家长的联系互动，欢迎并接受家长对学校与教师的评议；学校举办的家教研讨会和家风小故事征文活动，校园文化成为培养教育学生健康成长的重要途径和校园文化的组成部分。

学校重视组织学生开展科技活动。2005年起已先后举办10届科技节，采取邀请科技老师到校传授、师生共同参与方式，鼓励学生发明创造，有8项专利发明在市有关科技比赛中获奖。至2016年，组合式钥匙扣等15项学生发明获市知识产权局、市教委颁发的专利证书。

1999年4月，上海民办协和实验学校举办首届校园运动会，至2016年已举办16届，比赛项目有广播操、田径、球类等，20余个比赛小项，创造（保持）学校个人（集体）运动纪录57项。学校还组织运动队参加奉贤区运动会、教育系统中小学各种球类、跳踢比赛和田径达标赛。1999—2016年，有58个集体运动项目在区级体育比赛中获团体前三名，30名运动员获男子跳远比赛项目奖牌。学校坚持每日不少于1小时的体育活动时间，保证学生身体健康发展。学校文化体育活动的展开，凸现上海帕丁顿双语学校先进的文化理念和发展方向，推动全校教育教学取得新的业绩。

第一节　校园文化

一、校旗　校徽　校服

1. 学校校旗

1998年9月，上海民办协和实验学校校旗由学校设计。底色为白色，旗中心的校名字体为蓝色。后学校2次易名，更换校旗。2015年4月，学校更名为上海帕丁顿双语学校，重新制作的新校旗为红底黄字。

上海民办奉浦学校校旗

上海帕丁顿双语学校校旗

2. 学校校徽

2005年10月，上海民办奉浦学校校徽制成，校徽为圆形，由绿色、白色相间颜色组成，校徽中间为1本翻开的书本左右张开，呈绿色，又恰似正待茁壮成长的嫩苗，内涵为“好好学习、天天向上”。外圈有两个绿色圆圈，圆圈内上方为英文上海民办奉浦学校，下方为中文上海民办奉浦学校，中英文校名均为绿色。2015年4月，学校更名为上海帕丁顿双语学校，重新制作新校徽。新校徽的含义为：上部盾牌代表勇气、自我强大、保护意识；博士帽代表智慧、知识；白玉兰花代表上海；中部有代表民族性的中

上海民办奉浦学校校徽

上海帕丁顿双语学校校徽

国结把两条代表和平、繁荣的莲叶草串联；下部许愿丝带代表未来的愿望；盾牌上方为英文校名帕丁顿、丝带上英文为双语。是年8月，帕丁顿双语学校中公办教师、学生析出，建立上海市奉贤区奉浦学校，沿用原校徽。

3．学生校服

1998年9月起，学校统一为学生制作校服，分为夏、冬季服装，校服颜色先后由绿白相间，红白相间为主，学校先后更名，学生校服也随之更换多套。

上海帕丁顿双语学校男生冬装

上海帕丁顿双语学校女生秋装

二、校训　校风　教风　学风

1．校训

2005年8月，学校决定制定校训："果行懿德"，它的含义是行为果决、道德高尚就是一种完美的人格。

2．校风

1998年9月建校时校风为"明理力行"。2005年8月，校风更改为"品行朴实，身体结实，学业扎实"，以"三实"概括为对学生德、体、智全面发展的要求。

3．教风

"关心学生、因材施教、严于治学、探索创新"，学校明确提出教师培养教育学生的4点要求。

4．学风

"志存高远、笃学不倦、勤思好学、求知求真"，鼓励学生从学习的动力到学习的方法、态度，归结到实现学习的目标。

三、石碑　壁画　浮雕　油彩画

1. 校训石碑

建于2006年夏季，校训石碑坐落于北校门左侧小花园内，由花岗石石材制成，呈△形状，高1.5米，宽3米，厚1.2米。石碑正面刻有红色“果行毓德”4字。“果行毓德”语出《易·蒙》，意思是行为果决、道德高尚就是一种完美的人格。石碑北面刻有校长撰文的“果行园记”。

2008年，民办奉浦学校校训石碑

2.“民族魂”红墙

2006年制作，红墙位于原教学楼二楼大厅右侧，高1.2米，宽0.9米，面积1.08平方米，圆弧形，墙面以红色作底。“民族魂”3字为金色，红墙前4个圆柱上分述“处世”“立身”“处事”的重要内容。红墙左侧为学校德育纲要前言。2016年因原教学大楼全面装修改为幼儿园而不再保留。

3.“文、武、德、艺”浮雕

2006年制作，位于原教学大楼一楼正厅左侧，由学校美术教师周华设计雕塑。浮雕由4组塑料材料制成，各高1.2米，宽0.9米，每帧面积1.08平方米。浮雕分为“文、武、德、艺”4个主题。“文”雕塑主像为孔子（中国古代教育家、孔孟之道始祖）录有孔子语“学而不厌，诲人不倦”“学而不思则罔，思而不学则殆”及孟子语“老吾老以及人之老，幼吾幼以及人之幼”的名言。“武”雕塑明代抗倭名将戚继光等形象。“德”雕塑主像为老子。“艺”的雕

2008年，民办奉浦学校教学楼内“文、武、德、艺”浮雕

塑为敦煌壁画，表现中华民族艺术源远流长。2016年，原教学大楼全面装修改办幼儿园而不再保存。

4. “丝绸之路”油彩画

2006年制作，丝绸之路油彩画位于原教学大楼一楼正厅右侧，由学校美术教师周华等共同创作。画面长9米，宽1.7米，面积15.3平方米。以西汉张骞出使西域途经地点为背景，分别描绘了长安门（今西安）、敦煌（位于今甘肃敦煌西）、楼兰（今若羌东北）、于阗（今和田一带）、大胝（今阿富汗）、安息（今伊朗）等题材。反映中国自公元前114年始已开辟一条古老而漫长的商路（称为丝绸之路），是连接世界古代文明发祥地中国、印度两河流域的重要纽带，意在教育莘莘学子放眼世界、振兴民族未来的宏图。2016年，原教学大楼全面装修改办幼儿园而不再保留。

2008年，民办奉浦学校教学楼内的丝绸之路油画

四、文化艺术节

1998年12月，上海民办协和实验学校举办首届文化艺术节暨元旦文艺联欢会，同时展出学生美术、书法、摄影、篆刻、泥塑、集邮等作品百余件。1999年9月28日，学校举办第二届艺术节暨迎国庆文艺演出活动。学校学生乐队表演了管弦乐节目。以后，学校每年举办文化艺术节。2001年12月，协和学校表演的管乐合奏在2001年上海市第三届艺术节中小学优秀节目调演中获得二等奖。2002年10月，协和学校表演西洋乐合奏“安娜波尔卡快速波尔卡”荣获2002年上海市布谷鸟学生音乐节中小学乐队比赛一等奖。2007年，学校艺术节主题为“扬我民族文化、秀我学生风采”。2008年，举办“艺术——让生命精彩”的艺术节。2009年，学校举办“奉浦学校——我们快乐成长的乐园”为主题的艺术节。活动从11月2日开幕，至12月29日举行艺术节闭幕仪式。整个艺术节期间，全校30多个班级1000余名师生参加，节目由歌舞、器乐、小主持人、语言、微评、书画等六大类组成，经过层层举办自编自演节目和评选，全校评出60个

获奖节目，其中一等奖9个，二等奖17个，三等奖27个，其他单项奖7个。在艺术节闭幕会上挑选21个获奖节目进行公演。2010年，学校举办的文化艺术节，10月20日开幕，至12月27日举行闭幕式，全校师生参与率100%，全校在歌舞、语言、器乐、影视节目欣赏、小主持人、书画专场方面评选获奖节目54个，其中一等奖9个、二等奖18个、三等奖26个、优秀组织奖1个。2011年，学校举办“开启艺术感知、打开情感闸门”为主题的艺术节。2012年12月29日，奉浦学校举办“积极向上、清新高雅、健康文明”为主题的艺术节。活动内容有经典艺术视频欣赏，“我是主持人”及语言类专场选拔赛、歌舞专场选拔赛、器乐类及其他专场选拔赛、书画作品专场比赛，快乐星期五作品展示，元旦文艺会演，评出一等奖节目8个，二等奖节目17个，三等奖节目28个。其中学校合唱队合唱节目在是年奉贤区合唱比赛中被评为第二名。2013年，学校艺术节的主题是“创和谐学校、展艺术风采”。2015年12月31日，帕丁顿双语学校举办“掌握羊毫留青史、奋挥猴棒辟征程”“亮教职工之情、展帕丁顿之彩”2016年元旦联欢晚会，参加联欢的节目有声乐、乐器、舞蹈、小品、戏曲、朗诵等节目20个，特聘2名教师演唱“新年好”“难忘今宵”歌曲。

2013年12月，民办奉浦学校迎新文艺汇演

2015年6月，上海帕丁顿双语学校举办“六一”少年儿童文化艺术活动

1998—2016年，学校先后举办文化艺术节18届，参加活动师生2万余人次，演出各类节目1000余个，通过层层表演与选拔、评选，挖掘艺体潜能推动学校特色艺术的发展，向高校输送一批艺术人才。2011年的高考中，全校录取本科生中被录取动画等艺术类高校的学生43名，占录取本科生总数的41%。

2013年上海民办奉浦学校艺术节获奖节目情况表

表11-1-1

表演者姓名	班级	节目类别	节目名称	获奖等第
施家雯(女)等	小学二（1）班	歌舞	舞蹈《我爱洗澡》	一等奖（小学组）
徐雅妮(女)等	小学一（3）班	歌舞	舞蹈《采蘑菇的小姑娘》	二等奖（小学组）
林伊杨(女)	小学二（1）班	歌舞	街舞	二等奖（小学组）
沈文茜(女)	小学二（4）班	歌舞	牛仔舞	三等奖（小学组）
陆毅然	小学一（4）班	歌舞	《月亮哪儿去了》	三等奖（小学组）
集　体	小学一（2）班	歌舞	合唱《感恩的心》	三等奖（小学组）
瞿弘研(女)、徐婷(女)	初二（1）班	歌舞	歌曲《WE CAN STOP》	一等奖（初高中组）
张静怡(女)	初一（1）班	歌舞	歌曲《虫儿飞》	二等奖（初高中组）
任　佳(女)	高一（1）班	歌舞	歌曲《孔雀飞来》	二等奖（初高中组）
沈晓迪(女)、贡心如(女)	高一（1）班	歌舞	《no no no》	三等奖（初高中组）
谢郅怡	小学六（3）班	歌舞	舞蹈《恰恰》	三等奖（初高中组）
徐霖(女)、蔡佳雯(女)	高一（2）班	歌舞	《青年纪念册》	三等奖（初高中组）
集　体	小学二（1）班	语言	诗朗诵《一株紫丁香》	二等奖（小学组）
集　体	高一（2）班	语言	相声《世界普通话》	二等奖（初高中组）
集　体	高二（4）班	语言	相声《正反语》	二等奖（初高中组）
集　体	小学二（3）班	语言	快板《学习常规》	三等奖（小学组）
集　体	六（3）班	语言	课本剧《凡卡》	三等奖（小学组）
集　体	初一（4）班	语言	《一场辩论赛》	三等奖（初高中组）
集　体	高一（2）班	语言	《一碗阳春面》	三等奖（初高中组）
贺菲菲	六（1）班	器乐	器乐表演	一等奖（小学组）
许思佳(女)、方舒(女)	六（2）班	器乐	器乐表演	一等奖（小学组）
陆　洲	高一（3）班	器乐	器乐表演	二等奖（初高中组）
胡毕华	初一（7）班	器乐	器乐表演	三等奖（初高中组）
余佳佳(女)	高二（2）班	影视欣赏	欣赏影视谈观感	一等奖（初高中组）
何婷婷(女)	高二（2）班	影视欣赏	欣赏影视谈观感	二等奖（初高中组）
杨宝慧(女)	初一（4）班	影视欣赏	欣赏影视谈观感	二等奖（初高中组）
李立娟(女)	初一（4）班	影视欣赏	欣赏影视谈观感	三等奖（初高中组）
戴晨涛	高二（2）班	影视欣赏	欣赏影视谈观感	三等奖（初高中组）
王　欢	初一（4）班	影视欣赏	欣赏影视谈观感	三等奖（初高中组）
集　体	初一（4）班	影视欣赏	欣赏影视谈观感	优秀组织奖
集　体	高二（2）班	影视欣赏	欣赏影视谈观感	优秀组织奖
钟欣烨	小四（2）班	小主持人	小主持人表演	一等奖（小学组）
葛茹菲娜(女)	小一（4）班	小主持人	小主持人表演	二等奖（小学组）
邓　乐	小二（2）班	小主持人	小主持人表演	二等奖（小学组）
林依杨(女)	小二（1）班	小主持人	小主持人表演	三等奖（小学组）
唐　吟(女)	小三（3）班	小主持人	小主持人表演	三等奖（小学组）

续表 11-1-1

表演者姓名	班级	节目类别	节目名称	获奖等第
汪思奇	小五（2）班	小主持人	小主持人表演	三等奖（小学组）
朱嘉豪	高二（1）班	小主持人	小主持人表演	一等奖（初高中组）
吴喻伦(女)	初二（1）班	小主持人	小主持人表演	二等奖（初高中组）
任　佳(女)	高一（1）班	小主持人	小主持人表演	二等奖（初高中组）
宋海欣(女)	六（3）班	小主持人	小主持人表演	三等奖（初高中组）
徐栎萌(女)	高一（4）班	小主持人	小主持人表演	三等奖（初高中组）
吴雷桢(女)	高一（2）班	小主持人	小主持人表演	三等奖（初高中组）
朱　然	小五（2）班	书画	书画展评	一等奖（小学组）
严国珍(女)	小一（3）班	书画	书画展评	二等奖（小学组）
林依杨(女)	小二（1）班	书画	书画展评	二等奖（小学组）
汪思奇	小五（2）班	书画	书画展评	三等奖（小学组）
黄倩慧(女)	小二（3）班	书画	书画展评	三等奖（小学组）
罗伟麟	小二（2）班	书画	书画展评	三等奖（小学组）
邵燕玲(女)	高二（2）班	书画	书画展评	一等奖（初高中组）
周　慧(女)	初一（1）班	书画	书画展评	二等奖（初高中组）
吴芷晴(女)	高一（3）班	书画	书画展评	二等奖（初高中组）
顾奕佳(女)	高一（3）班	书画	书画展评	三等奖（初高中组）
张丹源	初一（2）班	书画	书画展评	三等奖（初高中组）
陆　淼	高一（4）班	书画	书画展评	三等奖（初高中组）

附：2016年上海帕丁顿双语学校元旦联欢晚会方案（摘录）

一、晚会主题：“紧握羊毫留青史　奋挥猴棒辟征程”，“亮教职工之情　展帕丁顿之彩”。

二、参加对象：全体教职工

三、时间：2015年12月31日15时15分

四、地点：401室

五、组织领导：

1. 主办：学校党支部、校长室、工会

2. 总指挥：董俊平

3. 总策划：顾行健、陆桂英

4. 总导演：程涛、李若男

5. 总后勤：王益权、郎军红(女)、蒋敏、钱双英(女)

六、节目筹备：小学低年级部3个、小学高年级部3个、初中部2个、高中

各部各2个，各年级部集体节目必须有1个。演出总时间在2个小时内。

七、节目载体：声乐、器乐、舞蹈、小品、戏曲、朗诵等，内容清新向上。

1．声乐类：独唱、重唱、小组唱（8人左右）、大合唱等，唱法不限。

2．舞蹈类：民族舞、中国舞、街舞、健美操舞、现代舞、独舞、双人舞、三人舞、群舞不限。

3．其他类：相声、小品、哑剧、诗朗诵等。

4．器乐类：独奏、重奏、齐奏等，民乐、键盘、西洋乐器不限。

5．节目演出语言不限（普通话、英语、方言）。

6．固定节目《新年好》《难忘今宵》

八、晚会原则与要求：

1．节目筹备、排练、演出以年级部为单位，各年级部主任为责任人。

2．挂点领导（董俊平高三年级部、顾行健初中部、陆桂英(女)小学高年级部），音乐教师要深入学部进行指导，肩负起领导、辅导职责。

3．节目形式多样、短小精干、主题鲜明、品位高雅。

九、演出安排：

1．主持人致主持词

2．校长元旦致词

3．教师代表讲话

4．董事长王丹花(女)致词

五、读书节

1998年9月，学校建立图书阅览室1间，建筑面积120平方米，根据全校各年级学生读书需要，添置读书设备和各类书籍，订阅各种报纸杂志，为学生课余多样化读书提供条件。2003—2005年，学校投入图书购置费23.51万元，增加图书种类。2008年11月，学校自编适合高中、初中、小学学生课余阅读的《学生成长指导手册》，每个学生分发1册。是年起，学校组织读书节活动。2009年5月，学校结合德育工作要点，实施“贤文化”读书教育活动，深化学校“民族魂·现代人”德育课题研究，开展“读懂中国、弘扬贤文化、做高尚的奉浦学生”主题读书教育系列活动。学校出资上万元，为全校学生购买分别适合小学、初中、高中学生阅读的中华传统文化读本《读懂中国》1书3套共9册，分别向小学部、初中部、高中部学生发放。该书总顾问为国学大师和著名教育家任继愈。小学卷、初中卷分为伦理篇、文学篇、艺术篇、科学篇、民俗篇，高中卷分为思想篇、文学篇、艺术篇、科学篇、民俗篇。3卷书根据各学段学生学习成长的特点与需要，以深入浅出、图文并茂、生动活泼、穿梭古今的故事，使中小学生接受中华优秀传统文化的教育，陶冶品格、提升素质、享受茁壮成长的快乐。2011年4—6月，学校举办为期3个月的读书节活动。4—5月，举办由每个班级10名同学参加的5次读书讲座活动，由名师作“贤文化礼仪、贤文化民俗、贤文化知识”为主要内容的专题讲座，开展《读懂中国》一书读后征文活动，全校收到学生征文100余篇（规定每个班级选3篇）。同时进行“身边温馨小故事”读书演讲比赛，参加奉贤区“学习共产党人精神、争做自强廉洁新人”第七届红色经典小故事演讲活动，全校小学到初中二年级学生500余人次参加。学校还通过系列读书活动，根据小学部、初中部、高中部学生实际，分别组织“爱我奉贤知多少”贤文化知识竞赛，进行各种形式的志愿者实践活动与关爱弱势群体、关心绿化、环境保护为主的“贤文化、千里寻”活动，开展“我看贤文化”读书辩论赛，在每个班级推选1～2名小贤人基础上，评选学校“十大小贤人”。2013年12月，学校根据小学、初中、高中学生特点，选编《廉洁文化进校园》系列读本，内容分别为《革命先辈廉洁奉公的故事》

“读懂中国”系列

1999年10月，上海民办协和实验学校举行读书节授书活动

《中国古代的廉史》《知荣辱、践贤行》，按小学、初中、高中学生阅读理解能力分发每名学生。2014年，学校结合读书活动，在小学部开设“童声合唱”“烹饪入门”“跆拳道”“儿童卡通”4个校队，丰富读书活动方式，培养读书兴趣。2016年，学校图书室、阅览室的面积增加至428平方米，有书架110架，阅览桌121只，藏有1万余册各类书籍，可同时容纳240名同学同时读书阅览。

六、文化媒体

1. 学校广播室

1998年9月，学校在学校教学楼设广播室。自此广播室成为学校升国旗、早操及重大活动紧急疏散演练的指挥室。2005年，广播室自办以播送学校工作动态为主的学校新闻节目。在学生中培训一批批节目主持人。

2. 学校网站

2006年5月，学校投资2万余元建立校园网络网址。通过网站视频，播出（滚动播出）学校重大活动计划，重要政策措施推动校务公开，加快学校重大信息的传播。

3. 校报《果行园》

2012年12月，学校创办8开版面校刊《果行园》，主要登载学校重大活动，教育教学等各方面工作的交流，先进事迹简介等内容。至2015年8月学校公办、民办分设，共印行16期。分设后由公办奉浦学校续办。

七、文化社团

2003年，学校鼓励学生参加各类课外兴趣活动课，陆续组织高年级学生自选参加文化社团。2006年，为丰富学生校园课余文化生活，培养学生课外兴趣和爱好，学校以高中年级学生为主，按照自愿报名参加的方式，陆续组建学生文化社团17个，成员200余人。每个文化社团设社长1人，由学生担任，并配备1名指导老师协助开展活动。社团坚持每2周活动1次（时间1.5小时）。

上海帕丁顿双语学校播音社招新广告

1. 播音社

2006年成立，主要是通过组织初中以上学生进行新闻采写、参与校园广播，培养小记者与广播节目主持人等。2016 年有社员 7 人。是年末，小二（1）班学生杨宇轩在全市 1000 余名新华小记者选拔中，被确定参加次年全国人民代表大会、全国政协会议采访体验的小记者之一。

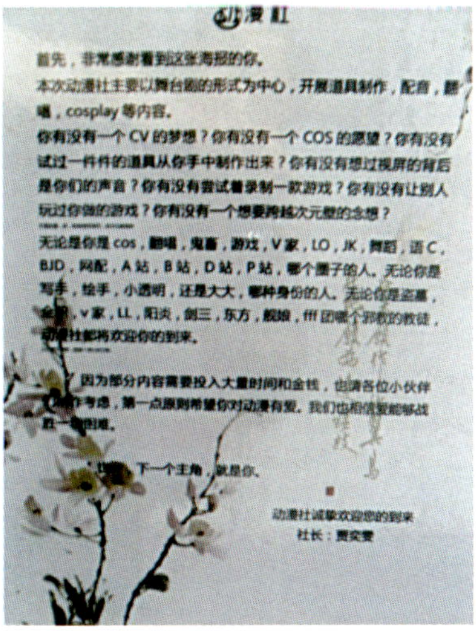

上海帕丁顿双语学校动漫社广告

2．**动漫社**

2006 年成立，通过组织成员欣赏动漫电影，培养动漫美术作品设计兴趣和爱好，进行动漫作品展览。2009 年，动漫社代表学校参加市动画配音比赛获三等奖。2015—2016 年，动漫社社员 14 人。2013—2016 年，全校有 30 多名学生考入吉林动画学院等高校动画专业。

3．**篮球社**

2006 年建立，主要是通过篮球训练，在校内组织各类篮球比赛，并代表学校参加校外篮球比赛活动。至 2013 年，学校初、高中男子篮球队在奉贤区级比赛中获得较好名次。其中 1999 年、2001 年在区中学生篮球比赛中两次获亚军。

4．**“小黄伞”义工服务社**

2006 年成立。通过培训，组织和开展义工活动，曾 10 次组织有 100 多人次参加的志愿者活动。培训学生奉献爱心的情操。

5．**动漫真人秀**

2006 年成立，主要是通过动漫 COSPIAY 的表演，丰富动漫表演内容，提升表演能力。2008 年暑假，该社获奉贤区动漫表演比赛第一名。

6．**摄影社**

2008 年成立，该社开展摄影技巧培训，开展摄影活动和摄影作品展览，增加业余爱好。2016 年有社员 15 人。

上海帕丁顿双语学校摄影社广告

7．**“绿箱子”环保社**

2009 年成立，通过学习和培训，承担校内外环保知识宣传，培训提高环保意识，开展社区内废旧电池收集活动。2009年，初一（1）班岳新宇（女）、徐卓（女）代表绿箱子社向全校发出绿箱子行动计划倡议书，提出保护环境的3条建议，得到全校同学响应。2010年，绿箱子社成员利用假期开展环保宣传活动被上海市中等学校系统团组织评为暑期优秀项目奖。2014年，获奉贤区“一团一品”优秀项目。

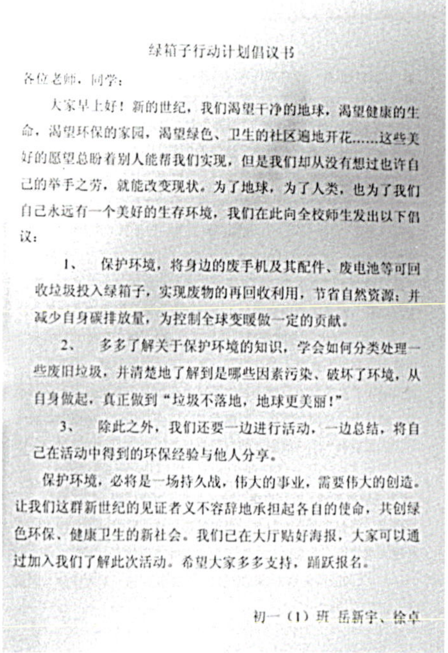

绿箱子行动计划倡议书

各位老师，同学：

大家早上好！新的世纪，我们渴望干净的地球，渴望健康的生命，渴望环保的家园，渴望绿色、卫生的社区遍地开花……这些美好的愿望总盼着别人能帮我们实现，但是我们却从没有想过也许自己的举手之劳，就能改变现状。为了地球，为了人类，也为了我们自己永远有一个美好的生存环境，我们在此向全校师生发出以下倡议：

1、 保护环境，将身边的废手机及其配件、废电池等可回收垃圾投入绿箱子，实现废物的再回收利用，节省自然资源；并减少自身碳排放量，为控制全球变暖做一定的贡献。

2、 多多了解关于保护环境的知识，学会如何分类处理一些废旧垃圾，并清楚地了解到是哪些因素污染、破坏了环境，从自身做起，真正做到“垃圾不落地，地球更美丽！”

3、 除此之外，我们还要一边进行活动，一边总结，将自己在活动中得到的环保经验与他人分享。

保护环境，必将是一场持久战，伟大的事业，需要伟大的创造。让我们这群新世纪的见证者义不容辞地承担起各自的使命，共创绿色环保、健康卫生的新社会。我们已在大厅贴好海报，大家可以通过加入我们了解此次活动。希望大家多多支持，踊跃报名。

初一（1）班 岳新宇、徐卓

民办奉浦学校绿箱子行动计划倡议书

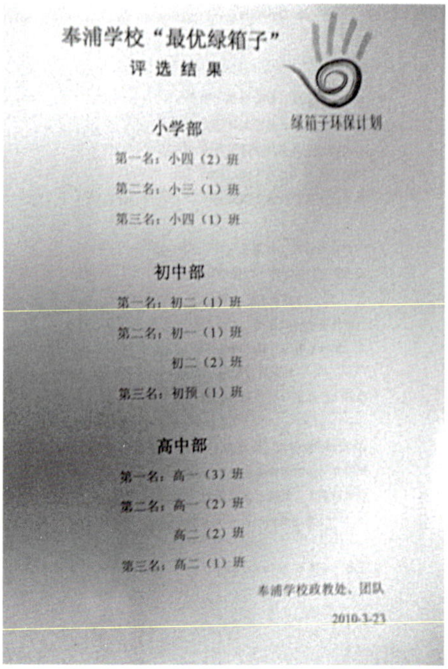

奉浦学校“最优绿箱子”

评选结果

绿箱子环保计划

小学部

第一名：小四（2）班

第二名：小三（1）班

第三名：小四（1）班

初中部

第一名：初二（1）班

第二名：初一（1）班

初二（2）班

第三名：初预（1）班

高中部

第一名：高一（3）班

第二名：高一（2）班

高二（2）班

第三名：高二（1）班

奉浦学校政教处、团队

2010-3-23

2010年，民办奉浦学校最优绿箱子评选结果

8.“清风”文学社

2009年成立，培养社员的文学爱好，参与编写、办好校刊，开展名著欣赏“文学套餐”等各种征文活动。

9．手指舞社

2009年成立，主要开展转笔、魔方等手指极限运动。该社评为2010年度奉贤优秀社团。

10．街舞社

2010年成立，主要进行街舞训练，参加街舞比赛与街舞展示活动。

11．DV社（校园电视台）

2013年成立，通过培训组织社员为学校电视台提供视频题材，丰富学校视频内容，学生自己

上海帕丁顿双语学校舞蹈社广告

采访编制的节目曾获奉贤区学生微视频作品三等奖。

12. 橡皮章社

2014年成立，通过学习培训掌握初步的橡皮章制作技巧，参加橡皮章作品展示。2015年被评为奉贤区学生节优秀社团。2016年有社员14人。

上海帕丁顿双语学校橡皮章社广告

13. 羲之文学社

2015年成立。2016年有社员11人，通过活动主要是培训文学、书法艺术爱好，传承文化艺术传统，提高书法水平。

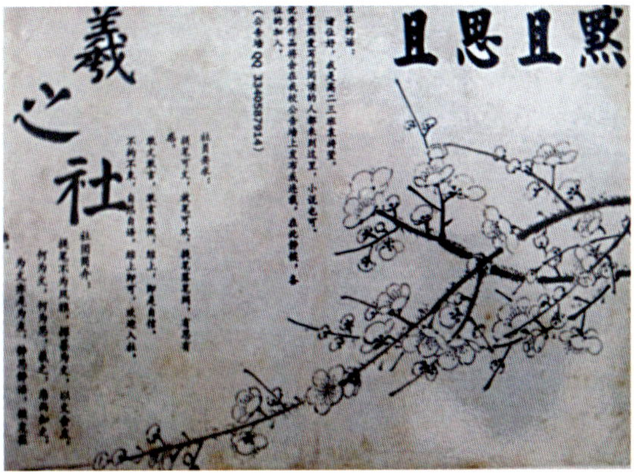

上海帕丁顿双语学校羲之社广告

14. 话剧社

2015年成立。通过活动主要是培养话剧兴趣爱好，提高话剧演技。2016年有社员7人。

15. 德尔塔社

2015年成立。2016年有社员15人。

上海帕丁顿双语学校话剧社广告

上海帕丁顿双语学校合唱社广告

16. 合唱社

2015年成立。2016年有社员15人，通过活动主要是培养学校合唱人才，组织学校合唱队活跃校园文化娱乐气氛。

17. 国学吟诵社

2015年成立。2016年有社员10人。

八、文化作品

1.《学生成长指导手册》

2008年，学校组织人员选编适合小学、初中、高中学生课外阅读的校本《学生成长指导手册》3册，分别分发至小学、初中、高中的每名学生。《学生成长指导手册》的内容以历史故事的形式，简明扼要向学生灌输“处世”“立身”“处事”的道理与方法，配合学校开展“聪明学习 · 智慧教学”活动，推动学生德、智、体全面发展。

2.《“聪明学习 · 智慧教学”案例集》

2009年6月，奉浦学校汇编《“聪明学习 · 智慧教学”案例集》第一册，收

2009年6月，上海民办奉浦学校汇编《聪明学习 智慧教学案例集》第一册

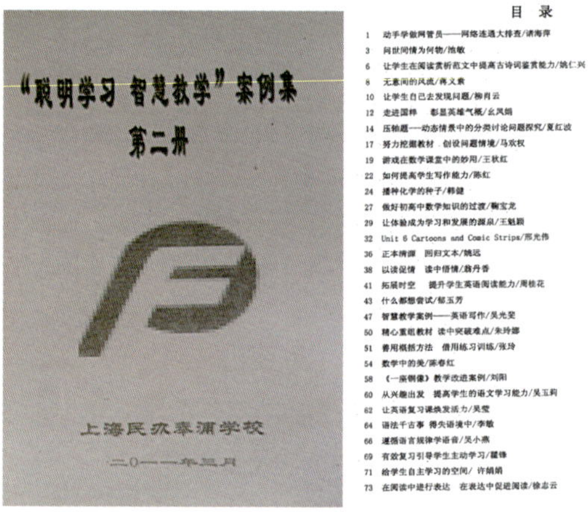

2011年3月，上海民办奉浦学校汇编《聪明学习 智慧教学案例集》第二册

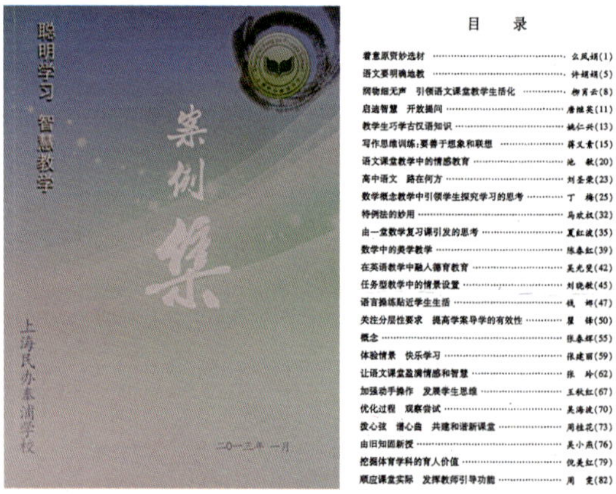

2013年1月，上海民办奉浦学校《聪明学习 智慧教学案例集》

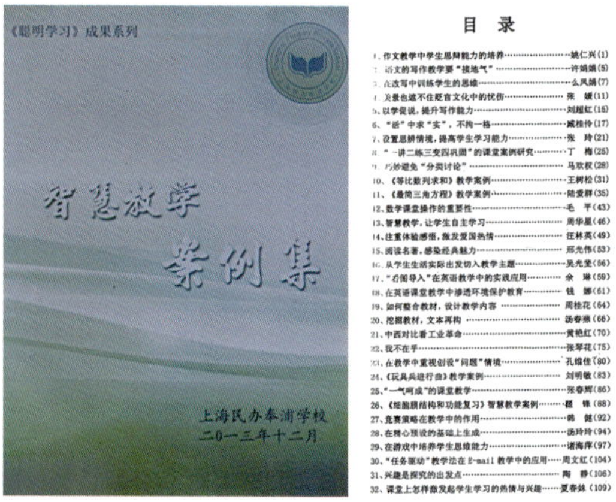

2013年12月，上海民办奉浦学校《智慧教学案例集》

2014年6月，上海民办奉浦学校《智慧教学案例集》

录柳肖云(女)等30名教师教学案例（见案例目录）。2011年3月，汇编第二册，收录诸海萍(女)等30名教师教学案例（见案例目录）。2013年1月，汇编第三册，收录么凤娟(女)等25名教师的教学案例（见案例目录）。2013年12月，汇编第四册，收录姚仁兴等32名教师的教学案例（附目录）。2014年6月，汇编第五册，收录张媛(女)等28名教师的教学案例（见附目录）。1～5册共收录145人次教师的145篇教学案例，共计431页44万文字，由校长戚盛伟作前言。

3.《"聪明学习·智慧教学"之班主任论文集》

2013年5月，学校收集选编《"聪明学习·智慧教学"之班主任论文集》，共收录全校从小学、初中、高中年级班主任论文28篇，从不同角度论述奉浦学校班主任老师教育成果与付出的心血，曹春华(女)、池敏(女)、柳肖云(女)、翁丹香(女)等4人的论文在全国性教育教学论文比赛中获奖。

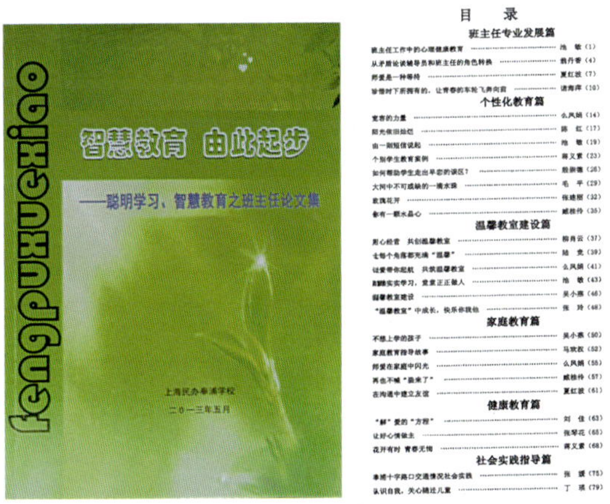

2013年5月，上海民办奉浦学校汇编《聪明学习智慧教学之班主任论文集》

4.《色彩静物技术突破》

2013年10月，学校教师张春辉以及徐韧刚共同编纂、由上海人民美术出版社出版的《色彩静物技术突破》一书，针对目前的美术高考竞争激烈，老师与学生都在寻找一种可以有效提升专业水平的方法。《色彩静物技术突破》全书分为6个阶段，分别为认识色彩、物体画法解析、色稿特

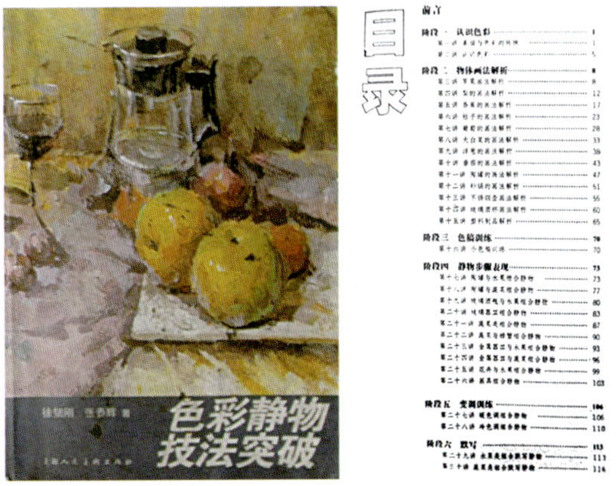

2013年10月，由奉贤区教师进修学院徐韧刚、奉浦学校张春辉合编的《色彩静物技法突破》一书由上海人民美术出版社出版

训、静物步骤表现、变调训练、默写。

5.《廉洁文化进校园》系列读本

2013年12月，学校自编《廉洁文化进校园》系列读本3册，分为小学、初中、高中读本各1册。小学读本的内容为《革命先辈廉洁奉公的故事》，收集毛泽东、刘少奇、周恩来、朱德等26名老一辈无产阶级革命家生活中的点滴小故事，却反映了他们博大的胸怀与高尚的情操，为学生幼小的心灵滋润廉洁养分。初中读本内容为《中国古代的好吏》，收录自先秦至清代的18名廉吏，叙述他们在漫长的封建社会中，为人民做了好事，他们廉洁奉公、公正执法的一面，为学生接受廉洁文化的陶冶和熏陶。高中读本内容为《知荣辱、践贤行》，收录当今社会的真人真事，他们之中有优秀共产党员，有一心为民的好干部，也有一些经不起物质诱惑、丧失原则而走向反面的人物，为学生指明人生的方向。3种读本为造就社会主义新人提供生动教材，3种读本由学校党支部书记作序，分发给在校每名学生。

“廉洁文化进校园”小学、初中、高中系列读本

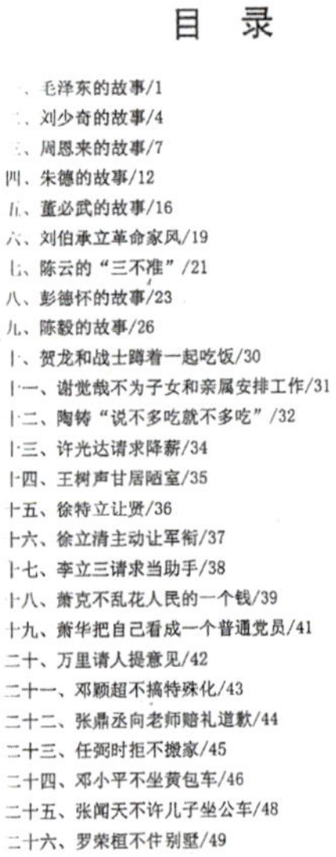

目　录

6.《为了智慧型校园的理想》

2014年4月，由学校戚盛伟为主编，顾行健、唐继英(女)为副主编，曹善明、曹春华(女)、高决心、么凤娟(女)、许娟娟(女)、吴玉莉(女)、王秋红(女)、周桂花(女)、陈春红、吴光斐、池敏(女)、马欢权、刑光伟、张建丽(女)为编委编写的《为了智慧型校园的理想》一书，由中西书局出版。该书概括总结上海民办协和实验学校成立以来，尤其是2005年后，开展“聪明学习、智慧教学”为主题的教学改革的实践活动。全书设9章25节53目，288千文字，9章的顺序为：绪论；智慧教学存在的问题；“聪明学习·智慧教学”的教学环境；教师智慧教学的策略；学生“聪明学习”的全攻略；智慧教学的氛围创设；智慧型教师的培养；智慧教

学实践篇；智慧教学的成效分析与反思。

7.《走进学生心里——教育教学微故事集》

2016年10月，上海帕丁顿双语学校根据历年开展德育教育的实践积累，专门汇编《走进学生心里》教育教学微故事集，书中收集全校83名教师（人次）的84个微故事。全书由学校党支部书记顾行健作序“走进学生心里世界”——读教师微故事有感。全书10万字，反映了老师以爱换回爱、以爱点燃爱、以爱赢得爱、心里装着学生、心里想着学生的情怀。

上海帕丁顿双语学校教育教学微故事集

2016年上海帕丁顿双语学校教育教学微故事集情况表

表11-1-2

微故事名称	作者	微故事名称	作者
宁可全抛一片心	黄艳红(女)	这是我的责任	孔维佳(女)
做一个幸福的摆渡人	杜　星(女)	漫漫数学路，师生携手过	蔡秋香(女)
我愿意等	诸海萍(女)	我的“高一”	方晓燕(女)
理解和宽容	刘晓敏(女)	教育需要等待	张静静(女)
地图的温度	曹晶晶(女)	坚守最纯粹的生命	张丽君(女)
欣赏学生是一种本领	王树松	撕心裂肺的震撼	李清华
200元	陈燕燕(女)	鼓励创造成功	王天玲(女)
花红自在开，柳眼春相续	任其兵	转弯遇到“爱”	么凤娟(女)
天上星，亮晶晶	刘圣荣	含着泪的野花	么凤娟(女)
他们是我学习的楷模	武秀丽(女)	摸着石头过“河”——路，就在脚下	刘　佳(女)
我身边的他们	张文明	在关爱中传递教育	高嘉旖(女)
完善自我　活出精彩人生	赵　丽(女)	“爱”和“鼓励”	陈晶晶(女)
心灵的艺术	李　茗(女)	和张小A的故事	陈燕茹(女)
让人又恨又爱的学生	黄瑞霞(女)	她	金晓芹(女)
左手写字的人	段华华(女)	她们	杨　华
让学生真正懂得教师的爱	王晓蓓(女)	放慢脚步，关注学生心灵	孙晓琼(女)
知识本身并不是力量	张伟国	那个她	尹　晶(女)
这个冬天不再寒冷——暖蛋事件	毛　平	师德——爱的奉献	郝玉婷(女)
阳光下的人	赵艳艳(女)	心灵碰撞	张　燕(女)
白纸与黑点	沈阳燕(女)	冷酷的外表、善良的心	李　平(女)
让教学因爱充满生命力	张丽君(女)	爱	姜凯夫
润物细无声	蒋义素(女)	一件小事	费文华

续表 11-1-2

微故事名称	作者	微故事名称	作者
微微一笑很倾城	藏桂伶(女)	可爱的人	张建丽(女)
甘为教育事业献青春	林　莹(女)	关注每一双眼睛	周华星(女)
我的姐妹，我的知己	施红妹(女)	要为他人着想要保护他们的自尊心	谢　杰
选择平凡	郑　妹(女)	无私奉献、以身作则的施红妹老师	李艳玉(女)
益师益友	刘瑜会(女)	奉献青春	吴海波(女)
爱在蓝天下	翁丽娜(女)	勤勤恳恳、兢兢业业的施红妹老师	徐青莲(女)
爱生如子送温暖 阳光雨露润心田	巴　欢(女)	我身边的好老师	曾倩倩(女)
和风细雨，但求事功	丁　瑛(女)	发现身边的美好	曾均婷(女)
不再抄人作业了	张荔婧(女)	身边那些闪光的人儿	吴小燕(女)
我身边的榜样	库月平(女)	高个施姐	刘超红(女)
牵着蜗牛赏风景	刘　玲(女)	我身边的党员教师微故事	翁　丹(女)
用“赞扬”扬起自信的风帆	郑　妹(女)	身边的感动	姚慧吉(女)
教学中的点滴小事	李素丽(女)	我的体育课堂	程　涛
学会夸奖每一个孩子	张　楚	我身边的好老师	顾俊杰
甜蜜的负担	孔　迪(女)	每个“特殊”的花朵都需要精心地浇灌	汪　宏
记周星华老师的先进事迹	汤春燕(女)		
理解他们宽容他们	李茵茵(女)	工作感悟	王　飞
学会等待 学会守候	翁丽娜(女)	在教学的路上不断	徐依凡(女)
我身边的榜样	丁　瑛(女)	我的音乐教学小故事	葛淑华(女)
表扬大于批评	严佳慧(女)	用赏识的眼光看待她	李若男(女)

8．教师获奖论文

1998年9月学校创办以来，全校教师在教育教学实践中积累和创造了许多教学经验，书写了不少教育教学论文，不少论文在区教育系统刊物上发表或获奖。2002—2014年，学校教师50余人次在区教育局系统以上刊物发表教育教学工作论文37篇，受到不同的奖励和好评。2003年教师池敏(女)“寄宿制学校学生存在的心理问题及应对策略”论文，被评为奉贤区德育教育论文评比一等奖、上海市中小学德育教育论文三等奖。2006年，教师柳肖云(女)的“痴心一片终不悔　心血浇开希望花”论文，在全国中小学德育教育论文评比中获一等奖。2008年，教师翁丹香(女)的论文获全国中小学德育教育成果评比一等奖。2009年，教师柳肖云(女)

2003年，奉浦实验学校教师池敏在全国中文核心期刊《思想·理论·教育》杂志上发表“寄宿制学校学生存在的心理问题及应对策略”获三等奖

的论文“用心经营、共创温馨教室”在全国中小学思想道德建设优秀成果展评比中获二等奖。2011年，教师曹春华(女)的“郊区学校学生西洋管弦乐队组建与训练的研究”论文在全国中小学音乐课程教学改革论文评比中获一等奖。2012年6月，教师唐继英(女)的“聪明学习教学案例的研究”论文在上海市中小学“高效教学经验”评比中获一等奖。2013年5月，教师戚盛伟“聪明学习的实践研究”论文在上海市第四届教科研成果评比中获三等奖。2007—2016年，收集到教师获奖论文34篇。

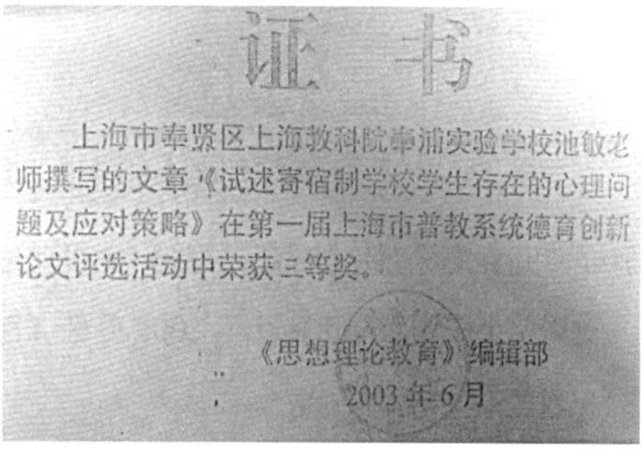

证书

上海市奉贤区上海教科院奉浦实验学校池敏老师撰写的文章《试述寄宿制学校学生存在的心理问题及应对策略》在第一届上海市普教系统德育创新论文评选活动中荣获三等奖。

《思想理论教育》编辑部

2003年6月

2003年6月，民办奉浦学校教师池敏获奖证书

9. 学生获奖作文

学校创办以来，在聪明学习活动中，学校坚持开展学生作文展示与评比活动，涌现不少优秀的学生作文。有42篇作文在区级以上比赛中获奖。2004年，奉浦学校学生桑雨晨(女)的作文获《中学生报》上海市作文竞赛一等奖。是年，奉浦学校学生柳霜(女)的作文获《21世纪中学生英文报》创刊3周年征文大奖赛中获排名第一的二等奖。2008年，奉浦学校学生刘雨桐(女)的作文在全国第十二届青少年作家杯作品比赛中获金奖。2012年，奉浦学校初三（1）班学生顾家(女)的作文荣获全国中学生作文比赛二等奖。

2012年4月，民办奉浦学校举办为李主一烈士扫墓学生优秀征文活动

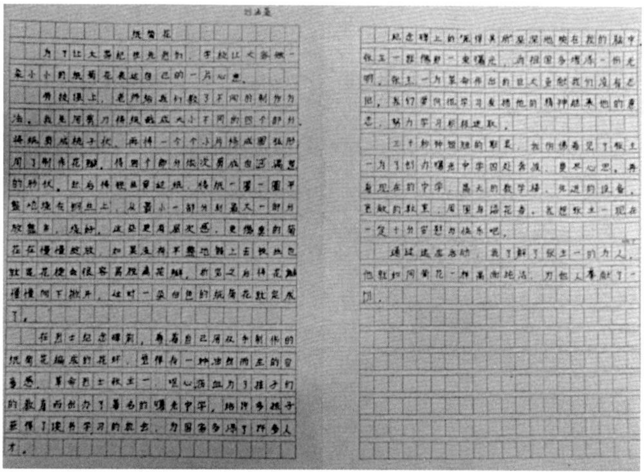

2012年4月，奉浦学校举办“为李主一烈士扫墓学生优秀征文选录”(作者刘涵藻同学)

10. 编写运动会歌词

2007年10月，上海工业综合开发区在奉浦学校举办第二届运动会，委托奉浦学校为运动会会歌作词。歌词内

容："奉浦，奉浦，开发的热土，四海的朋友在此相聚，五州的彩旗于此交汇，不同的颜色，同顶着一片蓝天，带着勇敢走上我们自己的路，我们同在开创未来，奉浦是和谐的大家园；奉浦，奉浦，开发的热土，春风催生开发的胚芽，夏雨繁荣着经济的枝叶，不同的语言，澎湃着共同的声音，带着憧憬走上我们自己的路，我们同在开创前程，奉浦是活力的大家园；奉浦，奉浦，开发的热土，智慧开启企业的征程，事业在我们手中延伸，不同的文化，涌动着共同的挚爱，带着热情走上我们自己的路，让更多的爱与奉浦同在，奉浦是幸福的大家园"。歌词内容不仅赞美了奉浦开发区这块热土，也舒发奉浦学校在开发区关心支持下成为奉浦幸福家园一员的真心表白。（作者戚盛伟）

九、家校文化

1．家长学校

1998 年 9 月，学校始建家长学校，由学校德育主任任校长。家长学校按年级组建。家长学校设家长学校委员会，委员由学校与有关学生家长协商确定。委员会设理事，由家长委员会协商产生。学生家长学校理事会成为学校与学生家长联系的桥梁，反映学生家长、社会需求的重要渠道。

民办奉浦学校家庭教育调查问卷封面

家长学校校长工作职责：全面负责家长学校的工作，指导督促各年级家长学校工作的开展；认真贯彻执行上级有关文件精神，提高家长学校管理水平，确保家庭教育规范化、制度化、科学化开展；制定家长学校教学、活动计划，确保按计划开展工作；组建家长学校相关机构，负责对教员进行考核；负责协调家长学校与学校有关部门之间的关系，保障家长学校的工作正常开展；多渠道筹措家长学校办学经费，确保家长学校正常运行，并督促做好专款专用；负责组织开

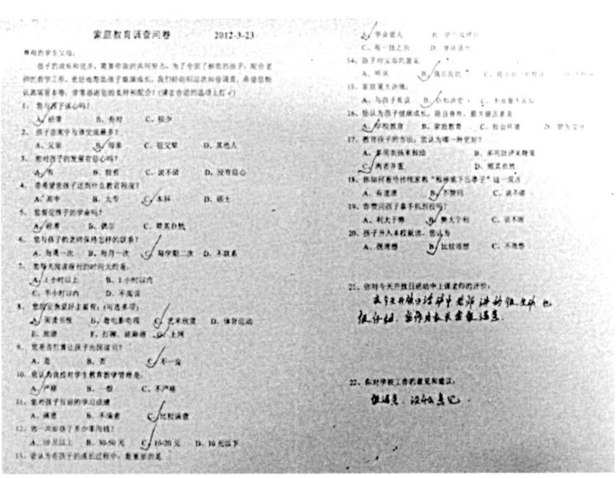
家庭教育调查问卷 2012-3-23

2012 年 3 月，奉浦学校在家长学校中开展家庭教育调查问卷活动的卷页选录

最近，地处奉浦工业区的协和学校积极开展家长一日活动，请家长来校与学生一起走进课堂，体验学校日常教学生活。

七彩校园　第55期

1998年12月10日《奉贤报》第3版七彩校园登载协和实验学校开展家长一日活动的报道

展家长学校先进班级、优秀教员、优秀学员等的评比工作；认真贯彻《家长学校工作规程》《家庭教育纲要》；协调各项工作，保障教学工作顺利进行；督促、检查教育教学活动；负责年度的家长学校检查、考核、评比、总结工作。

家长学校活动形式有家长会议，一般在新学期开学、学期结束，平时有家长代表会议。家长代表协商产生家长学校理事会，定期不定期开展家校活动。1998年学校开学后，即安排学生家长会议，向学生家长介绍学校发展计划和教育教学情况。2000年建立家长学校理事会，由学生家长代表组成。2005年起，坚持每学期召开学生家长会议，实行招生、收费公开，广泛听取学生家长意见，改进学校教育教学及住宿学生管理。2012年起，学校完善家校文化活动制度，形成家校工作常态化、规范化管理。把评优推优工作作为家校重要工作。2013年，学校积极参与奉浦社区“培育好家训好家风”活动，结合开展家校文化的实践。戚盛伟、黄艳红(女)、刘平(女)、李娟(女)等4名教师在《奉浦百姓谈家风》上发表。“培育好家风是以德立国的着力点”“对家风的几点思考”“传播正气风，传递正能量”“言传身教好家风，耳濡目染代代传”的文章，概述奉浦学校家校文化活动的体验与成果。

2002年12月，上海市教育科学院奉浦实验家长学校理事会第一次会议召开

2000年1月，协和学校家长学校被奉贤县教育局等机关认定为合格家长学校

2. 家教研讨会

2014年3月21日，经过一段时间的宣传组织发动，上海民办奉浦学校召开“传承好家训、培养好家风、弘扬贤文化”家庭教育研讨会暨“治家格言、小故事征文”颁奖活动在学校北大楼多功能厅举办。全校有79名学生的家长、学生参加，学校党支部书记作家庭好习惯培养的宣传讲话。家长代表进行了交流。经评议，79篇小故事征文中，韩志坚等13位家长的征文获一等奖，张仙红等20名家长的征文获征文二等奖，代谢飞等46名家长的征文获征文三等奖。

2014年民办奉浦学校治家格言小故事征文获奖情况表

表11-1-3

班级	学生姓名	家长姓名	获奖等第
二（1）	韩　涵	韩志坚	一等奖
一（3）	王博奕	王勇干	一等奖
三（4）	胡章琪	胡正辉	一等奖
六（3）	王娟娟(女)	王银根	一等奖
七（1）	沈双喆	朗军红(女)	一等奖
七（3）	李铭浩	沈秀华(女)	一等奖
八（1）	袁何斌	何翠娟(女)	一等奖
九（2）	周雨琪(女)	成　瑶(女)	一等奖
高一（2）	叶　梓	包卫平	一等奖
高一（3）	朱佳琳(女)	周国英(女)	一等奖
高一（3）	姚乾澎	朱　瑛(女)	一等奖
高一（4）	王一凡	赵　英(女)	一等奖
高二（1）	黄　意(女)	黄敬菊(女)	一等奖
一（1）	钱嘉妍(女)	张仙红(女)	二等奖
一（3）	李毅轩	毛丽婧(女)	二等奖
一（4）	葛茹菲娜(女)	热　娜(女)	二等奖
二（1）	金恩泽	韩晓凤(女)	二等奖
二（2）	曹　羽	万翠清(女)	二等奖
二（3）	江雨涵(女)	张　丽(女)	二等奖
三（2）	祝积武	祝建清	二等奖
四（2）	黄金璐(女)	盛妹珍(女)	二等奖
四（3）	李思妍(女)	陈欢花(女)	二等奖
四（4）	郁宸奕	俞庆美(女)	二等奖
六（1）	刘非凡(女)	李　娟(女)	二等奖
六（1）	赵嘉莉(女)	赵　进	二等奖
八（1）	叶婧彦(女)	沈红伟	二等奖
八（3）	唐　倩(女)	罗士永	二等奖

续表 11-1-3

班级	学生姓名	家长姓名	获奖等第
九（1）	易大睿	易万明	二等奖
高一（2）	蔡佳雯(女)	蔡　斌	二等奖
高一（3）	胡　禛	陈秀英(女)	二等奖
高一（4）	狄佳豪	周海红(女)	二等奖
高一（4）	刘　易	刘克林	二等奖
高二（2）	蒋金斯	蒋爱花(女)	二等奖
一（1）	杜欣冉	代谢飞	三等奖
一（1）	谭楚誉	陈媛媛(女)	三等奖
一（2）	李天佑	赵　炫	三等奖
一（2）	邹逸凡	邹　波	三等奖
一（2）	袁仁杰	施玉丰	三等奖
一（2）	程俊铭	林燕清(女)	三等奖
一（2）	程文喆	林雪英(女)	三等奖
一（3）	黄劭涵	邵　萍(女)	三等奖
二（1）	屠晟昊	宋　清	三等奖
二（2）	项佳瑜(女)	徐爱华(女)	三等奖
二（2）	罗玮麟	王晓燕(女)	三等奖
二（3）	成　鑫	唐文娟(女)	三等奖
二（3）	李安琪(女)	王海丽(女)	三等奖
二（4）	闻辰讯	闻　燕(女)	三等奖
二（4）	张浩然	张　燕(女)	三等奖
二（4）	黄杨莺(女)	黄晓娟(女)	三等奖
二（4）	李宇翔	吴玉婷(女)	三等奖
三（1）	沈施瀚	施红妹(女)	三等奖
三（3）	唐　吟(女)	王洪凤(女)	三等奖
四（1）	陆金雯(女)	金静兰(女)	三等奖
四（2）	陈剑涛	陈正坡	三等奖
四（2）	宋家乐	钱蓓丽(女)	三等奖
四（2）	戴佳雯(女)	周　静(女)	三等奖
四（2）	刘金岳	刘　伟	三等奖
四（3）	陈　云	蔡莉萍(女)	三等奖
四（3）	沈祎芸(女)	沈　敏(女)	三等奖
四（4）	蒋施繁	蒋燕燕(女)	三等奖
四（4）	何思宇	于春花(女)	三等奖
四（4）	胡语辰	胡晓峰	三等奖
五（1）	胡安琪(女)	胡德景	三等奖
五（2）	徐　缘(女)	徐长青	三等奖

续表 11-1-3

班级	学生姓名	家长姓名	获奖等第
六（1）	王 德	孙晓运	三等奖
六（3）	姚雪琴(女)	何桂红(女)	三等奖
七（1）	唐子悦(女)	唐建国	三等奖
七（2）	陈新元	陈玉文(女)	三等奖
七（2）	张雨桐(女)	钟群英(女)	三等奖
七（4）	李国庆	李华富	三等奖
七（4）	胡毕华(女)	胡加振	三等奖
八（2）	黄娜娜(女)	黄 涛	三等奖
八（2）	李冠男	李洪文	三等奖
八（2）	王静莹(女)	刘美丽(女)	三等奖
高一（1）	钱淑芬(女)	钱清松	三等奖
高一（1）	姚晓蓓(女)	徐 玲(女)	三等奖
高一（2）	郑雪涵(女)	庞 斐(女)	三等奖
高一（4）	杨渊译	潘燕华(女)	三等奖
高二（1）	沈 洁(女)	韩 芬(女)	三等奖

说明：未注明高中的为小学、初中年级

附：好家风小故事选

一、自立担当、学之以恒、严己宽人——韩志坚家庭家训

甲午春，接吾子涵奉浦学校有关家风、家训之征稿。遂忙里偷闲，整理多少年转辗求学、工作、治家之轨迹，有感而发。

试问吾家之家风，可从涵父成长之一小故事窥一斑。1980 整生于山海之滨，1995 年暑假曾陪涵爷爷三门湾畔出海运砂。空船出发晴空万里、风平浪静，为改善生计多载海砂超多超重，一并感天公作美之恩泽。船舷平海面，海鸥越浩瀚，年少心欢愉。满载归行海途中，风云突变浪逾尺高，卸砂避险犹不及。船上存三人，父、母、子，救生衣两件，取舍心纠结。父命母、子各穿好救生衣，沉着借浪使舵，约一小时后终于脱险。此事件后，出海均不带少年同往，然家事无论巨细，悉数备交给家之少年。少年感触至深，践行刻苦读书为跳出农门之不二捷径。

拟认为，吾家之家风：其一曰从小自立担当，不仅涵父如此，涵也更当如此。小小年纪入寄宿学校，为小家担当一己任，为父母的发展做出较大牺牲；其二曰持续好学，不管涵父、涵母，从最初的中专到自学大专、成人本科乃至研究生，及各项建造师等执业资格考试，持之以恒紧追社会之进步；其三曰严己宽

人，感恩社会主流文化，尽己之绵薄之力促团队之共同发展！

吾先人韩愈劝学解曾说："业精于勤荒于嬉，行成于思而毁于随"。家风当以家人久而久之之积累，身教大于言传。仓促作此短文，整合家训如下："自立担当、学之以恒、严己宽人"，与涵共勉之！

二、与人为善、待人真诚、吃亏是福——余庆美家庭家训

我出生于一个工人家庭，父母只生了我一个。但父母从不因为我是独生子而处处哄着我，惯着我，并且宠着我。河里摸鱼、田边捕鸟成为童年的记忆。家中，父亲慈祥、母亲贤惠。父亲经常说："要尊老爱幼，勤俭持家。"他特别强调要"与人为善、待人真诚"。

在我记忆中每当爸爸带我出去玩，坐在公交车上看到比我小的小孩或者一些老人，爸爸都会毫不犹豫的把座位让给他们坐；走在路上看到那些失去工作能力的人在路边要饭要钱，爸爸总会慷慨的拿出自己身上的钱给他们，村里谁家需要我爸爸帮忙，爸爸都会毫不犹豫的过去帮忙。家里要是有好东西了，总是乐呵呵地捧出去和乡亲们一起分享。

印象最深刻的是，在我刚读小学的时候，因我家前面有一点自留田，妈妈经常在上面种些瓜果、玉米什么的，也好给我解解馋。可是突然有一天我发现，怎么我家的自留田越来越少了，后来我才发现原来是隔壁的老人在田埂除草的时候一点一点的占我家自留地，我随即就问我爸妈，为什么不跟他们去理论。可我爸爸就跟我说，田少一点无所谓，我们做人不能因为一点点小事就跟人大吵大闹，这样会伤了和气。我们要记住"与人为善、待人真诚、吃亏是福"。

直到现在我还一直牢记着我爸爸的这条家训。

三、诚实为人、知恩图报、踏实做事、知错就改——朱瑛治家格言

家风，为成长奠基。

小时候，母亲常常对我说："不论贫富，一定要踏实做事、诚实为人。"似懂非懂的我只是含糊点头答应，并没有深深的烙印在脑海里，直到有一件事的发生。那是一个枇杷挂树技开始变黄成熟的季节，嘴馋的我和小伙伴们终于忍不住狂袭了邻居家的枇杷树，残枝落叶和所剩无几的涩果惹火了邻居，在邻居的责骂声和母亲的一再询问中坚决不承认错误，但头颈里的红杠和过敏出卖了我。从没

有责罚过我的母亲让我把手放在桌子上，用木尺狠狠地打了三下，愤怒、羞愧、心痛写满了她的脸，她那深重的话语令我至今难以忘怀："孩子，打你是为了让记住，人富不可有贪念，人穷更不可有偷念，只有自己劳动所得才得以安心、吃得香甜。做人更要诚实，做错了不怕，但要勇于担当改正……"家风如春雨，润物细无声。虽然是列形的，但它的力量却是巨大的，母亲虽然离开了我们，但她留给我们的记忆不仅仅是慈爱与怀念，更多的是敬重与庆幸。几十年来，我们的生活虽然平淡如水，但却踏实幸福的。

如今做了母亲的我在教育孩子时延续着"诚实为人、知恩图报、踏实做事、知错就改"的家风，处处体现着母亲的风范，我深知万贯家财不能保证子孙后代的幸福，但良好的家风能成为一个家庭世代传承和恪守的传统习惯。"百行孝先行"，古人的孝道，在今天就是感恩，今天的孩子们能否读懂风雨中等待孩子放学时那些长辈们的心情，能否理解父母望子成龙的期盼，我们不得而知，但我们可以用我们的行动让孩子在言传身教、耳濡目染、激荡砥砺中学会感恩、学会做人，形成一种共同的品质、人格、信仰，不求孩子个个成龙成凤，但求做一个踏实诚稳，与人善良。愿我们的传统美德在锐意进取，不断创新的今天代代相传，永远留存。

四、道德为先，邻里和睦——蔡斌家庭治家格言

父亲幼年时，跟随爷爷在部队生活了八年，爷爷奶奶从来都是严格管教子女的。除了在学校接受教育外，还在军营内熏陶，学习人民解放军的光荣传统，学会爱劳动、爱学习，尊师敬长。凡子女在外惹事生非或是不善待别人的事，爷爷奶奶绝不护短，严厉管教自己的子女。有一次，我父亲因为和爷爷部队的一位同事玩耍时，不小心脱口而出骂了一句不好听的话，事后被我爷爷知道了，除了严厉训斥、严格处罚外，还亲自领我父亲到被骂的这位同事家登门道歉，求得对方的谅解，使这位同事十分感动。虽然事小，但在我父亲的脑海里记忆犹新。从此，他无论是在学校里还是在单位里，同学之间、同事之间处处善待别人，严格要求自己，团结互助、勤奋工作、不计名利，受到同学、同事的一致好评。现在，他在区图书馆少儿部担任主任工作，凡是认识他的人都无不赞扬他是一位好同志、好领导、好党员。

我要继承和发扬我家的好家风，虚心真诚、勤奋努力地学习，使自己将来成为一个对社会有用的人，为祖国建设付出自己的绵薄之力。

第二节　校园科技

一、科技活动

1998年学校开办后，根据《国家中长期教育改革和发展规划纲要》精神，开展形式多样的科技活动。每年举办学生科技节，丰富学校科技文化。2006年，学校投资近万元购买单板机设备，培养单板机师资力量，使之成为奉浦学校特色科技项目，并为全区科技教师进行单板机培训，提高教师科技水平。为激发学生创造思维和创新兴趣能力，学校先后开展船模、车模、火箭模型发射、普及机器人、校园植物名录、学校减排节能方案和金钥匙科技创新活动。指导学生参加上海能力公开赛、未来工程师、机械奥运等活动。至2007年，举办10余届科技节活动，参与学生2万余人次。2012年，全校学生科技活动参与率达70%，其中五年级至七年级学生科技活动参与率100%。2008年6月，奉浦学校在第二届上海市中小学生“小科学家”创想英语擂台赛上被上海市科技教育中心评为优秀组织奖。

2009年，学校为引入外部科技资源，注入科技创新活力和动力，聘请奉贤区青少年活动中心教师金田

上海市教育委员会　上海市知识产权局关于命名
2008年度上海市知识产权示范
学校和试点学校的通知

各区县教育局、知识产权局，浦东新区社会发展局：

根据上海市人民政府颁发的《上海知识产权战略纲要（2004-2010年）》（沪府发〔2004〕33号）文件精神，上海市教育委员会、上海市知识产权局于2006年印发了《关于进一步加强上海市中小学知识产权工作的补充意见》（沪教委体〔2006〕28号），决定“十一五”期间继续在全市组织开展上海市知识产权示范学校和试点学校的评选工作。经市评审组评选认定并网上公示，现决定命名同济大学附属七一中学等6所学校为2008年度上海市知识产权示范学校，命名上海市复兴高级中学等6所学校为2008年度上海市知识产权试点学校（名单详见附件）。

希望上述学校在原有的基础上总结经验、不断创新，积极开展创造发明和知识产权宣传教育工作。各区县教育行政部门和知识产权管理部门要进一步加强示范学校和试点学校指导，推广发扬其先进经验，发挥学校知识产权教育工作在创新人才培养方面的积极作用，促进本地区学校知识产权管理工作深入扎实地发展。

附件：1. 2008年度上海市知识产权示范学校名单
　　　2. 2008年度上海市知识产权试点学校名单

上海市教育委员会　　上海市知识产权局

二〇〇九年四月九日

附件2：

2008年度上海市知识产权试点学校名单

虹口区	复兴高级中学
	华东师大一附中实验小学
静安区	育才初级中学
长宁区	长宁区少年科技指导站
杨浦区	平凉路第三小学
奉贤区	民办奉浦学校

2009年4月，上海市教育委员会、上海市知识产权局命名民办奉浦学校为2008年度上海市知识产权试点学校的文件

则担任学校科技导师，安排每周二中午时间，在学校举办贴近学生生活的创造发明专题讲座，激发学生创造发明热情。是年学校被上海市教育委员会、上海市知识产权局认定为上海市知识产权试点校。

二、科技成果

学校开办后，校园科技活动成为重要活动之一。教师何南友长期指导组织学生开展科技发明活动。至2009年4月，被上海市教育委员会、上海市知识产权局评审为专利发明的有11项。2012年，有5项科技发明。

2009年上海帕丁顿双语学校专利发明情况表

表11-2-1

专利名称	发明人	专利公开号	颁奖机关	获奖等级	时间
一种乒乓球拍	洪　森 何南友	CN201346376	上海市教育委员会 上海知识产权局		2009.4
一种组合式钥匙扣	彭　谦 何南友	CN201345937	上海市第十四届创新设计竞赛组委会	一等奖	2009.4
一种伸缩剪刀	马鑫海 何南友	CN201346780	上海市教育委员会 上海市知识产权局		2009.4
一种毽球拍	毕　洁 何南友	CN201346375	上海市教育委员会 上海市知识产权局		2009.4
一种圆规笔套	钟佳敏 何南友	CN201346923	上海市教育委员会 上海市知识产权局		2009.4
一种可调节椅背角度的椅子	管逸飞 何南友	CN201346021	上海市教育委员会 上海市知识产权局		2009.4
可更换刷头的刷子	韩萧鋆 何南友	CN201345979	上海市教育委员会 上海市知识产权局		2009.4
一种可调压的热水瓶塞	高　宇 何南友	CN201346152	上海市教育委员会 上海市知识产权局		2009.4
一种坐姿矫正仪	徐　涛 何南友	CN201346004	上海市教育委员会 上海市知识产权局		2009.4
一种黑板擦以及使用该黑板擦的黑板	徐　涛 何南友	CN201346937	上海市教育委员会 上海市知识产权局		2009.4
一种新型钥匙	彭　谦 何南友	CN101769092	上海市教育委员会 上海市知识产权局		2009.4

2012 年上海帕丁顿双语学校科技发明情况表

表 11-2-2

专利名称	发明人	颁奖机关	获奖等级	时间
能升降的洗手盆	吴 禛	上海市第二届“赛复创智杯”组委会	二等奖	2012
漏风广告牌	张博凡	上海市第二届“赛复创智杯”组委会	三等奖	2012
带手柄护手的黑板擦套	薛彧豪	陈嘉庚青少年发明组委会	二等奖	2012
旧牙刷变板刷	韩萧鋆	上海市第十五届创新设计竞赛组委会	二等奖	2012
带吸管的饮料瓶	薛昕悦	傲阳杯设计竞赛组委会	一等奖	2012

三、部分专利发明

1. 新型钥匙扣

在一个钥匙柄上装有多把钥匙，平时合在一起，装在小套子里，减小了体积，防止运动时相互撞击。使用时，将不用的钥匙向两侧按下，只剩下所选用的钥匙，这样1个钥匙柄上至少可以装6把（或以上）钥匙，这样很有效地改进了现有的钥匙扣，成为一个体积小易携带的组合式钥匙扣。

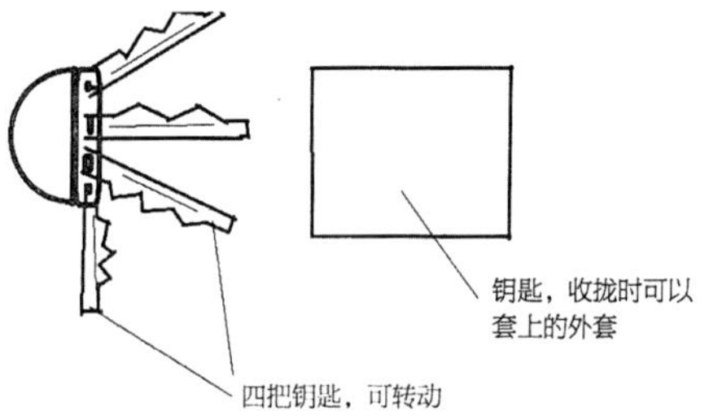

2009 年，民办奉浦学校学生彭谦设计的“组合式钥匙扣”，获市专利证书，并获上海市第十四届创新设计竞赛一等奖

2009 年由奉浦学校教师何南友、学生彭谦创新设计，获学生专利证书，并获得上海市第十四届创新设计竞赛一等奖。

2. 带吸管饮料瓶

设计的方案是：瓶盖比普通的瓶盖高一点，瓶口封闭，伸出吸管留 1 个不漏水的换气孔就行了。不用时拧上瓶盖，吸管口（略有弹性）可安全封闭。

2012年由奉浦学校学生薛昕悦设计发明，获傲阳杯设计竞赛一等奖。

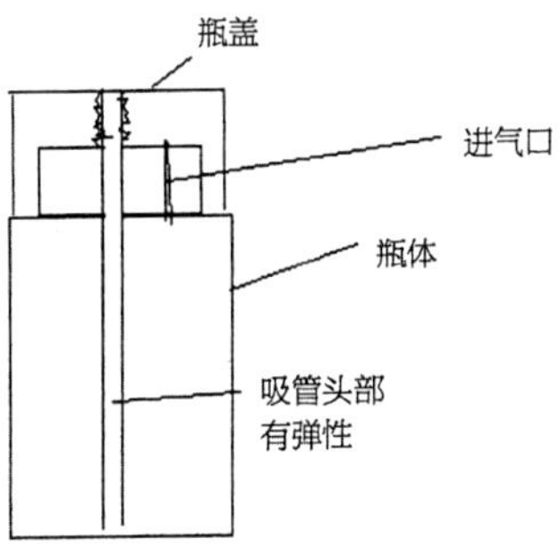

2009 年，民办奉浦学校学生薛昕悦设计的“带吸管的饮料瓶”，获上海市傲阳杯设计竞赛一等奖

3. 升降洗手盆

身材比较矮小的小朋友或有些残疾人，在洗手盆里洗手时会感觉很不舒服，有的太高，有的太低，公共场合的洗手盆一点都不人性化。于是设计1种可以升降的洗手盆，安装在公共场所，这样不

同身高的都可以方便使用，设计结构是靠摇把手来控制洗手盆高度，适用不同高度人群。

2012 年由奉浦学校学生吴祺设计，获上海市第二届“赛复创智杯”二等奖，奉贤区创新设计一等奖。

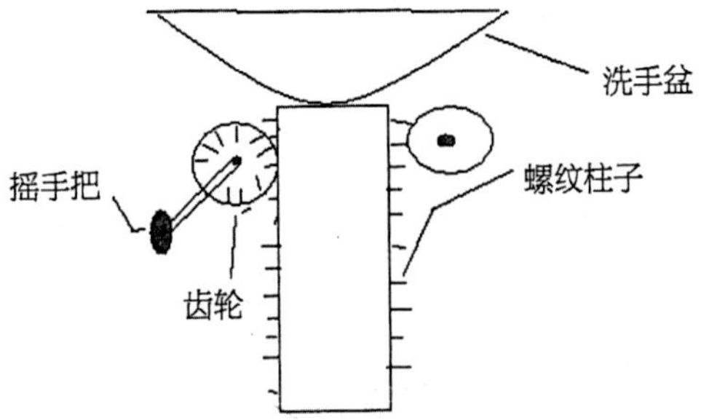

2009 年，民办奉浦学校学生吴祺设计的“能升降的洗手盆”，获上海市第二届“赛复创智杯”竞赛二等奖，奉贤区创新设计一等奖

4．漏风广告牌

设计的能漏风的广告牌，风吹来时可以将风力卸掉。主要做法是将广告牌分成许多片可以借风力自由转动的小片所组成，这样广告牌制作的难度会减小，加高的难度会减小。安装时只要把小广告串接起来就行了，在大风时每片小片都自由的摆动，卸掉了风力，保证了广告牌不会被风吹下来。

2012年由奉浦学校学生张博凡设计，获上海市第四届“赛复创智杯”三等奖，奉贤区创新设计一等奖。

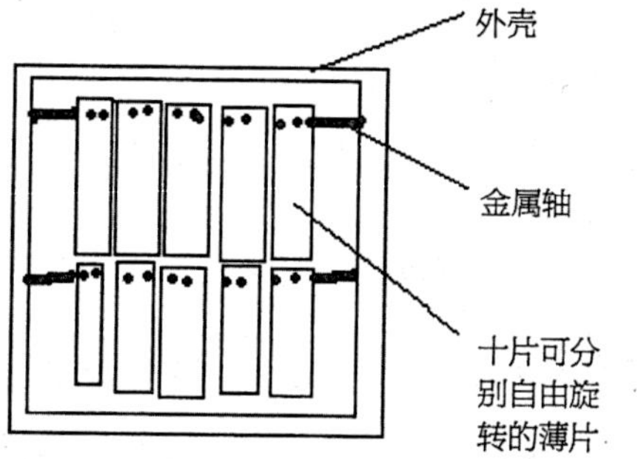

2009 年，民办奉浦学校学生张博凡设计的“漏风广告牌”，获上海市第二届“赛复创智杯”竞赛三等奖，奉贤区创新设计一等奖

5．带手柄护手黑板擦套

七年级以下的学生，不少身材比较矮小，在擦黑板时擦不到黑板上位置比较高的地方，踮起脚也擦不到。能不能发明一种黑板擦，给它按1个手柄，这样身材矮小的人也能擦到高处的黑板，另外加1个护套就可以保护手。于是用木材做了1个黑板擦的外套，背后装上手柄，最好可以变长，手柄上用软皮做一个护手套，可以起到保护手又能擦干净黑板的作用。

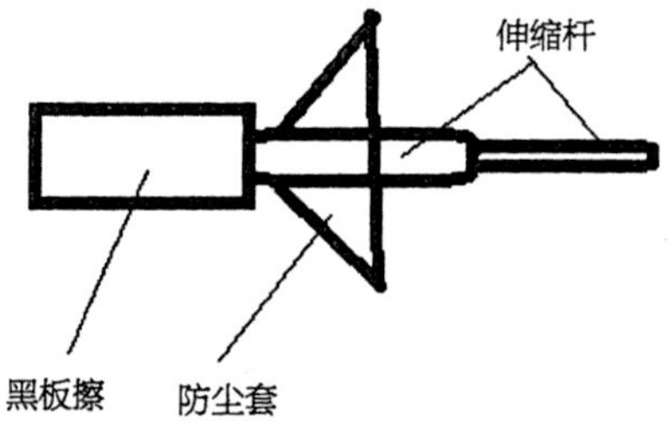

2009 年，民办奉浦学校学生薛彧豪设计的“带手柄护手黑板擦套”，获陈嘉庚青少年发明二等奖

2012 年由奉浦学校学生薛彧豪设计，获陈嘉庚青少年发明二等奖。

6. 旧牙刷板刷

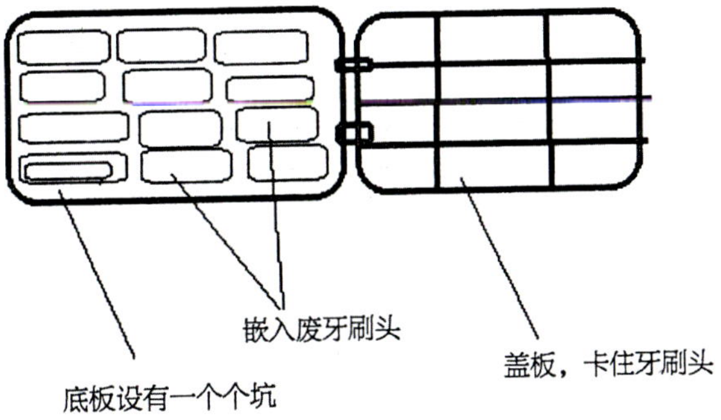

2012年，民办奉浦学校学生韩萧鋆设计的“旧牙刷变板刷”获市专利证书，并获上海市第十四届创新设计竞赛二等奖

生活中，经常要更换牙刷或牙刷头，然而换下的牙刷（头）经常是被扔掉的。而在洗衣服时碰到顽固污渍，经常要用板刷，而板刷的毛质量较差，用不了多久就会因脱毛厉害而无法使用。可牙刷一般不会脱毛，而且牙刷的毛弹性和质量都很好，能不能利用旧牙刷（头）做成板刷呢？于是将废旧的牙刷头集中起来，使它变成板刷。设计方案：图中小方块为废旧的牙刷头（有些是从牙刷上剪切下来，有的本来就是更换下的牙刷头），图中底板为带有空槽的板刷框，槽中正好装牙刷。只要将旧牙刷头依次插入槽中几个，最后将那个盖子盖好固定，就制成了一把性质优异的板刷了。2012年由奉浦学校学生韩萧鋆设计，获专利证书，并获上海市第十五届创新设计竞赛二等奖。

第三节　校园体育

一、体育教师队伍

1998年9月，学校创办开学后，即配备专任体育教师，并逐步优化体育教师队伍。2000年后，建立与完善体育教师专业培训与新体育教师培训制度，提高体育教学水平。为凸现学校体育特色，民办奉浦学校体育组编写《小学武术校本课程》2016年，学校成立奉贤区奉浦体育俱乐部，聘请游泳、篮球等专业教练员，并成立以上海市劳动模范王益权名字命

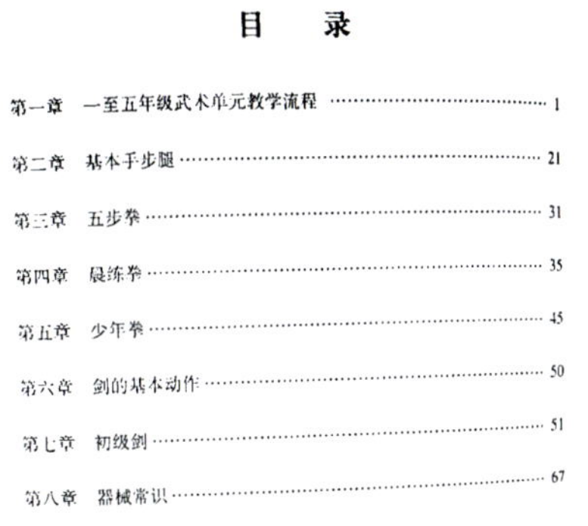
目　录

由上海市民办奉浦学校体育组编辑的《小学武术校本课程》

名的“劳模创新工作室”，聘请工作室成员10人。是年，上海帕丁顿双语学校有体育专任教师7人，其中篮球专业毕业教师1人，全校体育老师均具有体育教师合格证书。

二、体育设施

1998年9月，学校建有250米田径场，有室外篮球场2块。2006年，学校田径场、篮球场改铺塑料地面，各项体育设备逐步按标准建设配套。2016年，全校有250米标准的塑胶田径场1块，标准室外塑胶篮球场3块，小学生非标准篮球场3块，排球场1块，单双杠区1块，有单杠12副，双杠4副，力量健身房1间，形体房1间，有室内温水游泳池1座，篮球馆、羽毛球、击剑馆、桌球室等设施各1间，学校体育设施向公众开放。

三、体育社团

2003年起，学校体育社团陆续组建。学校体育组、团委、学生联合会先后组建体育运动队，以及篮球社、街舞社、羽毛球社、足球社、排球班、武术班、田径班等，300多人次参加。

体育俱乐部　2015年12月，上海帕丁顿双语学校与区教育局、体育局、奉浦社区、区老干部协会、兄弟区体育俱乐部开展合作建立。至2016年8月，已接待到校参加体育锻炼的有6.3万人次，其中游泳3.3万人次，桌球5000人次，乒乓1000人次，击剑3875人次，羽毛球1.2万人次，篮球5000人次，足球3200人次。

四、学校运动会

1999年4月，学校举办首届校园运动会，至2015年共举办15届，主要竞赛项目20多个，其中以田径项目为主。先后参加竞赛的运动员7800余名。在田径项目中保持学校纪录74项，小学男子

民办奉浦学校一（1）班迎校园运动会墙报

2008 年 10 月，民办奉浦学校举行第八届校园运动会

保持纪录 11 项，小学女子保持纪录 11 项，初中男子保持纪录 13 项，初中女子保持纪录 13 项，高中男子保持纪录 13 项，高中女子保持纪录 13 项。其中高中男子 100 米跑刘易创造的 12 秒 15 的成绩，王严钧的男子跳高 1 米 71 成绩保持至今。为迎接学校运动会，不少班级专门出运动会墙报专栏。

1999—2016 年上海帕丁顿双语学校运动会情况表

表 11-3-1

届次（届）	举办时间	宗旨	竞赛项目名称	参赛人员		
				合计	男	女
第一届	1999.4	开发学生运动潜能、选拔优秀体育人才丰富学生业余生活	篮球、广播操、田赛初中（预备班）、高中男女跳高、跳远、铅球、径赛初中（预备班）60 米、100 米、200 米、800 米、1000 米、1500 米、4 × 60 米、广播操比赛	360	192	168
第二届	2002.4	运动从现在抓起	广播操、小学生游戏、田径	310	160	150
第三届	2003.4	健身——人类的需要	广播操、小学生游戏、田径	300	156	144
第四届	2004.11.18	快乐健身　幸福成长	广播操比赛、小学生游戏、田径	312	160	152
第五届	2005.10	勇敢坚毅　体育本质	广播操比赛、小学生游戏、田径	295	155	140
第六届	2006.10.26	励志图强　谱写新篇	小学乙组：轻物掷、远保龄球、30 米迎面接力；小学甲组：60 米、100 米、立定跳远、仰卧起坐、10 × 50 米迎面接力；中学（分初中乙组甲组高中线）：60 米、100 米、200 米、400 米、800 米（女）1000 米（男）、4 × 100 米接力、跳远、立定跳远、跳高、实心球、仰卧起坐	604	340	264

续表 11-3-1

届次（届）	举办时间	宗旨	竞赛项目名称	参赛人员		
				合计	男	女
第七届	2007.11.30	健身育人	小学乙组：轻物掷远、30 米迎面接力、50 米、立定跳远、仰卧起坐、实心球；中学组：100 米、800 米（女）、1000 米、立定跳远、实心球、仰卧起坐、跳踢比赛	432	196	236
第八届	2008.10	健康快乐　放飞希望	小学乙组：轻物掷远、30 米迎面接力；小学甲组：60 米、30 米迎面接力、立定跳远、实心球；中学组：100 米、200 米、800 米、1000 米、4 × 100 米、立定跳远、实心球、跳高、广播操比赛、武术表演	562	281	281
第九届	2009.11.10	健康成长　实现超越	广播操比赛、小学乙组：轻物掷远、30 米迎面接力；小学甲组：50 米、100 米、30 米迎面接力、立定跳远、垒球、仰卧起座；中学组（分初中乙组高中甲组）：50 米、100 米、200 米、800 米、1000 米、4 × 100 米、立定跳远、跳远、实心球、跳高、仰卧起坐	434	217	217
第十届	2010.11.2	激扬生命之活力	广播操比赛、小学乙组：保龄球、轻物掷远、30 米迎面接力；中学组（分初中乙组高中甲组）：60 米、100 米、200 米、800 米、1000 米、4 × 100 米、立定跳远、跳远、实心球、跳高、仰卧起坐	468	234	234
第十一届	2011.11.4	健康生活　快乐成长	广播操比赛、小学乙组：保龄球、轻物掷远、30 米迎面接力；中学组（分初中乙组高中甲组）：60 米、100 米、200 米、800 米、1000 米、4 × 100 米、立定跳远、跳远、实心球、跳高、仰卧起坐	532	288	244

续表 11-3-1

届次（届）	举办时间	宗旨	竞赛项目名称	参赛人员		
				合计	男	女
第十二届	2012.10.22	绿色课程 阳光健身	小学乙组：传接球、轻物掷远、30米迎面接力；小学甲组：60米、20×30米迎面接力、立定跳远、垒球、仰卧起坐；中学组（分初中乙组高中甲组）：60米、200米、800米、1000米、4×100米、立定跳远、跳远、实心球、跳高、仰卧起坐、高中组加100米	636	337	299
第十三届	2013.10.31	丰富学生校园生活、提高运动技术水平	广播操比赛、60米、100米、200米、800米（女）、1000米、4×100米接力、立定跳远、跳远、实心球、跳高、跳绳	794	408	386
第十四届	2014.10.30	自信、阳光、健康成长	广播操比赛、小学甲组：60米、200米、立定跳远、4×100米接力、初中高中：100米、200米、800米（女）、1000米、跳高、跳远、立定跳远、实心球、4×100米接力	885	441	444
第十五届（上海帕丁顿语学校第一届）	2015.11.23	实施《上海市中小学生体育与健身课程标准》丰富广大学生校园生活，推动群体运动迈向一个新台阶	广播操比赛、小学甲组60米、200米、立定跳远、1分钟仰卧起立、掷垒球、50米×8（人）接力。初中、高中100米、200米、800米（女）、1000米（男）、立定跳远、实心球、4×100米接力。小学一、二、三年级设轻物掷准，传接球游戏，30米迎面接力等	429	219	210
第十六届（上海帕丁顿语学校第二届）	2016.10.16	实施《上海市中小学生体育与健身课程标准》丰富广大学生校园生活，推动群体运动迈向一个新台阶	小学甲组：60米、200米、立定跳远、1分钟仰卧起立、掷垒球、4×100米接力。初中、高中100米、200米、800米（女）、1000米（男）、跳高、跳远、立定跳远、实心球、4×100米接力。小学一、二、三年级设轻物掷准，传接球游戏，30米迎面接力等	524	293	231

1990—2013年上海帕丁顿双语学校体育项目纪录情况表（小学男子）

表11-3-2

纪录保持者	项目名称	所在班级	成绩	时间	创纪录运动会名称	地点
蒋贞滨	100米	初中预1	16秒8	1999.4	校运动会	协和学校
华　玮	200米	初中预1	31秒8	1999.4	校运动会	协和学校
刘广益	800米	初中预2	2分49秒4	1999.4	校运动会	协和学校
刘广益	1000米	初中预2	3分40秒1	1999.4	校运动会	协和学校
胡　伟	1500米	初中预1	6分20秒	1999.4	校运动会	协和学校
顾寒冰	跳高	初中预1	1米15	1999.4	校运动会	协和学校
华　玮	跳远	初中预1	4米11	1999.4	校运动会	协和学校
高　翔	铅球	初中预3	8米42	1999.4	校运动会	协和学校
集　体	4×60米接力	初中预1	40秒8	1999.4	校运动会	协和学校
陆　川	60米	初中预1	8秒34	2001.5	区田径达标赛	奉贤工业中专
姚星宇	立定跳远	五（1）	2米20	2013.10	校运动会	奉浦学校

1990—2010年上海帕丁顿双语学校体育项目纪录情况表（小学女子）

表11-3-3

纪录保持者	项目名称	所在班级	成绩	时间	创纪录运动会名称	地点
瞿佳君	200米	初中预3	34秒8	1999.4	校运动会	协和学校
徐薇婉	800米	初中预1	3分24秒	1999.4	校运动会	协和学校
徐薇婉	1000米	初中预1	4分17秒4	1999.4	校运动会	协和学校
孙雅文	1500米	初中预1	6分46秒3	1999.4	校运动会	协和学校
何丹红	跳高	初中预3	1米17	1999.4	校运动会	协和学校
干洁洁	跳远	初中预2	3米50	1999.4	校运动会	协和学校
何丹红	铅球	初中预3	6米80	1999.4	校运动会	协和学校
集　体	4×60米接力	初中预2	42秒09	1999.4	校运动会	协和学校
丁　楠	60米	初中预2	8秒9	2002.5	区第一届运动会	区体育中心
丁　楠	100米	初中预2	14秒85	2002.5	区第一届运动会	区体育中心
朱欣怡	立定跳远	五（2）	1米71	2010.11	校运动会	奉浦学校

2000—2009年上海帕丁顿双语学校体育项目纪录情况表（初中男子）

表11-3-5

纪录保持者	项目名称	所在班级	成绩	时间	创纪录运动会名称	地点
唐晓峰	400米	初三（2）	1分4	2000.4	校运动会	协和学校
叶　苗	1000米	初三（1）	3分21	2000.4	校运动会	协和学校
卫晓波	铅球	初三（2）	9米7	2000.4	校运动会	协和学校
李　诚	1500米	初二（2）	4分59	2000.5	区田径达标赛	奉贤工业中专
王严钧	跳高	初三（2）	1米65	2000.10	区田径达标赛	奉贤工业中专
褚　杰	800米	初二（1）	2分20	2001.5	区田径达标赛	奉贤工业中专
唐建鑫	跳远	初三（3）	5米22	2001.5	区田径达标赛	奉贤工业中专
黄　晨	60米	初三（1）	7秒5	2003.11	区田径达标赛	奉贤工业中专
黄　晨	100米	初三（1）	12秒2	2004.5	区田径达标赛	奉贤工业中专
陈　晟	立定跳远	初三（1）	2米69	2008.11	校运动会	奉浦学校
顾剑寒	实心球	初三（2）	11米8	2008.11	校运动会	奉浦学校
集　体	4×60米接力	初三（2）	53秒75	2008.11	校运动会	奉浦学校
施刘宇	200米	初三（1）	28秒48	2009.11	校运动会	奉浦学校

1990—2013年上海帕丁顿双语学校体育项目纪录情况表（初中女子）

表11-3-6

纪录保持者	项目名称	所在班级	成绩	时间	创纪录运动会名称	地点
何　群	60米	初二（2）	8秒9	1999.4	校运动会	协和学校
颜廷燕	100米	初二（2）	15秒9	1999.4	校运动会	协和学校
陈晓雅	跳远	初一（4）	3米86	1999.4	校运动会	协和学校
石　楠	铅球	初一（4）	6米22	1999.4	校运动会	协和学校
何　群	200米	初二（2）	33秒9	2000.4	校运动会	协和学校
李丰满	400米	初二（1）	1分20妙8	2000.4	校运动会	协和学校
张　莹	1000米	初二（1）	4分2秒8	2000.4	校运动会	协和学校
周　琴	1500米	初二（1）	6分26秒9	2000.4	校运动会	协和学校
李丽娜	跳高	初二（2）	1米22	2000.4	校运动会	协和学校
周　琴	800米	初二（1）	2分56秒8	2001.5	区田径达标赛	奉贤工业中专
彭　娜	立定跳远	初二（1）	2米18	2008.11	校运动会	奉浦学校
集　体	4×100米接力	初二（2）	1分7秒6	2010.11	校运动会	奉浦学校
夏雪妍	实心球	初三（1）	7米9	2013.10	校运动会	奉浦学校

2000—2013年上海帕丁顿双语学校体育项目纪录情况表（高中男子）

表 11-3-7

纪录保持者	项目名称	所在班级	成绩	时间	创纪录运动会名称	地点
陈　凯	1500米	高二（4）	5分14秒7	2000.4	区田径达标赛	奉贤工业中专
万春波	400米	高二（3）	1分2秒6	2000.4	校运动会	协和学校
乔　辉	铅球	高二（1）	9米98	2001.5	区田径达标赛	奉贤工业中专
赵　璇	跳远	高三（3）	6米10	2001.5	区田径达标赛	奉贤工业中专
王严钧	跳高	高三（3）	1米71	2002.5	区第一届运动会	区体育中心
范燕明	800米	高三（3）	2分19	2002.5	区第一届运动会	区体育中心
孙　尧	60米	高二（1）	7秒57	2010.11	校运动会	奉浦学校
董　翔	1000米	高三（1）	3分11秒7	2012.4	校运动会	奉浦学校
阮家豪	立定跳远	高一（3）	2米93	2012.11	校运动会	奉浦学校
刘　易	100米	高一（4）	12秒15	2013.10	校运动会	奉浦学校
刘　易	200米	高一（4）	25秒42	2013.10	校运动会	奉浦学校
徐少枭	实心球	高三（4）	14米2	2013.10	校运动会	奉浦学校
集　体	4×100米接力	高三（2）	51秒50	2013.10	校运动会	奉浦学校

1999—2012年上海帕丁顿双语学校体育项目纪录情况表（高中女子）

表 11-3-8

纪录保持者	项目名称	所在班级	成绩	时间	创纪录运动会名称	地点
刘秋凤	跳高	高一（4）	1米30	1999.4	校运动会	协和学校
陈晓英	1000米	高一（3）	4分5秒3	2000.4	校运动会	协和学校
朱　茵	60米	高一（4）	9秒78	2001.11	校运动会	协和学校
汤晴韵	跳远	高一（3）	3米95	2001.11	校运动会	协和学校
汤晴韵	铅球	高一（3）	8米68	2001.11	校运动会	协和学校
李颖超	100米	高三（3）	14秒6	2002.5	区第一届运动会	区体育中心
何　群	200米	高三（3）	30秒8	2002.5	区第一届运动会	区体育中心
李颖超	400米	高三（3）	1分12秒2	2002.5	区第一届运动会	区体育中心
张　瑜	800米	高三（3）	2分53秒3	2002.5	区第一届运动会	区体育中心
张　瑜	1500米	高三（3）	6分22秒9	2002.5	区第一届运动会	区体育中心
王怡怡	立定跳远	高一（2）	2米28	2012.11	校运动会	奉浦学校
张捷雯	实心球	高三（1）	9米10	2012.11	校运动会	奉浦学校
集　体	4×100米接力	高三（1）	1分4秒15	2012.11	校运动会	奉浦学校

五、校外运动会

1999—2016年上海帕丁顿双语学校先后派出运动队，参加奉贤区（县）各类体育运动比赛项目，取得名次的集体项目67个，个人前八名32人次。

1999—2016年上海帕丁顿双语学校参加区（县）级体育运动会获奖情况表

表11-3-9

年份	赛事活动名称	参赛项目	获奖名称	获奖单位
1999	奉贤县初高中男子足球联赛	高中男子足球	第三名	高中足球队
1999	奉贤县初高中男子篮球联赛	初中男子篮球	第二名	初中篮球队
1999	奉贤县学生田径运动会	入场式广播操比赛	一等奖	学校代表队
2000	奉贤县初高中男子足球联赛	高中男子足球	第一名	高中足球队
2000	奉贤县初高中男子篮球联赛	初中男子篮球	第五名	初中篮球队
2000	奉贤县学生田径达标赛	高中男女团体总分	第四名	高中代表队
2000	奉贤县学生田径达标赛	初中男子团体总分	第二名	初中代表队
2000	奉贤县中小学生跳踢赛	高中团体	第四名	高中代表队
2001	奉贤区南桥地区第一届初中篮球邀请赛	初中男子篮球	第三名	初中篮球队
2001	奉贤区中小学生篮球比赛	初中男子篮球	第二名	初中篮球队
2002	奉贤区第一届运动会	男子跳远	第三名	协和学校
2004	奉贤区中学生民防运动会	团体	二等奖	实验学校代表队
2004	奉贤区中学生民防运动会	模拟逃生	第一名	实验学校代表队
2004	奉贤区中学生民防运动会	包扎抢救	第五名	实验学校代表队
2004	奉贤区中学生民防运动会	定向越野	第五名	实验学校代表队
2004	奉贤区中学生民防运动会	野外宿营	第三名	实验学校代表队
2007.10	上海工业综合开发区体育运动会	足球	第三名	学校男子足球队
2007.10	上海工业综合开发区体育运动会	男子4×100米	第一名	学校代表队
2009.12	建桥杯上海国际跳棋冠军赛	女子幼儿甲组跳棋比赛	第二名	陈颂诺
2009.12	建桥杯上海国际跳棋冠军赛	女子幼儿甲组跳棋比赛	第三名	陈颂诺
2011	奉贤区阳光体育大联赛	男子排球	第一名	高中男排
2011	奉贤区阳光体育大联赛	女子排球	第一名	高中女排
2011	奉贤区阳光体育大联赛	羽毛球团体	第一名	高中羽毛球队
2013	奉贤区篮球赛	男子篮球	第五名	学校篮球队（男）
2013	奉贤区排球赛	女子排球	第一名	学校排球队（女）
2013	奉贤区第二届体育运动会	男子200米	第六名	刘易
2013	奉贤区第二届体育运动会	男子跳远	第一名	陈杰
2013	奉贤区第二届体育运动会	高中男子中足球	第三名	学校男足代表队
2013	奉贤区第二届体育运动会	羽毛球	高中组第六名	吴修远

续表 11-3-9

年份	赛事活动名称	参赛项目	获奖名称	获奖单位
2013	奉贤区第二届体育运动会	男女混合气步枪40发	第三名	金晓婷
2013	奉贤区第二届体育运动会	男女混合气步枪60发卧射	第三名	金晓婷
2013	奉贤区第二届体育运动会	男子50米自由泳	第二名	顾屹闻
2013	奉贤区第二届体育运动会	男子100米自由泳	第二名	顾屹闻
2013	奉贤区第二届体育运动会	女子耐力跳	第七名	天恬怡
2013	奉贤区第二届体育运动会	青少年国际象棋	第五名	郑宇翔
2013	奉贤区第二届体育运动会	青少年象棋	第八名	曹哲骁
2013	奉贤区第三届运动会	跳高	第四名	陈杰
2015	奉贤区中小学阳光伙伴集体跑赛	集体跑比赛	三等奖	学校代表队
2015	奉贤区“李秋平杯”篮球赛	男子篮球	第四名	学校高中男篮
2015	奉贤区“李秋平杯”篮球赛	女子篮球	第三名	学校高中女篮
2015	奉贤区“新视界眼科杯”足球赛	男子足球	第五名	学校高中男足
2015	奉贤区“新视界眼科杯”足球赛	男子足球	第二名	学校初中男足
2015	奉贤区“附小杯”围棋赛	初小围棋	第三名	学校小学部
2016	奉贤区综合素质大赛	综合素质赛	第三名	学校三年级学生
2016	奉贤区国际象棋赛	国际象棋	第一名	许芮菡
2016	奉贤区国际象棋赛	国际象棋	第四名	蒋艺
2016	奉贤区“新视界眼科杯”集体跑	阳光伙伴集体跑赛	二等奖	学校小学部
2016	奉贤区“新视界眼科杯”集体跑	阳光伙伴集体跑赛	三等奖	学校初中部
2016	奉贤区“南桥杯”中小学篮球赛	男子篮球	第三名	学校高中男篮
2016	奉贤区“南桥杯”中小学篮球赛	女子篮球	第一名	学校高中女篮
2016	奉贤区“南桥杯”中小学足球赛	男子足球	第二名	学校高中男足
2016	奉贤区“南桥杯”游泳赛	男子50米自由泳	第一名	李蕴麒
2016	奉贤区“南桥杯”游泳赛	男子50米自由泳	第四名	郁灏天
2016	奉贤区“南桥杯”游泳赛	男子100米自由泳	第一名	李蕴麒
2016	奉贤区“南桥杯”游泳赛	男子100米自由泳	第四名	郁灏天
2016	奉贤区“南桥杯”游泳赛	男子50米蛙泳	第三名	程雯靖
2016.1	上海市学生运动会	击剑比赛	第二名	小学女子团体
2016.1	上海市学生运动会	击剑比赛	第六名	小学男子团体
2016.1	奉贤区田径运动会	高中男子4×100米	第六名	高中男子组
2016.1	奉贤区田径运动会	小学男子4×100米	第三名	小学男子组
2016.5	奉贤区中小学生国际象棋赛	国际象棋	第一名	许芮菡
2016.5	奉贤区中小学生国际象棋赛	国际象棋	第四名	蒋艺
2016.10	上海市学生运动会	击剑	第四名	杜欣冉
2016.10	奉贤区田径运动会	高中男子跳高	第一名	瞿弘杰
2016.10	奉贤区田径运动会	男子400米	第二名	王昕元

续表 11-3-9

年份	赛事活动名称	参赛项目	获奖名称	获奖单位
2016.10	奉贤区田径运动会	高中男子铅球	第二名	毕晨浩
2016.10	奉贤区田径运动会	高中男子跳远	第四名	蒲逊
2016.10	奉贤区田径运动会	高中男子3000米	第四名	杨振东
2016.10	奉贤区田径运动会	高中女子铅球	第四名	沈雯琦
2016.10	奉贤区田径运动会	小学男子400米	第一名	刘颖杰
2016.10	奉贤区田径运动会	小学男子200米	第四名	刘颖杰
2016.11	上海市肯德基三人篮球赛	男篮	三等奖	高中男篮
2016.12	奉贤区中学生冬季长跑	长跑	三等奖	程涛

2013—2015年上海帕丁顿双语学校校外运动会成绩情况表

表 11-3-10

时间	项目名称	成绩	运动会名称	授奖机关
2013.7	青少年组高中女子排球	第一名	奉贤区第三届运动会	运动会组委会
2013.7	青少年组高中女子羽毛球团体	第五名	奉贤区第三届运动会	运动会组委会
2013.7	青少年组高中男子羽毛球团体	第七名	奉贤区第三届运动会	运动会组委会
2013.7	青少年组羽毛球比赛	道德风尚奖	奉贤区第三届运动会	运动会组委会
2013.7	青少年组篮球高中男子组	第五名	奉贤区第三届运动会	运动会组委会
2013.7	青少年组足球高中男子组	第四名	奉贤区第三届运动会	运动会组委会
2013.10	上海市学生武术操比赛	二等奖	上海市学生武术操比赛	上海市学生武术操比赛组织委员会
2014.5	小学生阳光伙伴乙组集体跑	二等奖	奉贤区学生阳光体育大联赛	区教育局体育局
2014.6	广播操比赛小学组	三等奖	奉贤区学生阳光体育大联赛	区教育局体育局
2014.6	广播操比赛中学组	三等奖	奉贤区学生阳光体育大联赛	区教育局体育局
2014.7	篮球比赛高中男子组	第五名	奉贤区学生阳光体育大联赛	区教育局体育局
2014.10	足球高中男子组	第四名	区学生阳光体育大联赛	区教育局体育局
2014.10	武术操比赛初中组	三等奖	区学生阳光体育大联赛	区教育局体育局
2014.10	足球初中男子组	第七名	区学生阳光体育大联赛	区教育局体育局
2014.11	冬季长跑高中混合团体	第六名	区学生阳光体育大联赛	区教育局体育局
2014.11	田径运动会高中女子组	团体总分第六名	区中小学生田径运动会	区教育局体育局
2014.11	冬季长跑高中男子团体	第六名	区学生阳光体育大联赛	区教育局体育局
2014.11	高中男子组团体总分	第七名	区中小学生田径运动会	区教育局体育局
2014.11	冬季长跑高中女子团体	第六名	区学生阳光体育大联赛	区教育局体育局
2014.12	跳踢拍比赛高中组	第五名	区学生阳光体育大联赛	区教育局体育局
2015.9	新视界眼科杯足球初中男子	第三名	奉贤区首届学生运动会	区教育局体育局

六、日常体育保健

为保证学生每天有1小时体育活动，学校成立由校长任组长的“奉浦学校保证学生每天1小时体育活动领导小组”，规定无特殊原因不得占用学生体育活动时间。

1．早操

每天在升旗仪式结束后全校师生做早操（广播操）时间30分钟。

2．眼保健操

每天上午第二节课后做眼保健操，时间5分钟，每天下午第六节课后开展课间体操（高中部室内操）时间20分钟。

3．课余体育活动

每天第八节课后，学校安排为学生自主拓展时间，学生可以在校园体育操场（室内体育活动室）进行自选篮球、足球、单双杠等体育活动项目，时间40分钟。

坚持早操锻炼是学校师生体育健身的主要形式

第十二章　人物　荣誉

本章设人物简介和荣誉两节。人物简介记载收集到的建校19年来各方面代表人物641名。其中，有热爱、关心、投资办学的企业（单位）主要负责人；有在教育战线辛勤耕耘几十年退而不休的老校长、老教师；有国外来校支教的外籍教师；有勤奋学习、德智体全体发展的优秀校友以及考入重点高中、大学本科的部分同学。荣誉一节收集学校（部门）获得的集体荣誉36次，以及上海市劳动模范王新其等为代表的一批先进人物101人次。

第一节　劳动模范　先进个人　先进集体

一、上海市劳动模范

王新其　1952年3月生，上海市奉贤区人，大专学历，土木建筑工程师。1969年5月参加工作，1973年2月加入中国共产党，曾任胡桥乡自来水厂厂长。1994年11月调入开发区工作，先后聘任为奉浦市政工程公司经理、公用事业有限责任公司经理、奉浦房地产开发公司经理、上海营巢房产开发有限公司董事长、上海申生投资有限公司董事长。

1994—2003年，参加开发区首批农民征地动迁安置工作，负责开发区首期市政道路（奉浦大道、环城东路等）建设的工程实施和开发区首期标准厂房的工程项目建设，以及开发区首批样板住房小区建设。脚踏实地，认真负责，为开发区发展赢得时间、信誉和效益，累计负责建设道路16千米、桥梁8座、标准厂房3万平方米、动迁房屋面积18万平方米，以及建造绿化面积30余万平方米。在工程建设和监管中遵纪守法，严以律己；热爱公益事业，多次赞助教育和社会福利事业，赢得群众好评。2004年，被上海市人民政府授予“2001—2003年上海市劳动模范”称号。2011年8月至2016年，上海申生投资有限公司投入4.5亿余元，建造学校教师公寓、食堂、高中部教学楼，国际教育交流中心、游泳球类馆等。

王益权　1968年10月生，上海市奉贤区人，中共党员，小学高级职称，大学文化。1998年8月调入上海民办协和实验学校。任教20余年中，在课堂对学生循循善诱，做好教学工作，课外以教师的慈爱之心关心学生成长进步。经常走访学生宿舍，帮助同学解决生活起居中的各种困难。担任工会主席后，对区教育局提出的“五不准”“五倡导”首先身体力行，关心教职工切身利益，争取资金改善教师的生活条件，做党政领导联系教职员工的桥梁。2010年，主管的师生餐厅被评为示范单位。是年8月，在干细胞捐献活动中，首先报名参加，2012年2月配对成功。3月为云南省1白血病患者输送干细胞，成为奉贤第七位干细胞捐献者，也是干细胞捐赠者中年龄最大的人员。2012年被评为“上海市优秀园丁”。2015年4月，被上海市人民政府授予2010—2014年度劳动模范称号。

2012年4月29日，奉浦学校副校长王益权捐献骨髓配对成功，获捐献荣誉证书

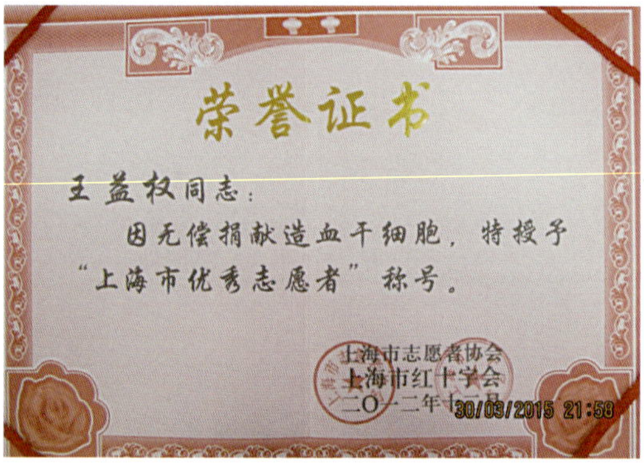

2012年12月，王益权获上海市志愿者协会、上海市红十字会授予无偿捐献造血干细胞“上海市优秀志愿者”称号

二、先进个人

上海帕丁顿双语学校创办19年来，涌现一批区教育系统以上先进个人。2000—2016年收集到的先进人物99人次。

2000—2016年上海帕丁顿双语学校区级先进个人情况表

表 12-1-1

姓名	荣誉名称	授评机构	授评时间
沈靖华	奉贤区荣誉称号	奉贤县人民政府	2000.4
曹春华(女)	奉贤区优秀中青年教师	奉贤区教育局	2000.4
曹春华(女)	奉贤区中青年骨干教师	奉贤区教育局	2001
曹春华(女)	记大功	奉贤区人事局	2001
李永卫	奉贤区园丁奖	奉贤区教育局	2001
李永卫	三等功、记功	奉贤区人事局	2001
吴 莹(女)	奉贤区优秀班主任	奉贤区教育局	2002
吴 莹(女)	奉贤区新长征突击手	共青团奉贤区委员会	2002
周时青	荣誉称号	奉贤区人民政府	2002.3
曹春华(女)	奉贤区德育先进个人	奉贤区教育局	2004.11
曹春华(女)	记大功	奉贤区人民政府	2004
唐继英(女)	奉贤区德育先进个人	奉贤区教育局	2004.11
钱 红(女)	奉贤区德育先进个人	奉贤区教育局	2004.11
丁 梅(女)	奉贤区德育先进个人	奉贤区教育局	2004.11
蔡国英(女)	奉贤区德育先进个人	奉贤区教育局	2004.11
蔡国英(女)	奉贤区思想品德教学评比一等奖	奉贤区教育局	2004
吴 莹(女)	奉贤区主题班会评比一等奖	奉贤区教育局	2004
倪美红(女)	奉贤区优秀中青年教师	奉贤区教育局	2005
王益权	记大功	奉贤区人民政府	2005.4
诸海萍(女)	优秀团干部	共青团奉贤区委员会	2005.5
诸海萍(女)	奉贤区十佳辅导员	奉贤区教育局	2006.6
诸海萍(女)	优秀德育工作者	上海市教育局	2006.6
江仁章	三等功	奉贤区人民政府	2007.2
池 敏(女)	三等功	奉贤区人民政府	2007.2
沈靖华	奉贤区园丁奖	奉贤区教育局	2007.9
沈靖华	奉浦开发区管理服务明星	奉浦开发区管委会	2008.12
吴莹夫妇	比翼双飞模范佳侣	奉贤区教育局	2008.3
池 敏(女)	三等功	奉贤区人事局	2008.4
曹春华(女)	奉贤区师德先进个人	奉贤区人事局	2008.6
曹春华(女)	三等功	奉贤区人事局	2009.11
马欢权	三等功	奉贤区人事局	2009.11
诸海萍(女)	教学节教学能力二等奖	奉贤区教育局	2009
吴玉莉(女)	嘉奖	奉贤区人民政府	2009
曹建军	行政嘉奖	奉贤区人力资源与社会保障局	2010.3
柳肖云(女)	行政嘉奖	奉贤区人力资源与社会保障局	2010.3
汪林英(女)	行政嘉奖	奉贤区人力资源与社会保障局	2010.3
何 芳(女)	行政嘉奖	奉贤区人力资源与社会保障局	2010.3

续表 12-1-1

姓名	荣誉名称	授评机构	授评时间
夏红波	行政嘉奖	奉贤区人力资源与社会保障局	2010.3
马欢权	行政嘉奖	奉贤区人力资源与社会保障局	2010.3
曹春华(女)	行政嘉奖	奉贤区人力资源与社会保障局	2010.3
诸海萍(女)	教学节青年教师评比一等奖	奉贤区教育局	2010
诸海萍(女)	市中青年教师教学评比二等奖	上海市教育局	2010
周　威(女)	奉贤区十佳师德标兵	奉贤区教育局	2010.6
周　威(女)	奉贤区教师“五表率”先进个人	奉贤区教育局	2010.6
江仁章	奉贤区教师“五表率”先进个人	奉贤区教育局	2010.6
诸海萍(女)	奉贤区师德先进个人	奉贤区教育局	2010.6
殷崇德	奉贤区师德先进个人	奉贤区教育局	2010.6
顾行健	上海市成人教育先进工作者	上海市教育局	2010
刘明坤	记大功	奉贤区人事局	2010
高决心	优秀共产党员	中共奉浦开发区工作委员会	2010
高决心	记三等功	奉贤区人力资源与社会保障局	2010
倪美红(女)	三等功	奉贤区人力资源与社会保障局	2010
沈靖华	三等功	奉贤区人力资源与社会保障局	2010.12
江仁章	三等功	奉贤区人力资源与社会保障局	2012.12
夏红波	三等功	奉贤区人力资源与社会保障局	2012.12
殷崇德	三等功	奉贤区人力资源与社会保障局	2012.12
唐继英(女)	奉贤区优秀骨干教师	奉贤区教育局	2012.01
诸海萍(女)	奉贤区第十五届教学节“育贤杯”中青年教学评比一等奖	奉贤区教育局	2012
诸海萍(女)	上海市教研室PIY计算机教师教学评比二等奖	上海市教研室	2012
林　莹(女)	奉贤区“课堂教学能力”优秀奖	奉贤区教育局	2012
李　敏(女)	奉贤区“课堂教学能力”优秀奖	奉贤区教育局	2012
翁丹香(女)	奉贤区“课堂教学能力”优秀奖	奉贤区教育局	2012
朱玲娜(女)	奉贤区“课堂教学能力”优秀奖	奉贤区教育局	2012
周华星(女)	奉贤区“课堂教学能力”优秀奖	奉贤区教育局	2012
刘　佳(女)	奉贤区“综合能力”优秀奖	奉贤区教育局	2012
王益权	市园丁奖、区园丁奖	奉贤区教育局	2012
王益权	师德“五表率”热心公益事业先进个人	奉贤区教育局	2012
吴玉莉(女)	三等功	奉贤区人事局	2012
唐继英(女)	三等功	奉贤区人事局	2014.3
夏红波	奉贤区优秀教师	奉贤区教育局	2014.4
李佳颖(女)	奉贤区优秀教师	奉贤区教育局	2014.4
周华星(女)	奉贤区十佳班主任	奉贤区教育局	2014.8
马欢权	奉贤区优秀教师	奉贤区教育局	2014.8

续表 12-1-1

姓名	荣誉名称	授评机构	授评时间
周华星(女)	奉贤区优秀教育工作者	奉贤区教育局	2014.8
张建丽(女)	奉贤区优秀教育工作者	奉贤区教育局	2014.8
张　玲(女)	奉贤区优秀教育工作者	奉贤区教育局	2014.8
郑　姝(女)	奉贤区优秀教育工作者	奉贤区教育局	2014.8
施红姝(女)	奉贤区优秀教育工作者	奉贤区教育局	2014.8
汤春燕(女)	奉贤区优秀教育工作者	奉贤区教育局	2014.8
诸海萍(女)	区教学能手	奉贤区教育局	2014
翁丹香(女)	2013 年度嘉奖	奉贤区人力资源与社会保障局	2014
池　敏(女)	2013 年度嘉奖	奉贤区人力资源与社会保障局	2014
王益权	2013 年度嘉奖	奉贤区人力资源与社会保障局	2014
唐继英(女)	奉贤区名教师	奉贤区教育局	2015.3
池　敏(女)	奉贤区优秀班主任	奉贤区教育局	2015.3
夏红波	奉贤区优秀骨干教师	奉贤区教育局	2015.3
黄艳红(女)	奉贤区优秀骨干教师	奉贤区教育局	2015.3
张　玲(女)	奉贤区优秀青年教师	奉贤区教育局	2015.3
么凤娟(女)	奉贤区优秀青年教师	奉贤区教育局	2015.3
刘　佳(女)	奉贤区优秀青年教师	奉贤区教育局	2015.3
王益权	2014 年度嘉奖	奉贤区人力资源与社会保障局	2015.3
王秋红(女)	2014 年度嘉奖	奉贤区人力资源与社会保障局	2015.3
池　敏(女)	2014 年度嘉奖	奉贤区人力资源与社会保障局	2015.3
李　宏	2014 年度嘉奖	奉贤区人力资源与社会保障局	2015.3
高决心	2014 年度嘉奖	奉贤区人力资源与社会保障局	2015.3
倪美红(女)	2014 年度嘉奖	奉贤区人力资源与社会保障局	2015.3
诸海萍(女)	2015 年奉贤区五四奖章	共青团奉贤区委	2016.5

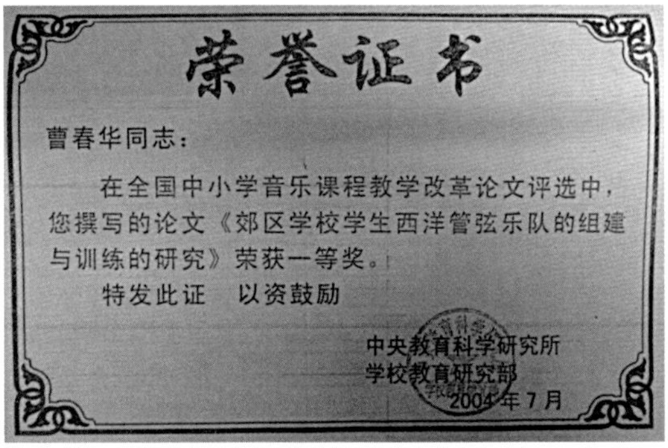
荣誉证书

曹春华同志：

在全国中小学音乐课程教学改革论文评选中，您撰写的论文《郊区学校学生西洋管弦乐队的组建与训练的研究》荣获一等奖。

特发此证　以资鼓励

中央教育科学研究所
学校教育研究部
2004年7月

2004 年 3 月，奉浦实验学校曹春华获“郊区学校学生西洋管弦乐队的组建与训练的研究”论文获一等奖证书

证书

HUO JIANG ZHENG SHU

上海市第四届学校艺术教育论文评选

三等奖

上海市奉贤区实验中学　徐音
上海市奉贤区奉浦学校　曹春华

《浅论初中音乐教学中的审美教育》

2005 年 12 月，民办奉浦学校曹春华等的“浅论初中音乐教学中的审美教育”论文获奖证书

2009年8月，学校教师吴玉莉作品“人是一撇一捺支撑起来的”获2009年全国中小学思想道德建设优秀成果展评活动优秀成果二等奖

2009年8月，教师戚盛伟、曹春华作品“树魂立根”获2009年度全国中小学生思想道德建设成果展优秀成果一等奖

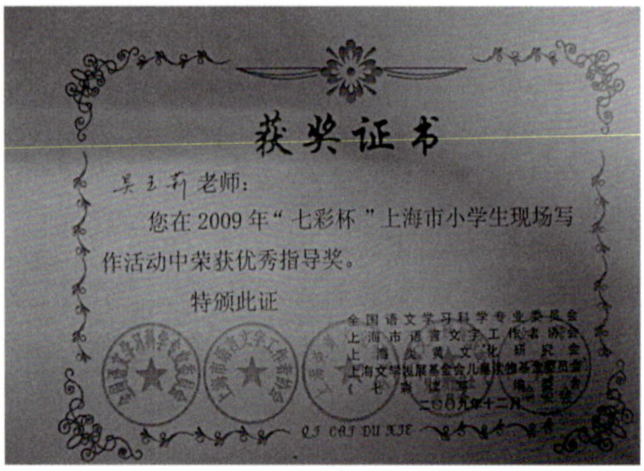

2009年12月，学校教师吴玉莉获上海市小学教师现场写作活动优秀指导奖

2013年10月，教师唐继英、许娟娟作品“教师教学行为优化”获2013年“中小学幼儿园课题情报总述”征文评选二等奖

2013年10月，教师唐继英被评为奉贤区第十届教育科研先进个人

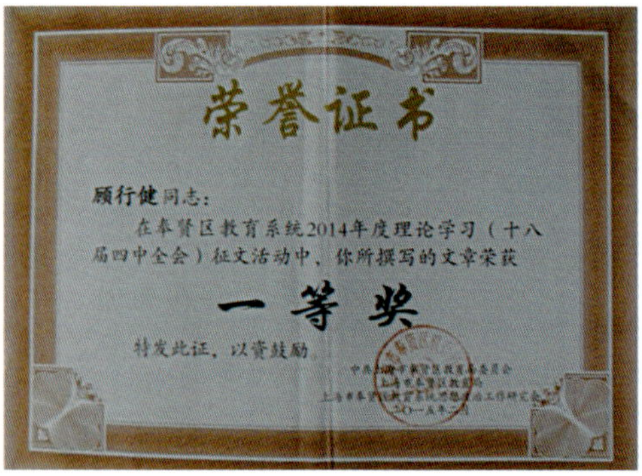

2015年2月，教师顾行建在奉贤区教育系统2014年学习十八届四中全会征文活动获奖证书

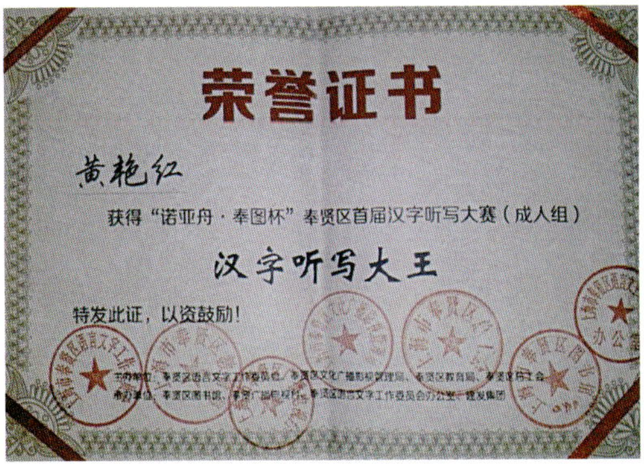

2014年7月，教师黄艳红获奉贤区首届汉字听写大赛成人组汉字听写大王证书、奖杯

三、先进集体

1999—2016年，上海帕丁顿双语学校，先后获得奉贤区（县）教育局等领导机关授予（评选）荣誉36项。

2000—2016年上海帕丁顿双语学校荣誉情况表

表12-1-2

授评名称	授评机关	授评时间
奉贤教育系统文明班组室	奉贤县教育局	1999.12
中小学优秀节目调演专访二等奖	上海市第三届学生艺术节组委会	2001
中小学音乐比赛一等奖	上海市学生音乐会组委会	2002.10
上海市绿化合格单位	上海市绿化委员会	2003.2
二星级行为规范示范校	奉贤区教育局	2003
奉贤区文明单位	奉贤区人民政府	2003—2015年
《提供适合学生发展的学习经历》课程方案二等奖	奉贤区教育局	2006.04
学校体育场地开放单位	奉贤区教育局	2008.11
奉贤区师德先进学校	中共奉贤区教育局委员会	2009.1
知识产权试点学校	上海市知识产权局、上海市教育委员会	2009.3
2007—2008学年度行为规范学校（三星级）	奉贤区教育局	2009.4
奉贤区等级达标校（二级甲等）	奉贤区教育局	2009.4
奉贤区文明单位	奉贤区人民政府	2009.4
小学、初中、高中课程教学奖	奉贤区教育局	2009.10
2009年度贯彻落实科学发展观、加强改进学校德育工作优秀学校	奉贤区教育局	2009
教育科研管理验收优秀学校	奉贤区教育局	2009
上海红十字达标校	上海市红十字会	2009.12
奉贤区合格家长学校	奉贤区教育局	2000

续表 12-1-2

授评名称	授评机关	授评时间
教研科研优秀学校	奉贤区教育局	2010
2008—2009 年上海市安全文明校园	上海市综治委周边治安领导小组	2010
少先队奉贤合格队	少先队奉贤区工作委员会	2010
2009 年中小学课程教学工作奖	奉贤区教育局	2010
小学、初中、高中课程教学奖	奉贤区教育局	2011.10
教学课程初中二等奖、高中三等奖	奉贤区教育局	2012.9
奉贤区先进班集体（高一 1 班）	奉贤区教育局	2012.4
奉贤区德育工作一等奖	奉贤区教育局	2012
《聪明学习实践案例的开发与研究》三等奖	上海市教育科学研究院	2012.10
奉贤区师德建设“五表率”专业发展表率班组	中共奉贤区教育局委员会	2012
教育科研优秀校	奉贤区教育局	2013.10
奉贤区红旗队	少先队奉贤区工作委员会	2013
奉贤区教育共青团信息工作先进集体	共青团奉贤区委员会	2014
AAAAA 社会组织	上海市社会团体管理局	2014
“七彩校园快乐成长”奉贤区首届学生活动节优秀组织奖	奉贤区首届学生活动节组委会	2015.6
奉贤区优秀团支部	共青团奉贤区委	2016.2

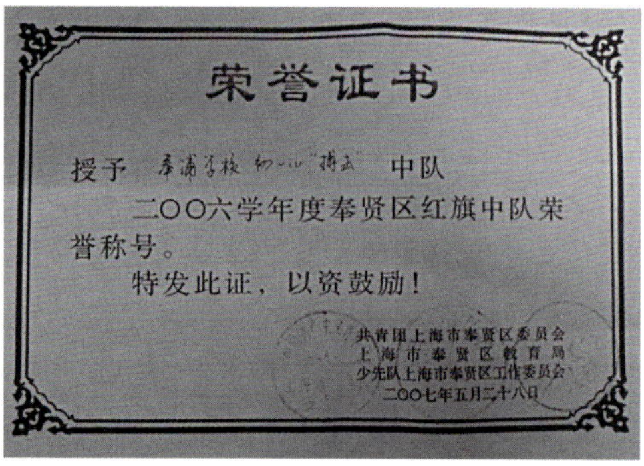

2007 年 5 月，学校初一（1）搏击中队获 2006 年度奉贤区红旗中队称号

2007 年 10 月，学校在上海市工业综合开发区第二届运动会上获男子 4 × 100 米接力赛第一名

2010年9月，学校中小学课程教育获2009学年奉贤区教学工作奖

2010年9月，学校获2009学年奉贤区中小学课程教学工作奖初中组三等奖

2011年9月，学校获2010学年奉贤区中小学课程教学工作奖初中组三等奖

2012年9月，学校获2011学年奉贤区中小学课程教学工作初中组二等奖

2012年3月，学校获2012年奉贤区第五届中小学生小科学家创想英语擂台赛团体二等奖

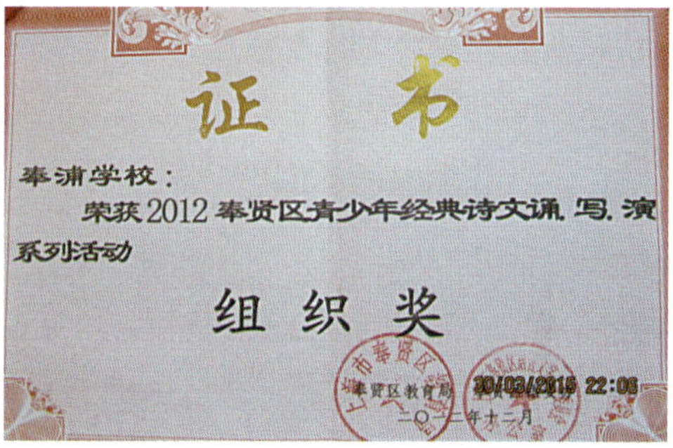

2012年12月，学校获2012年奉贤区青少年经典诗文诵、写、演系列活动组织奖

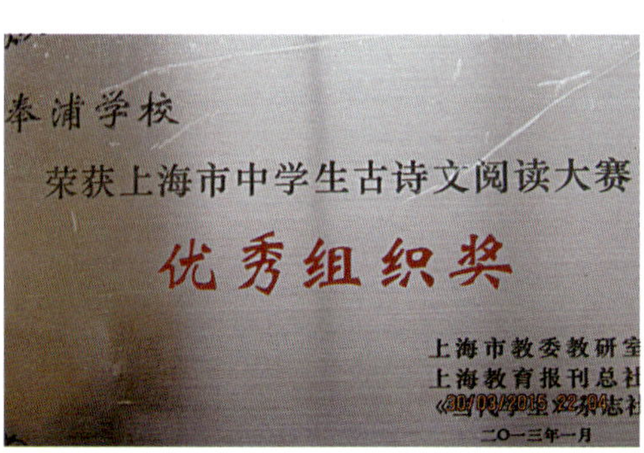

2013年1月，学校获上海市中学生古诗文阅读大赛优秀组织奖

2015年4月，学校五年级组获2013—2014年度奉贤教育系统巾帼文明岗

第二节　人物简介与名录

一、投资学校建设的单位负责人（以任职先后排列）

朱德龙　1952年2月生，上海市奉贤区人，大专文化程度。1973年2月加入中国共产党，次年3月起，历任奉贤县江海公社跃进大队党支部书记、大队长，江海公社植保站站长。1984年3月至1994年5月，先后任奉贤县江海乡人民政府乡长、中共奉贤县钱桥乡委员会书记。1994年5月起，先后任中共奉贤县委常委、中共上海奉浦经济发展实业总公司委员会书记、中共西渡镇委员会书记、上海市奉贤县奉浦工业区管委会主任、上海奉浦经济发展实业总公司总经理。期间，提出并决定投资建校。1998年2月，任中共奉贤县委常委、奉贤县人民政府常务副县长。2001年8月，任奉贤区人民政府副巡视员。2012年退休。

朱嘉骏　1960年9月生，上海市奉贤区人，大学文化程度。1980年进奉贤油脂厂工作。1985年10月加入中国共产党。至1992年2月，先后任中共奉贤油脂厂党支部书记、厂长。1992年2月后，历任奉贤县粮食局副局长、奉贤县人民政府经济协作办公室常务副主任、中共奉贤县四团镇委员会书记、四团镇人民政府镇长。1998年1月起，先后任中共奉贤县委常委、西渡镇党委书记、中共上海市工业综合开发区工委书记、上海市工业综合开发区管委会主任、上海市工业综合开发区有限公司总经理。期间，兼任学校名誉董事长。2001年8月至2003年1月，任奉贤区人民政府副区长兼开发区党工委书记。2003年1月至2014年6月，先后任中共南汇区委常委、副区长，上海浦东新区副区长，上海临港产业区管委会常务副主任、党委书记，浦东金桥经济技术开发区党组书记、管委会主任。2014年7月，任上海申虹投资发展有限公司总经理、常务副书记。2014年9月，任上海申虹投资发展有限公司党委书记、董事长。

管其昌　1950年12月生，上海市松江区人，在职研究生。1969年10月到黑龙江省呼玛县开库康公社插队，1972年7月加入中国共产党。先后任插队的所在生产大队党支部副书记、公社党委副书记、公安派出所指导员、县公安局边防科科长。1979年1月回沪，在松江县橡胶厂工作，先后任车间主任、副厂长、厂长。后任县工业局副局长、党委副书记、局长、工业总公司总经理，评为上海市劳动模范，是上海市第九届、第十届人大代表。1994年9月，任奉贤县人民政府副县长、党组成员、县委政法委副书记。2001年8月，任上海市工业综合开发区有限公司总经理、副董事长，主持开发区管委会工作。2002年5月离开开发区。

陈建庆　1956年10月生，祖籍浙江省绍兴市，从小在奉城长大。1981年1月至1983年8月，任奉城供销社科技股长。1984年12月加入中国共产党。1986年1月上海科技大学机械制造和设计专业毕业。1986年2月至1989年12月，任上海古华食品厂副厂长、奉城供销社副主任、上海华乐食品厂厂长、党支部副书记。1989年12月至1992年6月，任奉贤县供销社党委委员、副主任。1992年7月至1998年6月，任奉贤县平安乡党委副书记、乡长、平安镇党委书记兼人大主席。1993年8月，评为机械工程师。1998年6月至2002年5月，任江海镇党委书记。2002年5月，任奉城镇党委书记。2006年2月至2010年8月，任奉贤区人民政府办公室主任兼区政府法制办主任、外事办主任、合作交流办主任、地区办主任、人口办主任。2010年8月至2016年11月，任上海工业综合开发区管委会主任、总经理、党工委副书记。

庄锦荣　1939年1月生，祖籍江苏省无锡县，中共党员，大学文化程度。1959年毕业于上海师范学院数学专业，先后任教于四团中学、奉贤教师进修学校。1978年6月，任奉贤县教师进修学校副校长。1985年2月任校长。1990年8月，被上海市人民政府授予特级教师称号。1992年9月，任奉贤县教育局局长，党委副书记。1999年4月退休。1974年起先后参加上海市和全国小学教师进修中师的数学教学大纲和大纲拟订工作、上海市中学教材《数学》和全国小学教师进修教材《几何》及其教学参考书的编写工作。主持编写的“上海市郊区中小学设点布局和办学效益的研究”论文获上海市教科研一等奖。“县域范围内中小学目标管理系统的研究”获二等奖、“幼儿数学教育课程改革实验”和“上海郊区教育结构现状及优化途径的研究”获三等奖。1998年8月至2000年2月任上海民办协和实验学校董事会董事。其间，积极支持帮助学校的建设与发展。2001年6月被教育部、财政部、计委授予全国“两基”工作先进个人。

胡　卫　（详见本章第二节第二目第一子目）

王新其　（详见本章第一节第一目上海市劳动模范）

二、历任学校董（理）（名誉）事长（以任职先后排列）

朱嘉骏　（详见本章第二节第一目投资学校负责人）

沈金龙　1954年5月生，上海市奉贤区人，大专学历。1972年12月参加中国人民解放军，1976年6月加入中国共产党。1979年3月退伍。是年4月，在中共奉贤县委组织部工作。1984年3月至1995年9月，先后任中共齐贤乡党委秘书、宣传委员、副乡长、西渡镇党委委员、副镇长。1995年9月起，先后任上海市奉浦工业区管理委员会常务副主任、上海奉浦经济发展实业总公司常务副总经理，兼上海民办协和实验学校董事会董事长。2000年2月辞职离任。

蒋辉藥　1948年10月生，上海市奉贤区人，中共党员，中学高级教师，硕士研究生毕业，文学硕士学位。1968年高中毕业。是年9月插队落户于庄行公社光明三大队（今牛溇村）第一生产队。1969年9月至1978年9月先后在光明三大队小学、光明中学任教。1978年9月，考入上海华东师范大学中文系带薪脱产进修。毕业后在奉贤县教师进修学校任教，历任高中语文教研员、上海市中师语文中心教研组长、奉贤县中师班负责人。1984年12月调入奉贤中学，历任副校长、党支部副书记、校长、党支部书记。1968年获上海市优秀教育工作者称号。1990年获上海市劳动模范称号。1995年被评为全国教育系统劳动模范。1998年12月调任奉贤县教育局局长、党委副书记、县人民政府教育督导室主任。2000年2月至2002年5月，兼任学校董事会名誉董事长。2001年11月，任奉贤县人大常委会常委、教科文卫工作委员会主任等职。先后当选为上海市第十、第十一、第十二届人民代表大会代表，奉贤区第一、第二届人民代表大会代表、常委、国民经济和社会发展计划审查委员会副主任。还先后任上海市人民政府教育督导室兼职督学。先后撰写并发表于省市级刊物论文30多篇。主编内部印发《奉贤县全面实施素质教育行动钢要》等书籍。

胡　卫　1961年1月出生，上海市人，中共党员，本科学历，副研究员、全国政协委员、上海市教育科学研究院民办教育中心主任。1998年9月，任上海民办协和实验学校副董事长。1999—2000年，以上海市教育科学研究院民办教育中心的名义，筹集资金300万元，建设学校3号宿舍楼。2000年任学校董事会董事长。2003年8月，学校由奉浦经济发展实业总公司接管后离校。

王森龙　1961年3月生，上海市奉贤区人，中共党员，华东师范大学哲学系决策管理专业毕业。历任钱桥中心小学副校长，奉城中心小学校长，奉城第二中心小学校长、党支部书记，奉贤县教育局秘书、奉贤县政府秘书、南桥镇副镇长、党委副书记、镇长。2001年12月至2007年3月，任奉贤区教育局局长。2002

年5月至2009年2月，兼任学校名誉董事长。2007年4月至2016年先后任区教育局党委书记、区政府教育督导室主任，区总工会党组书记、常务副主席，区教育局调研员等职。1987年获上海市新长征突击手称号、上海市园丁奖。

王少峰　1963年12月生，上海市奉贤区人，中共党员，研究生学历。1982年8月至1998年9月在奉贤县公安局工作，历任刑队民警、钱桥派出所副所长、县公安局预审科科长等职。1998年9月，任青村镇党委副书记。2001年12月，任中共奉贤区纪律检查委员会常委、副书记。2011年10月，任中共奉贤区奉浦社区工作委员会书记、办事处主任。2012年9月任上海民办奉浦学校名誉董事长。2016年9月，调任奉贤区金汇镇人大主席。

李　臻　1954年7月生，上海市奉贤区人，大专文化程度。1972年12月，参加中国人民解放军，1975年4月加入中国共产党，1998年11月军队转业。曾任空军某部分队长、指导员、政治处副主任、教导员，中共奉贤县纪律检查委员会办公室主任。1991年2月起，历任奉贤县乡镇工业局副局长、对外经济贸易委员会副主任、头桥镇人民政府镇长。2002年5月起，先后任上海市工业综合开发区管理委员会主任、中共上海市工业综合开发区党工委副书记、书记，上海市工业综合开发区管理委员会副主任，上海市工业综合开发区有限公司总经理、副董事长，兼任上海民办协和实验学校董事会董事长。

陆建国　1963年8月生，上海市奉贤区人，中共党员，全日制大学文学学士、中学高级教师。1985年7月参加工作。历任奉贤区委组织部副部长，区社会工作党委书记，奉贤区教育局党委副书记、书记、副局长、局长，区教育督导室主任。1993年评为中学高级教师。1996年评为上海市劳动模范。2011年被评为全国成人教育先进个人，杰出贡献奖，被中央教科所聘为行政决策咨询专家，多次参与国家级教育规划课题研究。2014年9月，任奉贤区人大常委会副主任、区总工会主席。2012年9月至2015年8月聘为上海民办奉浦学校董事会名誉董事长。

王丹花　女，1976年10月出生，上海市奉贤区人，中共党员，工商管理硕士。先后毕业于上海陶行知师范学校、上海交通大学海外教育学院工商管理专业。1995年6月，在奉贤区实验小学任教。1995年8月至1999年12月，任共青团奉贤县委员会权益部长。1999年12月至2002年12月，在上海昆仑律师事务所工作。2002年12月，任上海营巢房产开发有限公司副董事长。2009年12月，任上海民办奉浦学校董事会董事长。1997—2003年，先后获得上海市新长征突击手、奉贤区优秀党员、奉贤区十大青年创业先锋等称号、上海市五四奖章。现任上海帕丁顿双语学校董事会董事长，上海营巢房产开发有限公司总经理、党支部书记。奉贤区政协委员，奉贤区青年创业协会副会长、秘书长。

三、历任学校校长（以任职先后排列）

夏明德　1930年3月出生，上海市川沙县（今浦东新区）人，大学文化，中共党员，中学特级教师。1949年参加工作。1949—1962年，在上海川沙中学任教，先后任班主任、学校数学教研组组长、教导主任。1962—1981年在上海市教育局教学处任中学数学教材编写组组长，并参与上海市重点中学理科教材编写。1981—1990年，借调上海市教育局教学处，任中学数学学科组负责人、教研员。1990—1998年，任上海民办前进进修学院教材组、政宣组负责人、教务长。1998年7月，任上海民办协和实验学校校长兼党支部书记。2000年4月离任。

马伯相　上海市区人，中共党员，大学文化，中学高级教师。曾任上海市第三女子中学教导主任、上海市虹桥中学校长等职。2000年4月，协和学校董事会聘任为校长兼党支部书记。2001年8月离任。

丰忠汉　上海市区人，中共党员，大学文化，中学高级教师。2001年8月应聘任民办协和学校校长。2003年8月离任。

杨连明　上海市奉贤区人，中共党员，大学文化，中学高级教师。2003年8月，由上海市奉贤区教师进修学校调入所属奉浦实验学校，任校长兼党支部书记。2005年5月离任。

戚盛伟　1945年生，上海市卢湾区（今黄浦区）人，研究生。1967年毕业于上海师范学院中文系。1998年3月，华师大高等教育学专业研究生班结业。1991年评为中学高级教师。2002年被评为上海市一级一等校长。曾获上海市优秀教育工作者、上海市教育科研先进个人、上海市园丁奖、奉贤区首批名校长、奉贤区优秀党务工作者等荣誉。记大功3次、荣誉称号1次。

1985年2月任奉贤胡桥中学校长。1990年8月任奉贤县教育局中教科长。1993年任奉贤县工业中等专业学校党支部书记。1998年7月任奉贤综合高中（今致远中学）校长，2000年兼党支部书记。2005年7月应聘任上海民办奉浦学校校长，2009年5月兼任党支部书记。2014年4月离任。

在上海民办奉浦学校任内，倡导“适合教育”，提出“聪明学习，智慧教学”的教学工作策略与“民族魂·现代人”的德育工作体系。2012年学校小学、初中、高中各部分别获区课程教学奖。

撰写的《提高农村初中办学效益的实践与思考》获上海市第三届教育科研成果三等奖；《县城内青年骨干教师培养的策略研究》获上海市第四届教育科研成果二等奖；《城郊型综合高中办学模式的实践研究》获奉贤区第六届教科研成果一等奖、上海市首届学校教育科研成果奖；《普通高中学生自主学习学业评价指标体系与操作方案的实践研究》获全国教育科学“十·五”规划教育部重点课题子课题；《“聪明学习”案例的开发与研究》获上海市第四届学校教科研成果三等奖。先后发表在《修辞学习》《语文教学》《上海教育》等杂志的论文30余篇。

顾行健　1952年6月生。江苏省启东县人，中学高级教师，中学一级二等校长资格，国家二级心理咨询师。1978年4月参加工作。上海师范大学教育管理本科、教育经济管理硕士研究生课程班结业，美国国际大学EMBA。曾任市农场局星火学校校长、奉贤区海湾镇成人学校校长等职。

2012年2月至2014年4月，任上海民办奉浦学校校长，2014年5月，任上海帕丁顿双语学校党支部书记，副校长。

1982年被上海市人民政府评为上海市职工教育先进工作者。2010年，被评为2006—2010年上海市成人教育先进工作者，多次被上海市农场局评为优秀教育工作者。2008年获上海市成人教育特色课题《塑造阳光心态》二等奖。2015年编写出版《奉贤农垦之路》，2010年参与奉贤区教育局“上海市中长期教育改革与发展规划纲要研究专项课题”，在市级刊物发表多篇课题研究论文。

董俊平　1976年4月生，上海闵行区人，文学学士、管理科学与工程学硕士（国家一级重点学科）、华东师范大学教育领导与管理学博士，中学语文高级教师，中共党员。现任上海交通大学教育集团副总裁、全国集团校总校长；上海交通大学奉贤现代教育示范园区总校长；上海交通大学湖州现代教育示范园区校长；上海帕丁顿双语学校校长；上海交大南洋中学校长。2014年3月，任上海帕丁顿双语学校校长。曾荣获团中央、文化部、教育部主办的“全国电视演讲大赛总冠军”，获市政府、区政府、交大教育集团特别嘉奖；教育部“全国特色兴校杰出贡献奖”；上海市十佳魅力教师。上海市中学二级二等校长，上海市优秀青年校长、上海市第三期名校长。

四、历任学校党支部书记（以任职先后排列）

夏明德　（详见第十二章第二节第三目历任校长）

马伯相　（详见第十二章第二节第三目历任校长）

张遴贤　上海市奉贤区人，中共党员，大学文化，中学高级教师。2001 年 8 月任协和实验学校党支部书记。2003 年 8 月离任。

徐　建　1960 年 6 月生，上海市奉贤区人，大专文化，中共党员，小学高级教师。2006 年 5 月到奉浦学校工作，任党支部书记。2009 年 8 月离校。

杨连明　（详见第十二章第二节第三目历任校长）

戚盛伟　（详见第十二章第二节第三目历任校长）

顾行健　（详见第十二章第二节第三目历任校长）

五、中学高级教师（以出生年月排列）

张　钰　女，1944 年 11 月生，上海市人。中共党员，大专文化。1963 年 7 月毕业于安徽省芜湖师范学校并参加工作。1986年在西北第二民族学院进修，大专毕业。1990 年评为特级教师。1989 年获第一届全国优秀教师称号，并获得宁夏回族自治区优秀共产党员称号，多次评为银川市优秀校长、优秀共产党员。1999 年获宁夏回族自治区人民政府颁发的“对宁夏有特殊贡献的知识分子”奖章、纪念章。2008—2010 年在上海民办奉浦学校初中部任教。

刘明坤　1945 年 2 月生，江苏省宿迁县人，大学文化。1965 年 9 月至 1970 年 7 月就读上海复旦大学物理系。1970 年 7 月至 1998 年 7 月，在贵州省都匀市有色物化操总队子弟学校任教。其间，1993 年被评为中学高级教师，任初中语文教师。

曾当选为都匀市人民代表大会代表和政协都匀市委员会委员。评为冶金部贵州省冶金局先进工作者。1998 年 7 月至 2005 年 7 月，应聘在奉贤区教师进修学院（校）附属奉浦学校（上海民办协和实验学校）任教，任初中历史、地理和高中地理教学。2005 年 2 月退休后，仍关心支持教育事业，返聘工作至 2012 年 7 月。2010 年被奉贤县教育局记大功 1 次。

程春影　女，1949 年 10 月生，上海市奉贤区庄行人，大学文化，中学高级教师。曾任奉贤区实验中学校长，奉贤区政协常委。先后被评为上海市劳动模范，奉贤区十佳女杰，奉紧区名导师，上海市三八红旗手，上海市先进教育工作者。

任教期间实验中学先后评为上海市文明学校、上海市三八红旗集体、上海市素质教育实验校、全国优秀体育学校、上海市行为规范示范学校。曾发表多篇论文及课题获区、市等第奖，在任数学教师期间，所带班级多次被评为上海市优秀集体。

2004年退休，2005年受聘于奉浦学校任副校长，分管教学工作，多次获得区课程教学奖，在教学常规管理中，培养一批中青年教师。

刘　平　女，1952年4月生，上海市静安区人，中共党员。1969—1974年在安徽省颍上县插队。70年代起先后获安徽省师范大学英语专业本科、上海师范大学教育管理专业本科学历。华东师范大学研究生进修班学习，中学高级教师，中学一级一等校长任职资格。奉贤区名导师，1991—2007年在奉贤区（县）实验中学任教，任党支部书记、副校长。任职期间，学校被评为上海市文明单位、上海市三八红旗集体。2007年退休，受聘上海民办奉浦学校。2004年被评为上海市优秀园丁，曾获上海市金爱心奖、奉贤区优秀党务工作者称号。

沈利德　1953年4月生，上海市人，大学文化，中学高级教师。毕业于云南省昆明师范学院外语系后在华东师范大学英语系进修。1976年起先后担任初中、高中英语教师。1998年7月调入上海民办协和实验学校工作，任高中英语教师，高一（4）班班主任，学校英语教研组组长。2000年所教的高二（4）班被评为上海市中等学校先进集体。被评为优秀班主任。2001年任高中年级组组长，每届高中毕业班高考升学率成绩良好。2014年高考升学率93.2%，2002年主持的教学科研课题《高中课堂英语教学中交际能力培训的研究和实践》被评为奉贤区第六届教育科学研究成果三等奖。是年，在《中小学英语教学与研究》期刊发表《英语写作教学的几种方法》论文。2006年撰写《中学英语课堂教学》论文，在奉贤区教育研究中心评比中获三等奖。

陆桂英　女，1958年1月生，山东省招远市人。东北师范大学政法专业本科毕业，中学高级教师。曾经历加拿大多伦多大学校长专业课程修学，华东师范大学教育管理研究生课程班、教育部校长培训中心中学校长高级研修班初中第六期等学习。现任上海帕丁顿双语学校副校长，分管小学、初中学部。历任上海市曹杨二中附属学校校长、上海市曹杨二中党总支副书记（主持工作）、嘉兴世合教育事业部副总监、教育部中学校长培训中心特聘教授、教师资质认证国考专家。曾荣获上海市园丁奖。主持的《建设民主集体，共创阳光人生》集体实践研究获上海市二等奖，此书由华东师范大学出版社出版。《教师自主发展机制的研究》获普陀区一等奖。上海市重点课题：阳光育人学校文化建设的实践研究。近期研究项目：国家（上海）课程的校本化实践研究（双语教学体系）、聚焦学生学习的课堂转型实践研究等。

郁玉芳 女，1963年6月生，上海市奉贤区人，大学文化，中国民主同盟成员。1981年7月至1985年7月就读于上海师范大学政治教育系，获法学学士学位。应聘于奉浦学校期间，先后任教高中、初中思想品德学科，长期担任政治教研组组长。多篇论文获区级奖项或在区级刊物发表，指导学生参加市、区各项竞赛获奖20余个。1998年3月被奉贤区人民政府记大功一次。曾4次评为中国民主同盟盟务工作积极分子，具有律师资格证书。2009年12月评为中学高级教师。

曹春华 女，1965年2月生，上海市金山区人，大学文化，中共党员，中学高级教师。1982年7月至1986年6月就读于上海师范大学艺术系专科。2001年获本科学历。1986年7月起先后在金山区罗星中学、奉贤南桥小学、奉贤工业中等专业学校任教音乐学科。1998年8月应聘到奉浦学校工作。教学中秉承“教师无小节，处处是楷模”的师德理念，引导教育学生。先后获得奉贤区优秀中青年教师、中青年骨干教师、师德先进个人等荣誉称号，受到记大功奖励。论文《运用主体性德育策略，提高德育工作的实践》在《上海教育科研》杂志发表。《郊区学校学生西洋管弦乐队组建与训练的研究》获全国中小学音乐课程教学改革论文一等奖。《浅谈初中音乐教学中的审美教育》获上海市第四届艺教论文三等奖。

高决心 1967年3月生，上海市奉贤区人，大学文化，中共党员，中学高级教师。1983年7月至1987年7月就读于上海师范大学数学系（专科）。1987年8月分配至奉贤县邬桥中学，先后任年级组长、教研组组长，期间，担任数学兴趣小组的辅导老师，指导学生参加市、县的多次数学竞赛。多人次获奉贤县数学竞赛一等奖、二等奖，上海市数学竞赛二等奖1次。所带班级获奉贤县先进集体称号。1987—1998年中3次获奉贤县教育局记功、园丁奖。1998年7月调入上海民办协和实验学校，任初中、高中数学教学工作，兼任班主任、年级组长和高中数学教研组组长。2007年任奉浦学校教导副主任，分管学校信息化和教师培训工作。评为上海工业综合开发区优秀共产党员，3次获区级记功和嘉奖。2009

年，参加市级课题“聪明学习、智慧教学”的研究工作。

唐继英　女，1967年7月生，上海市奉贤区人，大学文化，中共党员。1987年7月至2002年6月在奉贤齐贤小学任教，2002年7月至2004年6月在奉贤区教师进修学院附属学校任教。2005年7月应聘上海民办奉浦学校，任教语文，担任初中班和高中语文教学，任教班级的语文成绩在全区统考中名列前茅。担任学校教导主任期间，协助校长室制定学校课程方案、课程计划、教师奖励、过程性评价骨干教师评选等方案。2012年12月获中学高级教师职称。2002年9月，评为奉贤区第二批优秀中青年教师。2012年1月获奉贤区优秀骨干教师称号。2014年3月被区人事局记三等功。参与编纂《为了智慧型校园的理想》一书，担任副主编，《关于“聪明学习”的优化教师教学行为的实践研究》被列为奉贤区重点课题。2016年，该课题被评为上海市教育科学研究院第五届学校教育科研成果三等奖。中共上海市奉贤区第三届代表大会代表。

钱　红　女，1971年3月生，上海市奉贤区人，中学高级教师，2003年8月至2009年7月任奉浦学校初中部政治教师兼年级组长。现任奉贤区教育学院教育发展研究中心德育教研员。曾荣获上海市第三届“育德之星”、上海市园丁奖、奉贤区优秀中青年教师称号。参与编写《走进贤城——奉贤区中小学社会实践活动指南》《突发事件的应对与处理——奉贤区随迁子女民办小学班主任优秀征文集》《奉贤区“贤文化”教育读本优秀教案集》《奉贤区未成年人践行社会主义核心价值观故事读本》。所撰写的论文发表于《奉贤教育》《班主任工作大全》(华东师范大学出版社)、《中小学教师教育研究读本》(上海教育出版社)等刊物。

丁永花　女，1972年1月生，上海市奉贤区人。中学英语高级教师。2003—2005年在奉浦学校任教英语学科。2010年获“首届全国英语教学能手”“首届全国英语名师”。2008年、2012年、2015年连续三届评为奉贤区“名教师”。2012年、2014年、2016年连续三届被市教学教研室聘为“初中英语学科中心组成员”。2012年入选“上海市普教系统名校长名师培养工程”培养对象。2013年入选上海市教委组织的“上海—加州影子教师”，赴美国加州培训。2013年入选为奉贤区首届“初中英语首席教师”培养对象。2012年、2013年、2014年、2015年、2016年被奉贤区教育局聘为教师中级专业技术职务任职资格英语学科评审组专家。2016年被奉贤区教育局聘为教师高级专业技术职务任职资格英语学科评审组专家。

李永卫 1973年10月生，上海市奉贤区人，大学文化，中共党员。1994年7月至1998年7月，就读于上海华东师范大学体育系，获学士学位。1998年7月分配到上海民办协和实验学校任体育教师。1999年，担任学校人事干部，根据学校人事需要实际，协助学校搞好教师员工的招聘工作并关心学校体育教学工作。2004年12月，被评为中学一级教师，2005年担任学校党支部副书记兼人事干部。2006年11月，获奉贤区中学体育备课一等奖。2009年5月获奉贤区体育教学评比二等奖。是年12月，被评聘为中学高级教师。先后获奉贤区园丁奖，受到记三等功，记功等表彰奖励。撰写的多篇关于学校体育工作的论文在市、区教育杂志上发表。

柳肖云 女，1974年4月生，浙江省泰顺县人，大学文化，中学高级教师。1990年7月至1994年就读于浙江省温州师范学院中文系。2001年经自学和社会考试，获浙江大学汉语言文学本科文凭。2005年9月至2013年6月在奉贤区奉浦学校任语文教师。任教过三届初中毕业班，撰写过《浅谈对话理论指导下的语文阅读教学》《不妨这样口味语言》《扬起个性的风帆，驶向作文的彼岸》等一系列文章在刊物发表或交流、获奖。2006年，撰写《痴心一片终不悔 心血浇开希望花》获全国德育论文一等奖。2009年5月《浅谈集体文化、荣辱感陶冶下的家校合力》在中国教育实践与研究论坛荣获大赛一等奖。2009年8月《用心经营、共创温馨教室》在全国中小学思想道德建设优秀成果展评活动中获二等奖。2008年评为奉贤区优秀青年教师，2012年评为奉浦社区优秀班主任。

吴 莹 女，1975年3月生，上海奉贤区人，大学文化。先后毕业于上师大、华师大，中学高级教师。1995年7月在奉贤县柘林学校任教。2002年获奉贤区优秀班主任，奉贤区新长征突击手称号。2003年8月应聘至上海奉浦学校工作，任英语教师。所带的初二（2）班主题班会《我与诚信手牵手》获奉贤区教育系统评比一等奖。2008年3月吴莹夫妇因出色的教育教学成绩被评为奉贤区教育系统授予“比翼双飞模范佳侣”称号。是年8月，被授予“奉贤区优秀青年教师”称号。论文《打开学生英语听力的阀门》获奉贤区中学英语学科课堂教学论文评比三等奖。2010年6月与2014年11月，参加区级课题《初中现行牛津英语教材再发展的研究与实践》《初中牛津英语“减负增效校本练习编写”的探索与实践》结题。2011年1月，被学生家长评为“我心目中的好老师”“我心中最美教师”。

倪美红　女，1976年1月生，上海市奉贤区人，大学文化，中共党员，中学高级教师。1998年7月毕业后分配至上海民办协和实验学校任体育教师。长期在教育教学实践和研究中坚持科研先导作用，提高教科研能力。2010年5月《议分段体育教学的策略》论文在《奉贤教育》发表。《体育教学中如何培养寄宿制高中女生的自锻能力》发表在《学校体育发展》杂志。2011年5月《多学段学校体育教学中如何培养学生的自主学练能力》获奉贤区中学体育论文交流一等奖。2005年，评为奉贤区优秀中青年教师。2010年被记三等功。学校体育工作也取得一系列好的成绩。2010年2名女学生在奉贤区中小学生乒乓球比赛中包揽第一、二名。2011年学校排球队在全区阳光体育大联赛中获高中男子团体第一名，高中女子团体第一名，羽毛球高中男子团体第一名。

六、中级职称教师

1998—2016年，上海帕丁顿双语学校先后招聘（调配）的中级职称教师96人，其中中学一级教师60人，小学高级教师33人，讲师（幼高）3人。2016年，上海帕丁顿双语学校教师102人，有技术职称教师77人，占专任教师75.49%，其中高级职称5人，中级职称9人，初级职称63人。

1998—2016年上海帕丁顿双语学校中级职称教师名录（以进校时间排列）

表12-2-1

姓名	性别	籍贯	职称	政治面貌	姓名	性别	籍贯	职称	政治面貌
曹建军	男	上海奉贤	中学一级		赵淑坤	女	上海奉贤	中学一级	
王胜利	男	山东烟台	中学一级		张秀英	女	上海奉贤	中学一级	
刘德根	男	上海奉贤	小学高级	中共党员	汪六弟	男	上海奉贤	中学一级	
周时青	男	上海奉贤	小学高级	中共党员	盛伟宾	男	上海奉贤	中学一级	中共党员
冯志华	男	上海奉贤	中学一级	中共党员	汪思德	男	上海奉贤	中学一级	
姚仁兴	男	上海奉贤	中学一级	中共党员	陶宝娣	女	上海奉贤	小学高级	
何南友	男	上海奉贤	中学一级		王锡鳞	男	上海奉贤	中学一级	
杨　龙	男	上海奉贤	中学一级		谢华芳	女	上海奉贤	中学一级	
王益权	男	上海奉贤	小学高级	中共党员	夏庆华	男	上海奉贤	中学一级	
瞿　锋	男	上海奉贤	中学一级		詹　强	男	上海奉贤	中学一级	
陈桂杰	女	辽宁沈阳	小学高级	中共党员	宋建伯	男	上海奉贤	中学一级	
朱　峰	男	上海奉贤	中学一级	中共党员	吴玉莉	女	上海奉贤	小学高级	
陈美香	女	上海奉贤	中学一级		孙凤仙	女	上海奉贤	小学高级	
梁伯雄	男	上海奉贤	中学一级		范小莉	女	上海奉贤	小学高级	
宋建伯	男	上海奉贤	中学一级		江仁章	男	上海奉贤	中学一级	中共党员

续表 12-2-1

姓名	性别	籍贯	职称	政治面貌	姓名	性别	籍贯	职称	政治面貌
徐　英	女	上海奉贤	中学一级		张仪芳	女	上海奉贤	中学一级	
陈小红	女	上海奉贤	中学一级	中共党员	张向红	女	上海奉贤	小学高级	
胡荣海	男	上海奉贤	小学高级		顾　薇	女	上海奉贤	中学一级	
沈晓红	女	上海奉贤	中学一级	中共党员	金海琴	女	上海奉贤	中学一级	
吴新华	男	上海奉贤	小学高级		章　丽	女	上海奉贤	小学高级	
何新莲	女	上海奉贤	小学高级	中共党员	张顺军	男	上海奉贤	中学一级	
沈靖华	男	上海奉贤	中学一级	中共党员	邹丽琴	女	上海奉贤	中学一级	
孙美红	女	上海奉贤	小学高级		廖新伟	男	上海奉贤	中学一级	
何　芳	女	上海奉贤	小学高级		林　英	女	上海奉贤	中学一级	
马欢权	男	上海奉贤	中学一级		邵引龙	男	上海奉贤	小学高级	中共党员
刑光伟	男	上海奉贤	中学一级		王树松	男	安徽寿县	中学一级	
李　宏	男	上海奉贤	中学一级	中共党员	沈忠勤	男	上海奉贤	中学一级	
徐　建	男	上海奉贤	小学高级	中共党员	库月平	女	黑龙江	小学高级	
陶　静	女	上海奉贤	小学高级		相梅英	女	上海奉贤	小学高级	
夏春妹	女	上海奉贤	小学高级		王毅兴	男	上海奉贤	中学一级	中共党员
王立群	女	上海奉贤	中学一级		方玲英	女	上海奉贤	小学高级	中共党员
唐燕燕	女	上海奉贤	小学高级		黄艳红	女	湖南岳阳	中学一级	中共党员
马耀华	女	湖北枣阳	中学一级		洪　莲	女	上海奉贤	幼高	
余莉萍	女	浙江镇海	小学高级	中共党员	许娟娟	女	上海奉贤	讲师	中共党员
阮慧华	女	上海奉贤	小学高级		王一心	男	上海奉贤	中学一级	中共党员
唐国华	男	上海奉贤	中学一级	中共党员	周文红	女	上海奉贤	小学高级	
殷崇德	男	四川内江	中学一级		陈　红	女	上海奉贤	中学一级	
周　威	女	辽宁沈阳	中学一级		何　芳	女	上海奉贤	小学高级	
刘　霞	女	湖北武穴	中学一级		陆　竞	女	江苏南京	中学一级	中共党员
张琴花	女	上海奉贤	幼高		潘海鸥	女	上海奉贤	中学一级	
王秋红	女	上海奉贤	小学高级	中共党员	陈春红	女	上海奉贤	中学一级	
杨卫平	男	上海奉贤	小学高级		刘圣荣	男	安徽霍邱	中学一级	
徐志云	女	上海奉贤	小学高级		鞠宝龙	男	上海奉贤	中学一级	
吴光斐	女	上海奉贤	小学一级	中共党员	张伟国	男	山东莱州	中学一级	
汪林英	女	上海奉贤	小学高级		龚晓燕	女	上海奉贤	小学高级	
丁　梅	女	上海奉贤	中学一级		任其兵	男	安徽舒城	中学一级	中共党员
周桂花	女	上海奉贤	小学高级	中共党员	韩　健	男	上海奉贤	中学一级	
杜　星	女	浙江上虞	中学一级	中共党员	刘晓敏	女	安徽合肥	中学一级	中共党员

七、校友代表

岳新宇　女，四川省人，共青团员。2006年9月至2012年6月，分别在上海民办奉浦学校小学部、初中部就读。2012年6月，以总分612.5分（语文141分，数学150分，英语147分，物理90分，化学56分，体育28.5分）被奉贤中学录取，其中文化课成绩584分列奉贤区中考第一名。2012年9月至2015年6月，在奉贤中学实验班任班长，团支部书记等职。高中毕业时被奉贤中学授予2015年届荣誉毕业生称号，并考入复旦大学，就读于自然科学试验班。

徐　卓　女，四川省人，共青团员。2004年9月至2012年7月，就读于上海民办奉浦学校小学部、初中部，历任学校少先队大队部干部，初中部学生会成员、班长，活跃于学校的各种大型活动和组织，主持日常仪式、演出与工作会议。校内成绩名列前茅，多次参加各学科竞赛，曾获市、区级多项奖励。2012年7月，被上海建平中学（重点高中）录取，参加学校团委宣传工作，担任班级团支部副书记等职。2015年7月，考入南方医科大学生物医学工程系。

姚一凡　女，上海市奉贤区人，共青团员。2003年9月至2012年7月就读于上海民办奉浦学校小学部、初中部。2010学年第一学期评为优秀少先队员，2011学年第一学期，评为学校初三（1）班三好学生。2012年7月，考入奉贤中学，2013年，被学校授予学习之星称号。在上海民办奉浦学校、奉贤中学学习期间，先后参加各类学习竞赛，26次获奖。2008年，获第六届上海市中学生迎世博英语大赛初中低龄组优胜奖。2009年，获华罗庚金杯少年数学邀请赛奉贤赛区三等奖。2011年，获第二十二届中学生希望杯全国数学邀请赛上海赛区初中二等奖、第二届优赛联合杯海峡两岸中学生作文大赛总决赛初三年组优胜奖。2012学年第一、第二学期分别获得奉贤中学贤才奖二等奖。2013学年第一学期获奉贤中学贤才奖一等奖。在2013年度上海市TI图形计算器教学应用研究绘图学生作品评选中获二等奖。

李　强　上海市奉贤区人，共青团员。2008年9月至2012年7月，就读于民办奉浦学校初中部。2012年8月，考入奉贤中学。2015年8月，被华东理工大学录取。在奉浦学校学习期间，曾获“优秀奖学金”，担任过国旗升旗手和班干部。积极参加学校组织的各类活动，参与的小品表演获得好评，在多次参加的数学竞赛中获得好名次。

乔　坤　1995年12月生，上海市奉贤区人，共青团员。2008年9月至2011年7月，就读于民办奉浦学校初中部，担任学校少先队大队长和学校活动主持人。2011年7月，被上海市进才中学录取，担任班级文艺委员，获学校十佳寝室长。2014年8月，考入上海海事大学，担任班级心理委员，为学校社团联合会人事部成员，参与策划学校的集体舞大赛，华盛顿管弦乐团专场等多次活动。乔坤说“奉浦学校的学习生涯为我今后的人生指明了方向，是匆匆那年中最难忘的记忆”。

胡　伟　1987年2月生，上海市奉贤区人，中共党员。2002年9月至2005年6月，就读于上海民办奉浦学校高中部。2005年12月入伍，现任武警上海公安消防总队青浦支队徐泾中队副队长，副连职中尉警衔。2011年至2012年，连续两年获支队嘉奖。2012年，被上海市公安局授予“优秀青年”荣誉称号。2013年，被上海市公安局记三等功1次。

严鸿飞　上海市奉贤区人，共青团员。2003年9月至2012年7月，在民办奉浦学校完成小学部、初中部学业，2012年7月，以585分总成绩考入上海市位育中学，2015年8月，被上海工程技术大学录取，就读制药工程专业。在奉浦学校期间，热爱绘画，为素描七级。在上海市第三届中小学生古典诗词创作比赛中获一等奖，在作文、数学、物理的校级比赛中多次获奖，享受学校奖学金。2012—2015年，获奉贤区第12届古诗文大赛三等奖，位育中学第27～28届中学生作文大赛区三等奖，绍兴文化考察征文第一名，获南京考察小级三等奖。

施曼琳　女，1996年9月生，上海市奉贤区人，共青团员。2008年8月至2011年，在上海民办奉浦学校读初中，2011年8月，考入奉贤中学。2014年8月，为上海大学录取。在奉浦学校期间，担任过班级生活委员、心理委员，帮助同学解决生活、学习中的各种困难，获得学校奖学金。在大学学习中，经常参加志愿者活动，享受帮助他人的快乐。在给母校的信中说，“奉浦学校是我最珍贵的母校，承载了我青春的回忆”。

徐　涛　上海市奉贤区人，共青团员。2008年9月至2010年7月，就读于上海民办奉浦学校高中部。在奉浦学校学习期间，2007—2008年，评为校三好学生。2010年8月，被江西科技学院录取，攻读室内设计专业。在大学期间，2010—2011年，被评为三好学生，2011—2014年，连续获国家奖学金。2014年7月毕业后参加工作，现为上海君阳建设发展有限公司主案设计师。在上海中心大厦、漕河泾、浦江、长风公园、江苏溧阳等地留下他的设计作品。

吴燕静　女，上海奉贤区人，共青团员。2008—2010年，就读于上海民办奉浦学校高中部。2010年9月，考入吉林动画学院，攻读动画专业。2014年7月，以优异成绩大学毕业，是年9月，到松江区薛家小学任教。在奉浦学校学习期间，在作文竞赛中多次获奖。2009年，获奉贤区作文竞赛（高二组）二等奖，新纪元作文竞赛三等奖。大学学习期间，连续三年获学校奖学金。2010—2011年分别荣获吉林动画学院优秀学生干部，优秀共青团员称号。

蔡佳骏　1990年生，上海市奉贤人。2002年，就读奉贤区教师进修学院附属实验学校，2005年，以奉贤区中考第一考入复旦大学附属中学。2008—2015年就读华东理工大学，取得本科及硕士学位，现在外企担任安全管理工作。

八、部分考取重点中学、大学本科学生名录（以毕业先后排列）

2001—2016年，根据收集到的资料，有374名学生被录取为大学本科，2015届有20名学生被市、区重点中学录取。

2001—2016年上海帕丁顿双语学校高考录取本科部分学生名录

表12-2-2

姓名	性别	籍贯	考入学校（专业）名称	届次
马玲娜	女	上海奉贤	上海师范大学	2001
朱　玲	女	上海奉贤	上海师范大学	2001
陈晓燕	女	上海奉贤	上海师范大学	2001
唐建华	女	上海奉贤	上海师范大学	2001
殷方华	女	上海奉贤	南京美术学院	2001
凤　蓓	女	上海奉贤	宁波大学	2001
王薇薇	女	上海奉贤	宁波大学	2001
蒋袁妹	女	上海奉贤	西南科技大学	2001
宋丹青	女	上海奉贤	东北财经大学	2001
王艳青	女	上海奉贤	淮北煤炭师范学院	2001
吴　敏	女	上海奉贤	华东理工大学	2001
毛霞云	女	上海奉贤	合肥理工大学	2001
仰兰洁	女	上海奉贤	西安财经大学	2001
闵琪亮	男	上海奉贤	上海科技大学	2001
孟黎平	女	上海奉贤	哈尔滨理工大学	2001
徐莉群	女	上海奉贤	宁波大学	2001
卫　佳	男	上海奉贤	上海大学	2001
陈　杰	男	上海奉贤	华东交通大学	2001

续表 12-2-2

姓名	性别	籍贯	考入学校（专业）名称	届次
周如意	男	上海奉贤	武汉科技大学	2001
潘军辉	男	上海奉贤	江苏石油化工学院	2001
朱惠兰	女	上海奉贤	青岛化工学院	2001
严嘉叶	女	上海奉贤	上海理工大学	2001
张　晶	女	上海奉贤	上海理工大学	2001
胡伯川	男	上海奉贤	上海工程技术大学	2001
尹元勇	男	上海奉贤	上海电力学院	2001
孙文达	男	上海奉贤	昆明工学院	2001
顾文文	男	上海奉贤	中国矿业大学	2009
沈　俞	男	上海奉贤	海洋大学	2009
于自立	男	上海奉贤	复旦大学	2009
于桂桂	男	上海奉贤	云南大学	2009
王文清	男	上海奉贤	云南大学	2009
陈颖胤	女	上海奉贤	沈阳航空学院	2009
冯　源	男	上海奉贤	吉林动画学院	2009
朱润坤	男	上海奉贤	吉林动画学院	2009
沈宇浩	男	上海奉贤	江西蓝天学院	2009
陈旖旎	女	上海奉贤	上海农森学院	2009
蒋云婷	女	上海奉贤	景德镇陶瓷学院	2009
杨　燕	女	上海奉贤	上海剑桥学院	2009
干金磊	男	上海奉贤	上海工艺学院	2009
顾嘉宾	男	上海奉贤	南京师范大学	2009
陆云峰	男	上海奉贤	南京师范大学	2009
王　青	男	上海奉贤	云南大学	2009
孙　磐	男	上海奉贤	中央司法警官学院	2009
沈佳丽	女	上海奉贤	上海剑桥学院	2009
许怡珊	女	上海奉贤	扬州大学	2009
顾凯晨	男	上海奉贤	成都理工大学	2009
金纯真	男	上海奉贤	上海商学院	2009
鲍雯雯	女	上海奉贤	上海剑桥学院	2009
方静怡	女	上海奉贤	重庆师范大学	2009
朱　燕	女	上海奉贤	重庆师范大学	2009
郭　忆	男	上海奉贤	云南大学	2009
薛丹萍	女	上海奉贤	成都理工学院	2009
王正超	男	上海奉贤	新加坡国立大学	2010
邬铭远	男	上海奉贤	澳大利亚悉尼大学	2010
陈超杰	男	上海奉贤	福建厦门大学	2010

续表 12-2-2

姓名	性别	籍贯	考入学校（专业）名称	届次
朱文杰	男	上海奉贤	上海理工大学	2010
宋晓霞	女	上海奉贤	上海师范大学	2010
汤馨云	女	上海奉贤	湖南理工大学	2010
顾　伟	女	上海奉贤	湖南理工大学	2010
高夏妮	女	上海奉贤	上海健康医学院	2011
赵玉铭	男	上海奉贤	上海电力学院	2011
马怡婷	女	上海奉贤	南京农业大学	2011
宋依蕾	女	上海奉贤	上海第二工业大学	2011
王文杰	男	上海奉贤	上海立信会计学院	2011
马鑫海	男	上海奉贤	上海邦德职业技术学院	2011
王依莲	女	上海奉贤	上海中侨学院	2011
陈啸天	男	上海奉贤	上海工程技术大学	2011
顾陈宸	女	上海奉贤	上海工商外国职业学院	2011
夏伊婷	女	上海奉贤	江西省景德镇陶瓷大学	2011
陈鸣杰	男	上海奉贤	四川省成都信息工程大学	2011
陈晓悦	女	上海奉贤	同济大学	2011
邬家晟	男	上海奉贤	武汉大学	2011
叶强林	男	上海奉贤	江西省南昌理工学院	2011
黄若彤	女	上海奉贤	福建省泉州师范大学	2011
金　琳	女	上海奉贤	上海杉达学院	2013
沈思韵	女	上海奉贤	上海师范大学	2013
穆莅晔	女	上海奉贤	上海师范大学	2013
张　乐	男	上海奉贤	上海视觉艺术学院	2013
王翕男	男	上海奉贤	上海外国语大学贤达经济人文学院	2013
周　琳	女	上海奉贤	上海应用技术学院	2013
王润秋	女	上海奉贤	上海工程技术大学	2013
连佳璐	女	上海奉贤	上海工程技术大学	2013
姚明远	男	上海奉贤	吉林动画学院	2013
潘温琪	女	上海奉贤	江西科技学院	2013
张婧雯	女	上海奉贤	上海外国语大学贤达经济人文学院	2013
袁佳文	女	上海奉贤	江西科技学院	2013
郑宇翔	男	上海奉贤	上海师范大学天华学院	2013
金超凡	男	上海奉贤	江西科技师范大学	2013
阮文洁	女	上海奉贤	景德镇陶瓷学院科技艺术学院	2013
唐伊雯	女	上海奉贤	江西科技学院	2013
朱鋆秫	男	上海奉贤	江西科技学院	2013
范正磊	男	上海奉贤	上海建桥学院	2013

续表 12-2-2

姓名	性别	籍贯	考入学校（专业）名称	届次
沈瑜佳	女	上海奉贤	上海师范大学天华学院	2013
王玮灏	男	上海奉贤	景德镇陶瓷学院科技艺术学院	2013
曹哲骁	男	上海奉贤	江西科技学院	2013
阙春勇	男	上海奉贤	江西科技学院	2013
李怡晗	女	上海奉贤	景德镇陶瓷学院科技艺术学院	2013
蔡晓菁	女	上海奉贤	上海建桥学院	2013
陈盈盈	女	上海奉贤	江西科技学院	2013
卫文婕	女	上海奉贤	景德镇陶瓷学院	2013
汤　尊	男	上海奉贤	景德镇陶瓷学院科技艺术学院	2013
徐培鑫	男	上海奉贤	上海杉达学院	2013
余春薇	女	上海奉贤	上海杉达学院	2013
金　浩	男	上海奉贤	上海建桥学院	2013
沈清宇	男	上海奉贤	江西科技学院	2013
顾宇弘	男	上海奉贤	景德镇陶瓷学院科技艺术学院	2013
董　翔	男	上海奉贤	南京师范大学泰州学院	2013
吴凌超	男	上海奉贤	上海视觉艺术学院	2013
苏　畅	女	上海奉贤	上海工程技术大学	2013
韩佳敏	女	上海奉贤	上海师范大学天华学院	2013
卫佳莹	女	上海奉贤	景德镇陶瓷学院科技艺术学院	2013
朱　炜	男	上海奉贤	无锡太湖学院	2013
顾　亮	男	上海奉贤	南京师范大学泰州学院	2013
何佳俊	男	上海奉贤	吉林动画学院	2013
姚琪鑫	男	上海奉贤	上海外国语大学贤达经济人文学院	2013
谢晓洁	女	上海奉贤	上海建桥学院	2013
徐至天	女	上海奉贤	武昌理工学院	2013
孙　汤	男	上海奉贤	吉林动画学院	2013
吕若菁	女	上海奉贤	上海师范大学天华学院	2013
曹紫颖	女	上海奉贤	上海建桥学院	2013
龚雨松	男	上海奉贤	上海视觉艺术学院	2013
金鹏云	男	上海奉贤	上海工程技术大学	2013
朱嘉靖	女	上海奉贤	上海外国语大学贤达经济人文学院	2013
王玉珏	女	上海奉贤	上海外国语大学贤达经济人文学院	2013
尹丹羚	女	上海奉贤	南京航空航天大学金城学院	2013
万超逸	男	上海奉贤	宜春学院	2013
杨艺苓	女	上海奉贤	上海戏曲学院	2013
叶依婷	女	上海奉贤	景德镇陶瓷学院科技艺术学院	2013
薛雯昊	男	上海奉贤	南京理工大学紫金学院	2013

续表 12-2-2

姓名	性别	籍贯	考入学校（专业）名称	届次
郑婷婷	女	上海奉贤	上海建桥学院	2013
顾晨杰	男	上海奉贤	邵阳学院	2013
夏思羽	女	上海奉贤	南京农业大学	2013
潘荔芸	女	上海奉贤	上海视觉艺术学院	2013
梅自寒	男	上海奉贤	江西科技学院	2013
李嘉诚	男	上海奉贤	景德镇陶瓷学院科技艺术学院	2013
程晓韵	女	上海奉贤	上海师范大学	2013
陈一玮	男	上海奉贤	云南大学旅游文化学院	2013
马晨晖	男	上海奉贤	上海金融学院	2013
范雨琦	女	上海奉贤	上海师范大学天华学院	2013
周　聪	男	上海奉贤	云南大学旅游文化学院	2013
唐彦澜	女	上海奉贤	上海师范大学	2013
杨　奕	女	上海奉贤	景德镇陶瓷学院科技艺术学院	2013
吴佳妮	女	上海奉贤	江西科技大学	2013
季　吉	女	上海奉贤	上海建桥大学	2013
倪嘉辉	男	上海奉贤	景德镇陶瓷学院科技艺术学院	2013
王昭祺	女	上海奉贤	上海师范大学	2013
周　怡	女	上海奉贤	上海师范大学天华学院	2013
陆湘明	男	上海奉贤	华东政法大学	2013
陈倩妤	女	上海奉贤	上海师范大学	2013
平雪儿	女	上海奉贤	南阳理工大学	2013
陈依伦	女	上海奉贤	上海政法学院	2013
沈楚楚	女	上海奉贤	上海戏曲学院	2013
戴王豪	男	上海奉贤	景德镇陶瓷学院科技艺术学院	2013
陆嘉超	男	上海奉贤	上海理工大学	2013
宝雨贝	女	上海奉贤	云南大学生旅游文化学院	2013
谢嘉程	男	上海奉贤	上海杉达学院	2013
赵一轩	女	上海奉贤	上海大学	2013
盛一凡	男	上海奉贤	景德镇陶瓷学院	2013
肖文慧	女	上海奉贤	上海视觉艺术学院	2013
王潇丹	女	上海奉贤	上海应用技术学院	2013
黄　朴	男	上海奉贤	上海外国语大学贤达经济人文学院	2013
施曼琳	女	上海奉贤	上海大学	2013
袁和安	女	上海奉贤	上海电机学院	2013
朱心忆	女	上海奉贤	上海师范大学天华学院	2013
吴修远	男	上海奉贤	上海师范大学天华学院	2014
明　悦	女	上海奉贤	大连艺术学院	2014

续表 12-2-2

姓名	性别	籍贯	考入学校（专业）名称	届次
曹　宇	男	上海奉贤	江西科技学院	2014
聂傲宇	男	上海奉贤	云南大学游泳文化学院	2014
吴　禛	男	上海奉贤	上海杉达学院	2014
王　浩	男	上海奉贤	上海师范大学天华学院	2014
唐慧婷	女	上海奉贤	南京师范大学泰州学院	2014
孙长阳	男	上海奉贤	上海杉达学院	2014
张　迟	男	上海奉贤	上海杉达学院	2014
项夏虹	女	上海奉贤	上海杉达学院	2014
朱晨晨	女	上海奉贤	上海杉达学院	2014
王梦蕾	女	上海奉贤	上海大学	2014
茹莉莎	女	上海奉贤	上海杉达学院	2014
俞公璞	男	上海奉贤	江汉大学	2014
张　涛	男	上海奉贤	江西科技学院	2014
黄文娴	女	上海奉贤	上海大学	2014
钱唯一	女	上海奉贤	上海建桥学院	2014
黄　晨	女	上海奉贤	上海外国语大学贤达经济人文学院	2014
蔡一鸣	男	上海奉贤	江西科技学院	2014
杨　翊	男	上海奉贤	江西科技学院	2014
薛家栋	男	上海奉贤	江西科技学院	2014
潘　浩	男	上海奉贤	上海建桥学院	2014
徐　政	男	上海奉贤	景德镇陶瓷学院科技艺术学院	2014
郑　昊	男	上海奉贤	上海师范大学天华学院	2014
杨倩云	女	上海奉贤	浙江工商大学	2014
吴逾凡	女	上海奉贤	景德镇陶瓷学院科技艺术学院	2014
姚韵洁	女	上海奉贤	吉林动画学院	2014
周智斌	男	上海奉贤	上海师范大学天华学院	2014
匡　荣	女	上海奉贤	上海外国语大学贤达经济人文学院	2014
顾　煦	女	上海奉贤	上海建桥学院	2014
瞿怡妮	女	上海奉贤	江汉大学	2014
邱佳悦	女	上海奉贤	江西科技学院	2014
徐辰梦	女	上海奉贤	景德镇陶瓷学院科技艺术学院	2014
杨芝兰	女	上海奉贤	云南大学旅游文化学院	2014
杨玉琪	女	上海奉贤	上海师范大学天华学院	2014
王潇逸	男	上海奉贤	西安邮电大学	2014
李嘉玮	男	上海奉贤	上海电机学院	2014
陈昳昀	女	上海奉贤	上海师范大学天华学院	2014
陈家熠	女	上海奉贤	上海大学	2014

续表 12-2-2

姓名	性别	籍贯	考入学校（专业）名称	届次
滕梦旭	女	上海奉贤	上海视觉艺术学院	2014
叶韵钦	男	上海奉贤	上海师范大学	2014
林日盛	男	上海奉贤	江西科技学院	2014
陈啸天	男	上海奉贤	上海工程技术大学	2014
宋晓霞	女	上海奉贤	上海师范大学	2014
刘懿欣	女	上海奉贤	江西科技学院	2014
翁一帆	男	上海奉贤	四川传媒学院	2014
顾新竹	女	上海奉贤	上海商学院	2014
林木子	女	上海奉贤	上海工程技术大学	2014
苏依时	男	上海奉贤	哈尔滨商业大学	2014
裴天正	男	上海奉贤	吉林动画学院	2014
陈洁怡	女	上海奉贤	上海建桥学院	2014
曹心怡	女	上海奉贤	上海理工大学	2014
高逸凡	男	上海奉贤	景德镇陶瓷学院科技艺术学院	2015
许思聪	男	上海奉贤	上海外国语大学贤达经济人文学院	2015
谢家树	男	上海奉贤	沈阳化工大学	2015
郁　雯	女	上海奉贤	景德镇陶瓷学院科技艺术学院	2015
唐雨婕	女	上海奉贤	上海电力大学	2015
李　仕	男	上海奉贤	九江学院	2015
沈　琰	男	上海奉贤	广东海洋大学	2015
张旭杰	男	上海奉贤	上海建桥学院	2015
刘海嘉	男	上海奉贤	南华大学	2015
刘香宇	女	上海奉贤	辽宁医学院	2015
朱丽娟	女	上海奉贤	北京科技大学	2015
李屹宇	男	上海奉贤	上海应用技术学院	2015
褚佳妮	女	上海奉贤	上海视觉艺术学院	2015
姚正昊	男	上海奉贤	上海杉达学院	2015
汤佳佳	女	上海奉贤	天津中医药大学	2015
朱奕霖	男	上海奉贤	上海建桥学院	2015
杨雅芬	女	上海奉贤	广东海洋大学	2015
蒋肖辉	男	上海奉贤	上海中医药大学	2015
李彩虹	女	上海奉贤	上海工程技术大学	2015
景勇捷	男	上海奉贤	吉林动画学院	2015
张婕雯	女	上海奉贤	上海外国语大学贤达经济人文学院	2015
金　超	男	上海奉贤	吉林动画学院	2015
周　波	男	上海奉贤	景德镇陶瓷学院科技艺术学院	2015
王乐晖	男	上海奉贤	上海杉达学院	2015

续表 12-2-2

姓名	性别	籍贯	考入学校（专业）名称	届次
张思梦	女	上海奉贤	上海师范大学天华学院	2015
计思霞	女	上海奉贤	上海第二工业大学	2015
金晓婷	女	上海奉贤	南京师范大学泰川学院	2015
张　怡	女	上海奉贤	上海杉达学院	2015
刘　涛	男	上海奉贤	忻州师范学院	2015
陶　鑫	男	上海奉贤	吉林动画学院	2015
朱嘉豪	男	上海奉贤	吉林动画学院	2015
殷声强	男	上海奉贤	上海外国语大学贤达经济人文学院	2015
吴哲宇	男	上海奉贤	上海师范大学天华学院	2015
阮家豪	男	上海奉贤	上海杉达学院	2015
谢韵雪	女	上海奉贤	上海建桥学院	2015
陶文婷	女	上海奉贤	江汉大学	2015
范明明	男	上海奉贤	吉林动画学院	2015
汤伽铭	男	上海奉贤	云南大学旅游文化学院	2015
姜雨蝶	女	上海奉贤	云南大学旅游文化学院	2015
蔡卓瑛	女	上海奉贤	上海杉达学院	2015
陆红薇	女	上海奉贤	上海师范大学天华学院	2015
钱欣韵	女	上海奉贤	上海商学院	2015
何婷婷	女	上海奉贤	景德镇陶瓷学院科技艺术学院	2015
沈　静	女	上海奉贤	上海商学院	2015
王志贤	男	上海奉贤	上海视觉艺术学院	2015
吴姚雯	女	上海奉贤	上海师范大学天华学院	2015
张　磊	男	上海奉贤	吉林动画学院	2015
宗　莹	女	上海奉贤	上海外国语大学贤达经济人文学院	2015
蒋金斯	女	上海奉贤	上海理工大学	2015
王黎霞	女	上海奉贤	四川传媒学院	2015
闫路路	男	上海奉贤	上海师范大学天华学院	2015
李诺恒	男	上海奉贤	上海视觉艺术学院	2015
吴致远	男	上海奉贤	云南大学旅游文化学院	2015
奚晓蓉	女	上海奉贤	上海师范大学天华学院	2015
邵燕玲	女	上海奉贤	上海视觉艺术学院	2015
董成誉	女	上海奉贤	首都师范大学科德学院	2015
张　泓	男	上海奉贤	上海师范大学天华学院	2015
顾凯铭	男	上海奉贤	上海建桥学院	2015
陈璟玉	女	上海奉贤	上海建桥学院	2015
曹立人	男	上海奉贤	上海建桥学院	2015
杜泽域	男	上海奉贤	上海师范大学天华学院	2015

续表 12-2-2

姓名	性别	籍贯	考入学校（专业）名称	届次
顾轩成	男	上海奉贤	上海音乐学院	2015
陈洁瑞	女	上海奉贤	上海戏剧学院	2015
顾嘉祺	男	上海奉贤	井冈山大学	2015
周茹依	女	上海奉贤	上海建桥学院	2015
王哲安	男	上海奉贤	上海视觉艺术学院	2015
顾　夏	女	上海奉贤	上海师范大学天华学院	2015
詹　霞	女	上海奉贤	上海建桥学院	2015
倪　浩	男	上海奉贤	云南大学旅游文化学院	2015
范　懿	女	上海奉贤	景德镇陶瓷学院科技艺术学院	2015
王奕睿	男	上海奉贤	四川传媒学院	2015
顾姚望	男	上海奉贤	上海体育学院	2015
葛欣奕	女	上海奉贤	上海外国语大学贤达经济人文学院	2015
汪天智	男	上海奉贤	上海理工大学	2015
周玄刚	男	上海奉贤	上海应用技术学院	2015
汤伽斌	男	上海奉贤	上海外国语大学贤达经济人文学院	2015
梁卫倩	女	上海奉贤	江西师范大学科学技术学院	2015
黄天琦	女	上海奉贤	江西科技学院	2015
钱雨晴	女	上海奉贤	上海师范大学天华学院	2015
刘润东	男	上海奉贤	安徽大学	2015
徐　靓	女	上海奉贤	上海对外经贸大学	2015
郑明哲	男	上海奉贤	江西科技学院	2015
刘容序	女	上海奉贤	河南工业大学	2015
阮城龙	男	上海奉贤	江西科技学院	2015
王　波	男	上海奉贤	江西科技学院	2015
潘顾漪	女	上海奉贤	长沙学院	2015
褚天祺	女	上海奉贤	上海师范大学天华学院视觉转达专业	2016
瞿铭昊	男	上海奉贤	上海师范大学天华学院数字媒体专业	2016
钱淑芬	女	上海奉贤	上海师范大学天华学院数字媒体专业	2016
姚晓蓓	女	上海奉贤	上海杉达学院环境设计专业	2016
钱博闻	男	上海奉贤	上海杉达学院产品设计数字媒体专业	2016
陈寅峰	男	上海奉贤	九江学院体育教育专业	2016
陈嘉诚	男	上海奉贤	上海应用技术大学工商管理专业	2016
陆　怡	女	上海奉贤	景德镇陶瓷科技学艺术学院绘画专业	2016
宋海珍	女	上海奉贤	上海建桥学院珠宝设计专业	2016
邹　奇	男	上海奉贤	重庆大学城市科技学院工程造价专业	2016
沈啸宇	男	上海奉贤	江西科技学院视觉传达设计专业	2016
金怡琳	女	上海奉贤	江西科技学院服装设计专业	2016

续表 12-2-2

姓名	性别	籍贯	考入学校（专业）名称	届次
贡欣如	女	上海奉贤	江西科技学院视觉传达设计专业	2016
王金仙	女	上海奉贤	武汉工程科技学院视觉传达设计专业	2016
陆佳妮	女	上海奉贤	曲阜师范大学音乐学专业	2016
姚　悦	男	上海奉贤	湖南工业大学科技学院产品设计专业	2016
沈小迪	女	上海奉贤	无锡太湖学院数字媒体专业	2016
王晨鸣	男	上海奉贤	南京师范大学布泰州学院视觉传达设计专业	2016
郑智捷	男	上海奉贤	云南旅游大学视觉传达设计专业	2016
任　佳	女	上海奉贤	上海外国语大学国际教育专业	2016
蔡海林	男	上海奉贤	景德镇陶瓷大学科技艺术学院雕塑	2016
陈韦超	男	上海奉贤	首都师范大学科德学院摄影专业	2016
沈宏达	男	上海奉贤	上海杉达学院财务管理专业	2016
汪松峻	男	上海奉贤	吉林动画学院戏剧影视导演专业	2016
沈子骞	男	上海奉贤	云南大学旅游文化学院环境设计专业	2016
盛思昱	男	上海奉贤	景德镇陶瓷大学科技艺术学院雕塑	2016
万　幸	男	上海奉贤	景德镇陶瓷大学科技艺术学院视觉传达设计专业	2016
徐　霖	男	上海奉贤	江西科技学院音乐学专业	2016
周兆杰	男	上海奉贤	吉林动画学院工艺美术专业	2016
蔡佳雯	女	上海奉贤	湖南工业大学科技学院环境设计专业	2016
陈伊婷	女	上海奉贤	上海建桥学院数字媒体艺术专业	2016
慕静文	女	上海奉贤	景德镇陶瓷大学科技艺术学院陶瓷艺术设计专业	2016
吴雷桢	女	上海奉贤	吉林动画学院视觉传达设计专业	2016
夏邵洁	女	上海奉贤	江西科技学院视觉传达设计	2016
项佳晨	女	上海奉贤	景德镇陶瓷大学科技艺术学院陶瓷艺术设计专业	2016
杨紫薇	女	上海奉贤	上海师范大学天华学院数字传媒艺术	2016
郑雪涵	女	上海奉贤	上海建桥学院产品设计专业	2016
周思颖	女	上海奉贤	武汉工程科技学院产品设计专业	2016
朱宇晨	女	上海奉贤	上海师范大学天华学院视觉传达设计	2016
庄雅清	女	上海奉贤	景德镇陶瓷大学科技艺术学院产品设计专业	2016
叶　梓	男	上海奉贤	吉林动画学院产品设计	2016
徐祎涛	男	上海奉贤	云南大学旅游文化学院环境设计专业	2016
朱旭尧	男	上海奉贤	陕西科技大学设计与艺术学院设计	2016

续表 12-2-2

姓名	性别	籍贯	考入学校（专业）名称	届次
徐　平	男	上海奉贤	上海工程技术大学服装设计专业	2016
方正武	男	上海奉贤	吉林动画学院新媒体漫画专业	2016
朱笑奕	男	上海奉贤	上海师范大学天华学院数字媒体艺术	2016
盛志豪	男	上海奉贤	景德镇陶瓷大学科技艺术学院设计	2016
于嘉陶	男	上海奉贤	云南旅游文化学院视觉传达设计专业	2016
朱佳琳	女	上海奉贤	上海外国语大学贤达人文经济学院数字传媒艺术专业	2016
高丁洁	女	上海奉贤	北京工业大学耿丹学院艺术设计专业	2016
平俊杰	男	上海奉贤	景德镇陶瓷大学科技艺术学院产品设计专业	2016
徐　扬	男	上海奉贤	上海剑桥学院数字传媒 3+2 专业	2016
姚乾澎	男	上海奉贤	福建农林大学金山学院国际经济与贸易专业	2016
阮卫晨	男	上海奉贤	西南林业大学环境设计专业	2016
王静怡	女	上海奉贤	江西科技学院服装设计专业	2016
刘　东	男	上海奉贤	江西科技学院服装设计专业	2016
王　磊	男	上海奉贤	四川传媒学院公共艺术专业	2016
刘　易	男	上海奉贤	上海体育学院体育教育专业	2016
陆　森	男	上海奉贤	上海师范大学天华学院视觉传达设计	2016
卫　伟	男	上海奉贤	武汉工程科技学院产品设计专业	2016
钱之一	男	上海奉贤	江西科技学院音乐专业	2016
杨渊译	男	上海奉贤	吉林动画学院视觉传达设计专业	2016
张心悦	男	上海奉贤	湖南科技大学科技学院环境设计专业	2016
王　飞	男	上海奉贤	浙江工商大学视觉传媒设计专业	2016
吴贺鹏	男	上海奉贤	吉林省动画学院动画专业	2016
徐美娜	女	上海奉贤	江西科技学院环境设计专业	2016
张　卉	男	上海奉贤	景德镇陶瓷大学科技艺术学院绘画	2016
陆文静	女	上海奉贤	云南大学旅游文化学院服装设计专业	2016
丁一川	男	上海奉贤	首都师范大学科德学院影视摄影专业	2016
孙亚轩	男	上海奉贤	上海建桥学院数字媒体艺术专业	2016
陈逸蕾	女	上海奉贤	景德镇陶瓷大学科技艺术学院陶瓷与建筑设计专业	2016
张　震	男	上海奉贤	景德镇陶瓷大学科技艺术学院 07 动画	2016

2015年上海帕丁顿双语学校中考录取重点中学情况表

表12-2-3

姓名	性别	籍贯	考入学校名称	届次
袁何斌	男	上海奉贤	奉贤中学（市重点）	2015
戴家安	男	上海奉贤	金山中学（市重点）	2015
叶倩彦	女	上海奉贤	上海大学附中（市重点）	2015
刘涵藻	女	上海奉贤	建平中学（市重点）	2015
徐　晶	女	上海奉贤	奉贤中学（市重点）	2015
蔡雨萱	女	上海奉贤	上海师范大学附中（市重点）	2015
邵煌轩	男	上海奉贤	奉贤中学（市重点）	2015
瞿弘妍	女	上海奉贤	杨浦中学（市重点）	2015
周奇帆	男	上海奉贤	奉贤中学（市重点）	2015
程佩妮	女	上海奉贤	曙光中学（区重点）	2015
张忆敏	男	上海奉贤	曙光中学（区重点）	2015
张昭禾一	男	上海奉贤	曙光中学（区重点）	2015
李圣悦	男	上海奉贤	致远高中（区重点）	2015
顾　家	女	上海奉贤	致远高中（区重点）	2015
吴喻伦	女	上海奉贤	上南中学（区重点）	2015
廖欣雨	男	上海奉贤	致远高中（区重点）	2015
杨　洋	男	上海奉贤	致远高中（区重点）	2015
王静莹	女	上海奉贤	致远高中（区重点）	2015
何叶培	男	上海奉贤	致远高中（区重点）	2015
卫倩玲	女	上海奉贤	致远高中（区重点）	2015

附　录

上海市民办协和实验学校董事会章程

总　则

根据中国共产党第十四次代表大会关于“鼓励多渠道、多形式社会渠道办学和民间办学”的精神，以及根据《上海市民办学校管理办法》，上海奉浦经济发展实业总公司和上海市教科院民办教育中心联合创办上海市民办协和实验学校，并依法成立董事会。

组　织

1. 上海市民办协和实验学校实行董事会领导下的校长负责制。

2. 校董事会由上海奉浦经济发展实业总公司、上海市教育科学研究院民办中心、协和实验学校、教育界资深人士4方面组成。董事会成员暂定为6人，并设名誉董事长若干，分别是上海奉浦经济发展实业总公司2人、上海市教育科学研究院2人、协和实验学校1人、教育界资深人士1人。上海市民办教育中心的代表为董事长。

3. 董事会董事每届任期3年，可连聘连任。

职　权

上海市民办协和实验学校董事会是上海市民办协和实验学校的最高权力机构，有权决定学校的重大事宜，其职权主要如下：

1. 校长的聘任与解聘；

2. 制定学校发展规划；

3. 决定学校经费的筹划方案，审核学校的预决算；

4. 管理学校的基金和资产；

5. 决定学校教职工的编制总数和工资总额；

6. 接受助学捐资；

7. 修订学校的组织章程。

其　他

1. 校董事会例会一般每学期召开1次，特殊情况由董事长决定。董事会议由董事长召集主持。董事因故不能出席校董事会，可书面委托代理人出席，如届时本人不能出席、也未委托他人出席，则作为弃权。

2. 校董事会每次会议须作详细的书面记录，并由全体出席董事签字，代理人出席时，由代理人签字。记录正本由学校存档，副本分送各董事。

3. 校董事会的决议，应有过半数董事出席，并有出席的半数以上通过方为有效。

4. 本章程的解释权属董事会。

上海市民办协和实验学校董事会

一九九八年四月

上海市奉贤区教师进修学院附属奉浦学校董事会章程

一、学校董事会由上海市工业综合开发区管委会、奉贤区教育局、奉贤区教师进修学院3方组成。董事会由5～7名董事组成。董事会协商选举董事长1人，副董事长1～3人，董事每届任期3年，连选可以连任。董事会可以罢免董事长。

二、董事会对学校全面负责，并行使下列职权：

1. 聘任学校校长，根据校长提名，聘任学校副校长和其他中层管理人员（包括财务负责人），决定其报酬事项。

2. 制定学校发展规划。

3. 决定学校经费筹集方案。

4. 审核学校预算、决算方案。

5. 决定学校内部管理机构的设置。

6. 决定学校教职工编制定额与工资标准。

7. 制定学校的基本管理制度。

8. 决定接受捐赠。

三、董事长对董事会负责，并行使下列职权：

1. 召集主持董事会会议，主持董事会日常工作。

2. 监督董事会决议的实施情况，并向董事会报告。

3. 在董事会闭会期间，对学校的重大业务活动进行指导。

4. 提名校长人选，供董事会审议。

5. 董事会授予的其他职权。

四、董事长不能履行职权时，由董事长指定副董事长或其他董事代行其职权。

五、董事会每年至少召开两次会议，有紧急事项时，经三分之一以上董事提议应召开临时会议，董事会由董事长召集，于会议召开前10日书面通知全体董事。

六、董事会会议可以书面、传真、电话或类似通讯设备举行，只要与会董事能听清和理解其他董事的立场或观点，并进行交流，所有的董事应视作已亲自出席会议。

七、董事会会议应由二分之一以上的董事或代理人出席方可举行。

八、每名董事有1票表决权。董事会作出的决议，须经二分之一以上董事或其代理人通过。

九、对需要董事会会议通过的事项，如议案已派发给全体董事，并按第八条的规定经董事签字作出书面决议，无须召开董事会会议。

十、董事会会议上决定的事项应作为董事会决议，并由出席董事或其代理人签字。董事应对董事会决议负责，如因董事会决议违反我国法律法规或章程，而导致的严重损失，则作出决议的董事应承担赔偿责任，但经证明在表决时，曾表示异议并记载于会议记录的，该董事可以免责。

十一、本章程由董事会负责解释。

二〇〇三年十月

上海民办奉浦学校董事会章程

总 则

第一条 为了切实有效地依法管理和规范学校的日常活动，根据《教育法》《中华人民共和国民办教育促进法》《民办教育促进法实施条例》等法律、法规和有关规定制定本章程。

第二条 学校由上海奉浦经济发展实业总公司利用非国家财政性经费出资

5000万元举办，学校的开办资金300万元。上海奉浦经济发展实业总公司要求合理回报，按《中华人民共和国民办教育促进法》第51条、《民办教育促进法实施条例》第44、45、46、47条执行。

第三条 学校名称和地址

学校名称：上海民办奉浦学校

学校地址：上海市奉贤区奉浦韩村路333号

第四条 办学层次：小学、初中、高中

办学形式：全日制寄宿

招生对象：小学适龄儿童、小学毕业生、初中毕业生、高中生

招生范围：上海市

第五条 学校宗旨：遵守法律法规，贯彻国家的教育方针，确保教育教学质量，遵守诚信原则，信守职业道德，提供诚信服务，接受社会监督，为经济建设和社会发展培养人才。

第六条 学校接受奉贤区教育局、奉贤区民政局和有关部门的管理、监督、督导和检查。按教育行政部门的规定委托中介组织评估办学水平和教育质量。准时参加各有关部门召开的会议和活动，准时上报各类报表和信息。

第七条 学校的审批机关和业务主管单位是奉贤区教育局，登记管理机关是奉贤区民政局。

学校的组织与活动

第八条 学校设立董事会。实行董事会领导下的校长负责制。

第九条 董事会组成：

（一）学校首届董事会由上海奉浦经济发展实业总公司组建，董事长由上海奉浦经济发展实业总公司推荐。换届时的董事会成员由上海奉浦经济发展实业总公司和董事会推选，董事长由新的一届董事会选举产生。

（二）学校董事会由上海奉浦经济发展实业总公司、校长、教职工代表等组成。其中三分之一以上董事应当具有5年以上教育、教学经验。学校董事会由9人组成，设董事长1人。董事长、董事名单报奉贤区教育局备案。

（三）董事会每届任期3年。

（四）董事增补，由上海奉浦经济发展实业总公司或董事长提名，经董事会讨论通过，报奉贤区教育局备案。

（五）董事有下列情况之一的，经董事会表决通过可以罢免，并报奉贤区教育局备案：

1．严重违反国家法律、法规或本章程的；

2．因工作变动或健康原因，不能正常履行董事职责的；

3．本人要求解职的；

4．教育行政建议罢免的。

第十条 董事会职权：

（一）董事会行使下列职权：

1．聘任或解聘校长；

2．修改学校章程和制订学校的规章制度；

3．制订发展规划，批准年度工作计划；

4．筹集办学经费，审核预算、决算；

5．决定教职工编制和工资标准；

6．决定学校的分立、合并、终止；

7．决定其他重大事项。

（二）董事会不得干预在其职权外的学校内部管理和教育教学活动。

第十一条 董事会议事规程：

（一）议事程序和规则是通过董事会会议提出、讨论并通过，秉承公平、公正原则，遵守推进学校发展的根本利益的规则。

（二）学校董事会由董事长负责召开。董事长因故不能出席，应指定或委托其他成员负责召开。

（三）学校董事会每年召开3次会议。董事长认为有必要或经1/3以上董事提议，可以召集董事会临时会议。召开董事会会议，应提前一周通知全体董事。董事会会议应有2/3以上成员出席方为有效。

（四）董事会行使1人1票的表决权，董事会的决议需经全体董事的半数以上成员通过方能生效。

（五）学校董事会讨论以下重大事项，必须得到全体董事2/3以上同意方可通过：

1．聘任和解聘校长；

2．修改学校章程；

3. 制订发展规划；

4. 审核预算、决算；

5. 决定学校的分立、合并、终止；

6. 其他重大事项。

（六）董事会应对所议议题形成会议记录，一般由董事长签名即可。形成董事会决议的会议记录，出席会议的成员应在会议记录上签名。

第十二条 学校的法定代表人：

（一）董事长为学校的法定代表人。法定代表人代表学校对外发生法律关系，签署具有法律效力的文件。

（二）学校法定代表人的变更，按奉贤区民政局的有关规定办理。

第十三条 聘任校长应当经董事会讨论，并报奉贤区教育局核准。

第十四条 校长的任职条件：

（一）参照同级同类公办学校校长的任职条件；

（二）身体健康，年龄在70周岁以下，能确保到岗到位。

第十五条 校长的职权：

（一）执行学校董事会的决定；

（二）负责实施发展规划，拟订年度工作计划、财务预算和学校规章制度；

（三）聘任和解聘学校工作人员，实施奖惩；

（四）负责学校的教育教学和行政管理工作，保证教育教学质量；

（五）负责学校的日常管理工作；

（六）参加管理部门组织的会议、活动和完成管理部门布置的各项工作；

（七）学校董事会的其他授权和章程赋予的其他职权。

第十六条 学校依照《工会法》建立工会组织，并通过教职工代表大会或全体教职工大会等形式保障教职工参与学校民主管理和监督。

第十七条 学校建立健全行政管理制度、学籍管理制度、教育教学管理制度和财务、财产管理制度，制定各个岗位的岗位职责，并报奉贤区教育局备案。

第十八条 学校公示《民办学校办学许可证》《民办非企业单位登记证》《收费许可证》《税务登记证》《收费项目和收费标准》《退费规定》和《学校章程》。

第十九条 学校聘任的教师应当符合《中华人民共和国教师法》和国家有关教师资格、任职条件的规定。

第二十条 学校聘任教师、职员，应当签订聘任合同，并明确双方的权利、义务。聘任外籍人员按照国家有关规定执行。

第二十一条 学校按照教育行政部门的有关规定开展教育教学活动，不得开设教育法规禁止的专业和课程。

第二十二条 学校的招生简章或招生广告，报奉贤区教育局备案。

第二十三条 学校在每个学年度结束时，按市教委颁发的档案规定，建立学校档案。

学校的资产与财务管理

第二十四条 学校依法建立和健全财务、会计制度，资产管理制度，并按照《会计法》规定设置会计账簿，进行会计核算。

第二十五条 学校的收费项目和收费标准由学校制定，报奉贤区物价局审批并公示。学校收取的费用主要用于教育教学活动和改善办学条件。不得用于分配、转让、担保和校外投资。

第二十六条 学校对上海奉浦经济发展实业总公司投入的资金、受赠的财产以及办学的积累，享受法人财产权。学校存续期间，所有资产由学校依法管理和使用，任何组织和个人不得抽调、挪用和侵占。

第二十七条 学校经费来源：上海奉浦经济发展实业总公司的出资；学费收入；其他合法收入。

学校根据发展的需要，设立发展基金，用于学校的维修和教学设备的添置、更新等，以改善办学条件，促进学校发展。

第二十八条 学校资产的使用和财务管理，接受有关部门的监督。在每一会计年度结束时，制作财务会计报告，委托会计师事务所依法进行审计，并公布审计结果，同时报送奉贤区教育局。

学校的变更与终止

第二十九条 学校变更名称、层次、类别、校址、校长，由学校董事会报奉贤区教育局批准。

第三十条 学校变更举办者，须由举办者提出，在进行财务清算后，经学校董事会同意，报奉贤区教育局核准。

第三十一条 学校的分立、合并，在进行财务清算后，由学校董事会报奉贤区教育局批准。

第三十二条 学校自行终止，由学校董事会讨论通过，报奉贤区教育局批准。学校终止时，应当妥善安排在校学生。

第三十三条 学校自己要求终止时，由学校组织清算，清算期间不得开展清算以外的活动。

清算人员由学校举办者代表、学校法定代表人和教职工代表组成。根据需要可聘请国内注册会计师、律师参加。

清算结束后，写出清算报告，提请董事会审核通过，到奉贤区民政局办理注销手续。

第三十四条 学校财产按下列顺序清偿：

（一）应退受教育者学费及其他费用；

（二）应发教职工的工资及应缴纳的社会保险费用；

（三）偿还国家税收；

（四）偿还其他债务。

学校清偿后的剩余财产，按照有关法律、法规的规定处理。

附　则

第三十五条 本章程修改权属于学校董事会。修改后的章程，在30日内报奉贤区教育局备案，并向社会公示。

第三十六条 本章程与国家法律、法规相抵触时，以国家法律、法规为准。

第三十七条 本章程报奉贤区教育局备案，并经奉贤区民政局核准登记后生效。

上海民办奉浦学校董事会

二〇〇五年八月

上海帕丁顿双语学校章程

总　则

第一条 本单位的名称是：上海帕丁顿双语学校。

第二条 本单位是主要利用非国有资产自愿举办的，从事非营利性社会服务活动的社会组织。

第三条 本单位的宗旨：遵守法律、法规，贯彻国家的教育方针，依法维护受教育者、教师和其他教育工作者的合法权益，确保教育教学质量，遵守社会道德风尚，信守职业道德，遵守诚信原则，依法办校为宗旨。

第四条 本单位的登记管理机关是上海市奉贤区民政局，相关行业主管部门是上海市奉贤区教育局，本单位接受登记管理机关、相关行业主管部门和其他职能部门的监督管理。

第五条 本单位的住所地：上海市奉贤区八字桥路686号。

第六条 本单位的举办者：上海申生投资有限公司。

第七条 本单位的开办资金：伍拾万元，由举办者上海申生投资有限公司出资。

第八条 举办者的权利和义务：

（一）推选代表作为本单位第一届董事候选人或监事候选人；

（二）办理登记注册手续后，不抽回出资；

（三）对出资的财产不保留、不享有任何财产权利，不要求回报。

第九条 本单位的业务范围：小学、初中、高中学历教育。

第十条 本单位按国家有关规定和核准的业务范围主要在上海开展活动。

第十一条 本单位按照公平、公正、民主的原则，制定议事程序和规则。

第十二条 本单位设董事会，其成员为5人。

董事会每届任期4年，任期届满，连选可以连任。

第十三条 担任本单位理事的港、澳、台居民以及外国人，每年在中国内地居留时间累计不得少于3个月。非中国内地居民不超过本单位理事总数的三分之一。

第十四条 董事会董事的资格：

（一）坚持党的路线、方针、政策；

（二）有完全民事行为能力；

1. 在本单位业务领域内有较大的影响和较高的声誉；

2. 年龄一般不超过70周岁，身体健康，能坚持正常工作；

3. 有积极参与本单位工作的意愿，确保充足的工作时间；

4. 认同本单位的宗旨、发展方向、机构文化，有公益精神；

5. 非国家现职工作人员；

6. 诚实守信、乐于奉献、尽心尽责。

第十五条 董事会的产生和罢免：

（一）第一届董事会成员由举办者提名并协商确定；

（二）董事会换届改选时，由本届董事会推选产生新一届董事；

（三）罢免、增补理事由董事会表决通过；

（四）董事的选举和罢免结果报登记管理机关备案。

第十六条 董事会是本单位的决策机构，行使下列职权：

（一）制订、修改章程；

（二）选举、罢免董事长、副董事长；

（三）聘任或解聘本单位行政负责人及其提名的行政副职、财务负责人；

（四）审议听取行政负责人的工作报告，并对其工作进行检查；

（五）决定重大的业务活动计划；

（六）审定年度财务预算、决算方案；

（七）决定增加开办资金的方案；

（八）决定本单位的变更、分立、合并、终止及清算等事项；

（九）决定内部机构的设置；

（十）制定内部管理制度；

（十一）依法核定从业人员的工资报酬、福利待遇；

（十二）决定其他重大事项。

第十七条 董事会每年召开2次会议。董事会会议由董事长负责召集。

有三分之一以上董事联名提议时，必须召开董事会会议。如董事长不能或不召集会议的，提议董事可推选召集人。

第十八条 召开董事会会议，董事长或召集人需提前5日通知全体董事、理事。

第十九条 董事会会议应由三分之二以上的董事出席方可举行。董事会会议实行1人1票制。董事会作出决议，必须经全体董事过半数通过方为有效。

下列重要事项的决议，须经全体董事三分之二以上通过方为有效：

（一）章程的制订和修改；

（二）选举和罢免董事长、副董事长；

（三）变更开办资金；

（四）本单位的分立、合并。

第二十条 董事会会议应当制作会议记录。形成决定的，应当当场制作会议决议，并由出席会议的董事审阅、签名。董事会决议违反法律、法规、规章或章程规定，致使本单位遭受损失的，参与决议的董事应当承担责任。但经证明在表决时反对并记载于会议记录的，该董事可免除责任。

董事会会议记录、决议由本单位的档案管理工作人员存档保管。

第二十一条 董事会设董事长1名，副董事长1名。

第二十二条 董事长行使下列职权：

（一）召集董事会会议；

（二）检查董事会决议的实施情况；

（三）法律、法规、规章和本单位章程规定的其他职权。

副董事长协助董事长工作，董事长不能行使上述职权时，由董事长指定的副董事长代其行使职权。

第二十三条 本单位行政负责人为专职。行政负责人对董事会负责，并行使下列职权：

（一）主持本单位的日常工作，组织实施董事会的决议；

（二）组织实施本单位年度业务活动计划；

（三）拟订本单位年度财务预算、决算方案；

（四）拟订本单位内部机构设置的方案，协调内部机构开展活动；

（五）拟订内部管理制度；

（六）提请聘任或解聘行政副职、财务负责人，由董事会决定；

（七）决定各内设机构主要负责人的聘免和专职工作人员的聘用或辞退；

（八）章程和董事会赋予的其他职权。

本单位行政负责人列席董事会会议。

第二十四条 有下列情形之一的人员，不得担任本单位的董事长、副董事长、行政负责人：

（一）因犯罪被判处管制、拘役或者有期徒刑，刑期执行完毕之日起未逾5年的；

（二）因犯罪被判处剥夺政治权利正在执行期间或者曾经被判处剥夺政治权利的；

（三）曾在因违法被撤销登记的社会组织中担任负责人的，且对该社会组织的违法行为负有个人责任，自该社会组织被撤销之日起未逾5年的；

（四）无民事行为能力或者限制民事行为能力的；

（五）法律法规规章规定不得担任的其他情形。

第二十五条 本单位的法定代表人为董事长王丹花(女)。

第二十六条 本单位设立监事，其成员为3人。

监事任期为4年，任期届满，连选可以连任。

第二十七条 监事在举办者、本单位从业人员或有关单位推荐的人选中产生或更换。

本单位董事及其近亲属、行政负责人及财会人员不得担任监事。

第二十八条 监事的权利和义务：

（一）列席理事会会议；

（二）检查本单位财务和会计资料；

（三）监督理事会、行政负责人遵守法律、法规、规章和章程的情况；

（四）发现问题时，有权对理事会、行政负责人提出质询和建议，并向登记管理机关和相关职能部门反映情况；

资产管理、使用原则

第二十九条 本单位经费来源：

（一）开办资金；

（二）政府资助；

（三）在业务范围内开展服务活动的收入，如学费；

（四）利息；

（五）社会各界的捐赠；

（六）其他合法收入。

第三十条 本单位的开办资金由举办者出资。根据运作和发展需要，举办者可以继续投入。

第三十一条 本单位的资产受法律保护，任何单位、个人不得侵占、私分、挪用。

本单位的资产必须用于章程规定的业务范围和事业的发展，除符合规定的支出外，财产及其孳息不得用于分配，增值部分不得分红，注销时剩余财产用于公益性或者非营利性目的。

第三十二条 本单位从事社会服务取得的收入除用于合理的工资薪金、福利支出和与本单位有关的、合理的支出外，全部用于登记核定或者章程规定的公益性或者非营利性事业。

第三十三条 本单位开展社会服务活动的收费按物价部门核定的标准执行。对取得的应纳税收入及其有关的成本、费用、损失应与免税收入及其有关的成本、费用、损失分别核算。

第三十四条 本单位接受捐赠时如签订捐赠协议的，应在本单位的业务范围内，根据捐赠协议约定的用途和方式使用。接受捐赠的物资无法用于符合本单位宗旨的用途时，可以依法拍卖或者变卖，所得收入用于捐赠目的。

第三十五条 捐赠人有权向本单位查询捐赠财产的使用、管理情况，并提出意见和建议。对于捐赠人的查询，本单位将及时如实答复。

第三十六条 本单位执行国家规定的《民间非营利组织会计制度》，依法进行独立的会计核算，建立健全内部会计监督制度，保证会计资料合法、真实、准确、完整。

本单位配备具有专业资格的会计人员。会计不得兼任出纳。会计人员调动工作或离职时，必须与接管人员办清交接手续。

本单位接受税务、会计主管部门依法实施的税务监督和会计监督。

第三十七条 本单位在年度检查、变更法定代表人以及清算时，进行财务审计。

劳动用工制度

第三十八条 未与本单位建立劳动关系的理事和监事不得从本单位获取报酬。

第三十九条 本单位工作人员的工资福利开支控制在合理的比例内，不变相分配本单位的财产，其中：工作人员平均工资薪金水平不得超过上年度税务登记所在地人均工资水平的两倍，工作人员福利按照国家有关规定执行。

第四十条 本单位劳动用工、社会保险制度按国家法律、法规及人力资源和社会劳动保障行政部门的有关规定执行。

年度检查、重大事项报告及信息公开

第四十一条 本单位按照《民办非企业单位登记管理暂行条例》和《民办

非企业单位年度检查办法》的规定，自觉接受登记管理机关组织的年度检查。

第四十二条 本单位按照登记管理机关重大事项报告的相关要求和指引，履行报告义务。

第四十三条 本单位按照登记管理机关信息公开的相关要求，履行信息公开义务。

终止和终止后资产处理

第四十四条 本单位有下列情形之一的，应当终止：

（一）完成章程规定宗旨的；

（二）无法按照章程规定的宗旨继续开展活动的；

（三）发生分立、合并的；

（四）自行解散的；

第四十五条 本单位终止，应当在董事会通过终止的决议后15日内，成立清算小组，清理债权债务，处理剩余财产，完成清算工作。清算小组一般应由本单位法定代表人或者董事会确定的相关负责人、债权人代表、行业主管部门和其他职能部门代表等共同组成。根据需要可聘请国内注册会计师、律师等参加。

第四十六条 清算工作的顺序：

（一）退还应退的服务性收费；

（二）支付本单位职工工资和缴纳社会保险等费用；

（三）偿还本单位债务；

（四）开展终结审计；

（五）处理剩余财产；

（六）撰写清算报告。

第四十七条 本单位清算期间不开展清算以外的活动。如遇民事诉讼的，由清算小组代表本单位参与民事诉讼。

第四十八条 剩余财产的处理：

（一）优先支付清算费用和清算组成员的酬劳；

（二）办理税务注销、银行销户等手续，结清税款、利息；

（三）在登记管理机关、行业主管部门和其他职能部门的监督下，将剩余财产捐赠给与本单位性质、宗旨相同的社会公益组织，并向社会公告。

第四十九条 本单位法定代表人或者负责人应当自完成清算之日起15日

内，向登记管理机关办理注销登记手续。

第五十条　本单位自登记管理机关发出注销登记证明文件之日起，即为终止。

附　则

第五十一条　本章程经2015年8月30日第1届第1次董事会会议表决通过。

第五十二条　本章程的解释权属董事会。

第五十三条　本章程的修改，须经董事会表决通过后30日内，报登记管理机关核准。

第五十四条　本章程自登记管理机关核准之日起生效。

第五十五条　本章程中的各项条款如与法律、法规、规章和政策不符的，以法律、法规、规章和政策的规定为准。

上海帕丁顿双语学校董事会

2015年8月30日

编后记

2015年6月，上海帕丁顿双语学校董事会决定编写《上海帕丁顿双语学校志》（以下简称《学校志》），并建立《学校志》编写机构。上海帕丁顿双语学校投资举办方上海申生投资有限公司董事长王新其为《学校志》编纂委员会主任，上海申生投资有限公司总经理王丹花(女)为主编，原中共奉贤县委常委、县政府常务副县长朱德龙等为顾问，聘请上海市奉贤区地方志办公室原副主任周生明为特约编审，上海民办奉浦学校原校长戚盛伟为执行主编、教师刘平为执行编辑。

上海帕丁顿双语学校是奉贤区一所民办学校。办校19年间，始终得到上海工业综合开发区管委会（上海奉浦经济发展实业总公司）、奉贤区（县）教育局、上海营巢房产开发有限公司及有关社会组织的大力支持与帮助。学校规模从初办时占地4.66公顷，建筑面积1.89万平方米发展到占地5.99公顷，建筑面积7.46万平方米。2016年，校区内有民办十二年学制上海帕丁顿双语学校、公办上海市奉贤区奉浦学校、上海帕丁顿外国语幼儿园及英国、美国、澳大利亚等高中课程中心等，成为奉贤地区教学环境优良、教师队伍稳定、教学质量逐步提升的校区。师生总人数超过2500人，其中上海帕丁顿双语学校师生1300余人。

学校董事会决定编写《学校志》，旨在记载办校19年来“顺势发展、困难曲折、改革进取、健康发展”四个阶段发展历程，记载学校创办发展中全校师生及社会组织、各界人士为学校建设发展所做出的贡献，同时也记载学校投资举办企业在发展壮大之后舍得投资办学回报社会的奉献精神，为学校留下一部展示民办学校特色，铭记发展历史，承前启后的生动教材。编者深感责任重大，任务光荣。

《学校志》编纂委员会始终关心编写工作。2015年6月至2016年，编纂委员会先后召开6次由编委主任、主编、顾问及学校部门负责人参加的编志动员会、培训会、交流会、研讨会，创造编志工作的有利条件。2016年2月，编委会决定聘请担任过多部志书主编的陈炳章参加编写组，并担任执行主编。编修人员根据民办学校特点，对原拟纲目进行调整，确定全书除总述、大事记外，共设12章，分别为第一章学校创办发展、第二章决策机构、第三章管理机构、第四章校务改革、第五章党群组织、第六章教职员工、第七章学校教学、第八章学生教育管理、第九章学校综合管理、第十章设施设备、第十一章校园文化科技体育、第十二章人物荣誉。是年7月，在原有材料基础上，按纲目要求边收集资料边编写。3名编修人员进行编辑的重新分工：戚盛伟负责编辑第六、七章，刘平(女)负责编辑第八章及协助收集有关资料，陈炳章负责编辑第一、二、三、四、五、九、十、十一、十二章，以及修改补充大事记、编辑总述、编后记、收集拍摄、制作有关照片、图表等资料，并负责志书总纂。《学校志》的编修坚持贯彻以人为本的指导思想，先后收集到创办以来为学校争光添彩的各方面代表人物1300余人次，同时注重记述学校发展与教学业绩，展示民办学校特色。2016年12月，全书大事记及正文十二章大部分已形成初稿。经过对初稿的多次调整、修改和补充。志稿基本达到记述清晰、体例规范、详略得当，展现学校特色，全书融为一体的要求。

2017年3月，《学校志》文字稿由编委分送区教育局、奉浦街道、学校历任部分领导，征求意见补充修改。经总纂，7月文字稿与卷首、随文照合成。于8月15日召开评审会议，出席会议的有姚金祥等方志专家、有关领导20多人。由方志出版社专家审稿后进行再修改，12月付印出版。

在《学校志》编写中，编委主要领导经常关心编志工作进展。《学校志》编委会顾问朱德龙自始至终关心支持编修工作，不仅参加编志工作的各种会议、听取工作汇报了解进展情况，还亲自修改稿件，通过牵线搭桥，在有关部门间开展协调，帮助编者收集学校已散失的历史资料，丰富志书的内容。《学校志》编委会副主任、校党支部书记兼副校长顾行健日常事务已很繁忙，但对于编者提出的提供资料请求总是有求必应，利用休息时间仔细认真地从电子档案或文字资料中寻找，先后收集各种史实资料原件或复印件、照片100余幅（份），不少内容为许多章节所摘录采用。上海申生投资有限公司职工徐晓华(女)，本身承担公司交办的不少工作，愉快接受《学校志》稿件打印任务，做到公司工作与稿件打印两不误，对于志稿的反复修改补充与时有的增减删改、文字移动穿插，总是不厌其烦、认真及时地完成。现在公办学校任教的教师刘德根，在编者查阅档案资料时，热情介绍档案资料情况和自己了解的信息，使编者查档少走弯路，不少可入志的原始资料得以收集。初稿形成后，原奉贤县教育局局长、奉贤区教育学会会长蒋辉藻，上海申生投资有限公司董事长王新其分别为《学校志》作序。校名、目录、总述的英语翻译工作由上海瑞尔翻译有限公司朱红燕(女)担任。在此仅向关心支持《学校志》编写的学校领导和师生员工表示深切的感谢。

本志资料包括公开出版的教师作品、学校教学案例汇编中摘用，一部分摘自存档文书等。由于种种原因，学校不少资料已经散失而无法收集，致使部分章节的内容比较单薄或者错漏，加上编者水平有限，志书中难免有不尽人意之处，敬请读者、用者谅解。

编者

2017年12月